ETHICS AS
GRAMMAR

ETHICS AS
GRAMMAR

Changing the
Postmodern Subject

BRAD J. KALLENBERG

University of Notre Dame Press
Notre Dame, Indiana

Designed by Wendy McMillen
Set in 11.3/13 Electra by Em Studio Inc.
Printed in USA by Sheridan Books, Inc.

Manufactured in the United States of America

Library of Congress Cataloging-in-Publication Data
Kallenberg, Brad J.
    Ethics as grammar : changing the postmodern subject /
Brad Jeffrey Kallenberg.
        p.   cm.
Includes bibliographical references (p.   ) and index.
    ISBN 0-268-02760-9
    1. Christian ethics. 2. Wittgenstein, Ludwig, 1889–1951.
3. Hauerwas, Stanley, 1940– I. Title.
    BJ1251 .K245 2001
    241'.0404'092 — dc21   2001001291

∞ *This book is printed on acid-free paper.*

To Jeanne

In whose story I am happily and inextricably embedded

CONTENTS

Abbreviations

WORKS OF WITTGENSTEIN

BB   *The Blue and Brown Books*

CE   "Cause and Effect: Intuitive Awareness"

CV   *Culture and Value*

LC   *Lectures & Conversations on Aesthetics, Psychology and Religious Belief*

LE   "A Lecture on Ethics"

LW I   *Last Writings on the Philosophy of Psychology*. Vol. 1. *Preliminary Studies for Part II of the Philosophical Investigations*

LW II   *Last Writings on the Philosophy of Psychology*. Vol. 2. *The Inner and the Outer, 1949–1951*

NB   *Notebooks, 1914–1916*

NPL   "Notes for the Philosophical Lecture"

OC   *On Certainty*

PESD   "Notes for Lectures on 'Private Experience' and 'Sense Data'"

PG   *Philosophical Grammar*

PHIL   "Philosophy"

PI   *Philosophical Investigations*

PR   *Philosophical Remarks*

RC   *Remarks on Colour*

RFGB   "Remarks on Frazer's Golden Bough"

RFM   *Remarks on the Foundations of Mathematics*

RPP   *Remarks on the Philosophy of Psychology.* Two Volumes

SRLF   "Some Remarks on Logical Form"

TLP   *Tractatus Logico-Philosophicus*

WL   *Wittgenstein's Lectures: Cambridge, 1930–32*

WVC   *Wittgenstein and the Vienna Circle: Conversations Recorded by Friedrich Waismann*

Z   *Zettel*

OTHER WORKS

NASB   *New American Standard Bible.* La Habra, CA: Lockman Foundation, 1977.

NEB   *New English Bible.* Oxford and Cambridge: Delegates of the Oxford University Press and the Syndics of the Cambridge University Press, 1961.

NRSV   *New Revised Standard Version Bible.* Oxford and New York: Oxford University Press, 1989.

PREFACE

Whenever I read Wittgenstein I cannot help but hear him speaking to me with a *Welsh* accent. Of course, this Austrian-born Cambridge scholar had mastered the language well enough to teach in English, but he never completely divested himself of a German accent and certainly preferred to write in his native tongue. Whether one reads him in German or in English, one is advised to pay attention to his instruction that his writings *must* be read at the right *tempo*. As a student I marveled how puzzling passages would suddenly become crystal clear when my teacher, the Welshman D. Z. Phillips, would read Wittgenstein aloud. I count myself fortunate to have never quite recovered from the urge to mimic Phillips's style when I read Wittgenstein for myself. Perhaps the greatest compliment I can pay Phillips is that, when it comes to Wittgenstein, I think that he has gotten matters right.

But there is more to Wittgenstein than what he has said and written, and there were destinations he intended to reach beyond those at which he had arrived at life's end. For this reason I wish to bring Wittgenstein into conversation not with D. Z. Phillips—as ubiquitous as his voice may be for contemporary studies in Wittgenstein—but with another voice altogether: that of the theological ethicist, Stanley Hauerwas. The fact that I have brought these two thinkers together—an Austrian-born, Neo-Kantian Cambridge don and a Yale-educated, high-church Mennonite from Texas—requires some explaining. Perhaps the best way to introduce this study is simply to describe my methodology.

It is not uncommon to find in the great art museums of the western world aspiring artists meticulously copying the works of the masters as if to learn their style by rote. Yet some misguided students try to imitate abstract art in the same way—for instance, using a triple-aught brush to reproduce the detail of paint blobs originally left in the trail of a six-inch palette knife—not realizing that the point of abstract art is not the artifact-as-representation but a method, or skill, of expression. The goal of studying this kind of art is to master the method. Much the same could be said for Wittgenstein's artistry. His works do not state philosophical theses and, therefore, cannot be outlined for their cognitive content. Rather, they aim at changing the sensibilities and skills of the reader.

The promise of real change was one I found worth investigating. I came to Wittgensteinian studies by way of theology rather than philosophy. As it turned out, my philosophical naivete was particularly fitting for the task. Wittgenstein himself did not consider his own lack of philosophical breadth as detrimental to his task. (On the contrary, much of his energy was directed at *undoing* the havoc modern philosophy had wreaked on his students' minds.) Moreover, Wittgenstein himself once remarked to Maurice O'C. Drury that he had done everything from a *religious* point of view. As this perspective is frequently passed over in Wittgenstein studies, I hoped that my theological fluency might pick up threads in Wittgenstein that otherwise would be overlooked.

One of my earliest desires in my graduate program in theology was to attempt a justification of narrative theology by appealing to what I was beginning to understand as "postmodern" philosophy. This hope was dashed very quickly. After a brief encounter with Wittgenstein, I realized that using his works to "justify" any philosophical thesis would be to miss the point of his entire project. The more I read of him, the more I was filled with a sort of terrifying fascination; I was intrigued by the vigor of his genius but was cut to the quick by the probings of his grammatical investigations, probings which threatened to leave none of *my* sacred stones unturned.

In the midst of this initial reading it began to dawn on me that Wittgenstein was more concerned with the *manner* (including attitudes, intentions, and stance) in which his students read him than with their grasp of any putative philosophical "theses." Consequently, he deliberately crafted his writing, not for the purpose of explicating and defending tenets of a philosophical system, but with an eye toward effecting a change in the way his readers perceived the world.

I could not resist likening this hoped-for outcome to "character transformation." Not surprisingly, I began to wonder about the possible relation between Wittgenstein and virtue ethics. Of course, when I inquired whether any attention had been paid to the impact of, say, Aristotle upon

Wittgenstein's thought, my question was laughed down, for Wittgenstein had prided himself in the fact that he had never read a lick of Aristotle.

As I studied, and eventually came to teach, Christian ethics, I became increasingly familiar with the writings of Stanley Hauerwas. Hauerwas's concern to change the fundamental question of ethics from "What ought X do?" to "What sort of people ought we to be?" had more appeal to me than merely the relief it offered from tiresome case-book approaches to philosophical ethics. Hauerwas appeared to be a postmodernist of the "good" sort. Under the tutelage of philosopher and theologian Nancey Murphy, I had begun to deliberately seek alternatives to epistemological foundationalism, metaphysical reductionism, and representational theories of language. And in this regard I found Hauerwas's works very promising. Moreover, Hauerwas turned out to be a self-proclaimed Aristotelian whose concern for shaping the "character" and outlook of his readers resembled that of Wittgenstein.

This book is my attempt to understand Christian theological ethics through the lens of Wittgenstein. In the reading of first Wittgenstein, then Hauerwas, I was unable to evade their meddling with my own way of thinking. As a result, I have become an unwitting interlocutor in a conversation that travels both through time (the corpus of each writer spans roughly three decades: Wittgenstein wrote from 1920–1951 and Hauerwas from 1968 to the present) and through conceptual space. Because their written works function as the roadmap of their conceptual travels, I hoped that by reading their works in chronological order, I might have duplicated these journeys.

Of course, I cannot pretend to begin my journey from "no where." I cut my teeth on Wittgenstein under the tutelage of philosopher of science Nancey Murphy, analytic philosopher D. Z. Phillips, and the "small 'b' baptist" theologian and ethicist, James Wm. McClendon, Jr. That I write as one rigorously trained to think in the manner of my teachers is a mark of bias in my study. But this bias cannot count against it, for, as Wittgenstein and Hauerwas both maintain, objectivity and comprehensiveness are always out of reach. For this reason, I did not trouble myself with endless debates between mostly conflicting "schools" over which of them gets Wittgenstein right. Sufficient for my purposes was that I master the language spoken by one of them in order that I might compare one particular language (namely, that exemplified by D. Z. Phillips, Rush Rhees, and Peter Winch) with my other first language, theology, as an insider to both.

My methodology is neither systematic nor comprehensive—and this too is fitting. Both Wittgenstein and Hauerwas consciously wrote in ways

that defy systematization, since they share the view that theoretical systems tempt us to think that the "character" of human subjects is inconsequential to what is being understood. Moreover, both thinkers expressed
a profound concern that we not overlook the fact that the human proclivity toward creating totalizing systems of thought is evidence of a disease for which we are desperately in need of a cure. Thus I do not pretend
to offer a line-by-line comparison of their respective theses. Rather, my
methodology is autobiographical and conversational. It is autobiographical in that these pages bear the marks of my own conceptual journey as I
have learned to see each thinker under the aspect of the other. It is conversational in that my goal is not to distill and compare philosophical or
theological theses as much as to assemble reminders which tell a story, or
history, the telling of which, I hope, will impart to my readers a working
fluency in the languages of Wittgenstein's therapeutic philosophy and
Hauerwas's Christian ethics. (Thus my title points in several directions at
once.) But this present volume is conversational in another way as well,
for it represents as much my conversations with others as those I have had
with myself.

I must admit that one of my greatest fears in undertaking to write
about Stanley Hauerwas was that I would not be able to read as fast as he
is able to write! More than once a letter from Stanley showed up at my
home with a few "inclusions," namely, long manuscripts which he had
just written for some occasion or other. But what astonished me even more
than his production capacity was the way Stanley went out of his way to
encourage my work with long letters or phone calls.

D. Z. Phillips and Stephen Toulmin were kind enough to give written responses to earlier drafts of my work. Friends and colleagues at Fuller
Theological Seminary and elsewhere (Christian Early, Paul Cho, Steve
Green, Steve Jolley, Anne Collier-Freed, Randy Parks, Ronni Schwartz,
and Art Hurtado) provided a wonderful sounding board for earlier versions of these chapters. I am especially grateful to Nancey Murphy and
James McClendon for years of dialogue that opened up Wittgenstein to
me in the first place.

What cannot be adequately expressed is my appreciation for Jeanne, my
wife, who patiently endured from me the symptoms of a book in progress:
vacant stares in the middle of dinner, tantrums over computer glitches,
perpetual forgetfulness (such as which kid to pick up from which sport at
what time), the habit of jotting notes on a bedside pad at 3 A.M., countless
dollars spent on books and library photocopiers, and the endless struggle

to make myself clear without trespassing into "heresy." Throughout the journey it was she, more than all others, who by her unceasing devotion and good humor, kept my ship aright.

NOTE ON READING WITGENSTEIN

In the not too distant past, the Wittgensteinian *Nachlaß*, consisting of hand-written notebooks, slips of paper bundled together, and a few longer typescripts, were scattered between private collections, the Wren Library of Trinity College, Cambridge, the Bodleian Library, Oxford, and the Österreichsche Nationalbiliothek in Vienna. In addition, the bulk of this disparate collection was microfilmed for Cornell University. During this early period, the greatest difficulty facing scholars who wished to study Wittgenstein was neither the scarcity of the collection (bound photocopies of the Cornell microfilm are available, for example, in the University Research Library at UCLA) nor the difficulty of his German (Wittgenstein strove to make his point in the simplest German possible). The greatest difficulty was making sense out of the unfinished state of Wittgenstein's curious redaction process. Today, the rise in number of scholarly translations by other Anglo-American philosophers as well as the progress of critical projects (e.g., *Wiener Ausgabe*) has made Wittgenstein's work readily available in English. This is not to say that forays in the original German are unfruitful, but rather that the task of reading his translated works is more than simply respectable; in some cases the best way to access the thinking of this one-time Cambridge scholar is simply to read him in English. Unless otherwise noted, all citations are from the published English translations of Wittgenstein's works.

INTRODUCTION

In March 1999, *Time Magazine* published its picks for the top two dozen or so thinkers of the twentieth century. Among such notables as Albert Einstein and Jean Piaget was one surprising name: Ludwig Wittgenstein. Wittgenstein's inclusion is not surprising because it was out of place — as *Time* had been wrongheaded about their "Man of the Year" in 1938, Adolph Hitler — but because Wittgenstein's work is so enigmatic that most readers who have stumbled upon his writings simply pick themselves up, dust themselves off, and move on. Not so for theologian and ethicist Stanley Hauerwas. Hauerwas once remarked that "God gave us that troubled soul Ludwig Wittgenstein to think through all the dualisms of modernity so that we really could have 'another side'."[1] Indeed, for a handful of "postmodern" theologians in the Anglo-American vein, Wittgenstein has proven to be the key that has unlocked a whole new world.[2]

Part of the promise of Wittgenstein's legacy is that his work can be fruitfully viewed under a number of different aspects. For example, Fergus Kerr shows that among the fundamental ideas that occurred to Wittgenstein very early in life was the repudiation of Cartesian psychology that seemingly hides the real world from the solitary ego by a veil of ideas.[3] In contrast, Wittgenstein averred that language so permeates our thinking processes that there is no way of stepping outside language to construe it as one thing and the world as another, or language-using subjects as one thing and experiential objects as another.

Others find in Wittgenstein the echoes of Aristotle's preference for *phronēsis* over *technē*. These readers gravitate toward the innumerable

1

comparisons Wittgenstein made between philosophy and architecture, painting, poetry, and, above all, music. Can a composer specify *in advance* what will be the shape of his or her composition (as the Socratic definition of *technē* that Aristotle inherited seemingly implies)? Yet artists in the creative process do, in fact, "know what they are doing." Wittgenstein contended that language use is governed by a skill not unlike the *phronēsis* of artistic know-how.[4]

> Is there such a thing as "expert judgment" about the genuineness of expressions of feeling?—Even here, there are those whose judgment is "better" and those whose judgment is "worse."
>
> Correcter prognoses will generally issue from the judgments of those with better knowledge of mankind.
>
> Can we learn this knowledge? Yes; some can. Not, however, by taking a course in it, but through "*experience*."—Can someone else be a man's teacher in this? Certainly. From time to time he gives him the right *tip*.—This is what "learning" and "teaching" are like here.—What one acquires here is not a technique; one learns correct judgments. There are also rules, but they do not form a system, and only experienced people can apply them right. Unlike calculation rules.[5]

Such a skill enables us to navigate our world without requiring that we first overcome finitude in human knowledge by means of general explanations of ontology, epistemology, metaphysics, and the like.

Still others find a haven in Wittgenstein's "method" of doing philosophy, which, in opposition to articulating overt philosophical theses or general explanations, became his self-proclaimed resting place.[6] Wittgensteinians of this sort take it as their business to intervene in the unending string of conversations bewitched by confusions. Especially at risk, they insist, are conversations in philosophy, theology, and ethics.[7]

But no matter how the story is told, there are a number of aporias which remained for Wittgenstein and against which his legacy struggles. Not that struggle is bad! Wittgenstein himself thought that linguistic struggle was simply the nature of the beast, and to give up the struggle would be cowardly, if not downright irreligious.[8] Kierkegaard once wrote that his own mission was not to make difficult things easier for his reader's comprehension but to make easy things more difficult for the sake of his reader's character.[9] Perhaps Wittgenstein, who admired Kierkegaard, had something of the same purpose in mind. Wittgenstein sought to free his readers from the spells cast upon their minds by breaches in the grammar of ordinary language. He thus confronted his readers with aporias which could not be surmounted except by fervent struggle; for in struggling with language one simultaneously acquires enough familiarity with language's deeper grammar to discern the range of legitimate senses underlying what formerly appeared aporetic. Some brief examples may help clarify this strategy.

At first blush, Wittgenstein appears to hold two contradictory views. On the one hand, he seemed to hold that we think with language, namely, we have no prelinguistic, or extra-linguistic, thought. Yet, on the other hand, he also seemed to hold that instances of "tacit understanding" (to borrow Polanyi's term)—such as the ability to recognize the sound of a clarinet or the aroma of coffee—elude human attempts to put these into words. How can we "know it" if we cannot "say it"? What was Wittgenstein up to? Perhaps this: when one puzzles his or her way through the *Investigations*, it may dawn upon the reader that the tacit dimension of thought is not outside language per se, but only outside the *representational* uses of language. To wrestle through to this conclusion is to get clearer on how extensive Wittgenstein views the linguistic shape of human life to be.

Consider a second example. Wittgenstein characterized his project as purely descriptive, one which left everything in its place. His words seem particularly promising for theology: "if you believe, say, Spinoza or Kant, this interferes with what you believe in religion; but if you believe me, nothing of the sort."[10] However, if language is the only means by which we are able to think at all, how are we able to perceive the sense of divine mystery (*das Mystische*), which on Wittgenstein's account lies *outside* of language? Conversely, if theology is nothing but the tracing of the grammar of particular religious claims, then is not our talk of God, at the end of the day, simply talk about people in loud voices? Perhaps. Yet the careful reader will learn that "language" for Wittgenstein was a more widely ramified concept than simply strings of words and their attending "rules" of use; language is, in a very important sense, continuous, coterminous, and identical with our world. Therefore, the frustrations we feel about the coarseness of our language epitomize our reaction to the finitude of our human condition. And surely we are right to say that we are without the means to adequately represent in language the ways in which our God is above all that. But the astute reader may also catch a glimpse of why Wittgenstein often lamented his inability to write poetry, since poetry is able to *show* what cannot be *said*. Wittgenstein's close friend Paul Engelmann understood the significance of this difference. He wrote,

Wittgenstein passionately believes that all that really matters in human life is precisely what, in his view, we must be silent about. When he nevertheless takes immense pains to delimit the unimportant, it is not the coastline of that island which he is bent on surveying with such meticulous accuracy, but the boundary of the ocean.[11]

In other words, theologians need not become tongue-tied having taken a course in Wittgenstein. Rather, Wittgenstein begs us all to sharpen our skills at seeing the presence of the divine that, to put it crudely, lurks in camouflage among the ordinary.[12]

Thus, perhaps such aporias dissolve by means of progress that given students make. The aporias with which Wittgenstein expresses himself, therefore, are neither lapses nor deficiencies in pedagogy. Rather, they are the heart and soul of his dialogical approach. Wittgenstein laced his writings with aporias so as to more deeply engage his readers in conversation. When one is able to recognize these as *pedagogical* aporias rather than as flat-out contradictions, one has gained sufficient fluency for recognizing the senses in which both sides of such aporias may be true.

However, having said all this, there are other aporias that are more profoundly mystifying. For example, on the one hand, Wittgenstein seems to regard attention to ordinary language usage as a safeguard against all sorts of illicit ways of speaking. Imagine overhearing someone asking a friend, "What is the color of the letter 'e'?" The friend replies, "Do you mean a long 'e' or a short 'e'?" We could only imagine such a conversation occurring between children or between foreigners trying to learn English. But for ordinary English speakers, the letter 'e' no more has a color than the color brown has intelligence or honesty a mass. The proper range of a word's application is shown by actual use, not by a theory that proscribes its use. Yet on the other hand, it is fair to ask, "*Whose* use shows proper application?" For Wittgenstein claims that ordinary language itself may go awry on the broad scale.

Language sets everyone the same traps; it is an immense network of easily accessible wrong turnings. And so we watch one man after another walking down the same paths and we know in advance where he will branch off, where walk straight on without noticing the side turning, etc. etc. What I have to do then is erect signposts at the junctions where there are wrong turnings so as to help people past the danger points.[13]

If language practices are so susceptible to confusion, how can some practices of some speakers be regarded as the benchmark for normal use? Here the aporia in Wittgenstein is not merely a pedagogical one.

As a second example, consider a problem in ethics. A deep problem that faced the later Wittgenstein was his reticence to give an account of moral obligation that carried more weight than simply the hypothetically imperative "rules of a game." Consider this passage from 1929:

> What does the word 'ought' mean? A child ought to do such-and-such means that if he does not do it, something unpleasant will happen. Reward and punishment. The essential thing about this is that the other person is brought to do something. 'Ought' makes sense only if there is something lending support and force to it—a power that punishes and rewards. Ought in itself is nonsensical.[14]

Wittgenstein seems to think of morality as purely conventional. Similarly, he thought that the "binding force" of logic was nothing more determinate than the happy chance of human agreement within a particular form of life.[15] But here a profound problem emerges: How are we to understand someone such as Kierkegaard (not to mention Kierkegaard's Abraham), who felt *obliged* to move in a direction diametrically opposed to the social cooperation in terms of which Wittgenstein conceives all obligation? Whence *this* obligation?

Wittgenstein's description of the grammar of 'ought' seemingly removes the force we ordinarily take it to connote. A third and analogous problem arises in his analysis of religious language. Wittgenstein carefully avoids making either universal or quasi-empirical claims about God, souls, and so forth (despite the fact that believers have a use for such claims within their specific history and form of life). Wittgenstein must stop short of making first-order claims and content himself with grammatical descriptions. Thus he will say of the human soul that it is not a something, yet not a nothing either. But Wittgenstein cannot say that the word 'soul' is *merely* a part of a language-game—for that would cheapen the religious outlook and make it appear as if the believer could simply choose to give up soul language in favor of some other "metaphor." So by the terms of his own project, Wittgenstein must refrain from criticizing linguistic practices except those conversations to which he is privy. The puzzle then remains: sometimes Wittgenstein, himself a citizen of no community,[16] challenges "mistakes" from the outside, while at other times he insists that so long as the game can continue to be played, all is well.[17]

Finally, in Wittgenstein's view, there is a groundlessness to language that admits a fourth aporia. On the one hand, language originated not by some form of ratiocination but through an extension of the way human animals instinctively reacted to their environment.[18] "Does a [nursing] child believe that milk exists? Or does it know that milk exists?"[19] Of course not. Rather, the newborn's behavior (crying) is an instinctive reflex, or primitive reaction, to the tactile, olfactory, and visual stimuli in his or her environment. Similarly, it belongs to the primitive reactions of the mother to attend to the pain behavior of her child. Her clucking and cooing are on the same order as speaking the sentence: "There, there. I know it hurts." Both types of vocal behaviors are outgrowths of her prelinguistic primitive reactions. On the other hand, these primitive reactions that human beings happily share, are themselves shaped by the language that we speak. How can both sides of this aporia be asserted? Are primitive reactions basic to language or is language basic to primitive reactions?

In each case, there is no *general* way to surmount these puzzles. Yet the ones who can *ask* what Wittgenstein was up to (and do so only by means of words) are those for whom a language is already in place. *This* must be accepted as the given; particular people have been gifted by their particular community with a particular language which is the unique correlate of reality.[20]

With an eye to these aporias, let me disabuse my readers of potential misreadings of what I am up to. First, I am not suggesting that Hauerwas went beyond Wittgenstein by concocting general solutions to aporias that puzzled Wittgenstein at life's end. Nor am I simply comparing Hauerwas with Wittgenstein in a straightforward thesis-by-thesis fashion. Rather, I hope to display the family resemblance between them and, in so doing, make the tentative suggestion that the gift of Christian particularity enabled and enables Hauerwas to do theology by means of Wittgenstein and yet also to surmount the aporias with which Wittgenstein expressed himself for the sake of his readers who lacked a determinative enough community to be addressed nonaporetically.

When I once remarked to a contemporary philosopher that my project was to show the presence of Wittgenstein in Hauerwas's theology, his response was telling: "Hah! That will be a very short book!" As it turned out, there was much more to my suspicion of family resemblance between the two than I could have ever anticipated. Hauerwas admits quite unashamedly that Wittgenstein's influence on him was of an entirely different order than that of other contemporary thinkers.

[Wittgenstein] slowly cured me of the notion that philosophy was primarily a matter of positions, ideas, and/or theories. From Wittgenstein, and later David Burrell, I learned to understand and also to do philosophy in a therapeutic mode. But there were also substantive matters to be learned from Wittgenstein. Originally sparked by my interest in history, I had begun to work on issues in the philosophy of mind such as the relation of "mind-body problem," "intentionality," and "motivation." Wittgenstein . . . helped me see that "mind" did not relate to body as cause to effect, for "mind" was not a singular thing or function. Moreover, Wittgenstein ended forever any attempt on my part to try to anchor theology in some general account of "human experience," for his writings taught me that the object of the theologian's work was best located in terms of the grammar of the language used by believers.[21]

In an early essay Hauerwas established that what he learned from Julius Kovesi and Iris Murdoch was the same as that which he learned from Wittgenstein, namely that description is everything. And, as there is no such thing as objective or disinterested description, religion could never be incidental or ornamental to his work in ethics. Rather, issues in ethics become clear as they are viewed through the thick spectacles of religious conviction. Thus Hauerwas's own particular Christian identity—"evangelical Methodist" or, more playfully, "high-church Mennonite"—has proven to be equally determinative for Hauerwas's scholarship.

I would like to suggest that . . . contemporary theological ethics has perhaps been too preoccupied with relatively peripheral issues. It should again turn to an investigation of basic religious notions such as repentance, forgiveness, guilt, in order to reemphasize their relationship to the moral life. For the Christian moral life, like any other moral life, is not solely the life of decision. It is also the life of vision—a vision that is determined by the religious and moral notions that constitute it. To be a Christian in effect is learning to see the world in a certain way and thus become as we see. The task of contemporary theological ethics is to state the language of faith in terms of the Christian responsibility to be formed in the likeness of Christ.[22]

The entanglement of these two influences was present from the very beginning.

What I intend to show is that these two strands—his appropriation of Wittgenstein and his rich Christian convictions—do not simply coexist in Hauerwas. Rather, Hauerwas is able to do ethics precisely because he has been enabled to think *through* Wittgenstein *by means of* the particular language of Christianity. On the one hand, there are three aspects under which Hauerwas's work in ethics may be illumined by the conceptual journey Wittgenstein himself underwent. In the first chapter I show that Wittgenstein's work bears the character of autobiography. His turning toward a therapeutic method of philosophy that effectively moved particular human subjects from the periphery to the very center of the philosophical stage was the result of work he had done on himself. When the dust settled, he could no longer speak of philosophy-as-artifact. Rather, he spoke of philosophy-as-artform: "The nimbus of philosophy has been lost. For now we have a method of doing philosophy, and can speak of *skillful* philosophers."[23] In chapter 2 I show that Wittgenstein's efforts to change the subject of philosophy can be detected in the aesthetic dimension in Hauerwas's ethics.

In chapter 3 I trace the metamorphosis of an oft-repeated concept in the Wittgenstein corpus: "form." Each successive revision of the notion served as a rung on a ladder which Wittgenstein ascended and eventually discarded. Thus, while "form" denoted the logical structure of reality in the *Tractatus*, shortly after 1931 the term came to rest in language-games that spoke of the irreducibly social character of human life. The given for Wittgenstein's later views, namely, "form of life," focuses the "political" aspect under which Hauerwas's work in ethics may be fruitfully viewed. Thus chapter 4 displays the ways in which Hauerwas conceives Christians' primary moral task as learning what it means to inhabit the particular form of life that constitutes the believing community called "church."

The final chapter on Wittgenstein, chapter 5, discusses Wittgenstein's anti-theoretical bent. Here, the family resemblance with Aristotle is most striking—despite Wittgenstein's unfamiliarity with Aristotle's work. For example, Wittgenstein came to conclude that philosophy's inability to view things *sub species aeternitatis* was not its lamentable condition but a clue to the *phronetic* character of the philosophical task. Thus he opposed approaches to modern philosophy and contemporary science that treated both as versions of *technē*. But Wittgenstein left his criticism in the shape of aporias. In chapter 6 I try to show that Hauerwas's particularism attained what Wittgenstein hoped for: a realism that was free from the confusions of the "inside out" epistemology of contemporary empiricism.[24]

These pairs of chapters are not intended to imply that there is a strict one-to-one correspondence between Wittgenstein's works and those of

Hauerwas. Nor do they theorize a causal link. Rather, the enigmas characteristically present in both authors are mutually illumined by the light each writer sheds on the works of the other. The fog surrounding Hauerwas's work clears when exposed to a right reading of Wittgenstein. I conclude with a retrospective look at the light Hauerwas sheds on Wittgenstein's legacy and I suggest that Hauerwas's appropriation of the particular language of Christianity enables him to surmount the aporias with which Wittgenstein expressed himself. Wittgenstein's genius lay in doing philosophy aporetically; aporias are the only shape philosophy can take if one is to oppose totalizing schemes without falling into the trap of adopting their terms in order to refute them. For, such aporias can never have general solutions without simply collapsing into another totalizing schema. If aporias are dissolved at all, they may be dissolved only in the *particular* case. To the extent that Hauerwas brings to his reading of Wittgenstein the gift of grace — namely, his Christian particularity—he is thereby enabled to go on.

ONE

WORKING ON ONESELF

A book is a mirror; if an ape gazes into it, of course no apostle looks back out.

—Lichtenberg

Working in philosophy . . . is really more a working on oneself.
—Wittgenstein, *Culture and Value*

There is an oddness to Wittgenstein's corpus that derives from its history. For many years the bulk of its unsorted stacks lay in a steamer trunk under G. E. M. Anscombe's bed. These stacks are indicative of Wittgenstein's perfectionist and labor-intensive editing process (a process which prevented him from publishing anything in his lifetime after the *Tractatus*); they render apt the book title *"Zettel"* (the German word for "scrap of paper")[1] and deprive his later works of any sense of finality—a trait symptomatic of all his posthumously published writings. The closest thing to a "finished" manuscript after 1929 appears to have no more structure than a series of numbered paragraphs. This oddness can tempt us to think of Wittgenstein's later writings as nothing more than an aggregate of stand-alone aphorisms.[2] The carefree stance we are often guilty of taking toward his work assumes that

any remark by his hand merits equal attention for the light it throws on his philosophy; as if his genius were a natural phenomenon which could not fail to express itself with equal power in all its manifestations. This attitude, however, makes one neglectful of Wittgenstein's own intentions, of the fact that he was actively striving to develop his thought in certain directions, as is made evident by the continual revising and reordering to which he subjected his remarks.[3]

With these words, Lars Hertzberg advises us to be alert to marks of ongoing development in Wittgenstein's thinking as we read the later corpus. I suggest that any development in Wittgenstein's later thought cannot be fully appreciated if his later works are read in isolation from the high point of his early period, the *Tractatus Logico-Philosophicus*. Granted, Wittgenstein's later thought constituted a revolution against the received philosophical paradigm of the early twentieth century. However, the nature of this revolution is widely disputed. I maintain that Wittgenstein's revolution is best told as the story of character transformation and conceptual metamorphosis that assumes one kind of unity between Wittgenstein's early and late works.

The suggestion of unity between the "early" and "later" Wittgenstein is certainly not new. There is enough ambiguity in Wittgenstein's writings for nearly any philosophical position to find a resting place. Yet many who argue for a unity do so either by conceiving it in terms of a conceptual continuity (as if all the later works could be distilled into theses that oppose the earlier *Tractatus* on a common ground) or by trying to assimilate both periods in his thinking under a different rubric altogether. For example, soon after its publication, the *Tractatus* was hailed as the final piece in the logical positivist's jigsaw puzzle. Less famously, Bernard Williams and Norman Malcolm debate the lingering effect of Kantian idealism on Wittgenstein's writing.[4] But there is something very un-Wittgensteinian about all such projects.

Unfortunately, when we look for continuity in Wittgenstein's work we are tempted to look for a *theoretical* continuity. Thus Williams sees a latent idealism, Malcolm hedges toward realism, James C. Edwards sees Wittgenstein's progressive emancipation from "rationality-as-representation," Fergus Kerr locates Wittgenstein's work in reaction to the myth of the solitary wordless Cartesian ego, and so on.[5] But can any author claim to have uncovered what Wittgenstein is really up to by framing the putative "theory" lying underneath his writings? I suspect that each "discovery" of a supposed central feature of Wittgenstein's thought has the grip it does on each author not because he or she has an objective grasp on Wittgensteinian truths, but because Wittgenstein has a subjective grasp on them as readers; each "discovery" is but a manifestation of their particular "cure." Reading Wittgenstein rightly leads to diverse convictions because maladies differ; each author champions the "Wittgensteinian theory" that most reflects the way that he or she has escaped his or her own fly-bottle. Wittgenstein cannot be subsumed without remainder under any theoretical framework because, as we shall see, the unity his work displays is a *narrative* rather than a theoretical one.

Rush Rhees is said to have once remarked that the chief work of Wittgenstein's later period, the *Philosophical Investigations*, has the unity of a conversation. Ordinarily, it would not dawn on us to treat a conversation as an exercise in propositional logic. ("Yes, I see that your decision to set the orthodontist appointment for Tuesday follows from your claim that blue is your favorite color and that Siberia may still have snow on the ground.") If asked to "outline" a conversation we would be hard pressed to know what to do. Typically, conversations cannot be reduced to their "essence" without great loss nor can they be fully "explained" apart from simply repeating all the words of the dialogue. We can't even imagine that the topics touched on betray a thematic unity that might be thought to underlie a conversation. Rather, conversations are woven from a cornucopia of topics by speakers who detect ways in which each sentence has bearing upon the others. The only thing that guarantees the continuation of a conversation is the skill of the interlocutors to go on.

This metaphor aptly describes the unity of the entire Wittgensteinian corpus. The linguistic (or narrative) unity of his philosophy is an expression of Wittgenstein's own ability to "go on." Three unresolved tensions in the *Tractatus* foreshadow the direction of his conceptual development. For the remainder of this chapter I will show that his conceptual transformation involved the migration of the human subject to the very center of his attention. Wittgenstein's revolution in philosophy was not simply that he had succeeded in changing the topics of philosophy but that he sought to change its subjects. As Wittgenstein's outlook matured, it became more intentionally ethical—not in the sense of providing an ethical theory, but in the sense that he as philosopher functioned as a moral sage whose therapy assisted the character transformation of concrete human selves.[6]

MIGRATION OF THE SUBJECT

One of the ways Wittgenstein mystifies contemporary thinkers is that he defies classification within the theoretical space mapped out by Enlightenment thinkers. Whereas critical thinking seeks objectivity in knowledge, Wittgenstein's postcritical philosophy came to be preoccupied with the unavoidably messy way that particular human subjects are entangled with acts of knowing. Wittgenstein's conceptual journey along these lines was foreshadowed by tensions in the content, style, and "storyline" of the *Tractatus*. These tensions resulted in Wittgenstein's experimentation with pedagogy and ultimately precipitated a clear therapeutic method in philosophy. But the direction that his later philosophy was to take seems very difficult to envision, given the way the *Tractatus* treats human selves as virtually invisible.

The Invisible Self

There is some ambiguity in speaking of the "migration of the subject" in Wittgenstein's early works, since the *Tractatus* referred to human subjects in two distinct ways. On the one hand, there is the "psychological I," which is the human being, the human body, the human soul with all its psychological attributes.[7] This "I" is the human self whose identity is bound up with the history of a particular community. One outspoken Wittgensteinian commentator, D. Z. Phillips, explains, "As D.Z.P. I am one of a human neighborhood. I am given a name by my neighbors. I cannot ask, 'What is history to me?' My identity is my biography. It is one biography among many."[8] However, at another level, the fact that a person can call the world "my world" (as in TLP 5.62) leads many to assume there must be a metaphysical subject doing the possessing, a subject to whom the "my" refers. This is what Wittgenstein called, on the other hand, the "philosophical I":

> 5.641   The philosophical I is not the man, not the human body or the human soul of which psychology treats, but the metaphysical subject. . . .

In contrast to the psychological "I," the "philosophical I" has no character, no history, and no neighbors. Wittgenstein explained that the metaphysical subject is as elusive as mercury squeezed between one's fingers.

> 5.631   If I wrote a book "The world as I found it," I should also have therein to report on my body and say which members obey my will and which do not, etc. This then would be a method of isolating the subject or rather of showing that in an important sense there is no subject: that is to say, of it alone in this book mention could *not* be made.

5.632   The subject does not belong to the world but it is a limit of
the world.

5.633   *Where in* the word is a metaphysical subject to be noted?

As Phillips correctly points out, the metaphysical subject cannot be a part
of the world of experience, as the psychological "I" can be, because it is
the putative subject of *all* experience. Even the "mineness" of experience
is itself an experience. Therefore, this subject necessarily lies *outside* the
world of experience; or better, "it is a limit of the world." Whereas the psychological I is irrelevant to philosophy, the philosophical I appears to be invisible to philosophical scrutiny.

The Tractarian presumption concerning the invisibility of the subject
may be seen in the shocking transition seen from statements 5.641 to 6
(Routledge edition):

5.641   There is therefore really a sense in which in philosophy we
can talk of a non-psychological I.

The I occurs in philosophy through the fact that the "world
is my world".

The philosophical I is not the man, not the human body or
the human soul of which psychology treats, but the metaphysical subject, the limit—not part of the world.

6   The general form of truth-function is:
$[p, \bar{\xi}, N(\bar{\xi})]$.
This is the general form of a proposition.

In one fell swoop, Wittgenstein jumped from the nature of the self to symbolic logic. How could Wittgenstein tolerate this abrupt change of topics
in an otherwise predictably syllogistic argument? Does this constitute a
breakdown in the argument? I think Wittgenstein *does* proceed reasonably.
If the metaphysical subject is simply an extensionless point coordinated
with the world, then it is not worth troubling over; it simply drops out of
view. Wittgenstein wanted to discard the subject altogether and even proposed that language dispense with the word "I."[9] In statement 6 Wittgenstein was simply gathering threads from his earlier discussion about the
world and the logical form that makes talking about it possible.[10] Discussion about the philosophical self and "its" world reduces to discussion about
the world, which, in turn, reduces to discussion about logical form and
truth-functions.

The upshot of this tidy analysis is that the early Wittgenstein intentionally tried to minimize any attention paid to his own reader—the concrete human subject who willfully leafs the pages of the *Tractatus*. This conclusion is also supported by the physical structure of the *Tractatus*.

First, no first-person pronoun occurs in any primary statements (those numbered 1, 2, 3 . . . 7) or secondary statements (those numbered to the first decimal place, as in 1.1, 1.2, etc.).[11] The tenor of the logically important propositions is consistently objective, impersonal, and universal in such a way as to imply that concrete human persons are incidental to the discussion.

Second, the presence of first-person pronouns in the elucidatory remarks shows that concrete human selves attract Wittgenstein's reluctant attention only to the extent that their stupidity threatens to blind them to Wittgenstein's views. It is easy to get the impression that if everyone thought as clearly on matters as Wittgenstein himself, he could have trimmed the "ponderous" eighty pages down to seven simple statements, and then again down to just one: "Whereof one cannot speak, thereof one must be silent." Yet, the fact that Wittgenstein paid even reluctant attention to his readers foreshadowed the way concrete human subjects were to become his later obsession.

The primacy, here and now, of concrete human persons will be shown in later works by Wittgenstein's explicit attention to unraveling conceptual puzzles that entangle his particular students. But surprisingly, this shift is already anticipated by the concessions he grants to the readers of the *Tractatus*. His use of extra white space is deliberately arranged to assist *readers* to make connections between major logical sections. Thus, for example, he breaks the text this way:

5.5563 . . .
5.557 . . .
[*white space*]
[*four unnumbered lines of text*]
[*white space*]
5.5571 . . .
5.6 . . .

Indeed, the fact that he includes elucidation at all may be an indication of his willingness to compromise the philosophical silence for the benefit of the reader.

Of course, if the only challenge I can muster to a picture of Wittgenstein as one committed to the invisibility of the human subject in the practice of philosophy consists in the appearance of personal pronouns (coupled with judicious use of white space) in the elucidatory remarks aimed at accommodating obtuse readers, then the picture of Wittgenstein that emerges from the *Tractatus* is one of an Enlightenment thinker *par excellence*. To effectively defend my claim that the unity of Wittgenstein's philosophy can be narrated as the migration of the human subject that begins in the *Tractatus*, I must uncover three kinds of tension in the *Tractatus* that only make sense as anticipations of Wittgenstein's later turn to the subject. First is the logical puzzle of the book's conclusion. The second is the tension between the book's content and its style. The third tension arises from the hidden storyline of the *Tractatus*.

Surmounting the *Tractatus*

First, it is easy to feel cheated when one reaches the conclusion of the *Tractatus*:

> 6.54   My propositions are elucidatory in this way: he who understands me finally recognizes them as senseless. . . .

How does Wittgenstein imagine himself to have defended such a claim? He cannot say, "I have now accurately described the way the world *really* is and therefore you, Oh reader, are compelled to accept the conclusion that based on *this* structure of the world, spelled out in my former propositions, the former propositions themselves are nonsensical!" This is precisely what his teacher Bertrand Russell thought he was up to. During Wittgenstein's doctoral *Viva* Russell charged that Wittgenstein was inconsistent for claiming to have expressed ineffable truths by means of nonsensical propositions. Wittgenstein's reply is telling: "Don't worry, I know you'll never understand it."[12] Was Wittgenstein's reply an instance of sophomoric arrogance, or was something else going on? Surely Wittgenstein knew that the basis for accepting a set of propositions as senseless can never be the sense of those very propositions. That a proposition lacks sense means precisely this, that its "meaning" cannot enter into its own justification.

Yet when he reached the point in the *Tractatus* where he claimed that everything he has said up to that point was literally *meaningless*, we are tempted to play the part of Anselm's Boso and ask, "What did he mean by that?" Is this an unfair question? Not if there is another way that ineffable truths can be communicated to us. Wittgenstein claimed that language is coterminous with the world; the limits of language are the limits of the world.[13] If we take him literally for a moment, we must conclude that it makes no sense to *speak* about the limits, because both the boundary and what lies beyond the boundary are off limits to language. And if discursive reasoning is a function of language, then we cannot even "think" the boundary: "for, in order to draw a limit to thinking we should have to be able to think both sides of this limit."[14] Now, there is no problem in the fact that we are invited, even exhorted, to contemplate the world as a limited whole so long as contemplation (*Anschauung*) is linked to feeling (*Gefühl*) rather than thought.[15] But there is a problem in using *language* to make such an offer since the phrases "the world *sub specie aeternitatis*" or "the world as a limited whole" (6.45) are literally "inexpressible" (6.522). All such notions—the limits of the world, *das Mystische*, logical form, God,—are metaphysical terms; to speak them is to speak unintelligibly (*unsinnig*), for they are terms lacking reference (*Bedeutung*).[16] Wittgenstein concluded that correct application of philosophy is the policing of language: sentences must be restricted to those of natural science, while putative metaphysical claims must be debunked. However, the sentences of *Tractatus* belong neither to natural science nor to metaphysics. And for this reason, the *Tractatus* was just as self-stultifying as were the principle of verifiability (which was itself unverifiable) and the principle of falsifiability (which was itself unfalsifiable).

Somewhat surprisingly, Wittgenstein acknowledged this problem but did not confess it as a fault. Why not? Midway through the *Tractatus* Wittgenstein made the distinction between *form* and *content*. Propositions which are false with respect to their content can nevertheless precipitate trustworthy conclusions by virtue of their form.[17] The sentence, "The basketball is green," when, in fact, the basketball is orange, is an example of a sentence that is false with respect to content. However, such a sentence still correctly conveys the fact that basketballs are the sorts of things that are colored. This fact is conveyed by means of the sentence's participation in the logical form of basketballs. Apparently Wittgenstein thought the same possibility holds for *senseless* propositions.[18] The senseless propositions of the *Tractatus*, insofar as they express (*ausdrucken*) logical form, can still direct those who surmount them to see the world rightly.[19]

Thus the escape route taken by Wittgenstein to avoid the inconsistency with which Russell charged him had to do with the ability of language to show what it is unable to say:

4.022   The proposition *shows* its sense.

The proposition *shows* how things stand, *if* it is true. And it *says*, that they do so stand.

In this way language can possibly communicate the inexpressible. But there is another way to read the *Tractatus* that circumvents self-stultification. This can be best illustrated by a short detour into the literary method of Stanley Fish.

Fish makes a convincing case that a reader-response model of literary criticism can best account for what otherwise might be an embarrassing spot in Plato's *Phaedrus*. Translator Walter Hamilton reminds us that "the *Phaedrus* has sometimes been described as Plato's farewell to literature," largely due to Socrates' explicit conclusion in the final section of the dialogue:

> To believe, on the one hand, that a written composition on any subject must be to a large extent the creation of fancy; that nothing worth serious attention has ever been written in prose or verse . . . to believe this, I say, and to let all else go is to be the sort of man, Phaedrus, that you and I might well pray that we may both become.[20]

The problem, of course, is that Socrates' pronouncement against all literature seems to consign the *Phaedrus* itself to the same problematic status. However, Fish argues that the *genre* of *Phaedrus* demands that we look for its unity not in its formal structure, as if *Phaedrus* were a self-contained artifact, but in its coherence as a function of the interplay between the reader and the text. Taking this approach will enable us to see that

> Rather than a single sustained argument, the *Phaedrus* is a series of discreet conversations or seminars, each with its own carefully posed question, ensuing discussion, and firmly drawn conclusion, but so arranged that to enter the spirit and assumptions of any one of these self-enclosed units is implicitly to reject the spirit and assumptions of the unit immediately preceding.[21]

Fish is not simply saying that the reader imaginatively enters into the dialogue at the same level as a main character (Phaedrus), so that the growth of his or her knowledge is simply the same incremental, piecemeal path taken by Phaedrus. Rather, the reader stands in a dialectic *with the text as a whole*, something Socrates' student would have been unable to do.

For example, Fish explains that early on the reader is forced to deal with a contradiction of which Socrates and Phaedrus are simply unaware. Phaedrus recounts a speech he heard given by Lysias, which receives Socrates' just criticism for its sloppy structure. However, when Socrates offers a well-crafted substitute, he is forced to criticize his own version for being simply a piece of rhetoric. Fish summarizes: "In other words, Lysias' speech is bad because it is not well put together and Socrates' speech is bad because it is well put together." While the observant reader may detect that the criterion for "good" has changed between these two criticisms, the clever reader will realize as well that the introduction of the new standard "invalidates the very basis on which the whole discussion . . . had hitherto been proceeding."[22] However, the point of this tension in the reader's experience of the text, claims Fish, is to urge the reader not to *go back* and re-evaluate Lysias' speech by the new criterion, but to *go on:*

> At that moment, this early section of the dialogue will have achieved its true purpose, which is, paradoxically, to bring the reader to the point where he [or she] is no longer interested in the issues it treats—no longer interested because he [or she] has come to see that the real issues exist at a higher level of generality. Thus, in a way peculiar to dialectical form and experience, this space of prose and argument will have been the vehicle of its own abandonment.[23]

Fish's analysis of *Phaedrus* illustrates the difference between showing and saying that we have already encountered in Wittgenstein. Claiming that a text shows what it cannot say is an allusion to the performative nature of language. As the ordinary language philosopher John L. Austin put it, the written text becomes a speech-act whose felicity depends, in part, on the uptake by its readers.[24] To be sure, there are issues such as the reader's eyesight, intelligence, and literacy that affect uptake. But the reader's "vision"—the reader's penchant for seeing some aspects rather than others—plays a central role in his or her ability to "get it." The genius of Plato, as expressed in the pages of *Phaedrus*, is shown by the way he utilized the reader-text dialectic to shape the manner in which the reader perceives. The *Phaedrus* is not processing an argument but transforming the reader's vision.

Further, in order to transform the reader's vision effectively, the dialectic which exists between reader and the-text-as-a-whole must initially engage the reader at his or her particular point of departure. "Going on" from here is not a simple matter of the reader systematically abandoning "false" beliefs and embracing "true" ones, but a matter of transcending the conflict between rival beliefs by seeing matters in a deeper way. But this means that if the dialectic is successful, then, as the reader's outlook is changed, he or she will reach the end of a section of a dialogue and discard it as "elementary."

> To read the *Phaedrus*, then, is to use it up; for the value of any point in it is that it gets you (not any sustained argument) to the next point, which is not so much a point (in logical-demonstrative terms) as a level of insight. It is thus a self-consuming artifact, a mimetic enactment in the reader's experience of the Platonic ladder in which each rung, as it is negotiated, is kicked away.[25]

The question remains, "To what extent does the *Tractatus* function as a self-consuming artifact?" Wittgenstein appears to answer this question in an uncharacteristically straightforward manner.

> 6.54   My propositions are elucidatory in this way: he who under-stands me finally recognizes them as senseless, when he has climbed out through them, on them, over them. (He must so to speak throw away the ladder, after he has climbed up on it.)
> *He must surmount these propositions;* then he sees the world rightly.[26]

Yet we must also ask how much Wittgenstein thinks that the enlightening power of the *Tractatus* is wrapped up in its *structure*. In other words, is the "ladder" suitable for climbing because of its logical structure or, rather, because its "point" can only be gotten by the reader whose outlook has been transformed via engaging the text-as-a-whole, dialectically in the manner described by Fish? As evidence of the former, we can point to the meticulous attention Wittgenstein paid to the logical rigor of the primary propositions, each predicate becoming the subject of the following statement, and so on. However, there is at least one compelling reason for rejecting this option.

Gottlob Frege, who possessed one of the brightest logical minds of Wittgenstein's day, was judged by Wittgenstein to have entirely misunderstood the *Tractatus*. In a letter written to Russell dated August 1919 Wittgenstein confided that "I gather that he [Frege] doesn't understand a word of it all."[27] How can this be? Perhaps we have here a clue that a dialectical reading is more important to correct exegesis than attention to the logical

structure of the *Tractatus*. For surely Frege could have followed the logical machinations of the *Tractatus* as well as, or better than, anyone.

Frege has been credited with the removal of the human subject from
philosophy of language by discarding John Locke's "idea"-idea as mere
psychologism.[28] Locke had suggested that objects and events gave rise to
ideas in our mind. We then subsequently affix labels to these ideas in the
form of speech. The upshot of the Lockean scheme is the impossibility of
a public measurement of the correspondence between a speaker's ideas and
words, for only the speaker has unmediated access to his or her own ideas.
But in consequence of Frege's suggestion, modern philosophers of language
no longer troubled with the middle term of the "word—idea—world" chain
but purported, instead, to do philosophy of language "objectively," by considering only the relation between *public* sentences and *public* states of
affairs.

In telling correspondence with Wittgenstein, Frege claimed that Tractarian statements 1 and 2 had identical meanings. Wittgenstein responded,
"The sense of both propositions is one and the same, but not the ideas that
I associated with them when I wrote them."[29] By the words, "when I wrote
them," Wittgenstein may have been trying to draw attention to the stance
a given reader takes toward the text and the fact that any such stance could
(as his notebooks show to be true in his own case), and ought to, change.
Wittgenstein felt it absolutely necessary to get past the propositions of the
Tractatus as he himself had done. Only by doing so might one see the world
rightly.[30] The use of the adverb "rightly" (*richtig*) here to modify the verb
"to see" (*sehen*) was deliberate: Wittgenstein's aim was that the reader attain a correct *manner* of viewing rather than secure a correct picture of
reality, because, as he would summarize some years later, "the search says
more than the discovery."[31]

It should not be surprising, on this account, that Frege, who tried to engage the text on purely objective terms, was bound to miss the point. And
it is likewise not surprising that Wittgenstein himself should go beyond the
Tractatus in search of a more fitting pedagogy.

Content vs. Style

If we accept Wittgenstein's distinction between showing and saying, then
we can get past the question of whether the *Tractatus* is self-consistent in
what it *says* in order to address the second, deeper tension in the *Tractatus:* Does what the text *show* fit its manner of expression?

Imagine leafing through a philosophy journal which contains an article arguing that the "real" meaning of some particular poem can be stated by proposition X. Imagine further that the argument offered by this author analyzes the poem, line by line, reducing each line to symbolic logic. Once the symbolization is complete the author applies the appropriate logical calculus, retranslates the symbolic logic into propositional form, and "Presto!" the logically validated conclusion is miraculously identical to the author's thesis. Frankly, we wouldn't know what to make of such an article. The genre in which the poem is discussed is so distant from poetry that we would be justified in wondering, not merely whether the author is reading this particular poem rightly, but whether the author knows what it means to read poetry at all. This illustration shows the way genre and style must "fit" the message if the text is not to be self-defeating. Lawrence Hinman puts it in the strongest terms:

> what one is saying sets the limits of valid philosophical discourse. A philosophical style is wrong when it naively steps outside the limits which are being established by what is being said, i.e., when the presuppositions of a certain mode of speaking contradict what is being said.[32]

Are the style and genre of the *Tractatus* "wrong"? Wittgenstein certainly chose his style deliberately. Fearing the readers might miss the logical scaffolding of the text (by reading it as a uni-dimensional treatise), Wittgenstein refused to have the *Tractatus* published in stages (as one potential publisher offered[33]) and also refused to omit the decimals.[34] Only in its final form did Wittgenstein think that the *Tractatus* counted as both philosophy and the sort of literature that in its artform could show what could not be said, namely, the relation of language to the world.[35] Wittgenstein had already grasped the intrinsic difficulty of using language to *say* how language relates to the world (a "discovery" sometimes attributed to the Wittgenstein's "later" philosophy), since there is no way to transcend language to speak about it. The naive realist claims that language "pictures" the world but is then hard-pressed to produce a criterion by which the putative correspondence between a proposition and a state of affairs can be measured. (Where could one stand to make such a call? And with what language might *this* be expressed?) Thinkers from Bertrand Russell (Wittgenstein's mentor at Cambridge) to Polish logician Alfred Tarski have typically answered this objection by positing a higher order language (what Tarski calls *metalanguage*) comprised of words like 'represent' and 'correspond' in order to refer to the relationship between "lower-order language" and "the world." But, of course, it is always fair to ask for the criteria against which metalanguage can be checked for correct employment. Thus an infinite regress.

Wittgenstein avoided the problem of correspondence altogether. He began with the claim that there is no way to utilize language to describe the extra-linguistic means by which it corresponds with states of affairs.

> 4.12   Propositions can represent the whole reality but they cannot represent what they must have in common with reality in order to represent it—the logical form.
>
> To be able to represent the logical form, we should have to be able to put ourselves with the propositions outside of logic, that is outside the world.
>
> 4.121   . . .
>
> The propositions *show* the logical form of reality.
> They exhibit it.

Granted, Wittgenstein assumed that language models or "pictures" the world, but of greater interest to him was how this picturing works.[36] He reasoned that the way pictures represent is by holding something in common with what is pictured. Both the picture and the pictured have the same "form." For example, the form that a photograph shares with the room it depicts includes things like spatial relations (e.g., "to the right of") and color relations (e.g., "is bluer than"). For Wittgenstein, "form" connoted the entire logical space that a state of affairs embodies. The logical form marks the boundaries of the world, that is, of the limits of all logically possible arrangements. To the extent that language pictures the world, it too shares this form. Thus, the only correspondence worth troubling about is the correspondence between the form of the world and the syntax of language. Here it would be better to say that the "correspondence" of language to the world is the co-participation of language and world in logical form. This is why Wittgenstein could write that for all sensible propositions, "the propositions 'p' and '$\sim p$' have opposite senses, but to them corresponds one and the same reality."[37]

So then, in Wittgenstein's thinking, "reality" or "the world" encompasses all possible cases, and this world is bounded by logical form.

> 5.61   Logic fills the world: the limits of the world are also its limits.

However, since language also embodies this form, we cannot say what logically we cannot think.[38] The difficulty that faced Wittgenstein became apparent in his realization that if "form" is the means by which representation occurs, then form itself cannot be represented, pictured, or spoken. But by the same token, how can he claim to know it and even be so presumptuous as to give it a name? Again the distinction between showing and saying comes to the rescue.

In Wittgenstein's early view, we perceive form directly without the mediation supplied by language. To put the point differently, if we grasp a proposition (or a photograph) *as a picture*, rather than as an artifact, we have *already* grasped its form. We would not know what to make of a person who said, "Yes, I see that is a picture of Mt. Rainier, but how do I know the form is the same in both cases if I can't spell it out?" Form is not elusive for being unsayable but is everywhere immediately present to us in each recognition of a picture *as* a picture.

Wittgenstein hoped that for all its literally nonsensical propositions about unsayable things, the *Tractatus shows* what cannot be *said*. If the *Tractatus* is a picture, it must already embody in its crystalline structure the form of the world. Hinman describes it this way:

> Thus the grammatical simplicity of the main propositions in the *Tractatus*, the orderliness of the presentation, the way in which certain propositions stand out as fundamental and others are given as derivative, and the very finality that characterized Wittgenstein's pronouncements are all aspects of his style which seem to reflect the basic claims about the relationship between language and the world developed in the *Tractatus*.[39]

The logical structure of the *Tractatus*, which constitutes, in part, its genre, succeeds in showing the logical scaffolding of the world. Yet, in the midst of this showing, as Frege complained, the theses appear to lack adequate support.[40] This, of course, anticipates Wittgenstein's later claim that if there were such things as theses in philosophy, they would be self-evident.[41] But in the *Tractatus*, this lack shows something that is of the greatest importance to Wittgenstein. Seen in all its logical relief, the seven theses of the *Tractatus* display the *limits* of language.

Wittgenstein's style in the *Tractatus* is dictated by two considerations: on the one hand, the ultimately simple and univocal character of the relation between language and the world means that that which shows itself here can indeed show itself once for all in its fundamental form; on the other hand, the fact that saying must be replaced by letting something show itself means that language in this context must almost have the terseness of a gesture.[42]

So far, so good. Once Wittgenstein began to think in terms of the human capacity to perceive form directly, the focal point of philosophy also began to change for him. Increasingly, the big question of philosophy of language was not whether the correspondence between language and world could be demonstrated in some subject-neutral way, but whether we as human speakers were skilled enough to recognize the limits of language. Thus, the first two tensions in the *Tractatus* can be understood as anticipating Wittgenstein's turn to the subject. The third tension that undermines the apparent Tractarian message that human subjects are incidental to philosophy is the fact that the style of the *Tractatus* also displays the narrative shape of Wittgenstein's own conceptual journey. *This* tension became unbearable for Wittgenstein and ultimately drove him to return to academia after his premature "retirement" from philosophy.[43]

The Storyline of the *Tractatus*

In a letter to Ludwig von Ficker, probably written in November 1919, Wittgenstein explained that the *Tractatus* contained "that which really occurred to me—and how it occurred to me."[44] At face value this may only mean that Wittgenstein claimed these thoughts as his own. But it also may be an allusion to the fact that the "logical" progression of the *Tractatus* was roughly an autobiographical one. We can discover the relation between the logical progression of the *Tractatus* and the chronological progression of his sourcebook for the *Tractatus*, the *Notebooks 1914–1916*, by mapping the decimal number of each Tractarian statement against the date of the parallel entry in the *Notebooks*: statement 2.17 corresponds with the entry for October 20, 1914, statement 3.001 with that of November 1, 1914, and so forth.[45] What we find is expressed by the figure that follows.

There are two striking features of the distribution. First is the 198-day gap in entries between June 22, 1915, and April 15, 1916.[46] Second, despite this gap, the development of Wittgenstein's thought during the entire period is expressed by the straight line that diagonally bisects the graph. I am not suggesting that this correlation is proof positive of an explicit historical development in Wittgenstein's thinking. The correlation itself may reflect

Chronological-Logical Correlation: *Notebooks 1914–1916* and *Tractatus Logico-Philosophicus*

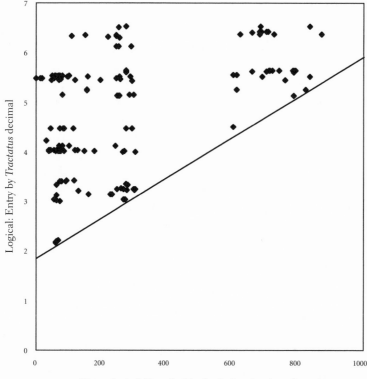

Chronological: Entry by *Notebooks* date (1 = Aug 28, 1914)

nothing more profound than that Wittgenstein simply stopped thinking about each Tractarian thesis once he had gotten it down on paper. Rather, I am suggesting that the figure illustrates the possibility of an intrinsic relationship between his life story and the logical structure of the *Tractatus*. On this view, Wittgenstein's own life reflected what the *Tractatus* advocates; as his thinking advanced in time he systematically discarded each "rung" of the ladder he had constructed. In other words, the *Tractatus* chronicles Wittgenstein's own conceptual transformation en route to the ineffable realm of *das Mystiche*. His decade-long hiatus from philosophy after writing the *Tractatus* is evidence that he had surmounted the entire ladder. This surprising result reveals that the *Tractatus*, despite its austere, objective, and totalizing logical structure, nevertheless contains a hidden map of Wittgenstein's own life. Far from being marginalized, the philosophizing subject— namely Ludwig Wittgenstein— is at the very heart of the *Tractatus*.

What can be concluded from these data? First, if my suggestion is correct, Wittgenstein's explicitly dismissive attitude toward human subjects engaged in philosophy stands in lasting tension with the autobiographical flow of the *Tractatus* itself, a tension that draws attention to the possibility that human subjects such as Wittgenstein could undergo profound conceptual transformation. The hope for such transformation was to become central to his rapidly maturing philosophical outlook. Second, the overt structure of the *Tractatus*—as shown by the decimals—barely conceals the narrative structure embedded in the elucidative remarks of the text. If the unity of the *Tractatus* is neither logical nor topical but *narrative*, then, *a fortiori*, the unity of Wittgenstein's early and later works is likewise the unity of Wittgenstein's own life. Third, Wittgenstein wrote in his preface that he expected only readers of the *Tractatus* "who have themselves already thought the thoughts which are expressed in it—or similar thoughts" would be able to understand the *Tractatus*. Therefore, if the *Tractatus* contains a record of Wittgenstein's own journey toward the ethical (and other aspects of *das Mystische* expressed by propositions 6 and 7), then it is possible—even preferable—to read the *Tractatus* as a manual for assisting its readers to make similar journeys.[47]

PLAYING WITH PEDAGOGY

I have spilled a lot of ink correlating tensions in the *Tractatus* with Wittgenstein's own early conceptual journey. Wittgenstein's later period began with an experiment in a pedagogical style that, in effect, inverted the priority of the *Tractatus*'s logical structure: the formerly insignificant elucidations became the chief means in dissolving philosophical puzzles, while the formerly paramount philosophical theses come to be exposed as language gone haywire. This can be seen very clearly in his "Lecture on Ethics" (1929), *Philosophical Remarks* (ca. 1930), and "Remarks on Frazer's Golden Bough" (begun in 1931). But perhaps the most important work for seeing his changing style is the so-called *Big Typescript* (1932–34).

The historical context of the *Big Typescript* is far different from that of the *Tractatus*. The latter was drafted in the isolated and austere mountains of Norway and then pieced together while Wittgenstein was on the Russian front. During this period, Wittgenstein was joined to the greater academic community only by an occasional letter. In contrast, the *Big Typescript*— the bulk of which has been recently published in English as the *Philosophical Grammar*—was constructed after Wittgenstein had returned to philosophy from a decade hiatus and deeply ensconced himself in Cambridge academic life, having honed his pedagogical skills on two years of live classroom lectures. The aroma of "lecture" permeates the *Big Typescript* and gives it more the look and feel of an introductory textbook than any of the rest of Wittgenstein's writings. Wittgenstein himself admitted as much in a marginal note uncovered by Rush Rhees: "My book might be called: *Philosophical Grammar*. This title would no doubt have the smell of a textbook title but that doesn't matter for behind it there is the book."[48]

Among those features that contribute to the "textbook smell" is the attention paid directly to the reader-as-pupil. As in his Cambridge lectures, Wittgenstein does all the talking. The reader is treated as a merely passive recipient of information. However, that the reader is included in the frequent "we" and "us" that litter the pages is a notable departure from the terse gestures of the *Tractatus*. The *Philosophical Grammar* does not quite fit the dialogical genre of the later works (for instance, the *Investigations*), nor does it match the autobiographical musings of the *Philosophical Remarks*. Rather, the genre of *Philosophical Grammar* might more appropriately be labeled "transcribed lecture."

The organization also adds to the textbook feel of the *Philosophical Grammar*. Unlike the *Tractatus*, whose table of contents (had one been written) would have been identical to the book itself, the table of contents in the *Philosophical Grammar* does not summarize an argument but, rather, displays a collection of landmarks reminding one of the journey taken, or anticipating one to be taken, by the reader.[49] In this way, the *Philosophical Grammar* is organized "geographically" and the table of contents serves as its roadmap or guide book. However, the quest Wittgenstein imagined for his reader differs from the sort of transformation Wittgenstein will later seek for readers of the *Investigations*. For one thing, the starting points of the journey—those confusions that are bewitching the mind of the reader of the *Philosophical Grammar*—as well as the endpoints for each stage along the way are fixed by Wittgenstein in advance. This is why the *Philosophical Grammar* does not "live" like the later dialogical *Investigations*; the *Philosophical Grammar* can only engage a reader who fits Wittgenstein's stereotype of "the confused pupil." Perhaps this is also why he never was satisfied sufficiently with the manuscript to publish it: since the route was so clearly mapped out for the student in advance, the book smacks of being governed by the very sort of theoretical agenda that Wittgenstein was trying to repudiate.

Imagine that a former reader of the *Tractatus* picks up the *Philosophical Grammar* and, thumbing through it, pauses to read the conclusion to

Part I, Section III: "What interests *us* in the sign, the meaning which matters for us is what is embodied in the grammar of the sign." What Wittgenstein is talking about is ambiguous. This is because only an insider—one of the "us"—can properly decode the message. This is but one example of his new pedagogy: the summary statements at the end of each section of the *Philosophical Grammar* are not conclusions of arguments. If they were, anyone could get an inkling of their sense and take the further trouble to read the entire section only if he or she wanted to follow the justification of the position that the conclusion summarized. But the remarks which terminate a given section of the *Philosophical Grammar* do not function as the conclusion of an argument (let alone as a self-evident truism). Rather, they function as a quiz to test the student's clarity of thought at just this stage of his or her intellectual journey. As such, they are never final destinations, but rather temporary docking points that signal the completion only of a particular leg of a longer journey to be continued by engaging following sections. Thus what look like philosophical theses in the *Philosophical Grammar* are not, because they are not universally accessible.

While the conclusions are not universally accessible, Wittgenstein does seem to begin the book with a particularly afflicted student in mind. For students of philosophy since Frege have been carefully schooled to believe, mistakenly, that "understanding" (whatever *that* is) is separable from "language":

§1   How can one talk about "understanding" and "not understanding" a proposition? Surely it is not a proposition until it's understood? . . .

§2   We regard understanding as the essential thing, and signs as something inessential. . . .

The uninitiated reader is likely to answer the question of §1, "Surely it is not a proposition until it's understood?" in the affirmative, that is, as a restatement of Frege's view that a sentence achieves the status of "proposition" if and only if there can be correlated to it something called its "meaning." To such a person, §1 might also suggest that the technical term "proposition" be reserved for each string of words that possesses a correlative meaning. But surprisingly, and on the contrary, §1 expresses a *double entendre* foreshadowing where Wittgenstein wanted to take the reader. He was interested not in delineating the logical status of propositions (as he was in the *Tractatus*) but in clarifying the notion we commonly call "understanding." He plans to move the student from Frege's mistaken view to his own view that "understanding" is inextricably bound up with the *use* of language.

After this intentionally duplicitous start, Wittgenstein parades a series of illustrations and questions before the reader to nudge him or her from the received account of understanding as "seeing" to Wittgenstein's own account of understanding as that which is embodied in one's use of language. Consider the following progression of quotations (see p. 32) from the opening pages of the *Philosophical Grammar* coupled with descriptions of the reader's evolving conception of "understanding."

In a scant eight pages of text, the concept of "understanding" has metamorphosed several times. First, the notion of "mental seeing" changed to something like "translation" and then again to a concept so fluid it defies definition. Wittgenstein then drew attention to the behavioral component of understanding, and, by linking understanding with the ability to answer questions like "What does this sentence say?" he suggested that readers provisionally consider understanding as some type of *precondition* to application. Finally, Wittgenstein guided his readers to take the now manageable step to embrace his conclusion that understanding is best thought of as the *actual* application of language.

The ambiguity with which Wittgenstein began the *Philosophical Grammar* was central to his developing pedagogical method. First, the initial paragraph was deliberately open to a misreading which his following parade of remarks systematically untangled. Second, the fact that the opening sentence was vulnerable to contrary literal readings *showed* the point he tried to make explicit: to possess understanding is to possess the skill necessary for using a string of words according to a range of grammatically allowable combinations within a given context. Third, it served as a reminder of the lesson learned. Having read it once, the student who goes back to review sees something entirely different from the uninitiated person who reads it for the first time. The answer to "Surely it is not a proposition until it is understood?" (§1) is still "Yes," but the tutored student now realizes that the reason this is so is because "understanding the meaning" is bound up with the proposition (i.e., its use) and not separable from it, as initially presupposed.

The pedagogical style that the opening pages illustrate is consistently maintained throughout the *Philosophical Grammar*. To repeat, of all of Wittgenstein's writings, this one most resembles a textbook. The table of contents is not an analytical outline showing the logical relation of parts. The logical relations within §1 and between §1 and §2, as well as those between Section I and Section II, and again between Part I and Part II, are not

"... Understanding would be something like seeing a picture. . . . (§2)

- *(the assumed starting position of reader: understanding-as-mental-sight)*

"In certain of their applications the words 'understand', 'mean' refer to a psychological reaction while hearing, reading, uttering etc. a sentence. In that case understanding is the phenomenon that occurs when I hear a sentence in a familiar language. . . ." (§3)

- *understanding is taken to be a mental event but, importantly, a mental event which accompanies the activities of using language.*

"Understanding a sentence is more akin to understanding a piece of music than one might think." (§4)

- *understanding-as-hearing. What is required to achieve understanding may not be insight but a trained ear or skillful hearing.*

"How curious: we should like to explain that understanding of a gesture as a translation into words, and the understanding of words as a translation into gestures." (§5)

- *understanding as familiarity with the connection between words and gestures.*

"Do we understand Christian Morgenstern's poems, or Lewis Carroll's poem 'Jabberwocky'? In these cases it's very clear that the concept of understanding is a fluid one." (§5)

- *understanding as a fluid concept; what understanding amounts to depends upon each context in which language is used.*

"To understand a sentence can mean...to be able to answer the question 'what does this sentence say?'" (§6)

- *understanding as possessing a behavioral component (e.g., to give a verbal response in answer to a question)*

"We speak of the understanding of a sentence as a condition of being able to apply it. We say "I cannot obey an order if I do not understand it".... (§8)

- *understanding as a precondition to the application of language.*

"'Understanding a word' may mean: *knowing* how it is used; *being able* to apply it." (§10)

- *understanding as the skill of knowing how to apply language.*

"When someone interprets, or understands, a sign in one sense or another, what he is doing is taking a step in a calculus (like a calculation). What he *does* is roughly what he does if he gives expression to his interpretation." (§13)

- *understanding is identified with the actual application of language.*

self-supporting. Rather, the firmness of these logical connections is supplied by the incrementally enlightened mind of the reader. As a result, the table of contents is an assemblage of reminders—sometimes phrases, sometimes whole sentences—of the lessons to be learned in the reading of the whole.

In this way, the *Philosophical Grammar* is a "self-consuming artifact" in a different, though related, sense from that used by Fish: the *Philosophical Grammar* consumes not itself, but the human selves that move through the volume. The reading of the *Philosophical Grammar* presupposes at every point that the reader has reached a certain level of conceptual clarity requisite for the next pericope. For example, Section II of Part I asks, "Can what the rules of grammar say about a word be described in another way by describing the process which takes place when understanding occurs?"[50] This sentence only makes sense to someone who conceives understanding in terms of the rules of grammar and is not in danger of slipping back into the sort of mentalism that was discarded in the reading of §§1–13. An uninitiated reader cannot simply dive into a middle section and "follow the argument." This is not because the argument is untenable or unclear, but because participation requires a reader of a certain sort—one who has been acclimated to the discussion by the entire sequence of discussion which precedes a given section.

The pedagogical style of the *Philosophical Grammar* makes it very demanding reading. Its structure is hierarchical rather than logical: numbered paragraphs are rungs of a ladder scaling a section; sections are rungs on a ladder scaling a part; and each part is a rung on a ladder which scales the whole. The ladder metaphor is, of course, borrowed from the *Tractatus*. However, in the *Tractatus* the point of the metaphor was to urge readers to discard the ladder once a certain conceptual elevation had been attained, namely, a God's-eye view (*sub specie aeternitatis*). In contrast, here the point is in the climbing.

Climbing is strenuous, and one gets the feeling that Wittgenstein expected as much from his reader as he did from those live bodies who struggled along during his half-day lectures. One of his students reminisced:

> Usually at the beginning of the year Wittgenstein would warn us that we would find his lectures unsatisfactory, that he would go on talking like this for hours and hours and we would get very little out of it. Plainly he was sensitive to the sort of audience he had. He wanted a small group of people who, knowing what was in store for them, were prepared to put in a full strenuous year with him learning philosophy. Visitors, even distinguished visitors, who wanted to attend a few lectures

to "find out what sort of thing Wittgenstein is doing" were not welcome, but anyone was welcome who seriously wanted to learn [to *do*] *philosophy* (and not just to hear Wittgenstein). And, if we worked hard, Wittgenstein worked tremendously hard.[51]

Wittgenstein's emerging pedagogical style displayed in the *Big Typescript* betrayed the fact that he had shifted his attention in philosophy from striving after a view of the world *sub specie aeternitatis* to striving after an alteration of the sensibilities of concrete human beings.

So far, I have tried to show that the movement of the subject from the periphery to the center of Wittgenstein's philosophical vision is shown initially by tensions internal to the 1922 publication, the *Tractatus*, and more fully in his experimentation with pedagogical style after 1929. The shift in style shows that the point of doing philosophy had changed for Wittgenstein: "A present-day teacher of philosophy doesn't select food for his pupil with the aim of flattering his taste but with the aim of changing it."[52] The goal of doing philosophy is not to produce a literary artifact replete with timeless truths but to clear up confusions in others' minds. In 1933 he wrote "philosophy ought to be written only as *poetic composition*."[53] Although Wittgenstein was never satisfied that his work ever attained this level of artistry, nevertheless, his work does make the same sorts of demands on a reader that proper reading of poetry does. Readers have to approach his writings deliberately and creatively, with the commitment to invest time and attention to nuance and subtle detail. At times one's investment seems fruitless. But as Wittgenstein once commented to Drury, "Philosophy is like trying to open a safe with a combination lock. Each little adjustment of the many dials seems to achieve nothing, only when all is in place does the door open."[54]

Evidently Wittgenstein felt justified in placing large demands on his would-be students precisely because of the way he came to conceive philosophy. Students during the Michaelmas Term 1930 quoted Wittgenstein as saying: "The nimbus of philosophy has been lost. For now we have a method of doing philosophy, and can speak of *skillful* philosophers."[55] Wittgenstein did not have a philosophical theory. Rather, he proposed a *method* by which conceptual confusions in the minds of concrete subjects might be dissolved. Philosophy becomes, in short, a kind of conceptual "therapy."[56]

Wittgenstein felt that he had reached a "real resting place" in his conception of philosophy as therapy.[57] When philosophy is deemed "good," the term is not a stamp of approval on a book's argument but an adjective that praises the skill of the therapist who helps others clarify their cloudy think-ing. However, Wittgenstein grew uneasy with the textbook feel of these first attempts at therapeutic philosophy. What emerges in Wittgenstein's most mature works might be called *aporetic philosophy*. In these works we see Wittgenstein's true genius displayed. Rather than creating more textbooks to serve as self-help manuals for students beset by a particular set of confu-sions, in the later works Wittgenstein reproduced conversations he had had with himself that, because of their aporetic character, engage readers who suffer from a wide range of befuddlements.

CHANGING THE SUBJECT

The development of Wittgenstein's later thinking is partially obscured by the nature of his posthumously published works. In nearly every case, each volume was originally conceived as notes for lectures given during his tenure at Cambridge. The trouble with lecture notes, of course, is that as the years pass a teacher is constantly having to begin at the beginning with a new, which is to say uninitiated, batch of pupils. For this reason, any progress Wittgenstein himself made in cracking problems that were as "hard as granite" would be lost on new students until they had first worked through easy problems en route to grappling with the more difficult ones.[58] Of course, there can never be enough time in the course of even a bright student's tenure to catch up with the likes of Wittgenstein. Because of this distance, the lectures, even those he dictated, were for Wittgenstein the pedagogical equivalents of middle axioms, comments that were tailored to nudge a particular group of students along but for whom the step to con-ceptual clarity was too great to be made all at once. Therefore, these com-ments may be at times poor reflections of Wittgenstein's own thoughts. We are thus amiss to read the *Blue and Brown Books*, or the *Lectures & Con-versations on Aesthetics, Psychology and Religious Belief* as transcriptions of Wittgenstein's mature thinking. As he explained to Russell, he dictated the notes known as the *Blue and Brown Books* so that *his students*, not the rest of the world's readers, would have something to take home in their hands.[59] In fact, Drury reports that Wittgenstein feared that student notes might be published as a record of his considered opinions (such as was done in the case of *Lectures & Conversations on Aesthetics, Psychology and Reli-gious Belief*).[60]

I am not suggesting that Wittgenstein thought that publishing a philo-sophical book was impossible. Rather, he thought that it must be a work of genius. Only §§1–188 of the *Philosophical Investigations* came close to meeting Wittgenstein's own rigorous standards.[61] The distinguishing mark of the *Investigations* is its genre. Gone is the severe architectonic of the *Tractatus* and in its place is a string of numbered paragraphs that cannot even be summarized by a table of contents (as per *Philosophical Grammar*). The invisibility of an explicit organizing principle and the apparent lack of thematic unity give the *Investigations* the appearance of randomness—as if each pericope were a stand-alone aphorism or thought-for-the-day journal entry. However, Wittgenstein deliberately crafted the *Investigations* and regretted that its style in particular had become for him a source of vanity.[62] What was this style and why was it brilliant?

First, in a manner far more explicit than that found in the *Tractatus*, Wittgenstein's later style displays the *narrative*, or *autobiographical*, unity of the work. When Wittgenstein compiled the *Investigations* from his journal entries, he took great pains to preserve the diary-like quality of the text. He knew that his notebooks were not simply a compendium of isolated proverbs. Rather, his entries were the unified expression of his own story, his own "journey" to conceptual clarity; they were, so to speak, his own *Confessions*.

Wittgenstein was quite taken by Augustine's *Confessions*. Drury reported that he knew his way around the Latin text well enough to find favorite passages quickly.[63] Even the casual reader must acknowledge that the *Confessions* is not a theological treatise but an autobiographical account of the path taken by one who *came to be* "made gentle by [God's] books" and whose "wounds had been treated by [God's] soothing fingers."[64] But whereas Augustine's *Confessions* are retrospective musings after the fact of his character transformation, the *Investigations* is a record of conversations Wittgenstein had with himself in the course of his struggle toward character transformation. Only the transformation of character readied one for the search for truth, because character alone was the lens that could concentrate whatever light was available into a single "burning point."[65] Wittgenstein viewed character as the courageous and self-denying manner in which a person faced truth with practiced regularity:

> No one *can* speak the truth; if he has still not mastered himself. He *cannot* speak it;—but not because he is not clever enough yet.
>
> The truth can be spoken only by someone who is already *at home* in it; not by someone who still lives in falsehood and reaches out from falsehood towards truth on just one occasion.[66]

The quest for character, therefore, was for Wittgenstein a passionate quest for a certain kind of life. Quoting Lessing with great emphasis, Wittgenstein remarked to Drury:

> If God held closed in his right hand All truth, and in his left the single and untiring striving after truth, adding even that I always and forever make mistakes, and said to me: Choose!", I should fall humbly before his left hand and say: "Father grant me! the pure truth is for you alone."[67]

Wittgenstein acknowledged the unending nature of his struggle when he admitted that "My thinking, like everyone's, has sticking to it the shriveled remains of my earlier (withered) ideas."[68] The fact that Wittgenstein was aware of his own conceptual transformation, one which was both progressive and yet ever incomplete, gives the *Investigations* an open-ended texture. As we shall see, the *Investigations* was more than simply autobiographical. Clearly, the sense of progress one gets by moving from page to page through the text is not a property of the text *qua* text, as if the *Investigations* were organized topically or logically or chronologically. But it is also more than a record of Wittgenstein's journey. Rather, the sense of progress involves the self-awareness that I, as a reader, am also having my way of seeing re-tooled and thus I am coming to conceive the world differently; the progress is *my own* conceptual transformation. Only to the extent that the *Investigations* maps out my journey will I be able to see its narrative unity.

Second, Wittgenstein's style is explicitly *dialogical*. Jane Heal argues that if the typical aim of philosophy is to construct firmer positions on life's most important questions by means of discursive rationality, then Wittgenstein's choice of a dialogical genre is self-defeating.[69] It has been suggested that Wittgenstein's deliberate obscurity was intended to overturn "philosophy as discursive reasoning" in favor of insight gained some other way (perhaps by means of poetry or mysticism).[70] As we have seen, there is more than a hint of this strategy in the *Tractatus*. But Heal rightly notes that this alternative simply sets up a dichotomy between insight gained discursively and insight gained in other ways. In fact, the later Wittgenstein is challenging this dichotomy altogether; clarity in thinking is achieved not by a passive flash of insight (whatever that might mean), but by active participation of the human subject in both practical and theoretical activity.[71] Heal concludes that the dialogical form is particularly appropriate for Wittgenstein not just because it is lively and gets the reader engaged but because of something about the content of 'the message' he is trying to get across, or, better, something about the nature of the state which is the hoped-for upshot of an attentive and sympathetic reading.[72]

In other words, it is of no use to discuss *general* types of insight when the only species of understanding is that which is possessed by this or that human subject under this or that set of conditions. Wittgenstein is not trying to construct a stand-alone argument in the *Investigations*. Rather, he is trying to cultivate a skill (conceptual clarity) in his readers. While he bemoans that he lacks the sort of artistic genius that can coerce one to see a work of art in the right perspective, his strategy is no less brilliant.[73] He parades past the readers a seemingly endless series of paragraphs (which, at best, bear a family resemblance) and a battalion of 784 questions with only 110 answers, 70 of which are intentionally wrong![73] Although no text can guarantee that it will succeed in teaching its reader how to think rightly—and surely there is a bewildering variety of opinions as to what the later Wittgenstein was up to—nevertheless, one thing is certain: the attentive reader must *struggle* if he or she is to read Wittgenstein rightly.

The point of philosophy for Wittgenstein, then, is not the conclusion of an argument, but the struggle itself. As Stanley Cavell aptly quips,

> [Wittgenstein's] philosophy is interested in questions in its own way—call it a way in which the answer is not in the future but in the way the future is approached, or seen to be unapproachable; in which the journey to the answer, or path, or tread, or the trades for it, are the goal of it.[75]

Hence, while there are scattered and inconsistent marks of an interlocutor(s) in Wittgenstein's "dialogue," the true interlocutor of the *Investigations* is the reader whom Wittgenstein seeks to engage in life-transforming struggle.

This, then, shows the second way Wittgenstein's later-period writings express the centrality of the human subject for his philosophy.[76] Not only does his style admit to possessing a "narrative unity"; by employing a version of dialogue, Wittgenstein sets before his reader an obstacle course the purpose of which is to reconfigure his reader's way of seeing.[77] This way of putting things makes Wittgenstein out to be more of a moral sage than an analytic philosopher.[78] There is some credibility to this charge because, in addition to being autobiographical and dialogical, Wittgenstein's style of philosophy is, third, deliberately *therapeutic*.

Paul Engelmann, an architect by trade but, perhaps, one whose greater claim to fame was to have been numbered by Wittgenstein among the few who truly understood the *Tractatus*, notes in his memoirs the great similarity between Wittgenstein and the turn-of-the-century Viennese journalist Karl Kraus. Kraus insisted that the moral character of the artist was essential to his or her craftsmanship. When a defect was evident in an artist's work, that defect ought to be understood as a manifestation of a moral defect in the artist's character. Kraus further maintained that this happens nowhere more frequently than when the artistic medium is that of language. According to Engelmann, Kraus's claim that "I cannot get myself to accept that a whole sentence can ever come from half a man" shows that "Kraus adopts the only attitude that makes sense by judging the morality not of an individual act, but of the person acting, and it is the latter which is unerringly revealed to Kraus through language."[79] Kraus's primary concern was to "preserve the purity of a language born of creative poetical experience."[80]

That Wittgenstein shared Kraus's views concerning the relation of the artist's character to the quality of his or her work is evidenced by his comment published as the foreword to *Philosophical Remarks*:

> I would like to say "This book is written to the glory of God," but nowadays that would be chicanery, that is, it would not be rightly understood. It means that the book is written in good will, and in so far as it is not so written, but out of vanity, etc., the author would wish to see it condemned. *He cannot free it of these impurities further than he himself is free of them.*[81]

Wittgenstein intentionally poured his life into his writing. His writings were not simply an accidental reflection of Wittgenstein's character. They were the product of a certain kind of devotion, perhaps even religious devotion.[82] That Wittgenstein considered his book as needing to be purged of its impurities in order to be a fitting oblation was but an indication that he regarded himself as requiring purification. Although Wittgenstein was powerless to take his book further than he himself had gone, he had come this far. In the *Tractatus* Wittgenstein sought to protect language from the meddlesome hands of metaphysicians, logical positivists, and others who attempt to specify things that can only be shown. Wittgenstein's original project, as I read the *Tractatus*, was to circumvent defective use of language by showing the limits beyond which philosophical language cannot tread.

But his "revolution" consisted in this: From the *Blue Book* on Wittgenstein did not simply seek to prevent the expression of a speaker's moral defects in his or her use of language but sought rather to cure the moral defect itself, that is to say, to transform the speaker's character by engaging him or her in a struggle for conceptual clarity. Here "conceptual clarity" is not simply a cognitive state (for cognitively impaired people can develop character) but additionally involves adopting the right sort of stance (or "good will") toward the world—for example, the courageous surrender of one's craving for explanation or of one's craving to say what can only be shown—the progressive attainment of which stance constitutes one's character.

Perhaps now we are in a position to see the way in which "the centrality of the subject" in Wittgenstein's later work determined the similarity he saw among ethics, aesthetics, and philosophy. In the *Tractatus* 6.421 Wittgenstein wrote: "Ethics and aesthetics are one." This ambiguous claim is open to several lines of interpretation. First, a common turn-of-the-century reading assumed that ethics, religion, and aesthetics shared the common fate of being literally meaningless. A strict theory of representationalism delineated between those statements that could be empirically verified and those statements (not only ethical, religious, and aesthetic statements, but "countless" kinds of statements, as Wittgenstein would wryly observe later) whose only possible significance was assumed, by default, to lie in their function as expressions of human value, experience, or emotion. In this view, all such "pseudo-propositions" were unified by not being *about* anything at all.[83]

If the first way to read the enigmatic "Ethics and aesthetics are one" is to consign both to the fate of being about nothing, a second way to read this statement is to understand ethics and aesthetics as sharing equally multifarious origins. This is the tack taken by D. Z. Phillips in his essays collected under the title *Interventions in Ethics*.[84] While aesthetic taste can, to some degree, be schooled, ultimately words such as "beauty" name a family resemblance that defies general treatment. The same holds for judgments of ethical value. The real danger, warns Phillips, is the distortion that arises when we succumb to our craving for generality and try to subsume ethics (or aesthetics) under a general theoretical framework. Moral (and aesthetic) judgment can be schooled, but since each instance of moral education presupposes a correlative communal form of life, aspiring to trans-communal (or, in Phillips's case, acommunal) moral judgment would be pointless. If the real danger for ethics and aesthetics lies in the distortion that a unifying theory brings to incommensurable value judgments, then the philosopher is obliged to perform interventions to thwart theoretics and leave everything as it is.[85]

But there is a third way of understanding the unity of ethics and aesthetics that is more in line with Wittgenstein's emphasis on changing human subjects. Benjamin Tilghman links the meaning of the Tractarian maxim to the broader context of the *Tractatus* and shows that ethics and aesthetics are unified by a joint concern for the truly important in human life. Since the realm of value cannot be spoken, but must be shown, Tilghman speculates that for Wittgenstein, only through art can these values be shown. This is possible because art *expresses* the human spirit in the same way that my world is an expression of *my* spirit when I view it *sub species aeternitatis*.[86]

As described above, Wittgenstein abandoned the hope of viewing the world from a God's-eye view (*sub specie aeternitatis*), but retained the view that contemplating the interconnectedness and limited character of the world was of utmost ethical importance. The upshot of this line of reasoning is that the morally good life is one lived in agreement or cooperation with these limits. Art celebrates our ability to *see rightly*, or in the right perspective, by *showing* all the connections of an object with its surroundings. Conversely, grasping a work of art is much like contemplating a world in miniature:

> The work of art shows us the *essence*; it shows us the object in its necessary *connections* with other things and it shows the scene portrayed as the logically necessary unity of the various artistic elements that compose it. And it is tempting to believe that this is part of what it means to see the object in right perspective.[87]

And perhaps this is what Wittgenstein meant by saying, "a work of art forces us — as one might say — to see it in the right perspective."[88] Because a work of art manifests all the connections of an object with its context, it is, in one sense, a self-contained world. But in contrast to a work of art, whose hermeneutic key is internal to the work itself, life strikes us as an *unsolvable* riddle. Tilghman argues that Wittgenstein used this comparison of art (aesthetics) and life (ethics) to display the point that *there is no riddle for us to solve*.[89] The real problem is the *how*, not the *why*, of living. Consequently, on Tilghman's view, to live rightly is to look at the world rightly, which is to say, under an aspect that dissolves the "riddle." Tilghman describes Wittgenstein as seeing ethics and aesthetics internally related to the character of the human subject, because both require judgments that are expressions of character:

> A person's view of the world and that person's character are intimately intertwined; they are, to all purposes, one. A person's view of the world determines his character; his character and hence his view of the world, is revealed in his deeds. The important thing is not so much what is done, but how it is done and the spirit with which it is done. Without this link of character, spirit and vision to action there can be no ethics and no moral assessment of a deed.[90]

This is a good description as far as it goes. However, Tilghman misses the *social* character of ethical and aesthetic judgment. Wittgenstein is quite explicit on this point. In his *Lectures & Conversations* he (reportedly) said, "In order to get clear on aesthetic words you have to describe ways of living."[91] I contend that Wittgenstein maintained throughout his life that the unity of ethics, aesthetics, and religion was a unity derived from the fact that all rely on the same sort of skills upon which the social medium of language depends.

Certainly by 1933 Wittgenstein had come to think of aesthetics as descriptive. "All that Aesthetics does is 'to draw your attention to a thing', to 'place things side by side'."[92] Here the connections manifested by a work of art are such that to see it rightly means seeing its connections with life — though not connections with the artist's inner life only, but with the history, context, culture, and conventions of artistic practice as well. However, the person who has come to grasp these connections cannot be said to have a handle on the *causal* connections as if he or she possessed an answer for what *makes* something beautiful. Rather, those who grasp the connections between a work of art and its broader context can be said to have developed a sort of fluency in the language of the craft. Thus, Wittgenstein views the apprehension of a composition's "meaning" as a trained capacity or skill. For example,

> The direction: "Wie aus weiter Ferne" in Schumann. Must everyone understand such a direction? Everyone, for example, who would understand the direction "Not too quick?" Isn't the capacity that is supposed to be absent in the meaning-blind man one of this kind?[93]

Wittgenstein's point is that only the skillful are able to rightly judge what Schumann meant by "playing a piece as if from afar" or when the tempo is "not too quick." Such a skill, or fluency, is developed by a certain sort of training.[94] "You can make a person see what Brahms was driving at by showing him lots of different pieces by Brahms, or by comparing him with a contemporary author."[95] In other words, induction into the practice can tune one's ears to the language of music.

Suppose you hear a piece of music in which you judge the bass to be "too heavy." In making such a judgment, Wittgenstein observed that "what we are trying to do is to bring the bass 'nearer to an ideal', though we haven't an ideal before us which we are trying to copy."[96] Judgments of "beauty" are not straightforward procedures as one might check the spelling of words on this page by looking up each word in a dictionary. Rather, aesthetic judgments are expressions of *skill*. This is not to say that beauty in art is simply an expression of solitary human preference, for judgments are shared: agreement in judgment of beauty is one species of the reflexive sort of agreement upon which language depends.[97] Wittgenstein would later comment:

> There is a lot to be learned from Tolstoy's bad theorizing about how a work of art conveys 'a feeling'. —You really could call it, not exactly the expression of *a* feeling [i.e., the artist's emotional state], but at least an expression of feeling or a felt expression. And you could say that in so far as people understand it, they 'resonate' in harmony with it, respond to it. You might say: the work of art does not aim to convey something else [e.g., the artist's psychological state], just itself.[98]

Wittgenstein calls this an expression of "feeling" rather than of "*a* feeling" precisely because it is shared. Nevertheless, it is not feeling in general. Rather, art is conventional in nature and expresses the accidental form of a particular culture's life. We might say that for Wittgenstein, aesthetics is neither universal nor individualistic, but *ethnocentric*. G. E. Moore recalled Wittgenstein's words:

> He said that such a statement as "That bass moves too much" is not a statement about human beings at all, but is more like a piece of mathematics; and that, if I say of a face which I draw "It smiles too much," this says that it could be brought closer to some "ideal" . . . and that . . . would be more like "solving a mathematical problem."[99]

Aesthetics and ethics are judgments of value, but such a value is neither a self-subsistent ideal, nor the property of the lone individual, nor a general feature of humans *qua* humans. Rather, the values that aesthetic and ethical judgments expose are those shared by a community. In an important sense, these values (or at least, agreement in judgments of them) is what makes a group a community. This being the case, there is only a nominal difference between skillful aesthetic and ethical judgment and skillful participation in other social-conventional practices (such as mathematics and language), which together constitute membership in community. This way of viewing things shifts the focus of aesthetics (or ethics) from the values expressed by an artifact (or in an instance of moral reasoning) to the question of whether one has the skill deemed adequate for rendering judgments that stand in agreement with those of the community.

It is no secret that Wittgenstein considered mathematics to be *about* an agreement in judgments. In the late 1930s Wittgenstein described his brand of mathematical constructivism with these words: "a mathematician is always inventing new forms of description. Some, stimulated by practical needs, another from aesthetic needs,—and yet others in a variety of ways." This makes the mathematician out to be more of an inventor than a discoverer.[100] The mathematician is not a discoverer, since, on Wittgenstein's view, there is no uncharted wilderness ("out there") to explore. Similar claims could be made for ethics, aesthetics, and philosophy. Wittgenstein distanced himself from the common notion that ethicists, artists, and philosophers are pioneers into previously uninhabited metaphysical jungles. Ethical, aesthetic, and philosophical puzzlement are not instances of someone being lost or of something being hidden. Rather, puzzlement points to a deficiency in human skill to see what is already before one as the solution itself. In a parenthetical remark, Wittgenstein stated:

> Here we stumble on a remarkable characteristic phenomenon in philosophical investigation: the difficulty—I might say—isn't one of finding the solution; it is one of recognizing something as the solution. We have already said everything. Not something that follows from this; no, just *this* is the solution!
>
> This, I believe, hangs together with our wrongly expecting an explanation; whereas a description is the solution of the difficulty, if we give it the right place in our consideration. If we dwell upon it and do not try to get beyond it.[101]

Accordingly, the task of philosophy is to cure human subjects of philosophical barbarism: "A present-day teacher of philosophy doesn't select food for his pupil with the aim of flattering his taste, but with the aim of changing it."[102]

The goal of cultivating good taste—a goal which makes the human subject the centerpiece of the philosophical task—meant that Wittgenstein's approach in philosophy resembled training in art appreciation. Moore paraphrases:

> He went on to say that, though philosophy had now been "reduced to a matter of skill," yet this skill, like other skills, is very difficult to acquire. One difficulty was that it required a "sort of thinking" to which we are not accustomed and to which we have not been trained—a sort of thinking very different from what is required in the sciences. And he said that the required skill could not be acquired by merely hearing the lectures: discussion was essential. As regards his own work, he said it did not matter whether his results [concerning some particular grammatical investigation] were true or not: what mattered was that "a method had been found."[103]

No fine arts instructor can discursively prove the greatness of, say, Rembrandt's "The Return of the Prodigal Son." Rather, an instructor shows the students the painting itself and supplements this showing with descriptions that frame the painting in a family of other similar paintings and within the historical practice itself. This descriptive pedagogy at once leaves everything as it is and yet forever alters the students' way of seeing (even if this alteration goes no deeper than that the student thereafter takes Rembrandt as one benchmark for "good" art).

A reader of Wittgenstein's playful examples of language-games faces a similar opportunity. In order to grasp what Wittgenstein was up to in the opening pages of *Investigations*, the reader must, provisionally at least, come to conceive of *meaning* (e.g., of "Slab!") as *use* (i.e., the builder's request) *within a given form of life* (namely, the construction of a building). But to think this way requires the student to suspend both the craving for a general definition and the presupposition that general definitions cover all the cases. To learn, even imaginatively, the moves internal to Wittgenstein's initial (and simplified) example of a language-game constitutes a notion of understanding-as-mastery. Furthermore, this example of a language-game is followed by many others, each of which is but a single rung on the internal ladder that constitutes the *Investigations*. In surmounting each rung, progress can be made; Wittgenstein hopes that readers who scale the book will, at the book's end, have come to view things so differently that they effectively have kicked away the ladder. Readers who have attained that level of skill and clarity and who look back at the earlier pedagogical examples will immediately discern these examples to be confused, simplistic, or shallow.

The sort of progress Wittgenstein hopes for his readers lends irony to the complaint that Rush Rhees voiced in his essay "Wittgenstein's Builders." Rhees wondered if Wittgenstein's games analogy was too simplistic an account of what it means to speak. Speaking requires more than constructing grammatically correct sentences; it involves having something to say which "bears on" the rest of the conversation. Rhees charged that if the builders' language-game was imagined as a language complete in itself, as Wittgenstein enjoined us to do, then the builders would resemble puppets more than human beings. Wouldn't the builders talk about what the building was for, once the work day was over? Wouldn't they discuss at home snags encountered on the jobsite? Wouldn't they require entirely different language-games for teaching their children? And so on. Rhees concluded that Wittgenstein's analogy did not answer what it is to have a language because it failed to show how language is related to the *rest* of human living.

> . . . if [the builders] speak to one another, the meaning of the expression they use cannot lie wholly in the use or the reaction that it receives in this job. . . . But the remarks they make may have something to do with one another; otherwise they are not talking at all, even though they may be uttering sentences. And their remarks could have no bearing on one another unless the expressions they used were used in other connections as well.[104]

What sort of conclusion can this be? A better question is, What sort of person is drawing this conclusion? Until his recent death, Rhees was one of Wittgenstein's literary executors, not to mention a close personal friend and long-time student. We find in Rhees, therefore, one who has worked his way around the Wittgensteinian corpus many times and in many ways. In short, he is one who has learned to "go on." However, Rhees seems curiously unaware that his own mature facility was his teacher's intention for him all along. In §§1–188 of the *Investigations* (which stands out for being the only section of Wittgenstein's writings with which Wittgenstein was satisfied), the *provisional* character of the exercises is evident throughout. On the one hand, Wittgenstein constructs explicit permutations of the original language-game of the builders (cf. §2 with §8). On the other hand, Wittgenstein also explicitly expands on the *method* expressed in language-game §2 (as in §48). Both kinds of development manifest Wittgenstein's intention to lead his readers on a conceptual journey rather than express once and for all by a single example all that it means to speak. That his goal was for the reader to transcend the opening positions of the *Investigations'* master game is made explicit in the last reference to language-games in this section:

> §179 Let us return to our case (151). It is clear that we should not say B had the right to say the words "Now I know how to go on," just because he thought of the formula. . . . And now one might think that the sentence "I can go on" meant I have an experience which I know empirically to lead to the continuation of the series." But does B mean that when he says he can go on? . . .
>
> No. The words "Now I can go on" were correctly used when he thought of the formula: that is, given the circumstance as that he had learnt algebra, had used such formula before. — *But that does not mean that his statement is only short for a description of all the circumstances which constitutes the scene for our language-game. — Think how we learn to use the expressions "Now I know how to go on," "Now I can go on" and others; in what family of language-games we learn their use.*[105]

When juxtaposed with Wittgenstein's set of reader instructions, it is evident that Rhees's charge is beside the point for two important reasons. First, Wittgenstein's account of language-games in §179 *does* achieve the nuance that Rhees sought after; unlike language-game (§2), Wittgenstein here clearly linked the intelligibility of language-games with the circumstances and scenery of the rest of life. Second, this pericope also *shows* Wittgenstein's sense of "understanding" as an instance of mastery ("going on") by the explicit command to the reader ("Think . . .") to finish the string of exercises (which Wittgenstein painstakingly laid out for the reader over the course of these seventy-two pages of text) by going beyond the final position of the text. This Rhees has done.

Rhees's objection falls short in assuming that Wittgenstein's concept of "language-game" holds steady throughout the *Investigations*. The fact that he even makes the charge he does, given Rhees's own level of skill, corroborates the claim that Wittgenstein's philosophical method, as embodied in the *Investigations*, treats ethics and aesthetics as unified in the linguistic skill of actual persons. This unity is one which makes the transformation of the human subject the very heart of the philosophical task.

ETHICS AS AESTHETICS

Why is my speaking not clear to you? Because you are unable to hear my message.

—John 8:43

In the end, nobody hears more out of things, including books, than he knows already. For that to which one lacks access from experience, one has no ears.

—Friedrich Nietzsche

The armed eye beholds the stars; the unarmed only sees fog shadows.

—Robert Schumann

Wittgenstein made it clear that philosophy was above all a work that one performed on oneself. Only by removing the plank in one's own eye could one be fit to help another see clearly. That Stanley Hauerwas has thoroughly ingested Wittgenstein becomes clear in the first aspect under which Hauerwas's work may be viewed: ethics-as-aesthetics. I use the term "ingested" to differentiate Hauerwas from other commentators on Wittgenstein. On the one hand, Hauerwas is not someone who simply reproduces the views of Wittgenstein, circa 1951, seemingly unaware of the directions Wittgenstein intended his thought to develop even at life's end. But on the other hand, neither is Hauerwas the sort of generalist who picks up

Wittgenstein's tangled skein intending to improve on it by "solving" residual difficulties as if they were logical contradictions. Rather, Hauerwas is a perceptive reader of Wittgenstein who recognized that Wittgenstein's aporetic style was the mark of his genius, for by it Wittgenstein addressed a diverse audience in a way that engaged each reader in his or her context. Hauerwas in his own writing has tried to engage a diverse audience and in that regard replicates something of Wittgenstein's pedagogy. Yet Hauerwas neither mimics nor transcends Wittgenstein. Rather, Hauerwas absorbed Wittgenstein and undertook a grammarian's task, having benefited from the clarity brought by seeing Christian faith and practice through the lens of Wittgenstein. As we shall see, it was the very particularity of the Christian theological task that enabled Hauerwas to surmount the aporias without which Wittgenstein was unable to express himself.

Hauerwas's indebtedness to Wittgensteinian thinkers such as David Burrell, George Lindbeck, Iris Murdoch, Nicholas Lash, and others is evidenced by frequent citations throughout his writings. Yet overt allusions to Wittgenstein himself occur in passages nearly as terse as Wittgenstein's own writings. Hauerwas commented to me in private conversation, "How could one quote Wittgenstein?" Precisely. If one has read Wittgenstein carefully, one will catch Hauerwas's syncopated allusions. But no compact summary or excerpt of Wittgenstein's work can communicate his "point" to the uninitiated reader, since there is no "point" other than the sought-after conceptual transformation. To put it differently, because Wittgenstein's writings aim to gradually transform a reader's concepts, in most cases one could only do him justice by quoting *very* long passages—passages long enough to do some work. In the absence of such lengthy citations of Wittgenstein by Hauerwas, I must content myself with making the case for Hauerwas's affinity to Wittgenstein by showing the family resemblance between them. Rather than range over the entirety of Hauerwas's writings at once, I will describe his works as breaking naturally into three periods (1968–1983, 1984–1990, and 1991–1999). In each period, an enduring strand of his thinking shows the way Hauerwas came to do theology through the lens of Wittgenstein.

Hauerwas's view of ethics as a form of aesthetics is a prominent theme in the first decade and a half of Hauerwas's academic career. Hauerwas internalized Wittgenstein's conviction regarding the centrality of the human subject and shared Wittgenstein's conviction that human knowledge is a matter of contingency. That is to say, there is no such thing as necessary knowledge, nor is there knowledge in general—at least not in the way that Enlightenment thinkers had hoped; knowing is always the particular ac-

tivity of a local human knower. Thus Hauerwas thought that the predomi-
nant debate in ethics on the American scene in the 1960s and 1970s,
namely, whether moral quandaries were solved by attention to norms or
by attention to context, was wrongheaded. Rather, what matters is the fit-
ness of a given person's moral judgment. Hauerwas saw this judgment not
as computational prowess but as a skill akin to aesthetic taste. If philosophy for Wittgenstein was therapy for the illness of conceptual confusion,
ethics for Hauerwas is therapy for the disease of moral confusion. That
human subjects are central to the task of ethics shows itself in Hauerwas's
therapeutic approach to moral reasoning. On the one hand, the style of his
pedagogy is "self-consuming." To read Hauerwas rightly is to be transformed
in the process. On the other hand, the self that undergoes transformation is
not the punctiliar monad of modern political liberalism but the "eschatological" self. Thus Hauweras aims to train his readers to recognize that the
gift of selfhood results from seeing oneself as deeply embedded in the story
of Jesus, which is both broader and longer than one's life span.

THE CONTINGENCY OF KNOWLEDGE

Stephen Toulmin judges the Enlightenment's quest for indubitable knowledge to be nothing more than an Ω-shaped detour in the course of philosophy.[1] Accordingly, he applauds his former teacher, Ludwig Wittgenstein,
for returning philosophy to a place of studied skepticism—not the sort of
skepticism that doubts whether any knowledge at all is possible, but the sort
of skepticism that takes the knowledge we do have with a grain of salt. For
Toulmin, Wittgenstein is a kindred spirit with that other book-end to the
modern period, the Renaissance thinker Michel de Montaigne. Between
them lay the legacy of René Descartes, whose project fostered human pretensions of power and control. Descartes construed "mental" as so completely bifurcated from "material" that reason was thought to be purely
volitional, which is to say, subject to no necessity outside of itself. This picture was, of course, very appealing to seventeenth-century thinkers, since
a purely volitional reason appears to offer the objectivity imagined necessary for settling disputes born of differences in religion, culture, history, and
language. Thus, argues Toulmin, the Cartesian project took root in a desperate age.

The earlier epistemic modesty of Montaigne stood in stark contrast to
Cartesian optimism. For Montaigne, there was "no use laying down a

hard and fast line to divide bodily processes ('material') from voluntary activities ('mental'), since there is no way to be sure in advance of experience just which of our bodily functions we can or cannot bring under deliberate control."[2] The possibility that human minds may be bewitched in many, largely undetectable, ways meant for Montaigne in the sixteenth century, as it would for Wittgenstein in the twentieth, that no experience can justify asserting a single answer to the questions that plague human existence.[3] Given the limited control human beings exercise over all their psychosomatic processes, knowledge claims are bound to be uncertain, ambiguous, idiosyncratic, and diverse. Montaigne's holistic picture of the human person is a reminder that if "objective" knowledge is improbable on account of our bodily functions, then, *a fortiori*, objectivity is exposed as entirely illusory by the impact that the confluence of language, culture, social history, and religious practices has upon our sensibilities.

This road is well traveled. Hauerwas himself never seems to tire of quoting Alasdair MacIntyre's *After Virtue* to defend the claim that the Enlightenment project's attempt to define moral agency in terms of human ability to *evade* identification with anything particular or contingent has been utterly disastrous.[4] The fact that Hauerwas shows his concurrence with Toulmin's assessment by drawing on sources as distant as Aristotle, on the one hand, and as near as Julius Kovesi and Iris Murdoch, on the other, indicates that Montaigne's picture is not an anomaly in the history of philosophy. On the contrary, the Enlightenment view is out of step with the rest of intellectual history in that it "renders the contingent history of the agent irrelevant in moral judgment and evaluation; it demands that justification for our decisions be given from the perspective of anyone."[5]

From Aristotle Hauerwas learned that the quest for knowledge begins with the thick stuff of everyday life.[6] Although Aristotle's teacher, Plato, may have been guilty of trying to circumvent the contingency of knowledge by postulating an immutable and transcultural theory of forms in order to defeat the cultural relativism of his day, his work in *Phaedrus* is redeeming for showing what is normally overlooked in Plato, namely, his conviction that human reason (in particular, that of his reader) must first be *trained* to be able to apprehend universal forms.[7] Aristotle went beyond his teacher in two ways. First, the contingency of knowledge is shown by the fact that the "criteria" (i.e., the virtues) for evaluating one's skill in living in accord with reason are learned from no loftier source than one's friends.[8] Second, the uncertainty of reason is shown by the fact that one could never be sure one was not mishandling the very criteria one was using to evaluate one's ability to handle such criteria. This echoes what Wittgenstein penned in 1937:

You cannot write anything about yourself that is more truthful than you yourself are. That is the difference between writing about yourself and writing about external objects. You write about yourself from your own height. You don't stand on stilts or on a ladder but on your bare feet.[9]

Thus, Hauerwas takes Aristotle as unable to separate truthfulness, or character, from *knowing, choosing,* and the *manner* of one's acting; these are equal and simultaneous moments of the moral act.[10]

From Kovesi Hauerwas learned that description is everything. In an essay that, by his own admission, constituted his crucial turn away from the decisionism that still dominates contemporary ethics, Hauerwas wrote: "Prior to decision must come the idea of our moral notions, for without 'our moral notions there would be nothing to make decisions about; there would not even be a need to make decisions'."[11] In Kovesi's view, human decisions proceed by means of "notions." Notions precede decisions and contain a formal element that allows us to group under a single aspect things which may be empirically very dissimilar. For example, an "error" in tennis includes such things as a foot fault, missing the baseline, and double hitting the ball. In this instance, the notion of error is what it is because of the role that this notion plays in one particular human activity, the game of tennis. Our reliance on notions for recognizing tennis errors is analogous to our reliance on moral notions for recognizing behaviors as instances of moral error.

We do not perceive something called lying, but we know that certain acts are acts of lying in the same way that we know certain objects are tables and chairs. Moreover, this kind of knowing is already embodied within our inherited cognitive notions. We do not come to know the world by perceiving it, but we come to know the world as we learn to use our language.[12]

Here the difference between moral and nonmoral notions is *not* the difference between evaluation and description. All notions are descriptive in that they enable us to see matters under one aspect rather than another. Saying that some notions are "moral" refers, rather, to the way that we see with rule-like regularity a family resemblance between certain actions. And why should we see this? Because we have reason to: our notions are needed in a way of life.[13] In Hauerwas's estimation, the relationship between language, rules, and community is extremely important:

The way we learn to use a language depends almost totally on the community in which we learn it, for the "gap" between formal and material elements of our notions is not bridged by logical deduction but by the historical experience of a particular group of people.[14]

Any attempt to render moral judgment from the vantage of the disinterested spectator is simply pointless. Moral facts, like other facts, are never *simply* known; moral facts are knowable for the ways that they intersect with our lives. Such a knowing "takes place by learning the language that intends the world and our behavior as it ought to be that good may be achieved. The moral life is struggle and training in how to see."[15]

Hauerwas finds Kovesi's emphasis on training to see echoed in the writings of Iris Murdoch. From Murdoch Hauerwas learned to name as "sin" the human illusion that we possess the degree of control necessary to describe the moral life entirely in terms of decision. In an essay which foreshadowed his subsequent preoccupation with virtue, Hauerwas wrote:

> Under the guise of neutrality the moral life is reduced to matters of choice. But no ethic which ignores sin can provide an authentic account of man, for ultimately we are not "isolated free choosers, monarchs of all we survey, but benighted creatures sunk in a reality whose nature we are constantly and overwhelmingly tempted to deform by our fantasy." Thus our very attempt to avoid the reality of sin is a symptom of our sinfulness.[16]

Murdoch's analysis of the limits of human knowledge drove Hauerwas to construe moral life as an aesthetic mode of "seeing." Henceforth Hauerwas located the moral life in the *vision* and *virtue* of humans who are agents, rather than in the *decisions* rendered by humans who are mere spectators.

We have begun to get a glimpse of Hauerwas's reliance upon Aristotle, Kovesi, and Murdoch for his conception of the contingency of human knowledge. As a result of their combined influence, the young Hauerwas began to direct his energies toward altering the condition of particular human knowers, namely, his readers. In ways very similar to Wittgenstein, Hauerwas came to view real people as the very center of his ethical therapy. His commitment to reshape the vision of his readers—that is, his commitment to ethics as aesthetics—is reflected in his self-consuming pedagogy and his retrospective notion of the self.

SELF-CONSUMING PEDAGOGY

As can be seen in the earliest of his writings (1968–1983), Hauerwas conceives ethics in terms of aesthetics. Just as Plato's *Phaedrus* is a self-consuming artifact (see chapter 1), Hauerwas's pedagogy is "self-consuming" to the extent he succeeds in changing the character of his readers by reshaping their moral vision. Given this emphasis in his writing, it is not surprising that Hauerwas avoids writing in a style that gives the impression that he has the final word on a given issue. In fact, having the last word is the farthest thing from his mind, for he considers his work in ethics to be nothing other than bringing his voice to bear on a much longer conversation. This conversational style shows him to be more of a *bricoleur* than a systematician.[17] Jeffrey Stout made this term famous in his suggestion that ethics is analogous to the craft of the old-world street vendor who had the uncanny ability to repair broken household items by using whatever odds and ends had been squirreled away for just such occasion.[18] In like fashion, Hauerwas's essays have an ad hoc texture. When he brings Barth into conversation with Trollope or compares Christian social ethics to life in a rabbit warren, one gets the impression that he is able to bring to bear on conversations about honor, peace, and the like whatever he is reading and thinking about at the time.[19]

However, the fact that Hauerwas's work can be described in terms of *bricolage* does not imply a rampant arbitrariness in his method. The *bricoleur* is as skillful in the selection of resources as in the effecting of a repair. Similarly, there is a method in Hauerwas's madness. On the one hand, his conversational mode shows his commitment to participate in the Christian tradition in a manner befitting it as "an historically extended, socially embodied argument."[20] For example, Hauerwas objects to the way his former teacher, James Gustafson, thinks that Christian ethics differs from secular ethics only in the sorts of reasons it finds persuasive and not in the specific obligations it finds mandatory. Consequently, Gustafson thinks that Christian ethicists, if they are smart enough, can find ways to translate Christian convictions into terms understandable by nonbelievers. But, Hauerwas complains,

> as . . . society increasingly becomes secular, Christians, insofar as they endeavor to remain political actors, must attempt to translate their convictions into a nontheological idiom. But once such a translation is

accomplished, it becomes very unclear why they need the theological idiom in the first place.[21]

It is important to note that the force of Hauerwas's argument against Gustafson is *historical*.[22] Hauerwas relativized Gustafson's claims (which otherwise might strike the reader as self-evident) by situating Gustafson in a school of thought that began in Kant, was extended through the social gospel movement of Rauschenbusch, and continued to develop via the thought of Reinhold Niebuhr and Paul Ramsey. This move allowed Hauerwas to make his own challenge to Gustafson part of a longer argument about whether the development of Christian ethics as a theoretical discipline (one rendered distinct from theology by the Enlightenment) is itself in keeping with older Christian convictions.

Hauerwas's commitment to do ethics in the mode of conversation also aids his pedagogy. In this regard, his unsystematic approach is crucial to the task of shaping his reader's outlook, for ethics is not static (the stating of a position) but something dynamic, namely, the evolving of a reader's understanding. Reflecting on his early work, Hauerwas remarked in 1985:

> I have always tried to write in a way that defies summary. If a work can be summarized it is not a genuine exercise in understanding since the point can be grasped separate from the execution. In fact it is my conviction that the execution is more important than the point since I find I learn the most from others by attending not only to what they say but how they say it.[23]

In other words, Hauerwas wants to engage his readers in a linguistic struggle by which his or her moral vision is clarified. By and large he utilizes three techniques to do this, some more successfully than others.

First, and perhaps most successfully, Hauerwas seeks to perform a conceptual transformation in his readers by challenging the standard, or received, vocabulary of any given debate. In the example just discussed, Hauerwas wanted to convince his readers that there is no such thing as "Christian ethics" if one means by that term (as Gustafson does) a theoretical discipline divorced from reflection on distinctively Christian *practices*. In his phrase, the church doesn't have a social ethic, the church *is* a social ethic.[24] He made his case not by arguing theoretically from first principles but by arguing historically toward first principles, that is, toward an agreement in judgment. Thus, Hauerwas challenges Gustafson's vocabulary by employing a sort of linguistic archaeology. But notice that the use Hauerwas makes of history is not an attempt to certify what really happened. Rather, Hauerwas uses history in the same way one might use a paradigmatic story, that is, in a way that provides a schema for the whole enterprise and, in so doing, establishes the meaning of the parts (in this case, the meaning of the vocabulary). In other cases, Hauerwas uses nonhistorical narratives to effect a similar conceptual transformation. For example, he employs Richard Adams' story *Watership Down* to help communityless readers imagine what authentic community life might be like by recounting the behavior of rabbits.[25]

In addition to excavating history for the meanings of central terms, Hauerwas also delights in shifting the center of gravity within a discussion by elevating the significance of some terms over others. For example, he refuses to speak of ethical *decisions* that we face, but rather presses the question, "Who is the 'we'?" It is not by accident that Hauerwas's methodology exactly parallels that of Wittgenstein, who sought to defuse philosophical "bewitchment" by relentlessly probing the supposedly insignificant terms: "To whom does it look like that? And under what circumstances?"[26] In the case of ethics, everything hangs upon *who* is doing moral reflection, for what one ought to do is already contained in the description of one's identity.[27] This focus on identifying the subject of ethics means for Hauerwas that the central question of Christian ethics is "What kind of people ought we be?" and the central obligation of Christian ethics is for the church to be the church.[28]

A second technique Hauerwas employs to cultivate moral taste in his readers is the speaking of a different language. Just as one could never learn Chinese by reading English translations of Confucius, similarly, Hauerwas is convinced that his readers will never acquire requisite fluency unless he engages them in the language called Christian. For example, the concept "sinner" does not have unambiguous meaning. One must be *trained* to understand him- or herself as a sinner.

> We must be trained to see ourselves as sinners, for it is not self-evident. Indeed, our sin is so fundamental that we must be taught to recognize it; we cannot perceive its radical nature so long as we remain formed by it. . . . We are not sinful because we participate in some general human condition, but because we deceive ourselves about the nature of reality and so would crucify the very one who calls us to God's kingdom.[29]

Such training requires participation in the communal practices of confession and reconciliation. Language, after all, is learned in duplicating a form of life, not by reading a dictionary. Furthermore, such training requires that the word or concept be used in multiple settings; it is the combination of repetition and variety that habituates one in the art of "going on."[30] This fluency, an instance of "going on," requires one to see the family resemblance between uses of a term in various contexts so as to be able to imagine appropriate applications of it in a new context.

In order to sensitize his readers to their need to acquire a new language, Hauerwas recounts his own need to "go on":

> Even though these essays appear to be wide-ranging, each has been conceived to develop or illustrate my concern to articulate how Christian convictions form lives. I find the essay a congenial form in that it allows me to double back and pick up what was insufficiently developed in other essays. . . .
>
> I cannot pretend that this way of proceeding has answered all the objections or clarified all the unclarities about my positions, but it at least lets me write as though each essay is part of a conversation. For I depend on those readers who read or hear the essay and tell me what remains unclear or just seems wrong. I am then able to revise or write something else that attempts to clarify or meet the objection. The essay has its limits, but it seems the best form for a still-developing theological ethic.[31]

As the above quotation suggests, the third technique Hauerwas employs for the benefit of his readers' training is his choice of the essay as the preferred form of address. Of the two dozen or so books which name him as an author, only seven of these are not collections of his essays. If we disqualify the four books that he has co-authored we are left with only three volumes that are not essays. But the fact that he has published more than 250 essays is surely an indication that this genre is particularly apt for his purposes. I suspect Hauerwas's affinity for the essay is that the genre itself *shows*, more than states, the nature of moral reflection; the essay is limited in scope, occasional by design, and invites conversation. In contrast, books may pretend to be totalizing, universal, and doctrinaire.

Lest I be accused of reading too much into Hauerwas's choice of genre, let me resurrect a comment made by Wittgenstein. In 1947 he wrote, "Am *I* the only one who cannot found a school or can a philosopher never do this? I cannot found a school because I do not really want to be imitated.

Not at any rate by those who publish articles in philosophical journals."[32] Wittgenstein evidently insisted on writing in a "different spirit"[33] because the academic genre of his day itself lured one into the optimistic pretensions of formalism, the chief of which is the belief that everything "true" could be assimilated into a gigantic scheme. This pretension alone led many thinkers subsequent to Wittgenstein to misinterpret him. For example, Saul Kripke tried to understand Wittgenstein by assimilating him into the standard mid-century mode of reasoning. Kripke's reading is questionable on at least two counts. First, Kripke reads Wittgenstein's paradox[34] as an expression of a thoroughgoing (which is to say, Humean) skepticism: under the presumption that thinking precedes language-use, Kripke concluded that grammatical rules *must* be cognitively present prior to the formation of a particular sentence in order for it to be formed according to these rules. This logical priority suggests another, for one must know what "according to" means if one is to apply grammatical rules "correctly." In other words, some rule(s) for interpreting grammatical rules *must be* logically prior to the grammatical rules. Of course, this quickly degenerates into an infinite regress in which rules for interpreting rules of interpretation are required, and so on. Kripke thinks this regress betrays a latent skepticism in Wittgenstein. Second, and more damaging to his own case, Kripke adopts a theoretical mode of discourse that attempts to generalize the "basic structure" of Wittgenstein's torturous path through §§201–265 of the *Investigations*. But one of the points Wittgenstein was making throughout the *Investigations* was that "arguments" about "language in general" are self-stultifying because they presuppose an exceptionally facile implementation of language, which theorizing tacitly denies in the offering of conclusions reputed to be universally compelling (i.e., regardless of anyone's level of skill in a given language).[35]

The tension between style and content in Kripke's work haunts even those who, like Norman Malcolm, tried to follow more deliberately in Wittgenstein's train. James Edwards, another admirer of Wittgenstein, rightly takes Malcolm to task for offering on Wittgenstein's behalf an *argument* against Cartesianism, a move which turns on the traditional conception of the philosophical task as that of offering and defending generalized theses— the very conception of philosophy all of Wittgenstein's later work is aimed at undermining.[36] In other words, Malcolm gives the game away to the formalists—who claim that philosophy must be done in such-and-such a way—by adopting their mode of reasoning.

More recently, D. Z. Phillips has fared a little better. To his credit, he avoids composing philosophical arguments and instead, through the genre

of essay, brings to bear his insights about confusions residing in a given contemporary discussion.[37] However, from time to time even Phillips cannot
resist the temptation to make a generalized moral claim or two. For example, Phillips (with H. O. Mounce) correctly describes Wittgenstein's position in the *Investigations* as a patient defusing of Protagorean relativism.[38]
The inability of one to get "outside" linguistic systems shows that it is just
as confused to claim "superiority" for one system as it is to blandly deem all
systems "equal." Yet while Phillips works to divest philosophers (and theologians) of conceptual confusion, he seems unaware of the fact that conceptual puzzles are *particular* (that is, they are his or mine or yours) but not
puzzles *in general*. Thus, his intent to disabuse others of conceptual confusion makes the tacit assumption that what confuses Phillips is confusing
in all cases. When this is coupled with Phillips's intention to do philosophy
as a citizen of no community, one is left wondering how successfully Phillips
himself has escaped Protagorean relativism.

In contrast, Hauerwas shows better than Malcolm and Phillips what it
means to "go on." Like Phillips, Hauerwas has adopted the essay (and the
sermon) as his mode of discourse. But Hauerwas can deal with the notion
of "truthfulness" with greater sophistication than Phillips. For example,
Hauerwas makes truth claims that are universal in scope and does so boldly
and unapologetically precisely because he speaks from within a particular
tradition, knowing that only other insiders who have been adequately shaped
into hearers are skillful and truthful enough to rightly understand what
"true" amounts to in such a case.

> Thus the primary task of Christian ethics involves an attempt to help
> us see. For we can only act within the world we can see and we can only
> see the world rightly by being trained to see. We do not come to see just
> by looking, but by disciplined skills developed through initiation into
> a narrative.[39]

And again:

> Put more directly, we often think that a true story is one that provides
> an accurate statement, a correct description. However, I am suggesting
> that a true story must be one that helps me to go on, for, as Wittgenstein
> suggested, to understand is exactly to know how to go on. . . . It is im-
> portant to note in this sense I cannot make the story true by how I use
> it, but the story must make me true to its own demands of how the

world should be. . . . A story that is true must therefore demand that we be true and provide us with the skills to yank us out of our self-deceptions. . . .[40]

Thus, Hauerwas utilizes the genre of essay in order to contribute to a much longer conversation—one that makes human readers the very center of his ethics. By it he intentionally speaks *within* the Christian tradition in a way intended to reshape his readers' manner of seeing. Does he succeed?

This question cannot be answered in general, for in the period 1968–1983 we see Hauerwas groping to find his own "cultural-linguistic" mode of doing ethics. Despite the fact that his earliest works are essays, he purposely arranges the essays in both *Vision and Virtue* and *Truthfulness and Tragedy* so that discussion of theoretical and methodological issues is placed first. This gives the illusion that theory precedes practice—a move which stands in stark contrast to his later emphasis on ethics as reflection on the actual *practices* of everyday saints. Moreover, the early essays betray an ambiguity concerning whom he considers his primary audience. This is especially felt in his early essays on medicine. Sometimes Hauerwas appears to pronounce for, and to, the entire medical community with little or no regard for Christian convictions.[41] In "The Moral Limits of Population Control," Hauerwas bends over backwards to utilize one result of Enlightenment ethics (the language of "rights") in order to counter another (namely, the theory of utilitarianism).[42] Yet in "Medicine as a Tragic Profession," Hauerwas has discarded secular categories altogether and speaks as one who struggles to bring his Christian convictions regarding the sinful character of human existence to bear on medicine:

> By calling medicine a tragic profession I am suggesting that it reflects the limits of our existence. . . . Tragedy is not helplessness, but our helplessness may be a manifestation of the tragic as it reminds us of our finitude.
>
> Self-deception has only intensified the tragic nature of medicine by making us less able to subject medicine to its proper office for our lives. Medicine is not more tragic than other aspects of our lives, but if it fails to be formed by a proper sense of the tragic its potential for moral destructiveness is increased.[43]

By 1981 Hauerwas had begun to take seriously the ramifications of an aesthetic view of ethics. Rather than do his reader the disservice of structuring his books according to a Tractarian-like table of contents, he lets the hoped-for conceptual transformation contribute to the way the reader envisions the whole:

> For the essays make it clear to the reader that my project is anything but finished and I am anything but certain how it is all to be "put together." If the essays do what they are supposed to do, they invite the reader to enter into the project and think through the issues, perhaps better than I have been able to do. Without presuming that my work has anything like the power of Wittgenstein's, it remains my intention that the essays, like his aphorisms, should make the reader think at least as hard, if not harder, than the author has about the issues raised.[44]

What Hauerwas hopes for, of course, is that this struggle results in a reshaping of the reader's moral vision so that "if the reader, on finishing the book, were to reread the first chapter, I suspect it would take on new meaning."[45]

By 1983 Hauerwas attempted to recover ground lost by his earlier, more formalistic and theoretical approach by showing in *The Peaceable Kingdom* the differences that basic Christian convictions should make. So, ethics is a matter of therapy which is effected by a delineation of the "grammar" of Christian convictions. Nevertheless, it should be clear from this discussion that Hauerwas takes as the primary ethical task that of "changing one's point of view, the old way of thinking."[46] The metamorphosis he is trying to effect in his readers may be described aptly as the acquisition of a new conceptual language, the ability to see something under a new aspect, the recognition of a formerly overlooked family resemblance, and the cultivation of moral vision. Such a self-transformative, or "self-consuming," pedagogy exemplifies the perspective of ethics-as-aesthetics which stands out in this period.

THE ESCHATOLOGICAL SELF

Thus far, Hauerwas's "self-consuming" pedagogy bears a striking similarity to Wittgenstein's therapeutic philosophy. At life's end, Wittgenstein viewed philosophy as the conceptual aid given that enabled someone to "go on." By this phrase he meant, roughly, that philosophy is only successful to the extent it helps human subjects simultaneously dissolve their respective conceptual confusions and surmount the aporias with which he expressed himself. Wittgenstein used aporias that could not be solved in general, in order to effectively challenge the dominant view of philosophy he inherited from his teachers. Ironically, the reader who learned to appreciate (as it were, from within) the sense in which Wittgenstein intended the aporias thereby came to see what was objectionable in the received account.[47] For example, Wittgenstein sometimes wrote as if our notions and conceptual languages (moral and otherwise) are inherited directly from our respective communities. But at other times, he wrote not as one who had *inherited* a conceptual framework, but as one who was attempting to *craft* a conceptual language that might not be fully appreciated until an entirely different culture was in place—perhaps a century from now.[48] Which is it? Well, if one understands why Wittgenstein might express himself in either of these two ways, one is in the position to understand that which Wittgenstein considered the deeper philosophical myth—the Cartesian picture of the self, the acommunal spectator, the wordless "I." However, each manner of expression—"I inherit my conceptual language from my community" vs. "I craft a conceptual language that cannot but be unintelligible to the individualistic age in which I live"—runs contrary to the other in a way that refuses to clarify who or what the self is, if not the Cartesian ego.

It is just at this point that some followers of Wittgenstein—and I intend to discuss but one, James C. Edwards—try to "go on" by departing from Wittgensteinian ethics and unwittingly reading him from the standpoint of the "prospective self," a fiction born of the very milieu Wittgenstein sought to oppose. This stance has the unfortunate result of diminishing the force of the "ought" as used in the language-games of morality. Of course, what "going on" amounts to in this, as in any given case, cannot be expressed independently of those very skills gained by the struggle to go on. In contrast to Edwards, Hauerwas is able to surmount Wittgenstein's aporias in at least one respect: by being an insider to a *particular* conceptual language, in this case, the language called Christian, Hauerwas avoids the ambiguities surrounding selfhood that plague modern thinkers who have purposefully shrugged off all such rich conceptual languages. On Hauerwas's view the self is decidedly eschatological—which is to say, simultaneously retrospective and future-facing.

The problem of selfhood can be given sharper focus if we consider the way Kierkegaard has been (mistakenly) championed as the father of ethical individualism. Kierkegaard's writings formed a polemic against the totalizing spirit of an age grown heady under the influence of Hegel's "System." What was particularly bewitching about the System was its presumption to be the good toward which rationality (*Geist*) had heretofore been progressing. What could be better? This way of stating things resulted in a vision of ethics as an exercise of cooperation with universal reason. Such cooperation was thought to produce an inevitable social harmony among all those who occupy the "sphere of the ethical." In Hegel's day the ethical mode of living, that is, a life lived in cooperation with *Geist*, was easily confused with authentic Christian living. It was against this confusion that Kierkegaard raised his voice:

> It is said to be hard to understand Hegel, while understanding Abraham, why, that's a bagatelle. To go beyond Hegel, that is a miracle, but to go beyond Abraham is the simplest of all. I for my part have devoted considerable time to understanding Hegelian philosophy, believe also that I have more or less understood it, am rash enough to believe that at those points where, despite the trouble taken, I cannot understand it, the reason is that Hegel himself hasn't been altogether clear. All this I do easily, naturally, without it causing me any mental strain. But when I have to think about Abraham I am virtually annihilated.[49]

Kierkegaard's point in *Fear and Trembling* is that Abraham could never have been moved to sacrifice Isaac on the basis of universal reason. Rather, Abraham's faith consisted precisely in the fact that it was a passionate leap *against* the grain of common sense. Thus for Kierkegaard there was a grave discrepancy between the morality of the crowd and that of the individual. The greatest danger for Christianity was its increasing reliance upon the theoretical mode of reason, which was incommensurable with faith; while speculative thought centers on "objective" truth, authentic Christianity has its roots in subjective truth.

The upshot of Kierkegaard's ethical views is twofold. First, Kierkegaard understood willing the good as inherently rebellious—willing the good was living under the aspect of eternal responsibility *as an individual* against the moral judgments of the crowd.[50] However, it is a bit misleading to call Kierkegaard's ethic "individualistic." In the first place, one must be careful not to confuse the positions expressed by essays that were written under a non-Christian pseudonym too quickly with the views embodied in Kierkegaard's explicitly Christian writings.[51] Thus we must ask what difference does it make for Kierkegaard's understanding of the self as "a relation which relates itself to its own self" that it was written under the pseudonym of a *Christian* of the most extreme kind?[52] Typically, commentators ignore the Christian aspect and read into Kierkegaard a crass sort of individualism. However, in his Christian writings Kierkegaard is quite clear that the individual could not be conceived except as *in relation to God*.[53] It may be that Kierkegaard's conception of the individual in these relational terms anticipates the way Wittgenstein (and narrative thinkers such as Hauerwas) subsequently come to view the self neither in terms of an intrinsic essence (as in Descartes) nor in terms of a God-less transcendental self-relation, but as an emergent in a social-linguistic matrix.[54]

Second, there is an incommensurability between modes of rationality (for Kierkegaard, between the sphere of the ethical and the sphere of the religious) that prevents translatability of "reasons" from one mode to the other. Thus Hegel may be *understood* (for reason belongs to the realm of the ethical), but Abraham *slays*. For Kierkegaard the sphere of facts in which speculative reasoning operated was absolutely separated from the sphere of value in which the mind of faith operated. Indeed, the sphere of values could not even be spelled out in theoretical terms; rather it had to be *shown* through parables, aphorisms, and the like.[55] Allan Janik and Stephen Toulmin conclude that the project which had begun in Kant, namely, the "attempt to chart the limits of reason in all its various spheres of activity," was transformed by Kierkegaard (and others such as Schopenhauer and Tolstoy) into "an outright denial of the validity of reason within the realm of values."[56] Consequently, the core ethical view maintained by Kierkegaard was that "the 'meaning of life' is not a matter for rational debate, cannot be given 'intellectual foundations', and is more a 'mystical matter'."[57]

These same two features are abundantly manifest in Wittgenstein's dialogue with Friedrich Waismann in 1929. Consider these words:

> What is ethical cannot be taught. If I could explain the essence of the ethical only by means of a theory, then what is ethical would be of no value whatsoever. . . .
> *For me* a theory is without value. A theory gives me nothing.[58]

So completely did Wittgenstein conceive (initially, at least) the separation between the realms of fact and value that when it comes to values one is reduced to silent gestures. This was the significance of his action during the meeting of the Vienna Circle. Picture it: Rudolph Carnap, Moritz Schlick, and other notables were circled together theorizing about language when Wittgenstein abruptly stood up, turned his back on the circle of chairs, and while facing outward—as if toward *das Mystiche*—read aloud from the mystical poetry of Rabindranath Tagore. What was this if not a grand gesture that expressed his conviction that the boundary of the language of logical positivism—expressed by the tight circle in which they all sat—simultaneously traced the inexpressible *das Mystiche* which lay beyond it?

A similar gesture is made toward the significance that the individual plays in Wittgenstein's early ethical views. In the same conversation cited above, he reminded Waismann, "At the end of my lecture on ethics I spoke in the first person: I think that this is something very essential. Here there is nothing to be stated anymore; all I can do is step forth as an individual and speak in the first person."[59] There is a vestige of this individualism still present in the later Wittgenstein. He advises Drury, "Make sure that your religion is a matter between you and God only."[60] In fact, the later Wittgenstein may have been even more prone toward individualism, considering the fact that the human subject had moved to the very center of his philosophical attention.[61] For both the early and late Wittgenstein, ethics has to do with a mode of seeing through the world to that sense of wonder and mystery that lay beyond it. In §§119–115 of the *Investigations* he wrote as if to say that he had come to realize that the very mode of reasoning (what Edwards calls rationality-as-representation) he adopted in the *Tractatus* had the effect of *obscuring* the impressiveness of *das Mystiche* insofar as it (*das Mystiche*) was misperceived as a difficult, though solvable, riddle.[62] Thus the ethical task, in Wittgenstein's view, is to deliver each individual from enslavement to totalizing views of the world where each of such views has its throttling grip by virtue of the (invisible) illusion that it is the only game in town.

Second, Wittgenstein resembled Kierkegaard insofar as he acknowledged that there is no way to settle in advance the question of how to choose between systems. Rush Rhees recalls a conversation with Wittgenstein in 1942 concerning an imaginary man who belongs to no particular tradition but must choose between abandoning his wife or surrendering his career in cancer research. In such cases, Wittgenstein insisted that ethics was not a mode of deliberation prior to the decision. Rather, ethics concerns the attitude the individual must take in light of whatever horn of the dilemma he winds up choosing:

> Whatever he finally does, the way things then turn out may affect his attitude. He may say, "Well, thank God I left her; it was better all around." Or maybe, "Thank God I stuck to her." Or he may not be able to say "thank God" at all but just the opposite.
> I want to say that this is the solution of an ethical problem.[63]

However, it is possible that ethics may be qualified (for example, as Christian ethics or Marxist ethics) and that two such attitudinal systems may conflict deeply. Wittgenstein continued:

> . . . it is so with regard to the man who does not have an ethics. If he has, say, the Christian ethics, then he may say it is absolutely clear: he has got to stick to her come what may. And then his problem is different. It is: how to make the best of this situation, what he should do in order to be a decent husband in these greatly altered circumstances, and so forth. The question "Should I leave her or not?" is not a problem here.

This is as far as someone can go without resorting to judgments made from within some particular rich conceptual language. That being the case, it should be clear that the so-called problem of ethical relativism, as commonly put forth by modern thinkers, is regarded by Wittgenstein as simply unintelligible.

> Someone might ask whether the treatment of such a question in Christian ethics is *right* or not. I want to say that this question does not make sense. The man who asks it might say: "Suppose I view his problem with a different ethics—perhaps Nietzsche's"—and I say: "No, it is not clear that he must stick with her; on the contrary, . . . and so forth." Surely one of the two answers must be the right one. It must be possible to decide which of them is right and which is wrong.
>
> But we do not know what this decision would be like—how would it be determined, what sort of criteria would be used, and so on. Compare saying that it must be possible to decide which of the two standards of accuracy is the right one. We do not even know what a person who asks this question is after.[64]

Christian ethics demands loyalty to one's spouse. But is Christian ethics the *right* system? Such a question cannot even be asked intelligibly. Someone who insists that one of the ethical systems is "the right one" or "true" is, in fact, simply making a judgment of value that amounts to adopting some particular system.

Clearly, Wittgenstein's game metaphor illustrates his view that there can be "no one system in which you can study in its purity and its essence what ethics is."[65] The term "ethics" names a family resemblance (as does "games") that enables one to use the adjective "ethical" with respect to judgments and actions. Wittgenstein describes an ethical system as a collection of language-games, or linguistic system, that was complete in itself. Thus he advocated resisting the temptation to "interpret" or translate from one system to another:

> In considering a different system of ethics there may be a strong temptation to think that what seems to *us* to express the justification of an action must be what really justifies it there, whereas the real reasons are the reasons that are given. These are the reasons for or against the action. "Reasons" doesn't always mean the same thing; and in ethics we have to keep from assuming that reasons must really be of a different sort from what they are seen to be.[66]

However, Wittgenstein's contention that there appears no way to ask or answer the question of which system one *ought* to adopt threatens to reduce the ordinary force of the word "ought." Consider this passage from 1929:

> What does the word 'ought' mean? A child ought to do such-and-such means that if he does not do it, something unpleasant will happen. Reward and punishment. The essential thing about this is that the other person is brought to do something. 'Ought' makes sense only if there is something lending support and force to it—a power that punishes and rewards. Ought in itself is nonsensical.[67]

By the time he had written part I of *Remarks on the Foundations of Mathematics* little had changed in his views: the binding force of social "games" such as logic and ethics is thought to be derived from nothing more determinate than human cooperation:

> "Then according to you everybody could continue the series as he likes; and so infer *any*how!" In that case we shan't call it "continuing the series" and also presumably not "inference." And thinking and inferring (like counting) is of course bounded for us, not by an arbitrary definition, but by natural limits corresponding to the body of what can be called the role of thinking and inferring in our life.
> For we are at one over this, that the laws of inference do not compel him to say or to write in such and such like rails compelling a locomotive. . . .

Nevertheless the laws of inference can be said to compel us; in the same sense, that is to say, as other laws in human society. The clerk who infers . . . *must* do it like that; he would be punished if he inferred differently. If you draw different conclusions you do indeed get into conflict, e.g., with society; and also with other practical consequences.[68]

But now the real problem emerges: If the oughtness of ethical statements derives from one's community, *how are we to understand Kierkegaard (not to mention Kierkegaard's Abraham), who suffered under a sense of an obligation that moved him in a direction diametrically opposed to the social cooperation in terms of which Wittgenstein conceives all obligation?* Kierkegaard felt obliged to criticize his society in ways that made him unintelligible to his contemporaries. Whence *this* obligation?

Wittgenstein would undoubtedly be pleased by the raising of this objection, since it rests upon an exegesis of the grammar of "ought." However, it is tempting to mistake Wittgenstein's aporetic expression for a to-be-solved-flaw in a more general theory of ethics. Such a misreading is presumes the very concept of self (self as autonomous chooser) of which Wittgenstein is intent on disabusing us. Such is James Edwards's transgression.

Edwards appears to argue that the *Investigation's* advance over the *Tractatus* is best expressed in terms of the freedom of the self to see the world in more than one way; the upshot of divesting ourselves of rationality-as-representation wonderfully increases our options. Yet Edwards begins his argument on the wrong foot, since he presumes that Wittgensteinian ethics must be conceived entirely in terms of the self as construed by modernity—the spectator who is free from all communal, historical, and religious influences.[69]

Edwards concludes that the author of the *Tractatus* thought that the power to access the meaning of the world lies in the hands of just such an individual:

> Once the world is seen for what it is *sub specie aeternitatis*—a limited, contingent whole bounded by the willing self—then the self can assume the right attitude toward it; the world can be seen aright. And to see it aright is to see its inevitable limitation, in two senses. It is first of all to see that the sense of life lies, not in the world itself, but in the willing self that limits it; and that is to see that one's happiness is within—indeed, *is*—one's own power.[70]

Edwards reasons that the power of the willing self is limited so long as it is unaware that there are other modes of seeing. Edwards takes this tunnel vision to be the great error of the *Tractatus* which Wittgenstein later repudiated. The Tractarian mode of rationality-as-representation, therefore, distorts moral vision.[71] Moreover, the Tractarian picture is particularly bewitching because it masks the possibility of other "pictures" by which one might see and renders invisible what Edwards takes to be the conditions for a subject's perspicuity, namely, self-consciousness of one's own determining presence in all one's doings.[72]

However, Edwards himself is apparently bewitched by a picture of the self that is uncharacteristic of Wittgenstein. Edwards writes that the self set free from the sorcery of the *Tractatus* is a self whose "mind plays *freely* among a variety of images, moving from one to the other gathering illumination with a variety of lenses."[73] This notion of the self misconstrues what Wittgenstein reminds us of in OC §92, that one must be trained into alternative modes of seeing, not shuttle between them as a matter of choice. For, by what criterion can one be thought able to juggle all these spectacles while seeing through no one pair in particular? If the *Tractatus* appears to deny the contingency of moral vision given the lack of alternatives, as Edwards maintains, surely Edwards's account of the *Investigations* fails to recognize the contingency of moral vision entailed by the possibility that we may not be "free to choose" alternative modes of seeing at all.

Might not the notion of an autonomous self make sense of Kierkegaard, who, in Edward's eyes, passionally *chose* to live contrary to his culture? Yet Edwards must refuse this option because it gives away too much; the Enlightenment version of the self has no room for the deep and irreducible sociality that permeated Wittgenstein's vision. In fact, Edwards fears that Wittgenstein will remain an enigma so long as we lack a communal form of life commensurate with the insights of the *Investigations*.[74] But Edwards can offer no resources in this regard because he is hampered by an account of the self that is "prospective." For Edwards, the self has burned all its bridges to the past and is entirely constituted by the choices it makes while facing the future.

In contrast to Edwards, Hauerwas surmounted Wittgenstein's aporia in this case by providing the sort of determinative account of the self that can only be spoken of from within a particular linguistic tradition. Hauerwas's resulting view of the self might thus be called "eschatological." On the one hand it is retrospective: I learn who I am by looking backward and discovering my identity as a gift bequeathed to me by a narrative community. On the other hand, it is future-facing: part and parcel of the gift of self is the joyful prospect of being trained, by participation in the community's life and language, to fashion my character in ways that fit the community's master story. Hauerwas gestured toward this eschatological self when he described character paradoxically as both the qualification and the orientation of the self.

Character as the Qualification and Orientation of the Self

Hauerwas began his break with Enlightenment thinking in his 1975 book, *Character and the Christian Life*. There he noted that the Enlightenment's rejection of the Reformers' substance dualism resulted in a construal of the self as nothing but an existential chooser. Consequently, ethics reduces to mere decisionism. But, Hauerwas avers, more is at stake in ethics than simply the decisions one makes, for lurking beneath the surface of every decision is the deeper question, "What kind of person will I be?"[75] Putting matters this way fundamentally changes the point of view from which moral reflection takes place. Ethics is akin to aesthetics not simply because both entail a certain skill in seeing, but also because what is at stake is not the distanced survey of an well-informed spectator, but the close-up, aesthetically-trained judgment of an actual human agent.[76] While his early view of agency tolerated individuality and decisionism, Hauerwas's study of Barth helped him realize that words such as "faithful" and "kind" were labels that could be more aptly applied to the pattern manifested by a *series* of actions than to an isolated decision or act. In Kierkegaard's words, "Let us never forget that Christianity is a whole course of life."[77] Hauerwas concludes,

> Faith for Barth is not just a matter of this or that particular decision; it is the determination of our whole being and action to God—a determination of our entire life in its individual moments and duration. Nor is the Christian life simply a series of conversions, but rather it is the content and character of the whole act of man's life.[78]

Thus, Hauerwas rejected Bultmann's "ethics of discontinuity" in favor of Barth's "ethics of continuity."[79] For Bultmann, moral decisions were made by a self cut off from its past. But Barth gave theological permission for understanding the self in some sense continuous with the past and therefore capable of displaying a patterned series of actions. This continuity of the self, which Hauerwas calls "character," was central to the Aristotelian account of agency that was discarded in the Enlightenment in favor of conceiving the self in terms of brute autonomy.[80] Hauerwas finds the Enlightenment self reductionistic, for a self-determining being cannot help but acquire a moral history which reflects the way in which one's beliefs, intentions, and actions qualify each subsequent decision.[81]

Hauerwas's claim to an "ethics of continuity" leaves him with something of a puzzle. One the one hand, he describes character as the qualification of the self. This seems to require some sort of psychological metaphysics in order for character to be solid enough to function as a causal influence on the shape of human acts. On the other hand, Hauerwas purposely avoids a metaphysical conception of character and conceives of it instead as the *form* of human agency.

> Character is not an accidental feature of our lives that can be distin-
> guished from "what we really are"; rather character is a concept that
> denotes what makes us determinative moral agents. Our character is
> not a shadow of some deeper more hidden real self; it is the form of our
> agency acquired through our beliefs and actions.[82]

This way of putting things still leaves ambiguous the sense in which he can say character "determines" agency. Hauerwas attempts to dissolve this puzzle by attending to the grammar of the concept of "I." He concludes that the language of agency ("I did X") can never be reduced to the language of science ("X happened").[83] We must be hesitant to borrow the language of causation when describing the relationship between character and selfhood. And, at this point explanation comes to a full stop:

> There is, however, no need to posit a "cause" of man's actions. Men
> simply have the ability to act; no further explanation is necessary. To
> be a man is to have the power of efficient causation. The self does not
> cause its activities or have its experiences; it simply is its activities as
> well as its experiences. I *am* rather than *have* both my activities and my
> nonvoluntary traits and processes.[84]

If "causation" names an external relation between two states of affairs, then Hauerwas offers an account of the internal relation between character and action more aptly described by the term "embodiment." Thus, "volitions, motives, intentions, reasons do not cause or move men to act, but men acting *embody* them."[85] Embodiment is not an external relation, but an *internal* one:

> Once it is plainly understood that action and agency are internally re-
> lated in the sense that the agent defines and determines the activity, it
> is clear that there is no reason to look beyond our self-agency for an
> explanation of behavior. Men are not related to what they do as one ex-
> ternal cause to an event, for what men do is not separable from their
> agency.[86]

The grammar of these two undeniable features of human existence shows
that neither agency nor character can be described prior to, or independently of, the other. Rather, they are reciprocally related as two sides of one
coin: character both qualifies one's agency and is given its determinative
shape by the choices the agent makes and has made.[87] One cannot help but
wonder at this juncture whether Hauerwas has escaped determinism at too
high a price, for in what sense can either leg of this reciprocal relation be
thought to "qualify" the other? Unfortunately, this is not the only weakness
in his early account.

The pattern of one's character cannot be separated from the *descriptions* the agent offers of his or her motives, beliefs, and intentions.[88] These
descriptions are not causal (for they may be entirely retrospective),[89] yet they
make the action what it is: "For what the action is, or even that it is an action, can only be determined by the fact that I was acting under one description rather than another."[90] In this regard the agent has privileged status
in determining his or her character.

> The agent is able to form a whole life pattern using certain descriptions
> rather than others; as agents we become who we are because we act in
> some ways rather than others. . . .
>
> Because we can determine our action by our control of its de-
> scription, the description we use forms what in fact we are as men. In
> this sense we are profoundly what we do, for once action is understood
> in its essential connection with our agency [for there is no undescribed
> action] it is apparent that by acting we form not merely the act but our-
> selves in the process.[91]

The notion of an agent's description is obviously bound up with another central feature of Hauerwas's early ethics: his concept of moral vision,
for one can only describe what one sees. However, this feature in and of itself points to a second weakness in Hauerwas's early account. Not only does
the internality of the relation between character and agency weaken the

sense in which each "qualifies" the other, but such qualification is also limited by the fact that agents can only describe actions according to a limited "core of fairly set descriptions" available within a given society.[92] A sheepish Hauerwas will later admit that these weaknesses stemmed from his attempt to conceive agency in terms of action *qua* action.[93] Alasdair MacIntyre eventually convinced him that actions can only be recognized for what they are when seen against the context of a narrative.[94]

From my cursory treatment of *Character and the Christian Life*, it is clear that Hauerwas's retention of the notion of an agent's "control" in the matter of "choosing" descriptions makes his own criticism of Enlightenment ethics unconvincing (since both presuppose an autonomous self). Further, the fact that he insisted that the relation between character and agency is an internal one renders his answer to the question "Why choose one description rather than another?" unsatisfactory. For these reasons Hauerwas turns rather abruptly to "narrative" as a central metaphor for his ethics.

Narrative as the Qualification of Moral Vision

In 1987 L. Gregory Jones detailed the multiple ways MacIntyre used the notion of narrative in his *After Virtue*.[95] Unfortunately, Jones faults MacIntyre for not specifying a core definition of "narrative." Such criticism cannot carry much weight against MacIntyre, since essentialism is precisely that to which narrative approaches offer a radical alternative. In Wittgensteinian terms, MacIntyre's uses of "narrative" display a family resemblance rather than share a core idea. A similar polyvalence is detectable in the variety of ways Hauerwas uses "narrative" to describe aspects of ethics. However, the notion of "story" first appears in Hauerwas's work simply as one of the means by which aesthetic vision is shaped and the individual agent is "freed" from the illusion of autonomy and individualism:

> Our vision must be trained and disciplined in order to free it from our neurotic self-concern and the assumption that conventionality defines the real. Ethics is that modest discipline which uses careful language, distinctions, *and stories* to break our intellectual bewitchment.[96]

In Hauerwas's understanding, "story" qualifies moral vision in three important ways.

First, narrative governs the language in which we frame our descriptions. For example, Christians inherit from their past a term for killing the unborn—"abortion"—that sets the precedent for their moral descriptions. On Hauerwas's view, to counter this vocabulary requires on the part of pro-abortionists "nothing less than a language reforming proposal; i.e., that abortion is not abortion."[97] And we do see that pro-abortionists frame their position in the language of "pro-choice" rather than "pro-abortion." A breakdown in communication is the inevitable result.

> Pro- and anti-abortion advocates do not communicate on the notion "abortion" since each group holds a different story about the purpose of the notion. At least so far as "abortion" is concerned, they live in conceptually different worlds.[98]

In Hauerwas's estimation, Christians see abortion as horrific because it is *abortive*, a fact that shows that "the Christian moral life is determined more by the language we have learned to speak than by the decisions we make."[99] Abortive in what sense? Christian use of the term is informed by a theological narrative: abortion cuts short both the gift of life given by God as well as the historical extension of the community whose children are a witness of its hope in the goodness of God.[100] To put it differently, apart from the stories of creation and redemption embodied in Jewish and Christian discourse we have no means for understanding how abortion is abortive.

Second, narrative qualifies moral vision by determining the *mode of description*. In response to Wittgenstein's parenthetical comment, "theology as grammar," Hauerwas proposed "story as the grammar of theology."[101]

> Stories, at least the kind of stories I am interested in [namely, "canonical" ones], are not to explain as a theory explains, but to involve the agent in a way of life. A theory is meant to help you know the world without changing the world yourself; a story is to help you deal with the world by changing it through changing yourself.[102]

How stories can function as self-changers becomes clearer when we realize that "the emphasis on story as the grammatical setting for religious convictions" shows that just as the grammar of a conceptual language is embodied in a form of life, so too a story may become the form of one's life. To be story-formed implies that both what I do, and the descriptions I offer of what I do, will be isomorphic with the master story.

The difference between story-formed descriptions of our moral lives and foundational explanations of our actions can be illustrated by Augustine's account of his conversion. It is absolutely crucial that Augustine's account took the form of autobiography, which is to say, a story. Part of what was at stake for Augustine in his conversion was the *mode* of self-description he would utilize. Each of the earlier phases of his life was governed by a *theoretical* account of life (first Manicheism, then Neoplatonism) that claimed to be true on the basis of its putative objectivity and universality. Of course, the fact that he passed from one theory to the next, with no guidance from any transparadigmatic criteria, showed the contingency both of his life and of the theories which claimed to explain his life to him.[103] What was at stake, therefore, was not his discovery in Christianity of a better *theory* (one on the same order as that of Manicheism or Neoplatonism), but rather his discovery of some way of unifying his past (including his rebellious and licentious youth) with his present while simultaneously making sense of the cataclysmic transitions from his life as a professional orator to Manicheism to Neoplatonism to Catholic Christianity. But this task of making sense of his whole life required Augustine to shift from an explanatory mode of thinking to a narrative one.[104] In other words, Augustine gained a "self" only after he was able to see the previously disjointed chunks of his past as episodes in a longer story, a story which the gospel told him was best described as a life—*his* life—questing for God. Had Christianity offered merely another abstract and universal theory, its truthfulness would have been on the same order as the other theoretical systems he had investigated, none of which could account for life's contingencies.

> Any ethical theory that is sufficiently abstract and universal to claim neutrality would not be able to form character. For it would have deprived itself of the notions and convictions which are necessary conditions for character. . . . If truthfulness . . . is to be found, it will have to occur in and through the stories that tie the contingencies of our life together.[105]

In order to be a character and to have character, one must view one's past through the lens of a narrative which can manifest the very reasons, way of life, and context without which moral notions and convictions founder.

Thus, narrative is the only mode of description appropriate to the concrete claims of the gospel in light of the contingency of our lives and knowledge. Hauerwas summarizes:

> The narrative character of our knowledge of God, the self, and the world is a reality-making claim that manifests that the world and our lives in it have a created status—that is, our lives, and indeed, the exis-

tence of the universe are metaphysically contingent realities. Narrative is, therefore, not secondary for our knowledge of God; there is no point or meaning that can be separated from the story. He is that kind of God and the world is that kind of world. For narratives are required for those matters that defeat all causal explanations. That does not mean that stories are but substitute or deficient explanations that we hope someday to supplant with more literal accounts. On the contrary, narratives are necessary exactly for those aspects of our lives that admit of no further explanations—e.g., God, the world, and the self.

It is therefore not surprising that knowledge of God, the world, and the self seem to have the same epistemological status.[106]

To put matters slightly differently, "the narrative Augustine tells shows us how he was moved to accept the gospel story by allowing it to shape his own."[107] That Augustine recounts his conversion to Christianity in narrative form shows that he has found his "self" in God's story; his conversion is enabled by the exchange of a theoretical mode of rationality for a narrative one.

Third, not only does Hauerwas see narrative as governing the language of description and as constituting an alternative mode of description, he also sees narrative as crucial for cultivating the skills necessary for seeing our lives under some aspects rather than others.

I am suggesting that descriptively the self is best understood as a narrative, and normatively we require a narrative that will provide the skills appropriate to the conflicting loyalties and roles we necessarily confront in our existence. The unity of the self is therefore more like the unity that is exhibited in a good novel—namely with many subplots and characters that we at times do not closely relate to the primary dramatic action of the novel. But ironically without such subplots we cannot achieve the kind of unity necessary to claim our actions as our own.

Yet a narrative that provides the skill to let us claim our actions as our own is not the sort that I can simply "make mine" through a decision. Substantive narratives that promise me a way to make my self my own require me to grow into the narrative by constantly challenging my past achievements. That is what I mean by saying that the narrative must provide skills of discernment and distancing. For it is certainly a skill to be able to describe my behavior appropriately and to know how to "step back" from myself so that I might better understand what I am doing. The ability to step back cannot come by trying to discover a moral perspective abstracted from all my endeavors, but rather comes through having a narrative that gives me critical purchase on my own projects.[108]

At the heart of Augustine's conversion is the fact that the story of God gave him the skills of discernment and distancing that enabled him to own his past as an episode in the story of God. Moreover, this story directed his future actions by means of narrating to Augustine who (and whose) he was. For these reasons the story stuck. Augustine's conversion, therefore, stands in stark contrast to the "conversion" of Bertrand Russell, who claimed to have been convinced by the ontological argument of God's existence—for the span of three days! Wittgenstein may have had Russell in mind when he wrote,

> What does it mean to say, "What is happening now has significance" or "has deep significance"? What is a deep feeling? Could someone have a feeling of ardent love or hope for the space of one second—*no matter what* preceded or followed this second?—what is happening now has significance—in these surroundings. The surroundings give it its importance.[109]

Later in his career, Hauerwas quoted John Milbank with approval regarding the grip that the gospel came to have on Augustine's life, for by the gospel Augustine was given a new self:

> Thus, the "depth" revealed in Augustine's *Confessions* (as he is more than half aware) is the effect of reflections on past actions, of the realization that they might have been different, that they can be totally reread in the context of the more general story of the Church, and that he can transform himself in the future.[110]

Augustine's *Confessions* shows that depth is not a matter of discovering the inner form of human beings, but rather a matter of realizing that I can see, by means of the language and story of the church, another life in my past. This is not discovering an essence, but seeing under a different aspect what has always been before my nose. At this early stage in his thinking, Hauerwas saw narrative as crucial for training us to see the pattern which constitutes the true form of our lives. On the one hand, the irreducibly narrative form of human life enables the life of Jesus of Nazareth to be captured in print. On the other, the form of life embodied in those gospel narratives can be reenacted in human lives. Thus Augustine's conversion (and likewise ours) is nothing less that the gospel becoming the material content of our character:

> Put abstractly, a story is the material content which gives form to our character so that the changes and growth of the self can be said to have a narrative continuity. The problem is how to affirm consistently, as it seems we must, both the necessity of moral growth and the demand for the self to have integrity. The category of "story" helps us to do that, since it enables us to see how our growth is continuous and/or discontinuous with the narrative structure of our life.[111]

Put concretely, the question "Who am I?" is given an eschatological answer by the story of Jesus. Looking back with the help of the gospel, we see that we are already by grace adopted members of the body politic whose historical face, despite the warts, manifests Christ's presence by means of Christians' love for one another. Looking forward, we see through the lens of the gospel that we are not yet all that we, by virtue of the gospel, know we should be—and may in fact become—as followers in Jesus' footsteps.

Hauerwas did not speculate as to why stories possess aesthetic power, that is, power to cultivate our skill in seeing the resemblance between stories He simply noted that, "As we follow that story, we gain some insight into recurrent connecting patterns, and also some ability to assess them. We learn to recognize different configurations and to rank some characters as better than others." Moreover, such attention to the grammar of stories is a skillful seeing that becomes focused without assistance from philosophical systems.[112] This is so because seeing is not an intellectual exercise but a transformation of the self.

> For Christian ethics is not first of all an ethics concerned with doing, but its first task is to help us rightly see the world. Christian ethics is not just a narrative, but rather involves a very definite narrative with a determinative content. . . .
>
> Thus, the primary task of Christian ethics involves an attempt to help us see. For we can only act within a world we can see and we can only see the world rightly by being trained to see. We do not come to see just by looking, but by disciplined skills developed through initiative into a narrative.[113]

Narrative Unity of the Self

We are now in a position to see that proper cultivation of moral vision comes by finding an eschatological (which is to say, narrative) account of the self that trains one how to see. As far as Hauerwas was concerned, the "true" story is not one that provides accurate description (how could this be measured?), but one that helps adherents go on in the sense of providing them with "the skills to handle the basic ontological variable of our lives, e.g., fate, anxiety, tragedy, hope, and so on."[114]

In *The Peaceable Kingdom*, Hauerwas discussed tragedy as the test case for rival accounts of the self.[115] In the first place, modern thinkers since Kant have described the self in terms of raw volition, the power to choose.[116] On this view, one is responsible for a given moral decision only to the extent that one decided "freely"—with all the relevant information and without compulsion. Of course, practically speaking, this view implies that responsibility is a moral fiction because I can always evade responsibility by discounting my history. That evasion is at the heart of the modern malaise.

> This attempt to avoid our history . . . results in the lack of the self-sufficiency to claim our lives as our own. For as we look back on our lives, many of the decisions we thought we were making freely, seem now to have been more determined than we had realized. We say: "If I only knew then what I know now." Using this as a means to claim non-responsibility for our past, we imagine that *next time* we will really act "freely." As a result we tend to think the moral life and ethical reflection are concerned with prospective decisions and the securing of the conditions necessary to insure that those "decisions" will be free. We ignore the fact that the more important moral stance is retrospective, because it is in remembering and accepting that we learn to claim our lives as our own—including those decisions that in retrospect were less than free. Ironically, my freedom turns out to depend on my ability to make my own that which I did not do with "free choice" but which I cannot do without. For what we are, our sense of ourselves, rests as much on what we have suffered as what we have done.[117]

Evasion of responsibility through discounting one's history constitutes what Hauerwas calls "the most basic modern deception."[118] The deceptiveness of this view of freedom stems from a faulty understanding of the self—one which erroneously makes freedom the be-all and end-all of the moral life rather than understanding human selves in terms of qualities, skills, or powers that derive from well-formed character. When the self is understood entirely prospectively (in terms of decisions yet to be made), no sense can be made of the sentence "I am responsible," because the subject (the yet-to-be-realized "I") is absent.

In sharp contrast, Hauerwas's view of the self is "eschatological." On the one hand, the eschatological self is prospective: I [co-]author my future in accordance with the story with which I have been graced. On the other hand, the eschatological self is retrospective. The grammar of responsibility implies that we, as agents, possess already the means to own the events of our past—even those in which we were entirely passive. Such a resource clearly cannot be of our own doing. Rather, retrospectively attuned persons have been surprised by the gift of a story that has made their lives continuous with its plotline.

> But our moral lives are not simply made up of the addition of our separate responses to particular situations. Rather we exhibit an orientation that gives our life a theme. . . . To be agents at all requires directionality. . . . Such attention is formed and given content by the stories through which we have learned to form the story of our lives. To be moral persons is to allow stories to be told through us so that our manifold activities gain a coherence that allows us to claim them for our own. The significance of stories is the significance of character for the moral life as our experience itself, if it is to be coherent, is but an incipient story.[119]

The way "tragedy" is typically conceived overlooks the requirement of historical continuity for selfhood. In disassociating oneself from his or her past, the modern individual is left unclear as to what the sentence "I have suffered X" may mean. In contrast, Hauerwas maintains that owning one's own actions is identical to making them a part of his or her story via the description given to them: "My act is not something I cause, as though it were internal to me, but it is mine because I am able to 'fit' it into my ongoing story."[120] For lack of these narrative resources, the modern view of the self finds tragedy inexplicable and irredeemable. But those who have gained an identity by locating their history within the gospel story have also gained resources for seeing their own tragedy as redeemable through becoming isomorphic with the story of Jesus.

Thus, suffering offers us the opportunity for becoming real or "truthful" to the extent that we come to recognize ourselves through the lens of a truthful story, "for a truthful narrative is one that gives us the means to accept the tragic without succumbing to self-deceiving explanations."[121]

We are finally in a position to see that in his early period (1968–1983), Hauerwas's narrative account of the self at once described the social origins of moral obligation and also accounted for moral obligation in Kierke-gaard's case. Following Wittgenstein, Hauerwas construed the moral life as one of transformed vision. For the Christian, this transformed vision is part and parcel of an existence patterned after the gospel. As this story is em-bodied in the believing community's memory and present form of life, the force of moral obligation is none other than the requirement that one live faithful to the community's canonical story in order to retain one's iden-tity as member of this community. The identity of this social community determines what one must do and be in order to retain one's socially-determined identity.

Earlier I asked whether Wittgenstein's conventionalist view of ethics could account for the obligation that Kierkegaard felt to move against the grain of his contemporary community. One sort of response points to the aporetic quality of Wittgenstein's writing: Wittgenstein did not craft a theory of ethics that could explain the minutiae of morality, but rather he assem-bled a series of pedagogical conundrums that aimed at helping a given stu-dent think more clearly. But another response is given by Hauerwas, who, without avoiding Wittgenstein's aporias, showed that for those formed by the gospel narrative, one's link with the past may be more morally deter-minative than one's link with one's contemporaries. By identification with the *historic* Christian tradition, Kierkegaard could feel keenly a sense of moral obligation that fit this community's identity narrative as well as this community's answer to the question, "What is human life for?"[122] Retention of his identity as "Christian" (in Kierkegaard's understanding of the term) and pursuit of the Christian *telos* (as Kierkegaard understood the term) de-manded that he live counter-culturally, even if this meant being the lone subversive in a society marked by dead orthodoxy.

Ethics has an aesthetic component because of the givenness of lan-guage and narrative. We are each recipients of a communal way of life, of a stock of stories, of a conceptual vocabulary, and of a history of conversa-tion; against these linguistic stones the lens of our moral vision is being ground. And we cannot put off our spectacles. For without them we are not only blind to our past responsibilities and myopic about our future; with-out them there is no "we" at all.

THREE

THIS COMPLICATED FORM OF LIFE

For the searching and the right understanding of the Scriptures there is need of a good life and pure soul, and for Christian virtue to guide the mind to grasp, so far as human nature can, the truth concerning God the Word. One cannot possibly understand the teaching of the saints unless one has a pure mind and is trying to imitate their life. Anyone who wants to look at sunlight naturally wipes his eye clean first, in order to make at any rate some approximation to the purity of that on which he looks; and a person wishing to see a city or country goes to the place in order to do so. Similarly, anyone who wishes to understand the mind of the sacred writers must first cleanse his own life, and approach the saints by copying their deeds.

—Athanasius

A dog believes his master is at the door. But can he also believe his master will come the day after tomorrow?—And what can he not do here?—How do I do it?—How am I supposed to answer that? Can only those hope who can talk? Only those who have mastered the use of a language. That is to say, the phenomena of hope are modes of this complicated form of life.

—Wittgenstein, Philosophical Investigations

Sometimes the meaning of a word can shift for us in unexpected ways. For example, what counted as a "good" job in one's youth may not measure up to one's expectations at midlife. So, the fifty-year-old trades perks, salary, and benefits for an occupation with longer hours, less pay, and greater personal sacrifice but one that makes a more tangible contribution to society. In this example, the notion of what makes a job "good" has shifted from personal peace and affluence toward beneficence and altruism. This latter conception of "good" is, in large measure, incommensurable with goodness described from the former standpoint. And yet this transformation of concept occurred for one and the same person. It was this order of semantic shift that Wittgenstein experienced concerning the notion of "form." The metamorphosis of the concept is so radical that I am not able to spell out a core definition that persisted throughout the process of transformation. Rather, the conception at each stage of his thinking, at best, bears a family resemblance to conceptions which precede and follow. Yet throughout Wittgenstein's writings the same term is repeated: *form.* At the outset, the term "form" connoted the logical structure of reality. But by the time his journey was complete, the word came to rest in a phrase that epitomizes the hurly-burly of human socio-linguistic existence: "this complicated form of life."

THE LOGICAL FORM OF THE WORLD

The view that language works by pairing signifier with signified is very old. Wittgenstein's contribution to this legacy was his explanation of *how* it was possible for language to depict the world. His version of the picture theory began with the observation that in order for a picture to succeed as a representation, it must have something in common with what it represents (X) and by means of which the picture is recognized as a picture *of* X.[1] That which was thought to be shared by a picture and a state of affairs was called their "form." Form can be *shown* (*ausdrucken*)—after all, it is present in both the picture and the state depicted—but form itself can never be *spoken.* Why not? If speaking is representation, then "to be able to represent the logical form, we should have to be able to put ourselves with the propositions outside of logic, that is outside the world."[2] And if representation proceeds by means of logical form, then to stand outside of logic removes from language the very stuff it needs to do its job. So then, form has an ineffable, yet very real, presence in both the world and the language that pictures the world.

Wittgenstein initially conceived of the world, therefore, as a combination of form and content.[3] The content of the world is constituted by its "facts," which are objects-in-particular-configurations.[4] An object is recognizable only by reference to its location in some larger constellation.[5] Objects can only be objects by means of participation in some logically possible arrangement. For example, it is impossible to conceive of a spatial object apart from all space.[6] Because objects must occur in *some* arrangement of all arrangements possible, the object is, in this sense, dependent for its reality on the range of these logically possible arrangements. The range of logical possibility is said to be the logical space in which the object lies. Something seen truly (i.e., from a God's-eye view or under the aspect of eternity [*sub specie aeternitatis*]) is "the thing seen together with the whole of logical space." This space is not simply three-dimensional, but multi-dimensional: "A speck in a visual field need not be red, but it must have a colour; it has, so to speak, a colour space around it. A tone must have *a* pitch, the object of sense *a* hardness, and so forth."[7] To know an object, therefore, is to know both the actualities and the possibilities of its relations (heavier than, harder than, etc.). Because objects, by being real, "contain" the possibility of all these relations, objects don't simply "lie" in logical space, they possess it, or better, they participate in the logical form of the world.[8]

The world, in this view, is the sum total of all the facts (not things, *contra* realism)[9]. The factuality of the world *in toto* depends upon its participation in logical form in the same way each atomic fact is constituted by some particular constellation of simple objects. Form is the *a priori* structure of the world.[10] Form transcends the world and is logically binding in the sense that it enables the realization of possible worlds and disables the actualization of impossible ones.[11] The study of logic, therefore, leads to a true knowledge of the world.[12]

If this summary were all we had to go on, it might be easy to mistake Wittgenstein's intentions, as did his contemporaries in the Vienna Circle. While it is true that Wittgenstein showed the limits of language by using a linguistic model internal to language,[13] his purpose in doing so was not to turn attention away from the unsayable. Rather, if the realm of the sayable had any value whatsoever, any "point" at all, this must lie beyond the speakable world.[14] In a letter to Ludwig von Ficker, Wittgenstein wrote of the *Tractatus*:

> *The book's point is an ethical one.* I once meant to include in the preface a sentence which is not in fact there now, but which I will write out

for you here, because it will perhaps be a key to the work for you. What I meant to write, then, was this: My work consists of two parts: the one presented here plus all that I have *not* written. *And it is precisely this second part that is the important one.* My book draws limits to the sphere of the ethical from the inside as it were, and I am convinced that this is the ONLY rigorous way of drawing those limits.[15]

The sense, or ethical value, of the world must lie outside the world in this ineffable realm where form, aesthetics, ethics, and religion possess transcendence and significance.[16] Thus the unsayable ought to capture our attention.

Wittgenstein succeeded in absolutizing the division between fact and value. But rather than consign the ineffable to the metaphysical dust bin, as did the logical positivists, Wittgenstein concluded instead that the route to the beyond-the-world cannot lie within language. The logical positivists stood on the road toward the mystical (*das Mystische*) in order to block the way and turn travelers back toward home. However, Wittgenstein stood as a moral sage at the crossroads not to turn travelers back but to warn them which fork is a dead end. His intention all along was to *draw attention to the mystical* by showing that the limits of our worldly island are simultaneously the shoreline of a vast ocean. Form, then, is part of the *a priori* conditions of the world and comprises the backdrop against which the world as a logically limited whole makes any sense at all.

Form is the logical limit of the world. Insofar as language (and thought) depicts the world by means of its participation in form, form is also the limit of language. While it is possible everywhere to coordinate language with the world, it is not possible to speak what is logically impossible by means of language: "To present in language anything which 'contradicts logic' is as impossible as in geometry to present by its coordinates a figure which contradicts the laws of space; or to give the coordinates of a point which does not exist."[17] Objects in space must be depicted by a picture which is able to express spatial relationships (e.g., "to the right of"). Moreover, a picture shares logical limits with the spatial objects it depicts: neither sign nor thing signified can possess spatial arrangements other than three-dimensional relationships, "to the right or left of," "behind or in front of," and "above or below." This limitation on spatial depiction shows form simultaneously embodied in both the configured object and its representation. The same analysis could be carried out for colored objects. What we want to call something's color was understood by Wittgenstein as the object's arrangement or configuration in "color space." This logical space determines the limits of what colors are logically possible in the world and its representations.

These two illustrations show that form is not merely the limit of the world and language, form is also the precondition for human understanding. The sense of a statement terminates in form. That form becomes the terminus for understanding was further shown by Wittgenstein's conviction that propositions have a sense independent of the facts. Even false propositions convey truth about the world because they express logical possibility.[18] The sentence "There are 12 hippos in my office" is false on the whole but conveys the logically possible relation that hippos are the sorts of things that could be "in" offices. So, argued Wittgenstein, it is not the false but the *meaningless* propositions which do no work. And here the term "meaningless" goes proxy for "formless." For example, we wouldn't know what to make of a dinner guest who turns and says, with all sincerity, "Milk me sugar." Our guest's sentence is formless (i.e., lacking logical relations) and, therefore, idle.

The Tractarian notion of form has three implications for Wittgenstein's early philosophy of language. First, language functions by "picturing" the world. Wittgenstein conceded early on that there are multiple ways of picturing,[19] but in each case the picture has meaning by expressing the form of the constellation of objects it depicts. More importantly, while general propositions may refer to the structure of the *whole* world,[20] the meat of his early picture theory was his insistence that there is a one-to-one correspondence between each proposition and some possible (real or imagined) state of affairs. In 1914 Wittgenstein wrote, "Proposition and situation are related to one another like the yardstick and the length to be measured," and again, "In the proposition we hold a proto-picture up against reality."[21]

This way of thinking about how language functions points to a second ramification of the Tractarian notion of form, namely, the way it finally dichotomizes language and world. Of course, the "world" in question is not a world of "things," but a world of facts. Hence investigations into the truth value of sentences by *empirical* investigation are fundamentally on the "wrong track."[22] The distance between subject and world have been collapsed for Wittgenstein. On the one hand, "The subject—we want to say—does not drop out of the experience but is so much involved in it that it cannot be described."[23] And on the other hand, Wittgenstein maintained that all experience has a linguistic texture to it so that language and world are coterminous: "The limits of my language mean the limits of my world."[24]

We must read the following claim in the light of the internal relation that Wittgenstein saw between knowing subjects and knowable objects:

> 2.223   In order to discover whether the picture is true or false we must compare it with reality.[25]

If the reality to which one compares each linguistic picture is the world of my experience (i.e., a world *internally related* to language use), all is well. But, as we shall see shortly, once Wittgenstein resorted to describing the representative function of language in terms of a "method of projection," he seemed unable to avoid becoming tangled in a conception of language as one thing and the world as another.[26]

Saying that a method of projection bifurcates language and the world doesn't quite capture all that is implied by the Tractarian notion of form. Wittgenstein's conception of form results, third, in an investigation of the relation between the *form* of the world and the *syntax* of propositions about the world. On the one hand, in order for the meaning of the proposition to be fixed there must be a determinate method of projection between world and proposition so that the isomorphism between the two can be clearly expressed. On the other hand, it is tempting to wonder just how the form of the world is embodied in propositions. At the outset, the young Wittgenstein denied that the form of the world was shown by the form of a *system* of propositions; that insight came later. He initially thought that the form of the world was embodied in the syntax *of a single proposition*. However, this appears problematic. The form of Indo-European sentences appears limited to two types (subject-predicate and relational), while the form of the world is multiplicitous. The only conclusion open to Wittgenstein, it seemed, was that language works because the sense of the proposition is "projected" onto the physical artifact (bits of ink on a page or vibrations in the air) when we think the sense of the proposition.[27] In other words, we need both a *picture* and a *way of picturing* (i.e., method of projection) in order to understand the picture.[28] So, theoretically, there could be a multiplicity of pictures each depicting a single fact by its own method of projection so long as what is characteristic for the depicted fact will be the same for all the picture-projection operations. For example, the peaceful nature of my relationship with my friend can be represented by a picture of two people calmly shaking hands, but also by a picture of two persons fighting so long as the method of projection in the latter case specifies that this is how things are *not*.[29] Wittgenstein's bottom line was this: While the written or spoken sentence (picture) has a certain structure (subject-predicate or relational), its ability to depict does not depend solely on its syntactical structure. Rather, the determinateness of the sense of the proposition presupposes, in addition to the sentence having some form, a similarly ineffable, albeit fixed, method of projection.[30]

Each of these three ramifications stimulated Wittgenstein to revise his original views. The young Wittgenstein began with the common assumption that ordinary assertions have determinate meanings, which can be ascertained simply by taking the proposition as a picture of some subset of the experiential world. Thus, he reasoned that three conditions are required in order for language to picture the world of experience in a determinate way. First, complex propositions must be finally analyzable into elementary propositions that each possess determinate meanings by virtue of their being paired with atomic facts he calls "simples."[31] Second, not only must there be such things as simples (in order for language to avoid ambiguity), but each simple must possess autonomy from the other; any overlap between states of affairs must dissolve in the process of analysis.[32] Third, in order for a proposition to have a determinate sense, there must be no way to be mistaken about the means by which objects are correlated with their symbolizations. When he wrote in his *Notebooks* (October 30, 1914) that the method of representation must be fixed, he seems to have in mind the presumed necessity of there being only one set of coordinates per simple. For example, if we restrict our discussion to points in Cartesian space, the point A is what it is because of its position in its "logical," which in this case is identical to "geometrical," space. (The method of projection in this case consists of lines that are perpendicular to the Cartesian axes.)

Once Wittgenstein undertook to explain the mechanism of language by means of the picture theory, he had trouble preventing himself from speaking about language as one thing and the world as another. This resulting bifurcation was not a problem with which he began. But subsequent to the formulation of his picture theory, Wittgenstein realized the need for a "method of projection" between language and the world that guaranteed the faithfulness of the representation despite intrinsic limitations of all symbolic systems.[33]

For example, Wittgenstein asked us to imagine a method which projects rectangles in one plane onto squares in another, and similarly projects a variety of coplanar ellipses onto circles. The plane containing circles and squares is analogous to language. There are intrinsic limitations to language—only squares and circles can be formulated. Yet something of form is retained in the projection: right-angularity is preserved in the transformation of rectangles and curvature is preserved for the transformation of ellipses. Yet, what prevents a rival method of projection from projecting rectangles, say, into rhombuses, and ellipses into line segments? Wittgenstein concluded that only if the determinateness of the method of projection is also guaranteed, can the determinateness of a sentence's sense be accounted for.

Eventually, all three of these assumptions went up for grabs. First, as Wittgenstein later mused, "Our difficulty was that we kept on speaking of simple objects and were unable to mention a single one."[34] As his early theory of language hinged on the idea that linguistic analysis terminates in logical atoms that name simple objects, his inability to name even one such object threatened the very core of his model. At one point Wittgenstein wondered if maybe—just maybe—patches in our visual field are simples.[35] However, as Frank Ramsey observed, if color patches are examples of simples, then simples cannot possess autonomy.[36] In other words, there is tension between Wittgenstein's second assumption—that elementary propositions are logically independent—and the fact that it is logically impossible for two colors (i.e., two simples) simultaneously to occupy the same visual space. A ball that is uniformly red cannot also be uniformly green or blue or any color other than red. This is a very strong logical connection. Consequently, either (a) logical atoms and their ontological counterparts—simple objects—are not logically independent or (b) a sentence like "This is red" is not an example of an elementary proposition.

Third, on what grounds might it be asserted that a method of projection is fixed? What is to prevent us from specifying the location of a point in space by means of lines of projection that are 45° to the axes rather than perpendicular? Or indeed, what is to prevent us from projecting rectangles, say, into rhombuses, and ellipses into line segments?

These problems laid the tracks for the development of Wittgenstein's later thought regarding form. The unspecifiability of methods of projection opened up the possibility of understanding the pictorial character of thought as a function of the human subject's skill at seeing patterns and aspects rather than as the description of the whole world from a God's-eye view. Furthermore, the temptation to see "sense" as fixed (because, on the one hand, the form of the world is presumably fixed, and on the other, linguistic form together with its method of projection is presumably fixed) ultimately turned Wittgenstein's efforts toward untangling the grammar of ordinary language. Eventually he would conclude that the determinateness of sense rests firmly upon grammatical *conventions*. Finally, in lieu of identifying a single example of a simple, Wittgenstein would come to a full stop with the conclusion that complexes function as simples[37]—a fact which in its own right suggests that meaning, sense, justification, etc., have conventional terminations. But even with this concession, answering Ramsey's challenge (that simples are not logically autonomous) will, more importantly, constitute Wittgenstein's first step toward casting off the language-world dichotomy.

THE FORM OF PROPOSITIONAL SYSTEMS

After a nine-year absence from philosophy, during which he taught school-children in rural Austria, Wittgenstein returned to Cambridge in a frame of mind able to reconsider what he once held to be the "unassailable and definitive" truths of the *Tractatus*. Two short publications mark the beginning of this period and summarize much of his early views. Taken together, the two reflect the two major strands of Tractarian thought. In *Some Remarks on Logical Form* Wittgenstein attempted to summarize where he stood on the idea of form. Here we see that his attention was still firmly fixed on the form of the single proposition (rather than of a system of propositions):

> I have said elsewhere that a proposition "reaches up to reality," and by this I meant that the forms of the entities are contained in *the form of the proposition* which is about these entities. For the sentence, together with the mode of projection which projects reality into the sentence, determines the logical form of the entities. . . .[38]

Philosophizing, on this view, amounts to clarifying the form, or logical structure, of a proposition by replacing ambiguous terms with symbols.[39] The second work preserved from 1929 is his "Lecture on Ethics" given to the Cambridge Heretics Society. On the one hand, this audience made the lecture especially challenging since its members had no particular training in either philosophy, logic, or mathematics. On the other hand, Wittgenstein may have assumed that this lack of formal training was to their advantage, since it would have left their minds unclouded by the nimbus of modern philosophy. In any event, Wittgenstein set about the business of pointing them in the direction of the ultimately important, the realm of the mystical, a topic toward which the *Tractatus*, at best, gestured.

During this same year, Wittgenstein's ongoing conversations with Vienna Circle member Friedrich Waismann reflect the beginnings of a comprehensive revision of his Tractarian views. So rapidly did his views change that plans to publish a revised and "corrected" second edition of *Tractatus* with Waismann were doomed from their inception. By 1936 Wittgenstein had cut off communication with Waismann, having suspected him of distorting his views to other members of the Vienna Circle. But in 1929 Waismann was still one of Wittgenstein's closest confidants, and conversations recorded by Waismann are a good barometer of the impending change of seasons in Wittgenstein's thinking.[40]

At the heart of this series of conversations held between Wittgenstein, Waismann, and Moritz Schlick during Wittgenstein's first few years at Cambridge lay Wittgenstein's admission of an error in the *Tractatus:*

> I used to have two conceptions of an elementary proposition, one of which seems correct to me, while I was completely wrong in holding the other. My first assumption was this: that in analysing propositions we must eventually reach propositions that are immediate connections of objects without any help from logical constants, for 'not', 'and', 'or', and 'if' do not connect objects. And I still adhere to that. Secondly I had the idea that elementary propositions must be independent of one another. . . . In holding this I was wrong. . . .[41]

At this time, Wittgenstein still held that propositions depicted states of affairs by means of the correlation of the form and content of a proposition with the form and content of the world. A complex proposition can be dissected into its elemental parts where "the signs . . . go proxy for things" and the form of the state of affairs is "exhibited by the form of a proposition."[42] However, perhaps in response to Ramsey's charge, Wittgenstein no longer held the view that elementary propositions were logically independent of each other; conclusions about the status of one proposition *could* be inferred from the status of another.[43]

> If, then, I understand what the specification of a length means, I also know that, if a man is 1.6 m. tall, he is not 2 m tall. I know that a measurement determines only one value on a scale and not several values. If you ask me, How do I know that? I shall simply answer, Because I understand the sense of the statement. It is impossible to understand the sense of such a statement without knowing the rule.[44]

Every proposition is part of one or another system of propositions or of one or another system of description.[45] Both the form of the single proposition and the form of the system contribute to the sense of the "picture"; the former expresses the form of the state of affairs, the latter contains the method of projection. Thus, Wittgenstein could no longer speak of the single proposition "laid against reality like a ruler" but preferred instead to say that "a *system of propositions* is laid up against reality like a ruler."[46]

The implication of this change in terminology is that Wittgenstein had come to view the linguistic *system* as the final repository for meaning.[47] This raises something of a puzzle. In the *Tractatus*, Wittgenstein had acknowledged that there was a basic arbitrariness about systems of description and that the sense of a given proposition can only be understood in the context of its system.[48] Does not the arbitrariness of the system to which propositions belong threaten the determinateness of each proposition's sense? For example, if all I knew was "red," is it possible that I may never come to speak of it or of another color or of color in general?[49] Not necessarily. On the one hand, Wittgenstein conceded that "the sentence has completely different sense according to what method I allow as verification."[50] But, on the other hand, propositions are composite animals symbolized, for instance, as $\Phi(a)$, having both a function (Φ) and an argument (a). But the function is no more superfluous than the argument. Wittgenstein's insight that there is a multiplicity of functions ($\Phi, \Psi, Z, \ldots$) as well as a multiplicity of arguments ($a, b, c \ldots$) can be described in slightly different terms as multiple ways of picturing and multiple elements of pictures, or, better yet, as multiple methods of projection each coupled with allowable forms of propositions.[51] Thus, the determinateness of sense may be preserved in spite of the fact that the form of the proposition cannot be thought to express by itself a given configuration of objects in the world, because *the form is bound up with the method of projection*. The *couplet* (form plus method of projection) fixes the sense of a proposition, and our ability to apply a proposition as a picture means that we have a grasp on the couplet.

Sometime after 1929, then, fluency in language began to look to Wittgenstein more and more like tacit knowledge. It is the act of speaking, the act of putting up language against reality, that "makes the rod with marks on it into a *measuring rod*."[52] But as a form of tacit knowledge, we are not able to specify with precision either the mode of projection or the logical form of the world in isolation from the other. Wittgenstein resurrected the compelling example of ellipses and rectangles in space projected as circles and squares onto a plane. The point he wanted to make at this stage of his thinking was no longer the determinateness of logical form but its ambiguity. The regular planar figures (circle, square) are analogous to the two forms that dominate Indo-European sentences (subject-predicate and relational). We can infer from the projected image whether the original figure was an ellipse or a rectangle, but so long as we lack complete specification of the method of projection we cannot infer anything about the dimensions or location of the original figure. So too, we can infer a basic shape of possible states of affairs by looking at the form of propositions but cannot say much more than that, because there are "ever so many different ways" to project "ever so many different logical forms" into language.[53]

The difference between this and his earlier views is that Wittgenstein has come to think of propositions as belonging to systems and to believe that the method of projection itself belongs to this system. This revision effectively directed Wittgenstein's attention away from the "form of the world" to the notion of form as embodied in linguistic systems of description. To put it differently, Wittgenstein became less concerned with how language depicts and increasingly concerned with the means by which the "painting" is "painted." On this view, syntax is not quite identical to the form of the system, but there is a connection. Wittgenstein speaks of a linguistic "calculus" as a sort of sentence generator; understanding a sentence requires simply working the calculus in reverse.[54] This sentence generator is governed by a set of rules which ensure that the descriptions generated conform to a single system. Syntax, in this light, "is the totality of rules that specify in what combinations a sign has meaning." But by itself, "it describes nothing"; syntax simply "sets limits to what is describable."[55] When a sentence is generated according to these rules it conforms to the linguistic form.

There are two ways to apply a linguistic calculus. First, a calculus can be applied in such a way so as to yield the grammar of a language (or of a system of description).[56] If I write a sentence, its sense is simply a function of what the rules permit me to write *within that system* regardless of its truth value. Wittgenstein illustrates, "As an example we may take Euclidean geometry as the system of syntactical rules according to which we describe spatial objects."[57] Syntax may be viewed locally as that which sets up the opening position of the "game," specifies the rules of play, and establishes the boundaries within which the game can be played conflict-free.[58]

On the other hand, a second way of applying a calculus shows how local syntax is only part of a more comprehensive set of rules—one which "connects" language with the form of the world in an unambiguous way.[59] Just as soon as Wittgenstein described language in terms of a system of propositions he perceived the need for collating the "yardstick" with its application: "We could now lay down the [meta-syntactical] rule that the same yardstick may only be applied once in a proposition."[60] For example, we teach children to count apples according to the rule that each apple may be counted only one time. Once such meta-syntactical rules are recognized, the calculus can be applied in a way that yields actual information about the world: "A calculus can be applied in such a way that true and false propositions correspond to the configurations of the calculus. In this case the calculus yields a theory that describes something." Propositions written according to the calculus of Newtonian physics not only have a sense internal to that game, they also have a truth-value dependent upon their correspondence with results of physical experiments.[61] It is striking for our present purposes to note that what I have provisionally described as "meta-syntax" (i.e., the rules governing the correspondence between the configuration of the world and the configuration of the system of description) were rules that Wittgenstein quickly thought of as belonging to the "form" of *the system of description.* This represents a steady shift in Wittgenstein: he sees more and more of what makes language work as falling under the domain of the system. Although systems of description are somewhat arbitrary, what is not arbitrary (or so he thinks) is that the systems have the same multiplicity as what they describe. And it belongs to their syntax to ensure that the mapping is "one-to-one" in order to prevent the same coordinate from being mapped more than once.[62]

Thus, by the end of 1930 the apparent dichotomy between language and the world was still problematic for Wittgenstein, as was the picture theory of thinking and speaking.[63] Yet by this time his attention had steadily turned toward the syntax of ordinary language. He had become all too painfully aware that the trouble with our grammar is that we cannot get a bird's-eye view of it, but we must do the best we can from within our given linguistic system. We rightfully assume that the act of speaking calibrates our world—we do, after all, find ourselves able to navigate by means of language—and therefore we must undertake a study of ordinary, rather than "ideal," language. "All that is possible and necessary is to separate what is essential from what is inessential in *our* language."[64]

This turning toward ordinary language systems and their respective grammars is but another way of describing the migration of particular human subjects to the center of Wittgenstein's philosophical attention. Since grammar (i.e., rules of language use) dictates the hearer's "expectations" and since speaker "intention" is contained in the "meta"-syntactical method of projection, the study of language is the study of how particular speakers and hearers play the game.[65]

As a result of his changing views, Wittgenstein became increasingly difficult to classify within the scheme of modern philosophy. In saying that the *relation* between language and world itself belongs to the syntax of language, and in shifting his full attention to this grammar, Wittgenstein made the first step toward repudiating the language-world dichotomy upon which the modern realist-antirealist debate turns.

SEEING THE FORM OF CULTURE

In 1931 Wittgenstein began jotting down his reflections on Sir James George Frazer's *The Golden Bough*, a project which would hold his attention perhaps as late as 1948. These reflections, posthumously compiled, edited, and published in 1967 as *Remarks on Frazer's Golden Bough*, hint at ways in which Wittgenstein's notion of "form" was influenced by his admiration for both Johann W. von Goethe and Oswald Spengler.

Frazer attempted to interpret the variety of magical and religious views held by "primitive" cultures as simply cases of erroneous scientific hypotheses. Frazer speculated that when primitives performed a rain dance they acted according to the mistaken belief that there was a causal link between their ritual and the coming of rain. Of course, Frazer and his readers felt certain that there is no such link. Nevertheless, the primitives' misplaced trust could find soil in which to take root, argued Frazer, in the fact that occasionally rains do happen to come after one dances. Such anecdotal evidence contributes powerfully to the resilience of a backward people's mistaken beliefs.

Wittgenstein objected to the way Frazer completely assimilated religion under the scientific rubric; the identification of religious ritual as "proto-scientific magic" enabled Frazer to discard it as an anachronism. Because of this, Wittgenstein found Frazer

> much more savage than most of his savages, for they are not as far removed from the understanding of a spiritual matter as a twentieth-century Englishman. His explanation of primitive practices are much cruder than the meaning of these practices themselves.[66]

By telling the story of religion and magic as one which culminates in modern science, Frazer had, in effect, robbed religion of any nonscientific significance.

One turn-of-the-century writer who decried the totalizing claims of the scientific worldview was Oswald Spengler. Spengler contended that there were two attitudes one could take toward the world. The scientific outlook sought to describe the *world-as-nature* in terms of cause-effect pairs that operate on the microcosmic scale. From this vantage point, the human mind was thought to possess a technical and theoretical impulse which seeks to conquer and dominate the world-as-nature, by systematizing it until "thought itself rules, and its causal criticism turns life into a rigorous process, the living content of a fact into an absolute truth, and tension into formula."[67]

Spengler argued that science treated all its objects as dead things, and in doing so necessarily missed the presence of the life-force which pulsates through the *world-as-history* on the macrocosmic scale. For example, because Darwinism is a causal (i.e., scientific) explanation of origins, it must postulate the existence of transitional types between species, despite the absence of "missing links," simply because its explanatory force depends on the integrity of the entire cause-effect chain that links present microcosmic events with the past. Spengler offered a rival description. Spengler asserted that Life—a power that unifies all things—manifests a periodicity through the "forms" embodied in living things. Each species has a form which has an "energy level" (that which governs the species' ability to resist mutation) and a "life-duration" which together determine the time when a given "form" of Life (i.e., a particular species) becomes extinct.[68] Thus, not only are individual animals alive, the species itself has a kind of life-cycle. In Spengler's model, the lack of transitional types is not problematic, but rather to be expected. One species becomes extinct while another spontaneously bursts onto the scene, and both events evidence nothing other than the metamorphosis of an underlying *anima* called Life.

Spengler applied the same sort of model to his understanding of human culture. He construed human life as the progressive actualization of humanity's "form." This occurs not simply on an individual level but on a corporate one as well. Thus, cultures "evolve" in the same way that the animal kingdom evolves, namely, by the spontaneous emergence of new and unrelated "forms" of Life. Spengler contended that this was the only way to make sense out of the historic fact that empires rise and fall without "transitional types" to serve as causal links from one empire to another.[69] Spengler concluded that we can hope to do a "philosophy of the future" if and only if we repudiate the dead, mechanistic, scientific view of world-as-nature and embrace in its place a morphology of world-as-history. This latter standpoint

> reviews once again the forms and movements of the world in their depths and final significance, but this time according to an entirely

different ordering which groups them, not in an ensemble picture in-
clusive of everything known, but in a picture of *life*, and presents them
not as things-become, but as things becoming [i.e., actualizing their
form].[70]

For Spengler, Goethe's *Faustus* was a fitting symbol of western civilization
because, like Faustus, this civilization has sacrificed its soul by neglecting
the morphology of Life in its quest for technical mastery over a mechanical
universe. Spengler summarized this notion of form, and what was at stake
for the culture which neglected it, by quoting Goethe:

> "Form is something mobile, something becoming, something passing.
> The doctrine of formation is the doctrine of transformation. Meta-
> morphosis is the key to the whole alphabet of Nature," so runs a note
> of Goethe's, marking already the methodic difference between his fa-
> mous "exact percipient fancy" which quietly lets itself be worked upon
> by the living, and the exact killing procedure of modern physics.[71]

Apparently Wittgenstein concurred with Spengler's cultural pessimism.
Monk reports this comment made by Wittgenstein to Drury:

> I was walking about in Cambridge and passed a bookshop, and in the
> windows were portraits of Russell, Freud and Einstein. A little further
> on, in a music shop, I saw portraits of Beethoven, Schubert and Chopin.
> Comparing these portraits I felt intensely the terrible degeneration that
> had come over the human spirit in the course of only a hundred years.[72]

Wittgenstein found the spirit of western civilization to be "alien and un-
congenial" and bemoaned the way science had lulled it to sleep. In this he
concurred with Spengler's cultural diagnosis.[73] However, he chided Spengler for offering just as totalizing an account of the "facts" as Frazer's scientific one.[74] The "facts" that Frazer recorded are ambiguous and may be
pictured in several different ways.

> "And so the chorus points to a secret law" one feels like saying to
> Frazer's collection of facts. I can represent this law, this idea, by means
> of an evolutionary hypothesis [Frazer], or also, analogously to the
> schema of a plant [Spengler], by means of a schema of a religious cer-
> emony, but also by means of the arrangement of its factual content
> alone in a '*perspicuous*' representation.[75]

The belief that none of these pictures is inherently more compelling than the others reveals Wittgenstein's conviction that what counts in any representation is the perspicuity by which it "denotes the form of our representation, the way we see things." Such perspicuity may be attained any number of ways. For example, the contingency of human knowledge and apparent spontaneity of the natural world because of its lack of systematic predictability, a point that Spengler caught but Frazer missed, receives an equally vivid expression in the words of the Lord coming through the prophet Jeremiah:

> At *any moment* I may threaten to uproot a nation or kingdom, to pull it down and destroy it. But if the nation which I have threatened turns back from its wicked ways, then I shall think better of the evil I had in mind to bring on it. Or *at any moment* I may decide to build or to plant a nation or a kingdom. But if it does evil in my sight and does not obey me, I shall think better of the good I had in mind for it.[76]

If the point to be expressed is the contingent nature of things, then apprehending this can be achieved through either Spengler's words or Jeremiah's, and an argument over whose picture is "correct" is beside the point. Form enables understanding, on this account, because to apprehend the form expressed by Spengler or Jeremiah is to "see the connections."[77] Does this mean that Wittgenstein legislates against hypothesizing causal links? Not at all. On Wittgenstein's view, our perception of the pattern that exists between diverse "objects" (such as religious rituals) might, in fact, be aided by hypothesizing a causal or developmental link. However, such an approach is only useful to the extent it draws attention to the pattern of connections (form) rather than to itself:

> But an hypothetical connecting link should in this case do nothing but direct the attention to the similarity, the relatedness, of the *facts*. As one might illustrate an internal relation of a circle to an ellipse by gradually converting an ellipse into a circle; *but not in order to assert that a certain ellipse actually, historically, had originated from a circle* (evolutionary hypothesis), but only in order to sharpen our eye for a formal connection.[78]

Wittgenstein feared that a single picture may become so dominant that its architectonic impulse obscures, rather than elucidates, form. In this he sided with Spengler against the spirit of European and American culture that hankered after "building ever larger and more complicated structures" which try to grasp the world in its entirety. In contrast, Wittgenstein increasingly devoted his philosophical energies to the pursuit of simple clarity.[79]

While Wittgenstein could not express unqualified loyalty to Spengler's theory of culture, Wittgenstein was less reserved in his admiration for the work of Goethe. Unsurprisingly, there is an affinity between Goethe's and Wittgenstein's respective conceptions of form. For Goethe, form denoted an aspect of a life-force that, for example, throbs in the life-cycle of flowering plants. The form of the plant is not only shown in the uniformity of the shape of its leaves but also in its formal unity throughout each phase of its life-cycle. The perception of an enduring form enabled Goethe to classify all the parts of the plant as metamorphosed leaves.[80] The leaf-form, which is dormant in the kernel and manifests a "primitive" existence in the "piling up node upon node" in the first tender shoot, achieves a full-blown and manifold reproduction during the plant's leafy stage.

> Yet here Nature restraineth, with powerful hands, the formation,
>   And to a perfect end, guided with softness its growth
> Less abundantly yielding the sap, contracting the vessels
>   So that the figure ere long gentler effects doth disclose.[81]

Although foliation looks as though it could go on indefinitely, all at once leaves give way to flowers. Goethe described the life-cycle of the plant as the actualizing of the plant's form toward the telos of a particular pattern, namely, seed-shoot-leaf-flower-fruit. This pattern, then, constitutes the plant's "form."

Under Goethe's influence, Wittgenstein conceived form as the means by which we see something as a picture, or better, as the *pattern* we perceive when we see something as a picture. Just as we can discern the unity in the sequence seed-shoot-leaf-flower-fruit, so, too, we can discern unity in this sequence:[82]

The connections are formal in both cases, and elucidating these connections is the point of any system of description. Pattern-perception, or "seeing as," becomes an important feature of Wittgenstein's philosophy after 1932. What is clear at this stage of his thinking is that a "picture" is only useful to the extent that it helps to bring something else into focus. And there are multiple ways of picturing, no one way necessarily more compelling than another. Yet for every picture we devise, we almost inevitably overlook the conventional character of our picture and thus misconstrue it to be the only system of description.

FORM AND THE HURLY-BURLY OF LIFE

With an irony that characterized Wittgenstein's entire intellectual journey, the hard crystalline structure of the logical form portrayed in the *Tractatus* succumbed to a more nuanced notion of "form" manifested in four ways by the *Big Typescript* (written between 1932 and 1934), the long manuscript translated into English as *Philosophical Grammar*. In it we see him wrestle with the pictorial character of thought, the conventional character of pictures, the interplay between grammar and the hurly-burly of human life, and the self-involving character of linguistic fluency.

The Pictorial Character of Thought

First, in *Philosophical Grammar*, the one-to-one mapping, upon which the Tractarian picture theory was built, was entirely displaced by the admission that multiple systems of description are possible. Thoughts are not representations of reality, although our thinking does have a pictorial character to it. Our thoughts are "analogies" by which we "see connections"[83] and according to which we understand the world.

> Here instead of harmony or agreement of thought and reality one might say: the pictorial character of thought. . . .
> Anything can be a picture of anything, if we extend the concept of picture sufficiently. If not, we have to explain what we call a picture of something, and what we want to call the agreement of the pictorial character, the agreement of the forms.[84]

Wittgenstein criticized his former picture theory of language for being overly narrow in its range of application. There is much in experience that cannot be neatly pictured in the Tractarian way. For example, the blurredness of objects in our peripheral vision cannot be translated into a drawing of objects with fuzzy outlines.[85]

Once Wittgenstein acknowledged the possibility that "reality" may be pictured in multiple ways, he ruthlessly questioned his earlier theory. In his fourth appendix to the first section of the *Philosophical Grammar* he confessed that, "misled as I was by a false notion of reduction, I thought that the whole use of propositions must be reducible" to the calculus of logical atomism.[86] He went on to describe the strict representationalism of *Tractatus* as the "false and idealized picture of the use of language" that had coerced him into accepting a particular form of confusion: "The primitive forms of our language: noun, adjective and verb, show the simple picture into whose form language tries to force everything."[87] In other words, if language is thought to have only one function—that of being a snapshot of the world that leaves everything as it is—then it is very tempting to look at the basic structure of sentences (i.e., the subject-predicate form which utilizes nouns and adjectives and the relational form which emphasizes verbs) as evidence of an ontological structure of the world. In this conclusion we see Wittgenstein denying that language shares a form with the world. Language is itself problematic, not simply because it is too coarse to state *das Mystische*, but because we are too obtuse to perceive its polyvalent functionality.

> As long as there continues to be a verb 'to be' that looks as if it functions in the same way as 'to eat' and 'to drink', as long as we still have the adjectives 'identical', 'true', 'false', 'possible', as long as we continue to talk of a river of time, of an expanse of space, etc., etc., people will keep stumbling over the same puzzling difficulties and find themselves staring at something which no explanation seems capable of clearing up.[88]

The above citation sounds almost as if the problem of philosophical confusion could be blamed upon a deficiency in language. But a linguistic system neither measures nor fails to measure reality like a yardstick because language *users* do the measuring, not yardsticks.[89] Thus, after 1932 we see Wittgenstein accommodating his picture theory to the rising significance human subjects play in his thought. In the *Tractatus* the logical space was the sole determinant of the possible range of a proposition's sense. From the time of the *Philosophical Remarks* (1930), Wittgenstein saw meaning as determined by the grammar of the system in which the proposition originated. But in the *Philosophical Grammar* (1932–34) Wittgenstein asked, "To whom does it look like that? And under what circumstances?"[90]

The Conventional Character of Pictures

The second major thrust of the *Philosophical Grammar* has to do with Wittgenstein's assertion of the conventional nature of pictures, a move which completed the exorcism of the language-world dichotomy from his thinking.

> We might now express ourselves thus: the method of projection mediates between the drawing and the object, it reaches from the drawing to the artefact. Here we are comparing the method of projection with projection lines which go from one figure to another. — But if the method of projection is [e.g.] a bridge, it is a bridge which isn't built until the application is made. — This comparison conceals the fact that the picture *plus* the projection lines leaves open various methods of application.[91]

Wittgenstein came to consider the manner in which a picture is *applied* as having to do with "grammar." Thus, grammar "describes the *use* of words in the language."[92] On this view, grammar is determined neither by the form of the world nor by the form of the linguistic system as previously thought in *Tractatus* and the *Philosophical Remarks*, respectively. Rather, meaning has to do with rules of use upon which speakers (happily!) agree. By focusing on use, Wittgenstein succeeded in closing the gap between language and world. Consider the following passages.

> But it might be asked: Do I *understand* the word ['perhaps'] just by describing its application? Do I understand its point? Haven't I deluded myself about something important?
>
> At present, say, I know only how men use this word. But it might be a game, or a form of etiquette. I do not know why they behave in this way, how *language* meshes with their life.
> Is meaning then really only the use of a word? Isn't it the way this use meshes with our life?
> But isn't its use a part of our life?[93]

Since our use of language is part of our life, it makes no sense to pry it off the world as if it could be examined in a vacuum. To do so would be to overlook the way every explanation of the putative language-world link is itself a *linguistic* explanation. If what was hoped for by such an explanation is a clear picture of "how language relates to reality," then the fact that all explanations use some language or other smacks of a lamentable limitation: "The limit of language is shown by its being impossible to describe the fact which corresponds to (is the translation of) a sentence, without *simply repeating the sentence*."[94] Wittgenstein concludes, "language is not something that is first given a structure and then fitted on to reality."[95] Nor is meaning grounded in the "correspondence" between a proposition and a state of affairs. Rather, meaning is not "grounded" at all: "But we said that by 'meaning' we meant what an explanation of meaning explains. And an explanation of meaning is not an empirical proposition and not a causal explanation, but a rule, a convention."[96]

Wittgenstein can still say that "what belongs to grammar are all the conditions (the method) necessary for comparing the proposition with reality" because he assumes the reader has already been disabused of the notion of an external link between language and world, and is ready to accept in its place the notion of an internal link that Wittgenstein describes in terms of public criteria.[97] In other words, the "reality" being compared with our language is *our public life together*.

Grammar and the Form of Life

A third change is that in the *Philosophical Grammar* Wittgenstein's conception of form shades into what he means by "grammar." On the one hand, he speaks of grammar in ways that he previously reserved for speaking about form. "What kind of investigation are we carrying out? Am I investigating the probability of cases that I give as examples . . . ? No, I'm just citing what is *possible* and am therefore giving *grammatical* examples."[98] In this statement, it is grammar that traces out what is *logically* possible. On the other hand, he uses "form" to denote aspects of grammar. For example, he speaks of form as having the force of a "rule."[99] Form to Wittgenstein was no longer simply the property of the world, or even of a linguistic system, but is the shape or range of allowable actions within, or applications of, the calculus.[100] So form became analogous to grammar and the term "grammar" connoted the use to which concrete human subjects put language. For example,

> We say that we understand its [a word's] meaning when we know its use, but we've also said that the word 'know' doesn't denote a state of

consciousness. That is, the grammar of the word 'know' isn't the grammar of a "state of consciousness," but something different. And there is only one way to learn it: to watch how the word is used in practice.[101]

These words epitomize the "ordinary language philosophy" that characterizes Wittgenstein's mature work. Perhaps the most striking feature of Wittgenstein's magnum opus, *Philosophical Investigations*, is the rich promise that the term "form of life" holds for philosophy of language and, perhaps surprisingly, theological ethics.

For Wittgenstein, the rules that "govern" speakers' use of language are inextricably bound up with the manner of their daily lives, with their "form of life" (*Lebensform*). But just how much familiarity with the "stage-setting" or "surroundings" must a language user possess to play the game correctly?[102]

First, meaning is a function of the vocable context. A sentence gains its sense from the immediate context of the language-game in which the sentence is located. For example, the proposition "All men are evil brutes" has a different color in the language-game of theology than in the language-game of a jilted lover. But a language-game is only infrequently a complete conversation. Therefore, Wittgenstein maintained that the verbal context of a given sentence also included the "whole field of our language-games" and that "conversation flows on, the application and interpretation of words, and only in its course do words have their meaning."[103] One can imagine the impatience with which this proposition was met by "ideal language philosophers." "At this rate," some complained, "one can never arrive at the determinative meaning of a sentence." Wittgenstein consistently replied, "determinative enough to go on." Wittgenstein was concerned not with meaning-as-such, but with meaning-as-heard in more or less skillful ways by this or that particular speaker.

In addition to vocable context, Wittgenstein used the term "surroundings" to signify a behavioral context which contributes to the sense that a speaker gleans from a sentence. Thus, "a lie has a peculiar surrounding," because one cannot announce an intention to tell a lie and then succeed in fooling anyone. Rather, a lie succeeds as an act of deception only when other behavioral components are in place.[104] "Only when there is a relatively complicated pattern of life do we speak of pretense."[105] A wry grin, averted eyes, a blush, a shuffle, and the game is up! The fact that children require *practice* to become convincing liars shows how deeply enmeshed is the behavioral component of language use.

One easily-imagined behavioral component of grammar is gesturing. Norman Malcolm reported on conversations Wittgenstein held with Italian economist Piero Sraffa.

> Wittgenstein was insisting that a proposition and that which it describes must have the same "logical form" [or "grammar" depending on which version of the story is quoted], the same "logical multiplicity," Sraffa made a gesture, familiar to Neapolitans as meaning something like disgust or contempt, of brushing the underneath of his chin with an outward sweep of the finger-tips of one hand. And he asked: "What is the logical form of *that*?"[106]

Sraffa's gesture startled Wittgenstein. He concluded that "gestures no less than words are intertwined in a net of multifarious relationships."[107] Gestures and words are reciprocally related:

> How curious: we should like to explain our understanding of a gesture by means of translation into words, and the understanding of words by translating them into a gesture. (Thus we are tossed to and fro when we try to find out where understanding properly resides.)[108]

The manifest linguistic character of gestures suggested to Wittgenstein that if language had a basic behavioral root, language must be very deeply embedded in the "bustle of life."[109]

Parts of the weave of human behavior—that we sweat when it is hot, that we squint at bright lights, that we gasp when endangered—are so basic that a perspicuous description of language can go no deeper than a record of these. Wittgenstein called these behaviors "primitive reactions" in order to emphasize their givenness for the functioning of language. One way (and only one way) to think of this connection is to imagine language as going proxy for these other behaviors.

> How do words *refer* to sensations? . . . Here is one possibility: words are connected with the primitive, the natural, expressions of the sensation and used in their place. A child has hurt himself and he cries; and then adults talk to him and teach him exclamations and, later, sentences. They teach the child new pain-behavior.
>   "So you are saying that the word 'pain' really means crying?"—On the contrary: the verbal expression of pain replaces crying and does not describe it.[110]

Yet the concept of primitive reactions — in addition to vocable and be-havioral contexts of a sentence — doesn't quite capture all that influences the shape of human speaking. Part of the weave of human behavior is *learned, social,* and *conventional* rather than primitive, instinctive, and bio-logical. For example, "Children do not learn that books exist, that armchairs exist, etc., etc. — they learn to fetch books, sit in armchairs, etc. etc."[111] In my children's early years the furniture scattered throughout my house pre-sented to my children a natural obstacle course. They struggled to climb into chairs long before they could speak the word "chair." They would stretch and wriggle and grunt until finally, looking toward me, they would cry out. And their crying would not be quelled until I assisted their climb-ing into the chair. Soon they had me conditioned to carry on other tasks while absentmindedly standing by to give them a boost each time they strug-gled. Up, down, up, down . . . this activity went on day in and day out for months before they could speak. Interestingly, when they finally spoke, it was the word "up" (associated with bodily motion) rather than "chair" (as-sociated with an object) that first went proxy for their grunting. And this his-tory of activity, according to Wittgenstein, eventually enabled my children to use the word "chair" as well. Our use of language is "anchored in our way of living and acting,"[112] so that only by involvement in this pattern of living — which in the case of chairs includes sitting, finding, and stubbing one's toe — can a member of an aboriginal (which is to say, "chair-less") tribe learn to use correctly the western concept of "chair."

Thus, the "stage-setting" or "grammar" upon which successful lin-guistic interplay depends involves not only the relation of words within a sentence, but also the relation between the sentence and the rest of the lan-guage-game, the relationship of this language-game to the rest of the con-versation (hence, to the whole system of language-games), and the place of this conversation in the activities (both primitive and conventional) of our daily lives.[113] This complex weave is what Wittgenstein wants his read-ers to glimpse in the phrase, "form of life."

Language as Self-Involving

It is important, at this juncture, to remind ourselves that "meaning" is not that which is paired with language irrespective of the human speaker(s). Rather, meaning is in the use of language by human speakers.[114] Familiarity with the "grammar" of language enables one to anticipate the possible ways this or that sentence might be used by other speakers — and because the range of these possibilities is limited (albeit conventional), Wittgenstein continued to use the term "logic" to describe the boundaries of proper use.[115] However, still more is required to determine which of "a multitude of familiar paths off from these words in every direction" one *ought* to take in response to a given situation.[116] Here the restrictions that conventional linguistic boundaries place upon speakers is reminiscent of the sort of force we normally associate with moral obligation. Perhaps a better way to put it is to say that Wittgenstein sees very little difference between the skill of moral wisdom and fluency in the speaking of ordinary language. The appropriate moral response turns on a correct reading of the wider context.[117] Thus, *moral* concepts (such as "kindness" or "malice") are simply shorthand descriptions of the wider contexts which lend sense to a moral description.

> I see a picture which represents a smiling face. What do I do if I take the smile now as a kind one, now as malicious? Don't I often imagine it with spatial and temporal context which is one either of kindness or malice? Thus I might supply the picture with the fancy that the smiler was smiling down on a child at play, or again on the suffering of an enemy.
>
> This is in no way altered by the fact that I can also take the at first sight gracious situation and interpret it differently by putting it into a wider context. — If no special circumstances reverse my interpretation I shall conceive a particular smile as kind, call it a "kind" one, react correspondingly.[118]

The ability to correctly read and respond appropriately to contexts, moral or otherwise, is part of one's fluency in the grammar of a language. The greater one's fluency, the broader the range of contexts to which one is sensitive. The spatial context of an object in a painting, for example, may be the rest of the picture, or the story behind the painting, or even the culture and times and life of the painter.[119] The temporal context for understanding artistic and linguistic expression includes both its history and its future. A line in a play or novel must be understood not only in light of what precedes it, but also in light of what follows it. Similarly, in ordinary conversation a sentence's meaning may have to be gleaned retrospectively in the light of *subsequent* conversation.[120] Any alteration in the context of a sentence may drastically change its meaning.

While there is a great difference between the "grammar" of a word and the "context" which makes a physical object intelligible, I am trying to draw attention to the similarity of these notions for Wittgenstein; in the case of an object as well as a word, the "meaning" of the object or word is a function of its *contextual connections*. In the *Investigations* Wittgenstein explains that "grammar tells what kind of an object anything is"[121] because grammar expresses its "essence"[122] (as Spinoza might say), or, better, its connections.[123]

> Look at a long-familiar piece of furniture in its old place in your room. You would like to say: "It is part of an organism." Or "Take it outside, and its no longer the same as it was," and similar things. And naturally one isn't thinking of any causal dependence of one part on the rest. Rather, it is like *this*: I could give this thing a name and say that it has shifted from its place, has a stain, is dusty; but if I tried taking it *quite* out of its present context, I should say that it had ceased to exist and another had gotten into its place.
>
> One might feel like this: "Everything is part and parcel of everything else" (internal and external relations). Displace a piece and it is no longer what it was. Only in this surrounding is this table this table. Everything is part of everything.[124]

Is the scope of the "surroundings" which we must "see" in order to understand a concept as broad as the entire world? Well, not quite. But we must see broadly "enough." Language is an activity of human subjects, each of whom must be skillful[125] enough to weave the vocable with particular bits of the "stage" in order to recognize which game is being played so that it can be continued appropriately. "In a conversation: One person throws a ball; the other does not know: whether he is supposed to throw it back, or throw it to a third person, or leave it on the ground, or pick it up and put it in his pocket, etc."[126]

Sometimes enough of the context can be imaginatively supplied for communication to succeed. Wittgenstein relied on this in his discussion of Frazer's *Golden Bough* with his students; a description of the Beltane Fire Festival and of its "surroundings" is enough for Wittgenstein's students to follow his comments on Frazer.[127] In fact, it was none other than the descriptions of primitive cultures that Wittgenstein found most valuable in Frazer's work. Given our ability to imaginatively inhabit rival forms of life, a breakdown in communication may not indicate that two communities speak incommensurable languages, as Kai Nielsen's pejorative term "Wittgensteinian fideist" implies.[128] Rather, a breakdown in communication may simply indicate that greater direct (as opposed to imaginative) participation in the recipient form of life is required to achieve the ability to "go on."[129] A breakdown in communication, therefore, is not necessarily a deficiency in language (or in two or more language-games) but a deficiency of skill on the part of language users to properly read the "stream of life" which gives the words their proper respective senses.[130]

The suggestion that communication requires self-involving participation of speakers in the host form of life has interesting implications for Wittgenstein's views of religious language. In *Zettel* Wittgenstein makes the following very important comment: "How words are understood is not told by words alone. (Theology)."[131] Religious believers frequently complain that they are misunderstood by atheist dialogue partners, while atheists, for their part, claim to understand what is being said by religious believers well enough to challenge those religious claims. The ways that theologians try to accommodate atheists in conversations about the (im)probability of God's existence show that atheists have not yet come to terms with the nature of religious belief and that theists only confuse things in trying to accommodate them in this fashion. Wittgenstein remarked to Drury, "Can you imagine St. Augustine saying that the existence of God was 'highly probable'!"[132] This point may be taken as an admonishment to both sides of the discussion; both have overestimated the extent to which an atheist may have imaginatively crossed the communication gap so long as he or she cannot imagine how an immovable concept—a concept for which the language of (im)probability is idle—can function in one's life. It is not necessary for atheists to hold the conviction that "God" names such a concept (lest they cease to be atheists), but they must be familiar with the grammar of such a concept before engaging in conversation. *This* understanding may not be attainable by way of imagination. Rather, some direct participation in the theistic form of life may be required of the atheists, just as St. Augustine became a catechumen before baptism precisely to investigate Christianity on its own terms. Conversely, theists, to hold up their end of the conversation, must get clear on what it might be to live without such a concept. Too often theists assume atheists are simply theists in a state of denial.

The necessity of a self-involving participation in a given form of life for cultivating the skill of hearing the connections between a sentence and appropriate aspects of its context raises a significant challenge to expositors of Wittgenstein's own religious viewpoint. Opinions vary widely over the extent and significance of his religious beliefs. Yet nearly all agree that his religious beliefs were well insulated from his philosophical work. Sometimes it is assumed that the proportional decline in attention given to religion (and to ethics) in Wittgenstein's later period shows a similar decline in interest. And very often, Wittgenstein's comments in *Lectures & Conversations* are taken to be central to ascertaining his religious views. But attention to the two developments I have labored to describe thus far (namely, the centrality of the subject and the importance of form) shows two recurrent missteps taken by those who hold these opinions. First, the centrality of human subjects for philosophy reminds us that *Lectures & Conversations* was written in a therapeutic mode for a group of neophytes who needed to be cured of a number of conceptual confusions before they might think clearly about, say, God. Thus *Lectures & Conversations* ought to be taken not as the final word, but as the first word of Wittgenstein's religious views.

The second misstep is in failing to canvass a context broad enough for understanding Wittgenstein's enigmatic remarks on God. Thus, *Lectures & Conversations* needs to be placed in the greater context of Wittgenstein's life project. This requires understanding that he meant to take his students to the place where they could see what could only be shown. This objective remained fixed for Wittgenstein from the *Tractatus* on. In this light, it is ironic that commentators restrict conclusions about Wittgenstein's religious beliefs to what he *said*. In order to understand Wittgenstein on religion, it seems to me, we must look at what is *shown* by his own religious asceticism—his voluntary poverty, his early zeal for evangelism, his journey toward pacifism, his public "confession" of sin, his ever deepening prayer life—because, in his own words, religious beliefs can only be understood with reference to the difference they make in one's behavior.[133] Of course, it must be admitted that these features render an ambiguous picture. But the real question is, "Ambiguous for whom?" Possibly, the extent to which we will see the pattern of Wittgenstein's life as a deeply religious one requires us to have the sort of character necessary to see it. The fact that religious persons such as Drury and James Wm. McClendon, Jr., saw a different pattern and significance in Wittgenstein's "religious" behavior than have nonreligious expositors of Wittgenstein suggests that, very possibly, only those who are willing to participate in this form of living can understand this aspect of Wittgenstein's life. Malcolm was on the verge of clarifying this connection when he wrote,

Clearly, there is an analogy between Wittgenstein's view that our concepts rest on a basis of human actions and reactions, and his view that what is most fundamental in a religious life is not the affirming of creeds, nor even prayer and worship—but rather, doing good deeds—helping others in concrete ways, treating their needs as equal to one's own, opening one's heart up to them, not being cold and contemptuous, but loving.[134]

Malcolm has rightly pointed out that, for Wittgenstein, religion is *shown* in one's deeds. But what Malcolm falls short of saying is that the doing of "good deeds" is itself the precondition for an observer to understand Wittgenstein's specific ethical and religious vocabulary. The highly religious character of Wittgenstein's conversations with Drury is not, therefore, evidence of inconsistency (how can he speak of God when God can only be shown?) but evidence of Wittgenstein's real position: religion does not involve doing deeds instead of speaking, but doing deeds in order to speak about religion.

FOUR

ETHICS AS POLITICS

*You would like to attain faith, and do not know the way; you
would like to cure yourself of unbelief and ask the remedy for it.
Learn of those who have been bound like you, and are cured of an
ill of which you would be cured. Follow the way by which they
began; by acting, as if they believed, taking the holy water,
having masses said. . . .*

—Blaise Pascal

*Christians do not have a theory that leaves everything the way it
is, but we are part of the community that changes everything.*

—Stanley Hauerwas

*Help each one of us, gracious Father, to live in such magnanimity
and restraint that the Head of the Church may never have cause
to say to any one of us, this is my body, broken for you.*

—*The Oxford Book of Prayer*

In chapter 2 we saw that Hauerwas's conception of ethics-as-
aesthetics could be viewed under the same aspect as Wittgenstein's post-
1929 subject-centered therapeutic philosophy. Hauerwas's focus on particular
human agents is a perduring theme in his work and is frequently manifested
by his insistence that agents be shaped before they can see the world rightly.
In 1996 he wrote,

Jesus told those who believed in him: "If you continue in my word, you are truly my disciples; and you will know the truth and the truth will set you free" (John 8:31–32). He also said to them, "I am the way, and the truth, and the life" (John 14:6). Note that being formed as a disciple is prior to knowing the truth. As we submit to discipleship, we learn to be people who are truthful. Truth is not a set of propositions about the world; rather, truth is Jesus Christ. We know truth by coming to know this person and we know this person by learning to pray as he taught us.[1]

Clearly, Hauerwas's attention to the subject involves quite a different notion of "subject" than his liberal counterparts. If liberalism bases decisionist ethics on a prospective conception of the self, then Hauerwas eschews decisionism entirely because of his eschatological understanding of the self. The skill for facing the future can only be cultivated by the same gift that enables one to own one's past. Moreover, the gift of discovering oneself in the story of God shows how an individual might rebel against the tide of what poses for morality—not because one freely chooses to do so, but because one has been gifted with a determinative identity that is longer (and perhaps wider) than the collective identity of one's contemporaries.

The notion of narrative in Hauerwas's thinking supplied the initial conceptual resources for tying together themes of agency, character, action, and history. On this point Hauerwas maintained that

> it is a mistake to assume that my emphasis on narrative is the central focus of my position—insofar as I can be said even to have a position. Narrative is but a concept that helps clarify the interrelation between the various themes I have sought to develop in the attempt to give a constructive account of the Christian moral life.[2]

This disclaimer suggests a second aspect under which Hauerwas's work may be fruitfully viewed. For Hauerwas is not enamored with narrative *qua* narrative, but with narrative-as-embodied-in-a-particular-community. The emphasis on Christian community in Hauerwas's thought is nothing less than the realization that the narrative that unifies one's self simultaneously locates one in a story much older than one's lifetime. Whether or not Wittgenstein's thinking may have been headed in this direction is hard to say. But in practice he chiefly lived in isolation as a philosopher and also appeared to live in moral and religious isolation, a fact which made him, at best, a "quiet" Christian.[3]

That Wittgenstein was an outsider to his immediate academic community is shown by the fact that he was largely unintelligible to his Cambridge contemporaries who tried to follow what Wittgenstein was saying as if he were using language in the same representational and propositional modes as they. In an essay that manifested his own confusion, Kai Nielsen defined the problem this way: Wittgenstein insisted that concepts, particularly religious ones, are only understandable to those who have "an insider's grasp of the form of life of which they are an integral part."[4] In Nielsen's estimation, such a view both deserves the label "fideism" and earns Wittgenstein rightful ostracism by his fellows. Yet Wittgenstein was not without a community of sorts, for the students whom he had tutored were capable of both hearing him and carrying on the conversation he had begun. *This* conversation, precisely because of its aporetic character, engaged his followers, both near and distant, in ways that equipped them to avoid the confusions that he felt had so beguiled modern analytic philosophy. Hauerwas is one such follower.

My strategy in this chapter is to show that Hauerwas sidesteps the general charge of fideism leveled against him by his contemporaries (Gloria Albrecht, Max Stackhouse, and James Gustafson) by rightly conceiving communication as a *political* act. Because the argument is rather serpentine, let me summarize it as concisely as possible before examining the details.

Kai Nielsen charged that, on Wittgenstein's view, *either* one must have an insider's grasp on a rival community's form of life *or* communication will fail. Of course, communication had better not fail lest we succumb to another Thirty Years' War, or worse. Fortunately, on the liberal view, one need not have an insider's grasp on a rival form of life in order to obtain successful communication between rival communities (*pace* Wittgenstein), because (1) messages are translatable (Albrecht); (2) we're all citizens of one global human community (Stackhouse); and (3) rival descriptions are still descriptions of one, and only one, real world "out there"—which, incidentally, science alone accurately depicts (Gustafson). From Hauerwas's perspective these views comprise the standard Enlightenment wolf in religious clothing.

Now if "Wittgensteinian fideism" entails these two mutually exclusive options (either be an insider or fail to communicate), then Hauerwas is in deep trouble: he cannot hang on to Wittgenstein and still hope that the gospel can be received as good news by those who have not yet heard it. Or can he?

Hauerwas's response is twofold. First, he dismantles all three liberal lifeboats: he tries to disabuse his friends of their optimism that communication is guaranteed either by translation, universalism, or empirical realism. As a Wittgensteinian and a Christian, Hauerwas conceives conversion as the learning of a second first-language (namely, that of Christianity) rather than as the translation of an otherwise alien message into one's native tongue. Moreover, Hauerwas maintains that Stackhouse's views of universal brotherhood are unacceptable as they are decidedly unchristian; Christians are not members of a universal *polis* but of a radically different and minority *polis* inaugurated by Christ. Additionally, Hauerwas suggests that Gustafson heads down the wrong path by aligning theology with those representational views of language presumed by science. In Hauerwas's estimation, more mileage can be gotten for theology from the view that language is internally related to the world rather than externally related to it.

Where does this leave him? Granted, the misunderstanding that Hauerwas's detractors display appears to manifest the very failure of communication they fear Hauerwas's position entails. However, the first leg of his response simply shows that their ways for overcoming the communication gap between rival frameworks are unconvincing. But then, if his rebuttals stand, are we not faced with the other horn of Nielsen's dilemma: irreconcilable differences?

However, the second leg of Hauerwas's response shows that the way Nielsen framed the so-called problem of fideism is wrongheaded. Now, Nielsen is half right; it is true that if one has an insider's grasp on a form of life then communication *can* be attained. But, falling short of this "insider's grasp," there are other ways for enabling communication than those (faulty) suggestions made by Albrecht, Stackhouse, and Gustafson. Namely, one can also get a grasp on a form of life as an outsider by being *shown*, not told, the form of communal life. This is what Hauerwas's model of "embodied apologetics" or "ethics-as-politics" manifests.

Hauerwas may properly be called a fideist in the *weak* sense (namely, in maintaining that understanding has something to do with grasp on a form of life) but not in the *strong* sense, which is to say, not in Nielsen's sense that understanding is *only* available to those with an insider's grasp on a form of life. Hauerwas has transcended Nielsen's form of the problem by showing another (Wittgensteinian) access route for becoming familiar enough with a rival form of life so as to enable communication between otherwise untranslatable frameworks. Hauerwas's advantage in defusing fideism, therefore, is that he can locate his speech in close proximity to a particular Christian community, one whose form of life shows the sense of its language. Hauerwas himself is a practicing Christian. But one need not be a Christian for Hauerwas's recommendations to hold. Proximity to and recognition of a group's characteristic form of life, as might be the case for an anthropologist who lives among an aboriginal tribe for a decade or two, provide enough of an insider's grasp of the form of life—even if from the outside—to allow understanding to occur.

WITTGENSTEINIAN FIDEISM

Judith Genova observes, rightly I think, that "all his life, Wittgenstein had difficulty saying what he wanted to say."[5] In 1915 he despaired over what he could only call an "enormous . . . difficulty of expression."[6] Even five weeks before his death Wittgenstein wrote: "Here I am inclined to fight windmills, because I cannot yet say the thing I really want to say."[7] At the beginning of his career he tried to use words as the medium by which he might show the limits of thought and language and world, and by so doing gesture to what lies beyond these. So tongue-tied did his wrestling match with language (in the writing of the *Tractatus*) leave him, that when he returned from the war with his completed manuscript he sought help for a speech impediment—that of being unable to find the right word—a defect that only could seemingly be cured by painstaking private conversations with his friend Paul Engelmann.[8] In his later works Wittgenstein struggled to use ordinary language to train sound judgment in his students so that they might avoid bewitchment by the very language he had no other recourse but to use. But how does one train keenness in judgment?

> Is there such a thing as "expert judgment" about the genuineness of expressions of feeling?—Even here, there are those whose judgment is "better" and those whose judgment is "worse."
>
> Correcter prognoses will generally issue from the judgments of those with better knowledge of mankind.
>
> Can one learn this knowledge? Yes; some can. Not, however, by taking a course in it, but through "*experience*."—Can someone else be a man's teacher in this? Certainly. From time to time he gives him the right *tip*.—This is what "learning" and "teaching" are like here.—What

one acquires here is not a technique; one learns correct judgments. There are also rules, but they do not form a system, and only experienced people can apply them right. Unlike calculation rules.

What is most difficult here is to put this indefiniteness, correctly and unfalsified, into words.[9]

In one sense, Wittgenstein's difficulty of putting things into words was repeated with each student he encountered, because teaching involved not the passing on of a transferable technique (much less a set of propositional tenets) but the cultivation of a skill in philosophical judgment that was as unique to each individual as the form his or her intellectual bewitchment took. Because imitation was susceptible to concretization (especially by those who naturally crave generality), he feared that it would be nearly impossible for anyone to realize how to "go on." He bemoaned in 1947: "Am I the only one who cannot found a school or can a philosopher never do this? I cannot found a school because I do not really want to be imitated. Not at any rate by those who publish articles in philosophical journals."[10]

That Wittgenstein was not optimistic that his generation, or even the next, could catch on to what he was up to seems plain enough. In part, the fact that he was widely misunderstood seems to be the inevitable by-product (in light of his own views) of his largely isolated existence, for if language is internally related to a communal form of life, what are we to make of his parenthetical remark: "The philosopher is not a citizen of a community of ideas. That is what makes him into a philosopher"?[11] It is no surprise, therefore, that people found conversations with someone who "manufactured his own oxygen" to be a bit stifling.[12] Moreover, the problems that his students faced when trying to follow Wittgenstein may have been compounded by the outlook of a culture that prevented them from seeing *das Mystiche* toward which Wittgenstein gestured. Russell Nieli wondered if the temptation of the age toward religious privatism wasn't exacerbated on the one hand by "socio-historical situations in which religious and metaphysical language has become associated with various rival parties in a public dispute" and, on the other hand, by "the extreme, pathological state of consciousness occlusion that typified late nineteenth and early twentieth century Europe."[13] Wittgenstein himself clearly thought so; he described the modern *Weltanschauung* as "thwarting" his philosophical project.[14]

Wittgenstein's contemporaries were not only unable to understand him, they mistook Wittgenstein's response to their incomprehension as evidence of his "fideism." Of course, they do have a point. Since he considered it to be just as confused to argue against a metaphysical employment of language as it would be to argue for it, Wittgenstein really has nothing to say to his detractors; he can only respond to the metaphysicians' words as one might to whistling or humming.[15]

Nevertheless, I am not concerned in this chapter with theoretical questions of whether fideism can be explained or defeated. I am not even sure what a general explanation or general refutation might look like. Rather, I am concerned with a more practical question: Do those who find Wittgenstein's description of language persuasive thereby surrender the hope of finding resources by which they can make themselves intelligible to those who do not share this perspective? This is a very pointed question for Hauerwas, who has made a career of writing to "outsiders." If Hauerwas is necessarily unintelligible to outsiders, then his thinking may be of limited value for insiders as well, since the Christian identity (by his own admission) hinges upon the practice of *witness*.

In the rest of this chapter I will attempt to show that Hauerwas has learned to go on in ways that enable him to hold on to Wittgenstein's insights regarding language but to escape the problem of fideism insofar as he draws attention to the *political* character of ethics. This argument has three moments, each of which will be brought into relief by contrasting Hauerwas's views with those of thinkers who have accused him of fideism. First, because understanding requires language training by means of participation in a form of life, the charges of fideism leveled by outsiders against Hauerwas are wrongheaded in their illicit assumption that messages must be "translatable." Second, because the Christian message is that believers are citizens of a new *polis*, the charge of fideism misses the mark in being symptomatic of the very condition from which Christians consider themselves saved. Third, because the gospel message *requires* embodiment in a living political option, the charge of fideism fails for being conceptually dependent upon an inadequate philosophy of language.

THE POLITICS OF COMMUNICATION

James Gustafson's depiction of Hauerwas as "sectarian, tribalist, fideist" has stuck because the seeming insularity of language-games implied by Hauerwas's account threatens to make communication between rival traditions impossible.[16] By calling Hauerwas a fideist, Gustafson is not only decrying the way Hauerwas's narrativist approach renders theology and ethics virtually

immune to external criticism; Gustafson is also faulting Hauerwas for trying to preserve the historical integrity of Christianity "at the cost of *making
Christianity unintelligible* in a world in which fewer and fewer persons are
formed to the Christian language."[17]

I wish to press a bit on the verb "make." Gustafson seems to presume
that the Christian message would be intelligible (or capable of being made
intelligible) had not Hauerwas's meddling made it unintelligible. The object of the verb "make" in either case appears to be the Christian message.
Gustafson seems to be assuming that intelligibility is a property of the message *qua* message (i.e., apart from particular interchanges between speakers of a given language). This entirely overlooks Wittgenstein's insight that
understanding is a function of speakers' and readers' skill rather than a function of the text *qua* text. What Hauerwas has failed to do, in Gustafson's
estimation, is perform the necessary translation of the message into terms
that *anyone* can understand. This contrast can be drawn more sharply by
examining what Hauerwas opposes in the work of Donald Davidson.[18]

The assumption that messages can attain universal intelligibility by
means of translation has a long and respectable philosophical heritage. In
recent years, Donald Davidson has argued against the notion that rival
groups might embody *incommensurable* conceptual frameworks on the
grounds that the claim, "Their conceptual framework is incommensurable
with ours," is self-defeating .[19] So long as there exists within the rival groups'
behavior some recognizable pattern (from which we infer that their behavior is "rational," which is to say, underlain by a conceptual framework),
then there is enough overlap between the two belief systems to enable a
more complete translation to proceed. Davidson encourages us to approach
the sometimes difficult task of translation with a healthy dose of charity. For
if we recognize another group as possessing a conceptual scheme, it must
mean that they share with us a vast number of mostly true beliefs.

Hauerwas is patently opposed to the project of translation that Davidson has made so respectable.

> In contrast to this dominant outlook, I have repeatedly argued that the
> central theological task is to render the world intelligible to Christians.
> For me the question is not "How can theologians make Christianity in-
> telligible to the modern world?" but "How can theologians make sense
> of the world, given the way we Christians are taught to speak in and
> through our worship of God?" I therefore have very little sympathy with
> attempts to translate Christian speech into terms that are assumed to
> be generally available. I resist that project not because I think there is

some unchanging "core" of Christian convictions that must be protected come hell or high water, but because I have a number of theological and philosophical misgivings about the very idea of translation.[20]

What are these misgivings? On the theological side, for example, it does not
take much imagination to see that the dogma of translatability undermines
the possibility and particularity of Christian discourse. In fact, as two cen-
turies of liberal theology show, "any presentation of theism which is able to
secure a hearing from a secular audience has undergone a transformation
that has evacuated it entirely of its theistic content."[21] We are not Christians
for *general* reasons (i.e., those that translate easily); we have *Christian* reasons for being Christian. But Davidson's project is also specious on *philosophical* grounds.[22] Consider the following anecdote. Comedian Robert
Kline once reminisced how, as a child, he occasionally listened to his extended family, immigrants from the Old World, banter in Yiddish. Of course
he could not follow the conversation, but when the group exploded in
laughter he would plead for them to translate the joke. Inevitably, the
translation—broken English or not—struck him as nonsensical rather than
humorous. While the words of the joke could be translated, the joke as such
could not. In similar fashion, Hauerwas objects to the way the modern doctrine of translatability embodies simplistic views of how language works.

> There is no doubt about the possibility of translating some sayings; but
> this account assumes that there is something like English as such or
> Hebrew as such or Latin as such, and that each can be translated into
> another. But as MacIntyre argues, there are no such languages but
> only "Latin-as-written-and-spoken-in-the-Rome-of-Cicero and Irish-as-
> written-and-spoken-in-sixteenth-century-Ulster. The boundaries of a
> language are the boundaries of some linguistic community which is
> also a social community." Thus the Irish "Doire Columcille" can never
> be translated into the English "Londonderry" once it is recognized that
> even names for persons and places are used *as* identification *for* those
> who share the same beliefs and presumptions about legitimate au-
> thority. In fact, Doire Columcille resides in a different narrative tradi-
> tion than Londonderry.[23]

Hauerwas, following Alasdair MacIntyre, wants to clarify the differences
between language-as-such and language-in-use. "To know the latter is to
be part of practices and habits that allow one to know how to go on in a
manner that is poetic."[24] In Hauerwas's eyes, Davidson "fails to note that

languages depend on what Wittgenstein calls 'agreements and judgments'. That is only made possible against a background of skills and practices."[25]

Intelligibility cannot simply be thought of as a property of a text or message. Rather, "intelligibility" names the happy condition in which the skills of the recipient are found to be adequate for communication. The sort of misunderstanding that the charge of fideism is meant to spook us into denying is a real possibility. Real misunderstanding can and does occur in cases in which recipients lack adequate language skills for knowing what to make of the moves in a given conversation. But misunderstanding cannot be rectified by translation. Rather, the judgment of fluent speakers becomes normative in such cases, although such expertise cannot be described any more precisely than to call it simply "linguistic skill." Wittgenstein put it this way: "In philosophy it is significant that such-and-such a sentence makes no sense; but also that it sounds funny."[26]

When Wittgenstein wrote, "only in the stream of thought and life do words have meaning,"[27] he was indicating something of the skill required of the language user who sought fluency. This "know-how" involves more than vocabulary retention, but it certainly does not involve *less*. Wittgenstein asks, "How do I know that this color is red? — It would be an answer to say 'I have learnt English'."[28] In addition to vocabulary, fluency also requires familiarity with activities. That Wittgenstein had theology particularly in mind surfaces in this comment: "How words are understood is not told by words alone (Theology)."[29] Rather, it is practice which gives words their sense.[30] For example, if one is to use the word "God" correctly, one must be familiar with the place that the language-games of prayer and confession play in the activities of praying and confessing.

Beyond simple vocabulary and familiarity with practices, fluency also consists in recognizing statements in a conversation as moves within a language-game and, additionally, knowing how to "go on." The "meaning" of a sentence, therefore, is a function of *who* is playing *what* game in *which* context. Phillips supplies a helpful anecdote on this point:

> Bonhoeffer tells of an incident during a heavy bombing raid on a concentration camp where he was prisoner: "As we were all lying on the floor yesterday, someone muttered 'O God, O God' — he is normally a frivolous sort of chap — but I couldn't bring myself to offer him any Christian encouragement or comfort. All I did was glance at my watch and say: 'It won't last any more than ten minutes now'."[31]

In other words, Bonhoeffer rightly did not think that the man's cry was anything but a breaking down. He might just as well have said, "Oh no! Oh
no!" or "Mamma mia, Mamma mia!" As such, the cry that resembles a plea
to God was, in fact, an exclamation of sheer fear.[32] Bonhoeffer, a skilled
language-user, was able to detect that this occurrence of "God" was quite
different from that which is used in Christian prayer; the words "God" and
"God" were mere homonyms.

From Wittgenstein's viewpoint, ordinary language users are those who
have gained an ear for the language by repeated engagements with the use
of language in a particular stream of life. This makes *training*,[33] rather than
translation, the means for overcoming cases in which members of one linguistic group are unable to "find their feet" with members of another linguistic group.[34] To say, as Wittgenstein did, that "It is part of the grammar
of the word 'chair' that *this* [sitting] is what we call 'to sit in a chair'," is to
drive home the point that the grammar of a word (i.e., the pattern of its use)
cannot be conceived apart from the way the surrounding social group lives,
acts, speaks, sees, hears, and thinks.[35] Since the imagination of a language
is simultaneously the imagination of a patterned way of living together,[36]
the converse is also apt: the sort of "understanding" that enables a group
to live together in a determinate pattern is identical to the skill required to
read the community's formative texts as an insider.[37]

The Narrative Community, or, Story-Formed Politics

As far as Hauerwas is concerned, "making Christianity intelligible," *pace*
Gustafson, is not something done to the message, namely *translate* it, but
something done for the recipients, namely *train* them. Hauerwas attributes
his access to these insights to the influence of Paul Holmer during his
graduate studies. Hauerwas reminisces:

> Holmer was . . . slowly changing my idea of what it meant to be reli-
> gious. He did so by forcing us to read Wittgenstein. I was learning that
> to become "religious is, in part, a matter of learning a new language."
> Of course, to learn that is only to be placed at the beginning; for we
> must be de-schooled from the presumption, fostered by much of mod-
> ern theology, that there is something wrong with first-order religious
> speech. It means that we must get over the presumption that if our re-
> ligious language is not working, we must find some way to translate it

into another language. I began to understand that if you needed to translate it, something had gone wrong not with the language *but with the speaker*.[38]

Nor could the "speaker" rightly be shaped by any dosage of *self*-administered medication. Hauerwas recalls his own need for "de-schooling":

> I remember we had the following exchange numerous times.
>
> HOLMER: "There's a distinction to be drawn; learning about the things of faith is not the same as learning to be faithful. But if that seems too patent, it might be said that theology is the learning *of* faith, not the learning *about faith*. Thus the distinction is drawn with the help of two prepositions, *of* and *about*."
>
> HAUERWAS: "But where do I find this language 'of'?"
>
> HOLMER: "You read the Bible."
>
> HAUERWAS: "But some people tell me to read this part of the Bible and other people tell me to read that part of the Bible."
>
> HOLMER: "Well, you need to read a larger context."
>
> HAUERWAS: "But some people tell me that this is the larger context, and other people tell me that is the larger context. What do I do then?"
>
> HOLMER: "You need to ask your pastor."
>
> HAUERWAS: "Some people tell me I should ask this pastor and other people tell me I should that pastor. How do I know which pastor to ask?"
>
> HOLMER: "Stanley, are you sure you are praying enough? And by the way, what is it that you're afraid of?"[39]

Hauerwas would later admit that his blindness while in graduate school was one of failing to see the role that community played in the shaping of the Christian life.

> No one can become virtuous merely by doing what virtuous people do. We can only be virtuous by doing what virtuous people do in that manner that they do it. Therefore one can only learn how to be virtuous, to be like Jesus, by learning from others how that is done. To be like Jesus requires that I become part of a community that practices virtues, not that I copy his life point by point.[40]

Thus, communication is "political" precisely because training in communication takes place within the stream of community life. Perhaps Hauerwas is free to speak in ways that Wittgenstein was not, for Hauerwas is an insider to a concrete historical community, namely, the Christian community whose form of life is governed by the gospel narratives of Scripture.

The claim that a community's form of life (upon which its language depends for its sense) may be determined by its communal stories (which cannot help but be framed in the local language) is not viciously circular.[41] Such dialectical relationship between form of life and narrative is certainly allowed for by Wittgenstein. His suggestion that a form of life stems from "primitive reactions" that are themselves prelinguistic was a suggestion Wittgenstein made provisionally, *en route* to showing that the patterns of social behavior—even our most "primitive" reactions—are trained by means of the language we use. Since story-telling (or context-describing) may be attributed to all users of language, Hauerwas's suggestion that narrative plays a determinative role in shaping a community's form of life fits well with Wittgenstein's other views.

But Hauerwas wants to say more than this. For Christians, some of the stories we recount to one another are "canonical." In his earliest writings, Hauerwas understands the canonical story as the hermeneutical key to understanding what truthfulness amounts to. In 1977 he wrote (with David Burrell),

> Religious faith, on this account, comes to accepting a certain set of stories as canonical. We come to regard them not only as meeting the criteria sketched above, along with others we may develop, but find them offering ways of clarifying and expanding our sense of the criteria themselves. In short, we discover our human self effectively through these stories, and so use them in judging the adequacy of alternative schemes for human kind.
>
> In this formal sense, one is tempted to wonder whether everyone does not accept a set of stories as canonical. To identify those stories would be to discover the shape one's basic convictions take. To be unable to do so would either mark a factual incapacity or an utterly fragmented self.[42]

Hauerwas is quite taken with the way some narratives are inseparable from the form of life of the community which trains its members in the linguistic skill of reading these canonical stories rightly.

> To be a person of virtue, therefore, involves acquiring the linguistic, emotional, and rational skills that give us the strength to make our

decisions and our life our own. The individual virtues are specific skills required to live faithful to a tradition's understanding of the moral project in which its adherents participate . . . .For skills, unlike technique, give the craftsman the ability to respond creatively to the always unanticipated difficulties involved in any craft in a manner that technique cannot provide. That is why the person of virtue is often thought of as a person of power, in that their emotional skills provide them with resources to do easily what some who are less virtuous would find difficult.[43]

Thus the "truthful" story is the one that both tells me who I am by narrating my life to me and equips me to live faithfully to this narration.

The internal (rather than causal) relation that Hauerwas sees between narrative and community[44] allows him flexibility in how he uses the term "narrative." For example, he identifies the Christian narrative with the material content of the Christian convictions.[45] By this he means both that Christians living in community extend the plot of the gospel and that the story of the gospel points the way for the community to know how to go on. The gospel narrative binds individual believers into communities and equips both with the tools for identifying who they are (and whose they are) by virtue of their coming to own the past—tragedy and all.[46] In this sense the Christian master story encompasses their whole world. But neither "world" nor "story" exist independent of the other. Rather, Christians are gifted with a world, and a place in it, by the canonical narratives with which they have been entrusted; Christians say that we are saved by grace, first, because the gospel is not a story of our own making,[47] and second, because the arduous training by which we come to use the language of the stories skillfully comes also as a gift.[48] One can never learn French by reading translations. One can only learn to speak fluently by interactions with others. At first these interactions may be rote (audio cassettes) or predictable (classroom exercises). But sooner or later, if one is to become fluent, one needs an increased level of spontaneity in dialogue. This comes only as a gift from others who have the patience, humor, and grace to show the novice the ways one topic may be brought to bear on another topic within a single conversation. Ultimately all conversations lead into the community's canonical narratives, not so much because these narratives are all that the community can talk about, but rather because the sort of reflexes that fluency cultivates (for example, which conversations are worth having and which are not; what "bringing to bear" amounts to; what connections are worth making) are those which are habituated by having looked at the world *through* these narratives.

Conversation, then, becomes a form of training that is internal to the community which speaks the sought-after language, and the canonical narratives provide the paradigmatic case for learning what bearing each aspect of the world has on the others. This training transforms the individual with the result that it is impossible to distinguish between internal and external evidence for one's convictions.

> That the Gospels have such a [reality-intending] character or that they involve "foundational metaphysical beliefs" I have never sought to deny or avoid. Rather, my concern has been to insist, along the lines suggested by Wesley, that the kind of truth entailed by the Gospels, the kinds of demands placed on reality, cannot be separated from the way in which the story of God we claim as revealed in Jesus' life, death, and resurrection forces a *repositioning of the self vis-à-vis reality*. . . . I have tried to maintain that it is impossible to distinguish between "external" and "internal" evidence as the character of Christian belief requires the *transformation of the self* in order rightly to see the actuality of our world without illusion or self-deception.[49]

While there may be external evidence for the truthfulness of Christianity, evidence is only evidence for someone. To read this evidence rightly requires one to be in the right position, stance, or state.[50] To say the same thing differently, the "narrability" of self and world expresses Christian convictions regarding the contingent character of our world and of our knowledge of the world.

> By "narrability" I mean that the world must be a contingent reality that requires a narrative display. If the world existed by necessity, no such narrative would be required, for the world would be open to theoretical explanation. The metaphysical trick, from a Christian point of view, is to show simultaneously how 'what is' cannot be other and yet why 'what is' is contingent and finite. Finally, 'narrability' does not entail that Christians must provide a 'superhistory' that encompasses all other subhistories, but rather it requires that no account of the world is final, short of the second coming.[51]

Intratextuality and Nontranslatability

If understanding is an achievement to be attained only after one is trained by means of participation in a community's form of life, then the charge of fideism against such a view is wrongheaded for presuming that understanding can be attained equally well, or better, by simple phrase-by-phrase translation. This insight can help untangle the specific form of miscommunication that exists between Hauerwas and Gloria Albrecht. Albrecht's charge of fideism is based on a mistake; Albrecht misunderstands Hauerwas precisely because she misconceives the notion of intratextuality.

Hauerwas is quick to admit views that he shares with Albrecht: "that humans are socially constructed, that all human knowledge is historically situated, and that the character of the communities which shape us is a central concern for doing Christian ethics."[52] But these points of commonality mean little if they are abstracted from Hauerwas's theology (as he contends Albrecht has done). More illuminating, therefore, are the specific charges Albrecht levels against Hauerwas.

Albrecht accuses Hauerwas of complicity in a cover-up of sorts. Taking Foucault's hermeneutic of suspicion as a starting point, she thinks Hauerwas rightly eschews the myth of Enlightenment individualism but charges that he has substituted, wrongly, a totalizing ideology in its place. For example, despite his view of human beings as socially constructed, Hauerwas's account of sin strikes her as unfairly universalizing, a flaw which

> allows him to make no distinction in the nature of sin based on the very different historical contexts, for example, of Black Christians in a racist United States, or of white, affluent men, or of Christians in the base communities of Central America, or of abused women.[53]

Consequently, she thinks Hauerwas has fostered a false consciousness that stifles the multiplicity of voices.

> What has been hidden is that language, narrative, discourse, and human subjectivity, being truly social, are also the sites of political struggle. What has been hidden are the fundamental loyalties expressed by where one chooses to stand. From the perspective of a poststructuralist feminist liberationist ethics, the point at this cacophonic moment in history is neither the celebration of diversity for its own sake nor the need to establish a community of common character. The point is the rising to sight and sound of voices speaking their own histories of suffering, of repression, and of resistance. Each voice reveals some aspect of the intertwined, hegemonic powers of racism, heterosexism, class privilege, and sexism. And each demands an end to its oppression.[54]

From Albrecht's perspective, Hauerwas's solution to the fragmentation of the Enlightenment project, namely, "the establishment of a community grounded in unified moral tradition," is simply the Enlightenment song in a different key.[55] By failing to recognize the reality of domination and the silencing of the multivocal Christian story, Hauerwas has simply replaced "rational man and ahistorical reason with Christian man and a master narrative."[56] The basic problem that Christian ethics ought to address is the false consciousness shared by both Enlightenment thinkers and Hauerwas. What gets lost in the shuffle for both accounts, Albrecht insists, is the sheer diversity of minority experiences and the fluidity which exists among their multiple discourses.

> In attempting to understand this diversity of experiences and what this means for the possibility of social transformation, a poststructuralist feminist ethic of liberation describes human personhood and human consciousness as a fluid process constituted by one's activities and the organization and meaning one chooses to give to these activities from the variety of interpretive discourses available. There is no pre-existent human nature; there is only unformed potentiality. And all communities are multivocal.[57]

The problem, therefore, is that the false consciousness, which Hauerwas has nurtured,

> denies this dynamic sociality and imposes false ideologies of either individualism or of social (or "natural") control. Freedom, the capacity of the individual to participate in co-creating self and society, is replaced by roles of dominance or subordination. Violence describes the experience of the loss of power to co-create oneself-in-relation. Violence describes the experience of being defined by dominant discourses. The goal of a post-structuralist feminist ethics of liberation is, therefore, to expose and transform this violence by choosing (1) to embody those discourses which reject the asymmetrical dualisms created by systems of domination (historically: race, class, sex, and sexual orientation) and (2) to call into being practices of interdependence aimed toward equality of participation in the social construction of meaning.[58]

For this reason Albrecht calls for an "emancipatory epistemology," one which out-liberates liberalism by entailing the "concept of Christian community that rejects the exercise of hegemonic power."[59] Only then can viable alternatives to authoritarian hierarchy (Hauerwas) and individual autonomy (liberalism) be found.

In a recent article Hauerwas expresses great weariness for being misunderstood so completely by a scholar of Albrecht's caliber, one who has read Hauerwas widely and carefully but, in the end, simply reproduced "the debilitating theological and philosophical habits that I have been so long committed to resisting and breaking."[60] Albrecht has misstated Hauerwas's views in at least three ways.

First, while she rightly notes the central place that "learning the habits of Christian speech" plays in Hauerwas's views, she assumes, wrongly, that this conviction is driven by Hauerwas's epistemology. Hauerwas responds, "I would be the first to admit that thinking you need an epistemology is a hard habit to break. It took years of reading Wittgenstein for me to get over it, though I probably still revert from time to time into epistemological speech habits."[61] In contrast with his disavowal, Albrecht's program *is* driven by epistemological concerns. Thus she chastises Hauerwas for creating a new brand of foundationalism—one built upon the authority of a hierarchical community rather than upon the certainty of autonomous reason.[62] Yet perhaps Albrecht herself has not escaped foundationalism, since she takes as self-evident the givenness of "women's experiences."[63] There is tension in Albrecht's claim that human beings are socially constructed and her presupposition that our experience in the world can be assessed in such a way so as to call into question the very socially-constructed conceptual framework by which experiences are had in the first place. This problem is compounded by her notion that language *corresponds* to the world of experience. Furthermore, there is a problem with Albrecht's category of "women." All women? Which women? By universalizing this class, her analysis in the end simply reinforces the conceptual restrictions she wants to transcend, namely, a biological (hence reductionistic) description of the class "women."

Second, Albrecht conceives of language as symbolically representing the world and tries to foist this view on Hauerwas. But it does not fit. Hauerwas avers:

> I never use the language of "symbols" to characterize language, since I do not believe that language is about helping us "to see and understand our experiences." Indeed, that way of putting the matter creates the unbridgeable gulf between language and the world that I have argued is part of the problem.

... The language of "meaning and value" suggests, wrongly, that there is some deeper or fundamental reality and that is what we are "really about." Such a view is fueled by the presumption that there should be a place that allows us to stand outside, be free, of our speech. I assume by contrast that "we are spoken before we speak"—a theological claim that even some current philosophers are beginning to discover. That "we are spoken before we speak" seems to entail linguistic determinism only for those who do not attend with sufficient care to how languages work.[64]

We do not first have experiences and then later affix to them symbolic labels, such as words. Rather, all experience has a narrative texture because the habits of our language, which are bound up in the narratives we recount to ourselves, constitute the world we inhabit, give us our selves, and are the *sine qua non* for having, much less exegeting, our "experiences."

Third, while Albrecht expects Hauerwas to be sympathetic with her arguments, she employs notions of freedom, choice, and egalitarianism that are characteristic of the very liberal political theory Hauerwas eschews. Consequently, Hauerwas hears her feminist theology as simply "liberal Protestant theology in a different key."[65] Albrecht's alternative to autonomy of the individual and to authoritarian hierarchy is a vision of the *autonomous community*. But this proposal leaves unchallenged the assumption that freedom ought to be construed as autonomy. Ironically, Albrecht is blind to the way the language of liberalism has constrained the scope of how she sees these matters. It is this deeper problem that Hauerwas has expended so much energy untangling.

I have tried to help Christians, particularly in North America, discover in what ways liberal speech (and practices) subverts the way we must speak as Christians. I have done so not because I think liberalism is peculiarly perverse, but simply because liberalism has been and is the speech that dominates our lives. From my perspective, the challenge for Christians is to learn the habits of Christian speech by patient imitation of faithful speakers in the tradition as well as attending to the challenges before us today. Such a learning posits no "pure Christian speech," but rather *requires a politics* in which Christian speech, in all of its complexity, does work.[66]

As it stands, Albrecht's proposed autonomous community has simply replaced the autonomous individual in the liberal equation. As a result, her

proposal will be susceptible to the very same sorts of problems that moti-
vated Hauerwas toward a narrative account of the self and community in
the first place. For example, Albrecht cannot help but define the communal identity "prospectively," a move that deprives the community of historical resources necessary for owning communal tragedy in the same way
that a prospective account of the self robs individuals of the resources necessary for owning individual tragedy.

I have described Albrecht's criticisms of Hauerwas to show one way in
which her charge of fideism is mistaken. Albrecht's misunderstanding of
Hauerwas shows that she has overlooked the resources—such as language-
training in a narrative-shaped community—necessary for attaining understanding. Sharon Welch observed that Albrecht's views are driven by her
allegiance to poststructuralist theory.[67] If so, then to the extent that all poststructuralist theories are "modernist,"[68] Albrecht's project aims at being con-
text-free in the characteristic modern way, despite her repeated claims to
"approach ethics from the position of a white, middle-class, heterosexual,
feminist, clergywoman."[69] In contrast, Hauerwas's intratextual approach insists that one first be trained to "see" by the process of acquiring the language of a determinate community, which is to say, of a community with
determinative canonical narratives. The possibility of intratextual, or intracommunal, tutelage shows that not every hierarchy is a "bad thing," as
Albrecht supposes. For fluency-by-intratextuality is able to achieve what
Albrecht's position—namely, intelligibility-by-translation—cannot.[70]

> Moreover, it is exactly "resident aliens" who must become adept
> at being multi-lingual. My argument against "translation" as allegedly
> a necessary strategy for Christians to speak as "modern people" or to en-
> gage the "public" is a reminder that no such translation is possible. . . .
> Because of the material content of our convictions, Christians cannot
> help but be witnesses. To bear witness often requires that Christians
> acquire—to use MacIntyre's language—a second first language. But
> the mark of anyone who has learned to speak two first languages is their
> recognition "in what respects utterances in the one are untranslatable
> into the other."[71]

In conclusion, it is Hauerwas's view that there can be no evaluation of
truth claims without commensurate transformation of the subject doing the
evaluation.[72] Moreover, because the story which gives one a self is constitutive of the community which trains one to read this story rightly, "the sub-

ject of transformation for Christians is not [simply] the isolated individual, but a *community* living through time."[73]

Hauerwas has taken his cue from Wittgenstein in order to correct the sorts of misunderstandings that plague modern academia. The pattern of human social interplay, or form of life, that frames the grammar of the Christian community's language is at the same time the form of that community's canonical narratives. Thus, an incommensurability of language-games between rival communities is simultaneously a fundamental difference of stories. The distance between languages is not bridged by some form of translation (a case of semantics without syntax) but by human capacity to become bilingual. The centrality of the community for this tutoring process implies that salvation is therefore political in nature: outside the church there is no salvation.

THE POLITICS OF SALVATION

A second persistent theme in Hauerwas's writing that defuses the charge of fideism is the political character of salvation. Because the message of the gospel is that Christians have been given citizenship in a new *polis* (Col. 1:12–13), the charge of fideism from the outside is not damaging; it is merely symptomatic of the very condition from which believers understand themselves to have been rescued. What is unsettling is that the charge of fideism comes from the mouths of those who should know better. In Hauerwas's estimation, Max Stackhouse is a fitting spokesperson for theological liberalism since he, by so completely ingesting political liberalism, lacks the ability to appreciate the ways in which the *polis* in Christ is a radical alternative to the secular world order.

Although it is common to date the rise of liberal political theory to the publication of Hobbes's *Leviathan* in 1651, MacIntyre (and others) have noted that the liberal vision of the generic individual as something more fundamental than its collective counterpart ("society") has its roots in the Reformers' picture of the soul standing naked and alone in its accountability before God.[74] Hauerwas sees the turn toward interiority (itself a tendency present in Christian thought as early as Augustine) and individuality as the by-product of another confusion, namely, the tendency (fully realized after Constantine) to conflate church and *saeculum:*[75]

It has been suggested that satisfaction theories of the Atonement and the correlative understanding of the Christian life as a life of interiority became the rule during the long process we call the Constantinian settlement. When Caesar becomes a member of the Church the enemy becomes internalized. The problem is no longer that the Church is seen as a threat to the political order, but that now my desires are disordered. The name for such an internalization in modernity is pietism and the theological expression of that practice is called Protestant liberalism.[76]

When Christendom's political stability unraveled after the Reformation, Christian pietism was transmuted into a radical individualism in desperate hopes that agreement between warring parties could be procured by a form of knowing that was, in principle, accessible to "anyone," and that residual disagreement could be exposed simply as the lingering hegemony of the past over human volition. Crucial to the success of this enterprise, wrote Kant, was the achievement of autonomy by the individual by means of "enlightenment":

> Enlightenment is man's release from his self-incurred tutelage. Tutelage is man's inability to understand without direction from another. Self-incurred is this tutelage when its cause lies not in lack of reason but in lack of resolution and courage to use it without direction from another.[77]

The (putative) liberation of the individual from all forms of historical conditioning became know as liberalism:

> As an epistemological position liberalism is an attempt to defend a foundationalism in order to free reason from being determined by any particular tradition. Politically liberalism makes the individual the supreme unit of society, thus making the political task the securing of cooperation between *arbitrary units of desire*.[78]

The defining characteristic of liberal individualism is raw volition.[79] Although the loss of historical resources for making choices implies that self-making is arbitrary, taken more positively, the prospective posture of the self means that human beings are at once "self-creating, self-controlling, and self-directing."[80] In other words, *choice* becomes the *summum bonum* of human existence.

Put simply, the story of modernity is that you should have no story except the story you have *chosen* when you had no story. Thus, the modern presumption is that one never should be held responsible for commitments that we have not *freely chosen*, even if at the time we thought we were *freely choosing*. Compassion and the creation of compassionate societies try to make possible for each person in a society of individuals to have the social, economic, and political status to *choose* who they want to be. The project of liberal societies is simply to make the *freedom of choice* a necessity. Thus, we achieve the goal of making *freedom* the fate of each individual.[81]

The invention of the autonomous self, conceived as standing in isolation from all historical influences and as the fundamental unit of human reality, was coincidental with the rise to prominence of Cartesian dualism, which posited a bifurcation between "the inner" and "the outer." The discarding of historical aspects from the conception of the self—aspects such as language, practices, religion, and geography—was seemingly legitimated so long as such aspects were taken to be "accidents of the external" which failed to touch the "real," which is to say "internal," person. Ironically, the bifurcation of the inner and outer has had the effect of making political life equally accidental, fragile, and violent.[82] For in Hobbes's words, society is bound together simply by a common fear in a life that is solitary, poor, nasty, brutish, and short. Such fragility can only be overcome by a social coercion that runs counter to the very notion of freedom it aims at securing.

After divesting the self of the possibility of anything that might resemble training in judgment, "the Enlightenment tried to show that the mind was immediately appropriate to a factual world *without training*."[83] (In this regard, practices such as medicine or law are a perpetual embarrassment to the liberal story, since the first task of a medical or legal apprentice is to hold his or her own judgment in *abeyance*.)[84] In particular, it was maintained that "inalienable rights"—a philosophically confused notion—were *prima facie* knowable by all reasonable persons. These rights were counted on to be the trumps which protected human freedom.[85] However, "rights" are not self-evident, but, in fact, derive their content entirely from the regnant concept of the self. Thus, once the dyadic self of the medieval period is reconceived by Enlightenment thinkers as the generic human monad (the social position of each being accidental to his or her respective identities), only one option for measuring distributive justice was even conceivable—the "inalienable right" of equality.[86]

Ironically, the generic account of the self that precipitated allegedly neutral procedural rules for attaining the just society simultaneously created the conditions for insulating liberalism from criticism and thereby securing its long-standing hegemony. Jeffrey Stout, in his *Ethics after Babel*, argues that in our fragmented age the best moral reflection will take the form of *bricolage*—the assembling of an eclectic moral language and the bringing of it to bear on now this, and now that, moral problem. But Hauerwas objects to Stout's vision:

> The practice and institution that make the image of the *bricoleur* intelligible look far too much like liberal bureaucracy. Bureaucrats assume they can choose between "options" without having to stand in any particular place. Accordingly, their role is to domesticate conflict by subjecting disputes to procedural rules which are allegedly neutral. At the very heart of such liberal proceduralism lies the attempt to dehistoricize our lives by suppressing memory.[87]

By the phrase "domesticate conflict" Hauerwas signifies the liberal agenda to do away with anything that might pose a challenge to the liberal account of the goods of freedom, rights, and autonomy. In other words, even though the Amish or Native Americans "have stories to tell about goods more basic than freedom and/or rights," when such groups conflict they must be subjected to procedures which pretend to procure "justice" in complete ignorance of these thicker descriptions of the Good.[88] On the surface, this seems to imply that liberalism destroys community formation by destroying the art of remembering. In fact, liberalism does not seek to destroy communities so much as absorb them by a totalitarian control over the vocabulary of individuals' self-description, on the one hand, and by perpetuating a mythic story (freedom) through this procedural account of justice, on the other. What Stout overlooks, in Hauerwas's view, is that when liberalism functions as a meta-tradition, it tends to "level the distinctions among other identifiable traditions and make their coexistence a good in itself."[89] This means, first of all, that when liberalism functions at the level of a meta-tradition, it "inevitably loses its historical character, which in turn insulates it from criticism,"[90] since the only terms remaining by which it might be criticized are those of the ahistorical vocabulary which spawned liberalism in the first place. Second, by making (peaceful) coexistence of rival groups a good in and of itself, liberal society becomes its own *telos*, with the result that only a very fine line separates liberals from communitarians, who likewise make community an end in itself.[91]

The upshot of this discussion is not simply that the liberal "story" is imperialistic and totalitarian,[92] but that an account of the self that is prospective, autonomous, voluntaristic, and therefore generic, entails a conception of society that is monolithic; *e pluribus unum* applies equally to a collection of groups as it does to a collection of individuals. On the liberal view there is but a single community (namely, pluralistic liberal society). And the hegemony of this view is protected by its invisibility:

> liberalism can be characterized as the presumption that you should have no story other than the story you chose when you had no story. A society constituted to produce people who get to choose their stories cannot help but be caught in perpetual double-think. For what it cannot acknowledge is that we did not choose the story that we should have no story except the story we chose when we had no story.[93]

For the most part, theological liberalism—which has been the brunt of Hauerwas's polemic for the past thirty years—can be characterized as an attempt to express Christianity from within the parameters set by political liberalism. What irks Hauerwas is not that contextualization of the gospel was attempted in modernity, as it had been in Augustine's day, but that contextualization has failed; Hauerwas charges that theological liberalism has contributed to a massive distortion of the gospel. For example, by presuming the primacy of autonomy and choice, theological liberalism caters to a type of dualism.[94] As regards the internal, the presupposition of voluntarism has resulted in an experiential-expressivist model of religion.[95] In this vein, religion is thought to do with private, interior, prelinguistic experience. This has several consequences. First, salvation is thought to be the acquisition by the individual of a "belief system" that gives "meaning" to his or her life. (Hauerwas is quick to point out the similarities of this with forms of gnosticism that the church rightly resisted.)[96] Second, in good Enlightenment fashion, such religious experience is said to be equally available to every individual prior to, and independently of, any adequation of the individual to religious experience that might come through a process of training in a communal setting.[97] This means, third, that the form that communal life takes is largely irrelevant to matters of salvation. Voluntarism has as its ultimate consequence the production of milquetoast congregations held together by nothing stronger than their common interests.[98]

If gnosticism names the form that theological liberalism takes in its view of the private life, then "constantinianism" names the form it takes with respect to public life. By this term Hauerwas does not mean the historical moment that Constantine joined the Church, but rather the long-standing temptation (one which predates AD 313) for Christians to use power — economic, social, governmental — to enforce the range and rule of Christianity.

> With the Constantinian settlement, Christianity wanted to try to show that we could be a civil religion, in a way that Judaism could not, because we were a universal faith that could command the adherence of anyone if they just got the right information and thought hard enough about it. Therefore, we sponsored a sense of "truth" that was a kind of correspondence theory — that just said that this is the way things are, and you should be able to come up with it pretty quickly. That was of course against our own best practice, since inherent in Christianity is the assumption that in order to know the truth you must be converted. Christianity grew, not by saying people already believe what we know — we just have to make it explicit — but it grew by witness, and witness is primarily the power of lives. So I'm saying that the kinds of theories of truth we sponsored had a political purpose, namely, to underwrite our attempt to become a civil religion.[99]

Ironically, the drift of the church toward civil religion resulted in Christians adopting a *coercive* manner of witness that was contrary to the material content of the witness itself:

> I regard foundationalism and liberalism as the result of Christian bad faith. Christianity wanted to show itself to be a universal religion and we thought by being a universal religion that meant that we had the truth that everyone really knew but just had to be awakened to. So natural theology became our mode, and when we went to other societies we assumed that all we were telling them was something that they already knew and therefore they would just naturally respond. And when they didn't naturally respond, we said they must be morally obtuse and rationally unclear and so we could coerce them since, as a matter of fact, this was just universal truth we were trying to make them live in accordance with.[100]

Although early constantinian optimism in the church may have been tempered by the memory of those who had been martyred at the hands of the State, contemporary liberal theologians' constantinian proclivity is not marked by such a dis-ease since, like the political liberalism from which it sprang, it is ignorant of its own historical conditionedness.[101]

For Hauerwas, the constantinian agenda is expressed overtly in Walter Rauschenbusch's turn-of-the-century call to "Christianize the social order" and the mid-twentieth-century Christian realism of Reinhold Niebuhr.[102] Hauerwas notes that Christianity was especially susceptible to embracing the projects of liberalism when Christianity possessed social hegemony. Just as liberal Christians in Niebuhr's day deluded themselves into thinking that they had out-totalized secular liberals by construing democracy as the by-product and highest expression of *Christian* management of society, a residual smugness can still be found among contemporary liberal theologians, despite their steady decline in political influence in recent years.

For example, Max Stackhouse offers his account of "conciliar denominationalism" as an alternative to pre-Enlightenment Calvinist and Catholic views of church-state relations. Because his account assumes that America is the great experiment in applied Protestantism, it makes *America* the primary subject of religious ethics. However, by adopting the same stance as secular liberals, liberal theologians simply perpetuated the illusion that they were still in control. Hauerwas observes wryly: "Pluralism turns out to be a code word used by mainstream Christians to the effect that everyone gets to participate in the democratic exchange of ideas on his or her terms, except for Christians themselves."[103] Hauerwas insists that the proper subject of ethics is the Christian community. The self that undergoes transformation is not the punctiliar monad of modern political liberalism but the "eschatological" self. Thus Hauweras aims to train his readers to recognize that the gift of selfhood is the result of seeing oneself as deeply embedded in the gospel, which is more determinative than political history. In fact, Hauerwas's ability to explicate an alternative to the liberal vision is itself evidence that the constantinian vision is fatally flawed.

In contrast to the Enlightenment myth that all conflicts are, in principle, resolvable, Hauerwas counters that inter-communal conflicts are real, deep, and lasting. Therefore, it behooves Christians to train as if for war, beginning with a clear understanding of who is the "enemy" of our faith. In his 1995 essay "Preaching As Though We had Enemies," Hauerwas paints this picture:

> the project of modernity was to produce a people who believe they should have no story except the story they chose when they have no story. Such a story is called the story of freedom and is assumed to be irreversibly institutionalized economically as market capitalism and

politically as democracy. That story and the institutions that embody it is the enemy we must attack through Christian preaching.[104]

As an extension of political liberalism, liberal theology is likewise Hauerwas's "enemy" for its tendency to obscure authentic salvation:

> Insofar as that political arrangement underwrites a "nonconfessional God" and a non-ecclesial version of Christianity, it runs into profound conflict with Christianity. When "Christianity" becomes separable from the social form in which it is to be embodied, two things happen: one, Christian belief gets located in an interior, asocial sphere, "the heart" or "conscience" or some other private (i.e., non-public) space, and this degenerates into "mere belief"; and two, in consequence of the first, a "public" space is cleared away for a counterfeit form of "religion" to emerge that is said to be "common" and thus becomes "the religion of the nation." What gets obscured in this arrangement is the possibility of a Christianity the material form of which is located neither in a private space nor in a general public space, but in the body of believers, in the church.[105]

Of course, having enemies is something good liberal theologians cannot have, for having enemies—at least disruptive ones—shows that they have not yet succeeded in achieving the ideal of democracy in their management of the social order. It is therefore with some urgency that Max Stackhouse marginalizes Hauerwas as a "bumptious child of the Vietnam protest era, the one with the quick wit, the furnished mind, the clever phrase, the brazen tongue and the disarming effrontery of the clown."[106] If the difference between Albrecht and Hauerwas is that between philosophy and theology, the difference between Stackhouse and Hauerwas is that between religion and theology. It is a function of Stackhouse's inability to acknowledge two communities where he can see but one.

Stackhouse's longest sustained attack against Hauerwas, his review of Hauerwas's *Dispatches from the Front*, illustrates his inability as a liberal theologian *par excellence* to hear what Hauerwas is saying. Tucked away in the middle of Stackhouse's essay is a reference to *Fullness of Faith*, by Michael and Kenneth Himes, that helps us understand Stackhouse's optimism regarding the role he thinks theology plays in public life.[107] Stackhouse is quite impressed by the way the authors find in the doctrine of the trinity an account of the dignity and distinctiveness of individuals-in-community that can serve as a "charter" for Christian existence in the public sphere.[108] Twice in his short essay Stackhouse alludes to his conviction that Protestantism is directly responsible for the origin and flourishing of democracy. *Fullness of Faith* catches Stackhouse's eye because of his own liberal propensity to regard salvation as the process of being rescued from a meaningless existence by the supplying of information. This points to the first of three criticisms that he, like others cut from the liberal bolt of cloth, levels against Hauerwas.

Stackhouse faults Hauerwas for being insufficiently analytical, a trait that he thinks has earned Hauerwas a wide following among the intellectually impoverished:

> Some people do not want to be forced to give an account of the faith that is within them, or do not know how, or think it is improper even to ask for such an account. They like Hauerwas's convenient philosophical conviction that since all claims are equally without foundation, religious claims are immune to rational criticism. They want *theos* without *logos*.

Stackhouse contrasts himself with Hauerwas in this regard, numbering himself among those who see the use of the mind as intrinsic to the Christian faith.

> many of us believe that we are not bound to the cultural-linguistic traditions of the socio-historical contexts from which we come. Not only can we critically reflect on faith and morals handed down to us, but we can convert or transform what we inherit—and offer a reasonable account of why we do so.[109]

Of course, this robust optimism depends entirely on the human mind having unfettered access to "universal principles" by which to "critically reflect" upon, "influence," "reform," and "order" public life (even violently). Stackhouse has recently conceded that the question of whether universal absolutes exist has been met everywhere with doubt and skepticism. However, on the grounds that we simply *must* have the basis for declaring practices such as terrorism inherently wrong, Stackhouse calls for theologians to have what Hauerwas lacks, namely, "the cross-cultural intellectual moral amplitude" to think through these issues.[110] Stackhouse is appalled by Hauerwas's stated intention to make his students think just as he does rather than make up their own minds. Stackhouse simply asserts what to him is obvious: "Every believer has to 'do his own believing', as Luther says. Each of us finally has to make up his or her mind on the most important questions with the aid of evidence, logic and the gift of grace." In good liberal fashion, the right to freely *choose* one's stance, one's community, one's tradition, and one's narrative is taken by Stackhouse to be the self-evident ground of his injunction: "Evidence and logic can be judged, but it is wrong to demand conformity of conscience."[111]

In answer to this first objection, Hauerwas offers a radically different conception of salvation.

> I should not hide the fact that informing [my] account of the church is a quite different understanding of salvation than is assumed by many Christians today. I have little use for the current fascination with individual salvation in either its conservative or liberal guises. Such accounts of salvation assume that God has done something for each person which may find expression in the church. I do not assume that salvation is first and foremost about my life having "meaning" or insuring "my" eternal destiny. Rather, *salvation is being engrafted into practices that save us from those powers that would rule our lives making it impossible for us to truly worship God.*[112]

Salvation is political, not in the sense that the theory of theology enlightens the praxis of public life (as Stackhouse imagines), but rather in the sense that salvation is constituted by an entirely different *polis*. It is the christological shape of the church that makes it both a radical alternative to secular society and formally incommensurable with theological liberalism.

Hauerwas's 1981 collection of essays, *A Community of Character*, marked his intention to

> reassert the social significance of the church as a distinct society with an integrity peculiar to itself. . . . [whose] most important social task is nothing less than to be a community capable of hearing the story of God we find in the scripture and living in a manner that is faithful to that story.[113]

Hauerwas works on the assumption that there is, to put it inelegantly, a narrative texture to human life. The fact is, we write novels that inevitably resemble the lives of real people because this genre expresses the possibilities of how someone might actually live. Similarity is achieved when the "form" of a real life becomes embodied in the picture of the life we call a novel. In the case of the Christian story, Jesus of Nazareth is born, lives, dies, and rises again. The pattern of this life and its details (form and content) are captured by the four evangelists in writing. The good news is that this process can also be run in reverse. Not only is the form of Jesus' life embodied in the text, the form thus embodied can be reduplicated in the community that rightly extends this story:

> I have tried to show that if we pay attention to the narrative and self-involving character of the Gospels, as the early disciples did, there is no way to speak of Jesus' story without its forming our own. The story it forms creates a community which corresponds to the form of his life.[114]

If the cross epitomizes the form of Jesus' whole life, then the form of community life taken in imitation of him will be necessarily *cruciform*— which is to say, peaceful and nonviolent—even to the point of martyrdom.[115] Thus "pacifism" does not name a theoretical position for Hauerwas, but the manner in which Christians are to live with each other.[116] Pacifism can neither be defended nor justified. Pacifism "derives its intelligibility not from any one set of teachings of Jesus but rather from the very form of his life and death."[117]

Once again, to see things under the aspect of the gospel does not come automatically; it is a vision into which Christians must be trained. Pacifism requires the practice of forgiveness, and forgiveness (lest it become but another form of power we exercise over one another) requires of believers an ability to see themselves as sinners. Seeing oneself under the aspect of "sinner," in turn, requires surrender to the authority of the story embodied in the practices which constitute the distinctively Christian form of communal life:

> No one can become virtuous merely by doing what virtuous people do. We can only be virtuous by doing what virtuous people do in that manner that they do it. Therefore one can only learn how to be virtuous, to be like Jesus, by learning from others how that is done. To be like Jesus requires that I become part of a community that practices virtues, not that I copy his life point by point.[118]

Jesus' form of life makes the Christian community an entirely different body politic. This particular community is "not a community of egalitarian acceptance," nor one in which freedom derives from "choosing our own stories." Rather, it is a community in which we have been trained to understand that "salvation comes by giving us something to do"—namely, a set of practices that bespeak the story of Jesus.[119]

In addition to faulting Hauerwas for not seeing what "anyone" can plainly see (namely, that it is incumbent upon every individual to make up his or her own mind on religious issues), Stackhouse accuses Hauerwas of the "heresy" of exclusivism. Stackhouse can make neither heads nor tails of Hauerwas's denial that politics is finally about the use of power. Stackhouse contends: "Hauerwas writes that he refuses to believe that politics is about coercive power. But this refusal does not make it less so. Even if politics is not *only* about that, *it is not politics if it does not involve the accumulation and exercise of power*."[120] In Stackhouse's mind the genius of Protestant theology was that it paved the way for the understanding of democratic processes that apply universally.[121] Because the procedures that yield democratic relations are supposedly universal in the range of their application, the issue for Stackhouse can never be *whether* politics involves power, but only whether that use is *responsible*.

> When we think about modern society, we have to recognize that parts of it are rooted in theologies which regard responsible intervention in nature and in social history as an obedient reordering of a sinful world rather than a secular compromise with that world.[122]

Thus, in Stackhouse's eyes, Hauerwas is a heretic of the worst order: by denying the legitimacy of coercion and thereby excluding from the community of faithful those who are "constrained" to use the instruments of coercion, Hauerwas has blasphemed against the God upon whose character democracy is founded: "But the question remains as to whether we are most faithful the more we oppose the cultural, social and civilizational life, or whether the God witnessed to by the Bible and present in Jesus Christ lives among the peoples of faith in all walks of life."[123]

Once again Stackhouse profoundly misunderstands Hauerwas. As Hauerwas wryly remarked: "What Stackhouse thinks I must think is only what someone like Stackhouse can think I think because of the way he thinks."[124] Stackhouse can only conceive of political relations as the balance of power—whether between individuals within a group, between groups, or between groups of groups. Thus, for Stackhouse, political involvement of the church is, by definition, the use of power within the (single) *polis* defined as all that which falls under the scope of these universally binding political processes. But Hauerwas is conceiving a radically different *polis*—one that is not bound by coercive political process and in which liberation from the bounds of political process constitutes our salvation. This alternative mode of social existence is not only christological (or, christomorphic), it is *eschatological* as well.

We have already seen Hauerwas's description of the Christian self as eschatological in that it faces both past and future at once. In Hauerwas's understanding, the community also has an eschatological dimension to it. Following John Howard Yoder, Hauerwas uses the term "eschatological" to connote the characteristic way the church defines its present mode of existence in terms of a yet unrealized goal which gives it meaning.[125] This yet-to-be-realized goal was proleptically revealed in Christ. Thus, as discussed above, the *form* of Jesus' life as the eschatological Messiah—his obedience, his death, his resurrection—becomes the pattern of this new mode of solidarity.[126] Life in this community conditions us to see, in the Apostle's words, "a new world" (καινὴ κτίσις):[127]

> the primary ethical question is not, What ought I now to do? but rather, How does the world really look? The most interesting question about the Sermon [on the Mount] is not, Is this really a practical way to live in the world? but rather, Is this really the way the world is? What is "practical" is related to what is real. If the world is a society in which only the strong, the independent, the detached, the liberated, and the successful are blessed, then we act accordingly. However, if the world is really a place where God blesses the poor, the hungry, and the persecuted for righteousness' sake, then we must act in accordance with reality or else appear bafflingly out of step with the way things are.[128]

Samuel Wells notes that the difference between what the secular person sees and what the Christian sees makes irony (rather than comedy or tragedy) the genre of eschatology.[129] For example, the death of Jesus looked like the end for the movement called Christianity. The irony lies in the surprising fact that his death sounded the knell for the principalities and powers (Hebrews 2:14) and signaled the inauguration of a new Christian body. In like manner, the mode of living in the Christian *polis*—its "irresponsible pacifism"—is ironically the very key to its identity and endurance.

Of course it would be very easy to misunderstand Hauerwas's account of the community as a community-in-withdrawal. But as Phillip Kenneson helpfully points out, the objections of sectarianism and withdrawal trade on a spatial metaphor. In contrast, Hauerwas's use of "eschatological" is probably better understood as an allusion to the fact that the Christian community inhabits a new time rather than a different space.[130] Inhabiting a different time involves the notion of ordering of our lives according to a history whose plot is aimed at a different *telos* than that of the world. To cite but one example, the proliferation of nuclear armaments schools us to see this difference. Hauerwas writes,

> the basic problem with nuclear weapons is not that they threaten human survival, but rather [that] they are but the ultimate sign of the madness that makes war appear such a necessary part of our lives. For war is the sign and the result of our denial that we live in a world with God as its end. War is the desperate means we use to reinforce our self-deception that we, and not God, are the lords of history such that our eternal destiny can supply the right ending to the world's story; or in the absence of that power, to assure the world will never end.[131]

This alternative reading of history changes the Christian's sense of timing. Faced with a calamity, Christians say, "It is time to pray." Faced with injustice, Christians say, "It is time to forgive."[132] In this light the real, possibly incommensurable, difference between the two communities renders plausible the otherwise odd habits of Christians who pray, forgive, baptize, and break bread. Wells summarizes:

> the eschatological hope is embodied by a people who see heaven not so much as a "space" but as a way of understanding and acting in time — as a verb, rather than as a noun. The ethical implications of this last dimension of eschatology orient the Christian toward time, rather than away from time in search of timeless reward.[133]

The resulting differences between society and the Christian colony are real. Christians are those who contend that history has *already* turned out right in Christ and therefore, all attempts to enforce the outcome are quite beside the point. A crucial aspect of the "end" of the story was the decisive defeat of the powers rendered at Calvary; if our war against the principalities and powers was decided *then*, then the content of salvation is nothing less than the concrete community structured now in defiance of their tyranny. For example, in thinking about the sort of sway the threat of nuclear war holds over daily life, Hauerwas outlined an eschatological response:

there is no more powerful response to totalitarians than to take the time to reclaim life from their power. By refusing to let them claim every aspect of our life as politically significant, we create the space and time that makes politics humane. Therefore, there is nothing more important for us to do in the threat of nuclear war than to go on living—that is, to take time to enjoy a walk with a friend, to read all of Trollope's novels, to maintain universities, to have and care for children, and most importantly, to worship God.[134]

The existence of the christocentric, eschatological community is salvific because it exposes all totalitarian (hence idolatrous) claims—such as can be heard in liberalism's insistence that political relations are necessarily coercive—as deceptive since in this new community a real alternative exists.

The third main problem Stackhouse finds in Hauerwas's project is the way Hauerwas minimizes the importance of the secular social order. He writes, "For Hauerwas, God exists, persons exist, traditions and practices exist and the church exists . . . , but society as a system of interacting 'orders' sustained by the vocations by which God calls us to serve our neighbors in the world does not."[135] In Stackhouse's estimation, the real locus of action is not the church but the world. The church best serves the world by specifying for the world the creational assumptions upon which science, technology, democracy, and economics rest and by avoiding an ingrown focus on particular communal life.[136] Communities which failed in this task would be pathetically "embryonic," falling short of realizing their members' full identities as citizens of the world.

In other words, Stackhouse wants to explore the theological requirements needed to bring about a global community. He suggests that a broad, deep, and durable community requires a vision of its own realization provided by a theological viewpoint that is manifest in the Scriptures: " in the Prophets, who knew that the true God is a God of justice; in Ruth and Jonah, who know that God was for all peoples; and in Jesus, who knew that God sets moral integrity above religious particularism. . . ."[137] Given this agenda, Stackhouse's opposition to Hauerwas's "religious particularism" is understandable. For in striking contrast, Hauerwas maintains that the church will never be able to work itself out of a job; the church best serves the world by telling the truth that the center of God's salvific intention is the church rather than the world.

The centrality and primacy of the church is a permanent feature in Hauerwas's thinking and one that he came to realize was internally related to the therapeutic mode of his ethics. Chapter 2 outlined the way the concepts of agency and character helped Hauerwas move away from the dominant decisionist mode of ethical reflection to a model of ethics-as-aesthetics. In that early stage of his thought, community appeared to play second fiddle to the task of elucidating the nature of agency (*qua* agency). However, once his attention had been arrested by the fact that the virtues always require *narrative* display—an account that manifests the way an agent stands in relation to others—Hauerwas turned his energies toward an examination of the narrative shape of Christian community life. The configuration of this form of life—namely, one that was christological, eschatological, and incarnational—became the determinative category for Christian ethics; the Christian community was the cruciform community precisely because it was marked by a pacifism in imitation of Jesus: "From this perspective the church is the organized form of Jesus' story."[138] Because the church is bound together by a form of life that embodies the story of God, the church as a distinctive community cannot be irrelevant for moral reflection nor are its convictions matters of indifference.

The liberal account moves in the opposite direction. Presuming the self to be an autonomous chooser, theological liberalism reduces all political alliances to associations that are merely voluntary—which is to say, arbitrary. Hauerwas began his career in ethics already suspicious of the generic individualism espoused by liberalism. Thus he proudly called himself an "unrepentant Barthian," a label by which he affirmed (among other things) that there is an irreducible social component to human life that liberalism, as the heir to the Enlightenment project, continually overlooks.[139] Thus, in contrast to the merely voluntary association liberalism sees, Hauerwas quests for the proper way to speak about the more determinative ties that bind us.

His first sustained attempt to express the reality of social connectivity within a given community relied upon the concept of "narrative." Although Hauerwas confined himself to discussions of the way the Christian narrative formed Christian community, he was clearly sympathetic with some of the seemingly generalized conclusions of Alasdair MacIntyre's metanarrative regarding the narrative texture of human existence in general. On these grounds, the liberal account can be faulted for failing to see human beings as social animals bound together by the particular stories and practices that constitute their respective communities. Even the liberal political society itself is a community of sorts, held together by the flimsy tale about having no story other than the story which the storyless individual freely chooses.

However, in the middle of his career, narrative as a *general* descriptive category began to fall into disuse. Hauerwas realized that what saves us is not having *some* story but having one story in particular—the story of God Incarnate.[140] The fact that the church is formed by this story means that what the Scripture alternatively calls the presence of God, the kingdom of God, and the spirit of God has come near in the concrete community that instantiates the story of Jesus.[141]

His conviction regarding the nearness of God in the Christian community opened the door for Hauerwas to affirm a much stronger intracommunal connectivity than is possible to attain extra-communally or is possible to express in terms of narrative. In 1995 he wrote,

> The body politics of liberalism can make no sense of passages like 1 Corinthians 6:12–20. Paul did not think that we, as baptized believers, ought to view our bodies *as if* we were one with one another through Christ, but rather that our bodies are quite literally not our "own" because we have been made (as well as given) a new body by the Spirit. What is crucial, therefore, is not whether the Church is primarily understood as "the body of Christ" or "the people of God," but whether the practices exist through which we learn that our bodies are not our own.[142]

These words indicate, against all liberal intuitions, that the communal life within the church is more determinative for understanding one's physical body than is familiarity with one's own physical body for understanding the church.

The upshot of this inversion of liberalism's punctiliar view of the self is Hauerwas's conviction that the followers of Jesus are more profoundly interconnected than can be expressed by mere metaphor: "by being present to others in church I find that I am made more than I would otherwise be—I am made one in the faith of the church; my body is *constituted* by the body called the church."[143] More recently, he criticizes as mistaken the typical metaphorical understanding of "the body of Christ." Thus, "It is not as if the church is, *like* the body, interconnected needing all its parts even the inferior one. The church *is* the body from which we learn to understand our particular bodies."[144]

We can see that the direction taken by Hauerwas's developing conception of intracommunal relations affirms a connection that far surpasses in strength the voluntary association upon which the liberal vision of society hinges. In fact, when speaking of the church, "community is far too weak a description."[145] For the form of life within the Christian colony—in what it shows and what it says—incarnates the presence of God in ways that cannot be talked about except in Christian speech.[146]

Hauerwas's mature concept of the strength of interconnections within the Christian colony is so firm that it virtually guarantees continued misunderstanding from the side of liberalism. Thinkers such as Stackhouse cannot help but misconceive Hauerwas's project as long as they think about social relations in only two modes: *analytically*, in which the individual is taken to be the fundamental unit of reality, the building block of the whole, and *sociologically*, in which the aggregate achieves a level of reality in proportion to its size and comprehensiveness. From the vantage of these two modes, the church is relegated to the margins, on the one hand because it is less fundamental than the individual, and on the other hand because it is merely a subset of greater society.

If the misunderstanding between Gloria Albrecht and Hauerwas is one of philosophy vs. theology, the misunderstanding between Stackhouse and Hauerwas is one of civil religion vs. Christian theololgy. Ronald Beiner notes that "liberalism itself instantiates one particular vision of the good, namely, that choice in itself is the highest good."[147] Unsurprisingly, Stackhouse thinks that liberal theology validates this vision, and thus life in the church must only differ from life in the secular political order by degree, not kind. In Stackhouse's final estimation, salvation is something about which each of us must make up his or her own mind, and Christian congregations (just as society in general) are held together by nothing more determinative than voluntary association.

In contrast, Hauerwas thinks that the image of the autonomous self is that from which we must be saved. Converts may initially think that they "choose" to follow Jesus, but such self-description is only a vestige of the condition from which they have been rescued. Slowly, by the process of schooling-by-immersion, converts learn to speak truthfully: we confess that salvation comes not as something we have chosen (as liberalism claims) but as something that has surprised us as a gift. Such an admission can only dawn upon the inhabitants of a particular linguistic community:

> The confessing church, like the conversionist church, also calls people to conversion, but it depicts that conversion as a long process of being baptismally engrafted into a new people, an alternative *polis*, a countercultural social structure called church. It seeks to influence the world by being the church, that is, by being something the world is not and

can never be, lacking the gift of faith and vision, which is ours in Christ. The confessing church seeks the *visible* church, a place, clearly visible to the world, in which people are faithful to their promises, love their enemies, tell the truth, honor the poor, suffer for righteousness, and thereby testify to the amazing community-creating power of God. The confessing church has no interest in withdrawing from the world, but is not surprised when its witness evokes hostility from the world. The confessing church moves from the activist church's acceptance of the culture with a few qualifications. The confessing church can participate in secular movements against war, against hunger, and against other forms of inhumanity, but it sees this as part of its necessary proclamatory action. This church knows that its most credible form of witness (and the most "effective" thing it can do for the world) is the actual creation of a living, breathing, visible community of faith.[148]

First- and second-century readers would have easily recognized in the Apostle Thomas's words, "My Lord and my God," the declaration of loyalty (*Dominus et Deus noster*) that the Emperor Domitian demanded from citizens of the Roman Empire.[149] Thomas's words testify to the fact that the earliest Christians saw their fundamental membership in the church, not in the State.[150] If we follow their example, we must consider salvation as likewise "political," in the sense that Christians have been saved via their deliverance from one *polis* into another.[151] In the words of Cyprian (and Augustine), outside the church there is no salvation (*extra ecclesiam nulla salus*).

The charge of fideism—namely, that Hauerwas speaks a language that only "insiders" can understand—is in one sense justified. But fideism in this sense cannot count against him, since it simply confirms the existence of an alternative *polis* which is the necessary condition for the gospel Hauerwas espouses. As I will argue shortly, the real existence of such a *polis* is itself a necessary condition for outsiders to understand this gospel on its own terms.

THE POLITICS OF APOLOGETICS

The conversations that Hauerwas has carried on with two of his detractors qualify the degree to which the charges of fideism against him have bite. *Contra* Albrecht, if understanding requires intratextual (i.e., intracommunal) participation in the form of life out of which a given claim is made, then the charge of fideism is not false but misguided for presuming that all messages are, in principle, translatable. *Contra* Stackhouse, if salvation is constituted by one's enculturation into the *polis* of the church, then Stackhouse's polemic, one waged from within the ranks of liberalism, is simply symptomatic of the disease from which Christians are being saved, namely, the totalizing grip of the liberal concept of the self and of the liberal society this concept entails.

I turn now, finally, to Hauerwas's long-term conversation with his former teacher, James Gustafson, in order to show that since the gospel is intelligible only when it is "embodied" in the life of a community, the charge of fideism once again falls short of the mark, this time for being freighted with faulty notions of language.

Hauerwas is wearied, but not worried, by the fact that Albrecht misunderstands him for the sake of her philosophical commitments and by the fact that Stackhouse misreads him for the sake of his allegiance to political liberalism. But I suspect that he finds the allegations made against him by his former teacher, current friend, and fellow theologian, James Gustafson, more troubling. Indeed, Hauerwas and Gustafson share much in common: a conviction that human existence is historically conditioned;[152] a concern for the import that behavior (both individual and communal) has for understanding theological claims;[153] the urge to displace the anthropocentric prejudice of most contemporary Christian ethics with a "theocentric" perspective;[154] an eschewal of liberalism's "fictive community" of autonomous rational individuals;[155] a commitment to realism (although, as we shall see, Gustafson's version of realism is impaired by his confusion with regard to the workings of language); and a concern for "truth."[156] The fact that Hauerwas quotes from Gustafson frequently, and with approval nearly as often as not, stands as evidence that Hauerwas finds his conversation with Gustafson a family argument of the sort upon which he thinks the vitality of the Christian tradition depends.

But there it stands: in 1985 Gustafson slapped on Hauerwas the labels of sectarian, tribalist, and fideist.[157] How are we to understand these allegations? Surely the diversity and enormity of the Hauerwasian corpus, which consists almost entirely of occasional essays, many of which are written to those whom he considers "outsiders" in one way or another, shows, *pace* Gustafson, that Hauerwas *does* have something to say. I suspect Gustafson finds this fact curious; at least Paul Holmer had the decency to remain within the bounds of a Wittgensteinian-born confessionalism! But if Hauerwas's writes predominantly to "outsiders," how can Gustafson con-

clude that Hauerwas takes religious language as insular? Of course, Hauerwas disavows *that* position:

> I certainly do not believe, nor did Wittgenstein, that religious convic-
> tions are or should be treated as an internally consistent language game
> that is self-validating. What Wittgenstein has taught me, however, is
> that if we attend to the diversity of our language we learn to appreciate
> what a marvelously diverse world we inhabit and how complex claims
> about the way the world is will inevitably be.[158]

Whence this misunderstanding? I wish to show that Gustafson misunderstands Hauerwas (and therefore mislabels him) on account of modern pre-
sumptions about the way language works that are latent in Gustafson's
views. In other words, if liberals are those who follow Schleiermacher's lead
in trying to make Christianity intelligible to its cultured despisers, then the
substance of their accommodation will be evident in their philosophy of
language, and not just in their epistemological and metaphysical commitments. This can be illustrated from Gustafson's own work.

Gustafson admits to having inherited more from Ernst Troeltsch than
merely the notion of the Church-sect distinction. In his first volume of
Ethics from a Theocentric Perspective he acknowledged Troeltsch as the
source of his comprehensive strategy for knitting together the claims of theology with those of science: the idea of God, which arises in the context of
piety, must not be stated in ways which are incongruent with the well-
established claims of science.[159] Science has this exclusionary power over
theological claims because science, insofar as it offers a description of the
real world, is included in the domain of theology, for "to say anything theological is to say something about how *things really and ultimately are*."[160]
Gustafson's vision of compatibility between science and theology is not at
issue. At stake, however, is the way Gustafson seems to take for granted that
the truthfulness of a sentence—whether empirical or religious—is a function of its ability to *refer* to the world. As Gustafson insists,

> If religion is passionate subjectivity and not related to anything objec-
> tive such as the reality of a sovereign Deity, then whatever induces and
> nourishes those passions is free from critical scrutiny by other per-
> spectives on life. If it is [subjectively] meaningful, one does not worry
> about whether it is true.[161]

Now, Gustafson nowhere indicates that anyone has a vantage point outside the boundaries of the historically conditioned communities that we inhabit so as to be able to measure the correspondence between "language" and "world." In fact, much of the emphasis on piety in his writings is meant to counter the liberal pretense that just anyone, regardless of his or her present or past behavior, can get a perspicuous read on reality. However, the fact that there is only one world "out there" does signify for Gustafson that claims about the world that we accept as well-established (such as those of science) necessarily form parameters for what else can be meaningfully said, including what can be expressed theologically. That Holmer and company think otherwise is what Gustafson finds so ludicrous about their fideism.

> The [putative] incommensurability of scientific and religious language means that the same person or communities will have two very different ways of construing the [singular] reality of life in the world side by side. From this perspective of the division of languages one has no bearing upon the other.[162]

In short, if there is one reality, which all truthful uses of language aim to describe, then religious language is either accountable to the truthful claims of science or else it is rendered vacuous for failing to take an object at all.[163]

Gustafson has made it clear that his work aims at preventing theologians from making tacitly empirical claims.[164] There is but one world out there and it lies in the domain of science to make *empirical* claims about the matrices of powers (physical, social, economic, and so on) in which we find ourselves inextricably tangled.[165] But those with theological eyes, those with proper religious affections, can see something else in the configuration of ultimate reality as well. They are able to make out an "Other" in the midst of interactions with "others":

> The affectivity that "becomes" religious, however, is a response to very particular events and objects; in the religious consciousness these objects and events are perceived to be ultimately related to the powers that sustain us and bear down upon us, to the Ultimate Power on which all life depends.[166]

Unfortunately, that which piety sees so clearly it can say little about. Even biblical narratives are not empirical descriptions.

In my terms, these narratives express human consent to the powers that have brought life into being; that order the range of "objects" and experiences; that create the conditions for possibilities of human developments biologically (genealogies), historically, socially, culturally. The traditional myths and symbols express the awe *and* respect that the senses of dependence, gratitude, possibility and the rest nourish as a result of participation in the powers of life in the world. Religious affectivity is evoked by objects of experience, and in the religious consciousness of the Western religious traditions this evokes piety toward manifold powers and toward the powerful Other that is perceived to be present in and through the world.[167]

In the end, while particular religious claims must not contradict the well-established claims of science, the positive work that they do is reduced to this: religious claims express human consent, awe, and respect to the end that piety is evoked.

What I have just illustrated in the writings of Gustafson is the paradigmatic modern construal of language. Its major premise is that the truth of a sentence lies in its correspondence with some "objective" state of affairs "out there." Accordingly, not only is language learned by ostension, it is inherently representational in nature. Anti-religious thinkers, the most infamous of which was A. J. Ayer, complained that religious and ethical language failed when tested according to public criteria of meaningfulness. Earlier this century, Ayer called such "meaningless" sentences, those which were neither true nor false, "pseudo-propositions."[168] In response, conservative religious thinkers accepted the major premise (meaning-as-reference) but denied that criteria for meaning were universal and public. Thus, the noun "God" in the sentence "God was in Christ reconciling the world to himself" *does* refer, but is verifiable only by means of a non-ostensive faculty, namely, illumination by the Holy Spirit. In contrast, liberal religious thinkers accepted both the major premise (meaning-as-reference) and the minor premise (the criteria of reference are universal and public) but salvaged religious language from meaninglessness by positing religious speech as that which *gestures toward the ineffable* and *expresses the humanly significant*. Thus, religious speech might express human aspiration (Feuerbach), intention (Braithwaite), disposition (Hare), or piety (van Buren).[169]

This sketch ought to be sufficient to indicate Gustafson's affinity for a model of language that Wittgenstein spent over two decades trying to cure us of. At its heart is the belief that language is one thing and that which languages depicts is another. The belief in the singularity of the external world was thought to give purchase to the long-standing agenda of liberal apologetics, namely, the accommodation of Christianity to the contemporary mind.[170] It is for this reason that Gustafson, while distancing himself from the sort of apologetics that defends Christianity, nevertheless winds up faulting Hauerwas for the way his putative fideism "forecloses apologetics."[171] Yet, ironically, Gustafson's own translation of "God" into the language of modern science as "the power that bears down upon us, sustains us . . ." leaves one wondering whether Gustafson is not, in the end, as ineffectual as the early Wittgenstein who stood with his back turned to the Vienna Circle, reading from mystic poetry as a last-ditch attempt to express the ineffable with words.

It appears that Gustafson, despite many affinities with Hauerwas's theology, misunderstands Hauerwas's putative fideism precisely because he is tacitly committed to a purely modern conception of language. In the years between Gustafson's *Treasure in Earthen Vessels* (1961) and the first volume of *Ethics from a Theocentric Perspective* (1981), Hauerwas spent a year reading Wittgenstein's *Philosophical Investigations* line by line as part of a philosophical discussion group that included the Wittgensteinian theologian, David Burrell.[172] This year contributed powerfully to Hauerwas's conversion to an entirely different paradigm for thinking about language. It is unclear to me when this conversion was complete, if ever. I will take up the discussion of Hauerwas's views of language more completely in the final chapter. For the moment, I wish to point out two ways Hauerwas's notion of ethics-as-politics turns on a (later) Wittgensteinian view of language that renders the charge of fideism wide of the mark.

First, Hauerwas does not think that truthfulness has to do with a condition of correspondence that putatively exists between sentences and "reality." Rather, "truthful" names the community that is able to shape a people who, in Wittgenstein's words, can "see the world rightly." The use of the Tractarian phrase here purposely recalls Hauerwas's emphasis on right vision (ethics-as-aesthetics) and Wittgenstein's insistence on transforming the subject as the precondition for the same. With this in mind, consider Hauerwas's direct response to the sort of allegations that Gustafson makes:

> I have argued that the very content of Christian convictions requires that the self be transformed if we are to adequately see the truth of the convictions—e.g., that I am a creature of a good creator yet in rebellion against my status as such. Talk of our sin, therefore, is a claim about

the way we are, but our very ability to know we are that way requires that we have already begun a new way of life. That is why the Christian doctrine of sanctification is central for assessing the epistemological status of Christian convictions. Assessing the truthfulness of religious convictions cannot be separated from the truthfulness of the persons who make those claims.[173]

The transformation of the self that Hauerwas has in mind occurs as one is enculturated into Christian community, which is to say, as he or she becomes a character in this community's story, participates in the form of life constituted by this community's canonical narrative, and learns to speak this community's language as a second first-language.

Second, the narrative which constitutes the truthful community requires an *embodied* apologetic. Here Hauerwas has an advantage not open to Wittgenstein. Wittgenstein struggled tremendously to show what could not be said, expressing himself in the form of aporias that engaged readers in a transformative conversation. But Hauerwas, opting not to engage his opponents on *their* terms, has the advantage of the gift of Christian discourse which, being a particular language, is tightly bound up with the actual life and practices of a particular community. Consequently, the material content of the gospel narrative is displayed by the life of the faithful community, without which corporate life the narratives are unintelligible. He responds at length to Gustafson:

Christianity is no "world view," not a form of primitive metaphysics, that can be assessed in comparison to alternative "world views." Rather, Christians are people who remain convinced that the truthfulness of their beliefs must be demonstrated in their lives. There is a sense in which Christian convictions are self-referential, but the reference is not to propositions but to lives.

. . . the subject of transformation for Christians is not the isolated individual, but a community living through time. For the convictions that Christians hold about the way things are entail the existence of a people, since what we know can only be known through witness. Moreover, contrary to Gustafson's claim that such a community lacks any means to criticize its tradition, its worship of God requires it to be open to continual "reality checks." God comes to this community in the form of a stranger, challenging its smugness, exposing its temptations to false "knowledge," denying its spurious claims to have domesticated God's grace. Thus, one of the tests of the truthfulness of Christian convictions cannot help being the faithfulness of the church.[174]

In these two passages Hauerwas sounds suspiciously like the church's earliest apologists. Granted, many words were bandied about in the second century. However, the trump card of the earliest apologists was their ability to point to the embodiment of the gospel in the concrete life of the church.[175] For early Christian writers, theology was identical to ethics because the gospel embodied in the text was none other than the gospel embodied in the community that preserved *this* text as its canon. The highly abstract and philosophical character of later theology and the subsequent separation of ethics as a distinctive discipline can be traced to the waning of the community's vitality after the third century and exacerbated in the fourth by the merging of church and state under Constantine.[176]

The internal relation between the gospel "message" and the community of believers presupposed by the Patristics was nothing less than an expression of their conviction that salvation was *real*. Hauerwas explains it this way:

> Jesus saves from sin and death. Yet sin and death are embodied in a history that requires an alternative history if our salvation is to be anything more than a vague hope. The name we give the social manifestation that makes that history present is the *church*.[177]

"Sin" (as that from which we must be saved) names a pattern in our history; it describes what sort of character we individually and corporately have played. To be saved from this history requires that our past be retold as a subplot in a different story. However, since part of our lost condition is our inability to escape the confines of our story / history, salvation can only come to us in the form of a concrete gift. *The church is this gift*:

> Salvation is a political alternative that the world cannot know apart from the existence of a concrete people called the church. Put more dramatically, you cannot even know you need saving without the church's being a political alternative.[178]

Such salvation "is not meant to confirm what we already know and / or experience. It is meant to make us a part of a story that could not be known apart from exemplification in the lives of people in a concrete community."[179]

Hauerwas's failure to accommodate liberals by translating the gospel into terms that they can already understand is not an instance of fideism because the gospel can be more powerfully and clearly displayed in the actual life of the church, enculturation into which constitutes the whole of salvation.[180] Of course, the absence of such a church would severely weaken Hauerwas's position. But this danger only points to the fact that Hauerwas's least "scholarly" writings (*Resident Aliens, Where Resident Aliens Live, Lord Teach Us,* and articles such as "The Ministry of the Congregation," not to mention dozens of his sermons which have appeared in print) are actually more central to his project than are his more scholarly essays, since the former describe concrete churches that Hauerwas thinks embody the gospel message. The church is God's new language; it is the gesture in terms of which the story is understood and one which is simultaneously made intelligible by the story.[181]

In conclusion, Hauerwas's growing attention to Christian community in the middle period of his writing—what I have called ethics-as-politics—not only illustrates how deeply ingressed the concept "form of life" has become in his thinking but also overcomes the charge of fideism in three ways. First, as illustrated by Hauerwas's dialogue with Gloria Albrecht, because the attainment of understanding requires prior training in a language by means of participation in a community's characteristic form of life (a necessary requisite for gaining fluency), the charge of fideism misses the mark since it assumes that all messages are, in principle, translatable. Second, in contrast to the liberal vision exemplified by Max Stackhouse, because the content of the good news is that Christians are citizens of a new *polis*, the charge of fideism presupposes the very condition (necessary citizenship in a global community) from which Christians are rescued. Third, as attention to the writings of James Gustafson has shown, the allegation of fideism hinges on a "Fido"-Fido model of language. To the extent that Wittgenstein has convinced us to reject this model of language, the charge of fideism likewise loses its sting.

FIVE

BACK TO THE
ROUGH GROUND

*. . . we must be content . . . to indicate the truth roughly and
in outline. . . .*

*. . . it is by doing just acts that the just man is produced, and by
doing temperate acts, the temperate man; without doing these, no
one would have even a prospect of becoming good.*
　　*But most people do not do these, but take refuge in theory
and think that they are being philosophers and will become good
in this way, behaving somewhat like patients who listen to their
doctors, but do none of the things they are ordered to do. As the
latter will not be made well in body by such a course of treatment,
the former will not be made well in soul by such a course of
philosophy.*

—Aristotle, *Nicomachean Ethics*

　　What is the relationship of theory to practice? Clearly, this question lies at the very heart of ethics. In order to understand how Hauerwas
answers this question it will be helpful to explore the surprising connections
that exist between the internal relationship Wittgenstein saw between language and practice and the distinction that Aristotle made between practical and productive reasoning. As we shall see, the pattern of Wittgenstein's
objections to the mode of rationality adopted by contemporary technological

culture strongly resembles Aristotle's preference for practical reasoning over productive reasoning.

According to Aristotle, human rationality could be expressed in one of three modes: contemplative reasoning (*theoria*), productive reasoning (*technē*), and practical reasoning (*phronēsis*). Strictly speaking, for classical Greek thinkers *theoria* was the contemplation of purely necessary truths (perhaps geometry) and as such had virtually nothing to do with the hurly-burly of human affairs. Rather, anything belonging to the contingent realm of particulars fell under the purview of either *technē* or *phronēsis*. On the one hand, *technē* has to do with production (*poiēsis*), such as the construction of a house or a pair of shoes. *Phronēsis*, on the other hand, has to do with action (*praxis*) in the social sphere and can be distinguished from *technē* on several counts.

First, the end (*telos*) of technical production is something identifiable in itself. Shoes, for example, are complete in themselves and are ontologically distinct from the cobbler. In contrast, the ends of praxis cannot be distinguished from the doing of it or from the doer of it. For example, when I respond to my neighbor in a particular manner, say, that of kindness, this pattern of action is itself the goal of my acting in this manner. Furthermore, I as an agent have more at stake in practicing kindness than has the cobbler in shoes since my action is (partly) constitutive of my own character, whereas for the cobbler, they're just shoes. In his masterful study of Aristotle, Joseph Dunne explains that

> the agent . . . is constituted through the actions which disclose him both to others and to himself as the person that he is. He can never possess an idea of himself in the way that the craftsman possesses the form of his product; rather than his having any definite 'what' as blueprint for his actions or his life, he becomes and discovers 'who' he is through these actions. And the medium for this becoming through action is not one over which he is ever sovereign master; it is, rather, a network of other people who are also agents and with whom he is bound up in relationships of interdependency.[1]

We might say that the ends of *technē* are external to production while the ends of practical reasoning are internally related to the exercise of *phronēsis*.

Second, to be a technician one only needs "bare knowledge."[2] I can correct the spelling on this page armed only with a knowledge of how words ought to be spelled. There is no way to "overdo it" nor does correcting spelling require a sense of good timing. And, in fact, the technician can readily specify the ideal in advance by simply holding out a dictionary. Not so for *phronēsis*; praxis requires numerous on-the-spot judgments. As Aristotle lamented, "but to do this to the right person, to the right extent, at the right time, with the right aim, and in the right way, *that* is not for everyone, nor is it easy."[3] Because action, object, extent, intention, and manner all vary with each new situation, the end of a given phronetic judgment cannot be conceived in advance; a new judgment must be crafted for each new occasion.

Third, *technē* has to do with universalizing rules for procedures which govern production, as it were, from above: "if a man does wish to become master of an art [*technē*] or science [*epistēmē*] he must go to the universal and come to know it as well as possible."[4] The maxim, "Sharpen your wood chisel by holding it 35° to the whetstone" is a rule that generalizes the advice of countless master furniture makers. And it is for love of universals that *technē* comes closest to the theoretical knowledge (*epistēmē*) that characterizes contemplative reasoning. In fact, Aristotle does not shy away from using the terms interchangeably: "productive *epistēmē*" and "theoretical *technē*."[5] Nevertheless, universals are, in an important sense, defective; something is lost in any generalization. Moreover, *technē* masks differences and overlooks particularity on the assumption that universals "contain" the particulars. Yet, the perception of the extent, manner, and time of this "containment" is itself a *phronetic* judgment. Thus, Aristotle concludes that *phronēsis* is more fundamental than *technē*.

Fourth, the approach of *technē* rests on the assumption that the application of a universal is both straightforward and sufficient. On the one hand, objects Aristotle, a universal does not contain its own application, and therefore application of universals cannot be straightforward. In order for reason to move us to action, the (so-called) "syllogism" of practical reason must access particulars as well as universals, since action is about particulars.[6] This is the domain of *phronēsis*. For example, by the approach of *technē* it might be inductively determined that light meats are healthier than red meats. However, if a person lacks the ability to discriminate in this particular case — is *this* chicken breast light meat? — the grasp of the universal ("Light meat is wholesome to eat") cannot lead to action.

On the other hand, Aristotle questions whether one's grasp of the particular ("*This* is light meat") is *sufficient* to lead to action. Why should one choose to eat at all? Or, if one chooses to eat, why choose that which is healthy? As it happens, an endless array of minor premises must be supplied in order to achieve good deliberation [*euboulia*]. And it also falls to the lot of *phronēsis* to intuit both the relevant major and minor premises. In Dunne's words,

> A very essential part of the role of phronesis, then, is to supply appropriate and finely discriminated ultimate minor premises. (Its full role might be outlined as [a] supplying these premises; [b] mobilizing them within a context whose adequate explication, in the case of our example, would involve, in addition to the major premises . . . some ultimate major that would link 'wholesome' via 'healthy' to a conception of the good life [*eudaimonia*]; and [c] supplying this major which, when fully elaborated . . . will be quite a complex proposition, setting out a notion of *eudaimonia* that is 'irreducibly plural' in that it embraces several different virtues. . . .)[7]

However, those who are skilled in practical reasoning do not have to work out this series of judgments in linear order—a very time-consuming task indeed!—but are able to catch up the whole tangle in one fell swoop: "One must come to a stop somewhere. The stopping-point is an act of perception (*aisthēsis*) performed by *nous*."[8] Such a grasp is reasonable but it is not syllogistic.

> Aristotle can offer no more specific guidance than to say that it is to be "determined by reason [*logos*] and in the way in which the *phronimos* would determine it." That the *phronimos* can, in fact depend very little on logos in the sense of principle or reason is made very clear at the end of this discussion; for the matters he has to deal with are concerned with particulars, and so, as Aristotle bluntly asserts, "the decision rests with *aisthēsis*."[9]

Dunne goes on to show that Aristotle thought that practical reasoning springs from an aesthetic insight that is immediate and intuitive. When we perceive "Δ" as a triangle, we do so by an immediate grasp of the complex as if it were something elementary. We do not first observe, "This is a single geometric figure; this figure has three sides and three angles; the sides all meet in single points; the lines and angels are necessarily coplanar . . ." and only then deduce that it must be a triangle. Rather, we grasp the whole in a flash. Aristotle's stopping point, which is simultaneously the true *starting* point for practical reasoning, is an aesthetic apprehension of an "ultimate particular." Because this insight is a function of *phronēsis*, rather than *technē* or *epistēmē*, Aristotle's "theory" of ethics offers ways to free us from the assuming that ethics is necessarily a theoretical task.[10]

Although I have vastly oversimplified the differences between Aristotle's conception of *technē* and *phronēsis*, once we become convinced that there are some glaring differences, it does not take much to convince us, as Dunne attempts to do, that the hallmarks of the modern theoretical approach — one that concerns itself with knowledge that pretends to be "explanatory, generalized, systematic, and transmissible, and at the same time a source of reliable control over the facts that it brings within its ambit" — amount to nothing but an enthronement of *technē*. It is this enshrinement of *technē* that Wittgenstein opposed, like Aristotle, and he did so in three ways. First, the approach to *technē*, when applied to philosophy of language, yields four confusions that arise at the very points of difference between *technē* and *phronēsis*. Second, Wittgenstein's preference for *phronēsis* can be seen in his "religious" opposition to the scientism in the culture that had so thoroughly ingested *technē*. Third, not only are philosophical confusions avoided by honing one's phronetic-linguistic skills, but also the method of this honing must be aporetic in character.

OBJECTING TO *TECHNĒ*

Aristotle's treatment of *phronēsis* was not so much a theory of rationality as an objection to the Socratic tendency to reduce human rationality to mere *technē*. Aristotle never attempted to fully explicate *phronēsis*, for on his view there could never be a *technē*-like explanation of practical reasoning. Dunne has done a great service in showing that the entire Aristotelian corpus reflects a more complicated picture of practical and productive reasoning (*phronēsis* and *technē*, respectively) than can be gleaned from a first reading. On the one hand, the Socratic picture of *technē*, which was standard fare for Greek thinkers, turns out to be much less tidy than expected; crafts such as navigation and medicine, because they involve a critical sense of timing (*kairos*) in their execution, are much more akin to applications of *phronēsis* than other crafts. On the other hand, although Aristotle gives *phronēsis* a great deal of attention in Book 6 of the *Nicomachean Ethics*, he cannot circumscribe its domain with a tidy definition; *phronēsis* is internally related to both an agent's character and experience in the broadest sense of these terms. However, in his treatment of *phronēsis* Aristotle is able to offer a series of objections to the overly simplistic Socratic picture he had inherited from his teacher.

Similarly for Wittgenstein, *technē* makes a far easier target for objections than *phronēsis* does for positive treatment; because it is internally related to so many things, the phronetic-like skill of conceptual fluency must remain something gestured toward. In many ways, Wittgenstein's entire corpus constitutes this gesture. But we can bring Wittgenstein's notion of linguistic judgment into slightly better focus by specifying four objections Wittgenstein raised against seeing language as a form of *technē*.

Showing What Cannot Be Said

Instances of philosophical puzzlement are not hidden contradictions within the grand system of human knowledge but confusions in the head of particular human subjects who don't know their way about.[11] The therapeutic conversation in which Wittgenstein sought to engage his readers promised to achieve for them a certain clarity, but at a price: the conversation had to be a *self*-consuming enterprise in which the reader's vision was transformed. For, philosophy is a matter of "seeing, not proving,"[12] and the role of the philosopher is that of a therapist who leads the patient by means of "intermediate cases" from mystification to perception of "connections."[13]

In one sense, the agreement in phronetic-like judgment upon which language hangs is broader for Wittgenstein than for Aristotle. Aristotle's stopping point was an insight, or perception (*aisthēsis*), of an ultimate particular. But for Wittgenstein the stopping point need not be insight per se, but any number of actions that function as ultimates for us; *Im Angfang war die Tat*—in the beginning was the act.[14] The actions, or reactions, are in an important sense fundamental—even primitive. Nevertheless, they are aesthetically schooled. Thus Wittgenstein compares human understanding with the soundness in judgment that is achieved by the fully trained apprentice who is able to see a pattern, follow a melody, recite a poem, or go on in similarly relevant ways.[15]

In Wittgenstein's mind, language itself was an artistic medium that was able to show more than could simply be denoted. For example, in his celebrated "A Lecture on Ethics," Wittgenstein alluded to the fact that language (its form, its logic, its limits, its internal relation to experience) was capable of expressing one's wonderment at the existence of the world or one's feeling of absolute safety within the world, despite the apparent misuse of language by sentences such as "I wonder at the existence of the world!" whose contrary (i.e., the nonexistence of the world) is literally inconceivable.[16] Between those whose sensitivities have been adequately acclimated to the medium, such expressions disclose something very deep. Wittgenstein feared that his own hands were too coarse for this job, yet he hoped that Longfellow's poem might serve as a fitting motto for his work:

> In elder days of art
> Builders wrought with greatest care
> Each minute and unseen part
> For the gods are everywhere.[17]

Sadly, contemporaries of Wittgenstein, whose approach to language was marked by *technē*, not only disregarded the centrally important *phronēsis*, they perpetuated two sorts of confusion which profane the ineffable. First, metaphysicians attempted to say what could only be shown. Second, logical positivists attempted to proscribe in advance the boundaries of intelligibility.

In 1930 Wittgenstein noted that every explanation begins with a description.[18] Descriptions of *physical* facts enable the construction of models for prediction in physics. Descriptions of *grammatical* facts (i.e., descriptions of the grammar of descriptions of physical facts) are the basis of philosophizing and, by virtue of the form that is embodied in both the world and its descriptions, attention to grammar will yield trustworthy knowledge about the logical structure of the world. Thus, "grammar is a 'theory of logical types'."[19] Grammatical analysis is as deep as theorizing can go. From the stance of his earliest views on form, Wittgenstein thought that philosophy was a legitimate enterprise so long as its "explanations" converge on the logical limits of form from the side of language just as theories in physics converge on the logical limits of form from the side of phenomena. The co-participation of language and world in the same logical scaffolding renders the fear of slippage between physics and philosophy groundless. By the same token, this co-participation also debars philosophers from succumbing to any "metaphysical" impulse to construct a parallel universe cluttered with a fanciful ontology of "forces" and "entities" and "essences" in imitation of the methodology of physics, precisely because to do so would be completely disengaged from those formal considerations necessary to make the pictorial character of language work in the first place.

Consider, for example, the impossibility of two colors occupying the same space in a visual field. What kind of impossibility is this? A metaphysician might treat this as correlative to physical impossibility and explain it by positing fictions—laws of nature, space, time—which *prevent* (a type of causation) the simultaneity of two colors. But what work has been done by this explanation? It is idle on two counts. First, it uses the noun "law" in a way which has no criterion for its use. Second, this law is said to "prevent" a situation that we cannot even describe. For Wittgenstein, it is precisely our inability to describe this situation that shows the impossibility to be a logical one, rather than a metaphysical one. What cannot be said (i.e., described) also cannot be actualized, because both language and world embody a form — in this case, color form — whose logical structure excludes the impossible.[20]

Strictly speaking, what language pictures are not objects and events "out there" but our object-like and event-like experiences.[21] Because Wittgenstein conceived these experiences as themselves a function of language (we think in a language), he could say that language and that which it pictures are internally related. Nevertheless, ordinary language is functionally realistic if for no other reason than for the sake of convenience.[22] It is far easier to say, "The red ball is bouncing toward me," than it would be to precisely describe my perceptions in a piecemeal fashion: "I perceive a circular patch of redness (one that is increasing in size), an alteration in sphericity and compression, a parabolic pattern of motion, the sound of 'boinginess'," and so forth. Clearly, our functionally realistic language is a convenient shorthand for avoiding an "unmanageably complicated phenomenological description."[23]

The trouble with some metaphysicians, however, is their tendency to ignore the fact that all sentences "in no matter how complicated a way, still in the end refer to immediate experience."[24] By Tractarian standards, metaphysical claims that purportedly refer to nonexperiential realities are literally senseless.[25]

Where does this leave physics? Theoretical physics constructs sentences which, from the outside, have every appearance of being literally meaningless but, when taken in the context of linguistic models, show that signs may have a collective meaning which *does* correspond to the structure of human experience. Thus, Wittgenstein likens the theoretical physicist to the parent who draws pictures of chairs, chains, and choo-choos for a child to identify. But in an important contrast, the *meta*-physician is like the child who, in imitation of the parent, scribbles on a bit of paper and then asks, "What's *this?*"[26]

Does this mean that Wittgenstein espoused some sort of Kantian idealism (perhaps a linguistic form)? Not at all. But it is very difficult to imagine what Wittgenstein was up to without borrowing categories of modern philosophy to describe him. And therein lies the problem; the fact that Wittgenstein repudiated the picture theory of language meant that he did not occupy the same conceptual space as other "modern" thinkers, from Thomas Hobbes to Wittgenstein's own contemporaries. Of course, what Wittgenstein did envision could not be easily spelled out: "Not empiricism and yet realism in philosophy, that is the hardest thing."[27]

If Wittgenstein has little patience for metaphysicians, he is even less charitable toward the anti-metaphysical system-building of the logical positivists. Ironically, Wittgenstein's devastating attack on the intelligibility of metaphysics was quickly hailed as the missing link in the evolution of logical positivism. That logical positivism turned particularly surly toward metaphysics, ethics, aesthetics, and theology under the influence of the *Tractatus* can be seen in the writings of one charter member of the Vienna Circle, Rudolph Carnap. In 1922 Carnap had begun to write, in opposition to the eminent metaphysician Henrí Bergson, an essay called *Der logische Aufbau der Welt*, a piece he would not finish until 1925. Carnap's polemic was polite and even tentative. Russell Nieli summarizes the flavor of this essay:

> In *Aufbau* Bergson is treated as a respected philosopher, whose opposing views on the use of the term 'science' deserve serious consideration, and whose views on the nature of metaphysics are even quoted at one point to illustrate an area of agreement between the two philosophies.[28]

Yet Carnap credited a radical turn in his outlook to the reading of the *Tractatus* sometime before 1928. When he picked up his pen again in 1932, this time against Heidegger, his tone was far less amiable.[29] He flatly declared:

> Through the development of modern logic it has become possible to give a new and sharper answer to the question of the validity and justification of metaphysics. . . . In the realm of metaphysics (including all value-theory and norm-science) logical analysis leads to the negative conclusion that *the alleged statements in this area are totally meaningless.* Thus is achieved a radical victory over metaphysics. . . .[30]

Ironically, what began as an attempt to do away with one error of metaphysics, namely, that of simply not making sense, ended up reproducing another error; logical positivists were as dogmatic about what did not exist as the metaphysicians had been about what did exist. But at least the mystical metaphysicians were cognizant of their own limitations.

6.372   So people stop short at natural laws as at something unassailable, as did the ancients at God and Fate.

And they both are right and wrong. But the ancients were
clear, in so far as they recognized one clear terminus, whereas
the modern system makes it appear as though *everything* were
explained.

The false confidence of the logical positivists stemmed from the way that
they overlooked the necessity of skilled judgment at every level of human
perception, even in the perception of so-called simples such as patches of
color.[31] From this Tractarian remark we see that Wittgenstein never intended to *refute* the metaphysicians. He merely intended to *discipline* their
use of language. Wittgenstein thought that religious mystics (such as Tolstoy) were on to something of utmost importance. He contended that the
nature of language prevented direct talk about the mystical. But he never
disdained the role that religious mysticism played in the life of mystics. In
contrast, Wittgenstein did repudiate logical positivism for the way their scientism discounted that which is truly important.

In Wittgenstein's eyes, the scientific worldview was a chief contribu-
tor to the demise of culture, and he recoiled at the suggestion that the modern *Weltanschauung* was in any sense "enlightened." These facts had been
lost on Carnap when he read the *Tractatus*. He could only register shock to
learn later, upon meeting Wittgenstein in person, that the author of the
Tractatus was more mystical than scientific. Carnap reflects on this first encounter in his autobiography:

His point of view and his attitude toward people and problems, even
theoretical problems, were much more similar to those of a creative
artist than to those of a scientist; one might almost say, similar to those
of a religious prophet or seer. When he started to formulate his view on
some specific philosophical problem, we often felt the internal struggle that occurred in him at that very moment, a struggle by which he
tried to penetrate from darkness to light under an intense and painful
strain, which was even visible on his most expressive face. When finally,
sometimes after a prolonged arduous effort, his answer came forth, his
statement stood before us like a newly created piece of art or a divine
revelation. Not that he asserted his views dogmatically. . . . But the impression he made on us was as if insight came to him as through divine
inspiration, so that we could not help feeling that any sober rational
comment or analysis of it would be profanation.[32]

This citation draws attention to the two ways metaphysics has been historically opposed. In the first place have stood those such as the logical positivists who, when faced with a metaphysical claim, asserted with Otto Neurath that "one must indeed be silent, but not *about* anything."[33] In the second place stand those mystics who repudiate metaphysical theorems for the way each enunciation *profanes what is ineffable*.[34] If the *Tractatus* functions as a self-consuming artifact, and if we take its last five pages seriously, then we must conclude that Wittgenstein is anti-metaphysical in this second, mystical sense and that he intended the *Tractatus* "as a ladder in the mystical ascent along the via negativa."[35] Thus, when at 6.432 Wittgenstein wrote that "God does not reveal himself *in* the world," he was not claiming that the notion of "God" is entirely contentless but that it simply has no referent *in the world*. There is an "aboutness" to metaphysical claims, but only an "aboutness" *shown* by our incurable urge to make them![36] Wittgenstein's long-time close friend Paul Engelmann would eventually say that it was this perspective that radically separated Wittgenstein from the logical positivists.

> A whole generation of disciples was to take Wittgenstein as a positivist, because he has something of enormous importance in common with the positivists: he draws the line between what we can speak about and what we must be silent about just as they do. The difference is only that they have nothing to be silent about. Positivism holds—and this is its essence—that what we can speak about is all that matters in life. *Whereas Wittgenstein passionately believes that all that really matters in human life is precisely what, in his view, we must be silent about.*[37]

Thus the cardinal problem in philosophy for Wittgenstein was the problem of becoming skilled enough to perceive what can be shown, but not said.

The point of Wittgenstein's showing/saying distinction (as in TLP 4.022) can now be seen to serve a twofold purpose. On the one hand, the point of showing the logical form of language was to show that the world and language are isomorphic. Logic is the structure of both world and language. But as such, logic is also shown to be an in-the-world structure and, consequently, language is bereft of the means for transcending this limit to speak about the "beyond-the-world." On the other hand, to grasp the in-worldly nature of language and logic is also to be pointed to what lies beyond it; to Wittgenstein it may have suggested the possibility of *ekstasis*—a breaking out of this logical scaffolding in mystical religious experience.

Certainly a close reading of Wittgenstein's life leaves the reader startled by the stranger features of his narrative—his hermetic existence, the giving away of his share of the family fortune, his serious consideration of becoming a priest or monk, his retreat from academics to teach schoolchildren in rural Austria—features which may be understood by an appeal to a life-transforming encounter with the Christian gospel through the writings of Tolstoy. Unfortunately, the reverence with which Wittgenstein held his conversion experience also accounts for his reluctance to write about it. Besides the circumstantial evidence of his eccentricity, we only have his repeated recommendations to others that they read Tolstoy's *Gospel in Brief* as evidence that perhaps something like a mystical (perhaps even evangelical) religious experience occurred for Wittgenstein in 1914.[38]

The logical positivists stated clearly their conclusion that statements about God, the good, and so forth, were devoid of meaning and, as such, not worth troubling about. For Wittgenstein, however, the point of decrying, for example, ethical statements as literally meaningless was not in the conclusion that ethics was thereby not worth troubling about. Rather, the point of logical analysis was to show that whatever ethical statements were ultimately "about" must be gotten to by another way. What is shown both in the "primitive" religious rituals and in our incurable urge to make metaphysical claims with a severely limited medium (i.e., language) is an "aboutness" that lies beyond the world.[39]

"I'll teach you the differences"

The second way Wittgenstein's opposition to technical views of language runs parallel to Aristotle's own account of *phronēsis* can be seen in Wittgenstein's rhetoric against the totalizing aspirations inherent in contemporary culture's speculative mode of rationality.

Wittgenstein's misgivings about the totalizing impulse of theory were initially shaped by his early reading of Heinrich Hertz's *Principles of Mechanics*. Hertz observed that in order for any description of phenomena to be considered a system of mechanics it must, obviously, meet criteria of logical consistency and agreement with observations. However, more than one model can satisfy these two criteria. Hertz went on to argue that his model was superior to both Newtonian mechanics and the reigning nineteenth-century paradigm by virtue of a third criterion: functionalism, or expediency (*Zweckmäßigkeit*)—a term that included the ideas of conceptual clarity and the appropriateness of the model for its intended purposes. Hertz proposed a mathematical model of mechanics with the distinct advantage of its being subject to a criterion that was *internal* to the model itself. Furthermore, as Janik and Toulmin have pointed out, Hertzian models are, in effect, self-limiting (rather than totalizing), since their mathematical form largely determines the range of their application.[40] What is important to note for our purposes is that Hertz recognized both the possibility of rival systems of description and also the possibility that multiple descriptions (models) can be constructed from within a given system. In this case, "we can . . . have no knowledge as to whether the systems which we consider in mechanics agree in any other respect with the actual systems of nature we intend to consider, than in this alone—that the one set of systems are models of the other."[41] In this way Hertz avoided the problem faced by empiricists, namely, the inability to pronounce upon whether or not a model was "getting it right" as measured by its "correspondence with reality." For Hertz "getting it right" was none other than the success of the model in fulfilling its own purposes.

Hertz's conclusion suggests that no system of description can ever be objectively correct—where "objectivity" implies taking the mythical stance outside both the model (language) and the world (reality) in order to evaluate their correspondence. In the *Tractatus* Wittgenstein managed to avoid this explicit denial by asserting that the criterion for correct language use (what Hertz called *Zweckmäßigkeit*) was internal to logical form (thereby rendering it impossible that the "clear and appropriate" system judge itself mistaken).[42] Yet, after disowning the Tractarian implications of a language-world dichotomy (sometime after 1930), Wittgenstein made even more explicit his adherence to Hertz's conclusion. In *Philosophical Remarks* Wittgenstein observed that the totalizing tendency of any theoretical model stemmed from the fact that comparisons between two systems can be made only if one first forms a new system that includes them both.[43] However, such a system would have no privileged status over the rival systems it claims to envelope:

> I can play with the chessmen according to certain rules. But I can also invent a game in which I play with the rules themselves. The pieces in my game are now the rules of chess, and the rules of the game are, say, the laws of logic. *In that case I have yet another game and not a metagame.*

Each system is a game in its own right and "while I can play, I can play, and everything's all right." But, "if inconsistencies were to arise between the rules of the game of [say] mathematics, it would be the easiest thing in the world to remedy. All we have to do is make a new stipulation to cover the case in which the rules conflict, and the matter's resolved." So the worry to "prove" a mathematical system to be consistent is ill-conceived. Mathematics is a calculus, and one plays the game until there is conflict, at which point one simply adjusts the rules of play. But in so doing, one simply has made up a different game.[44]

Wittgenstein thought that the same features of model-making that hold for mathematics hold for language as well. Unsurprisingly, about the time Wittgenstein made plain his rejection of foundationalism in mathematics, opting instead for a "conventional" approach, the game metaphor became dominant in his thoughts on language. Just as mathematics is a calculus and philosophy of mathematics amounts to elucidating its rules, so too, language is a calculus and philosophy of language amounts to elucidating its grammar.[45] Speakers use the linguistic calculus until there is a problem, and then simply make adjustments to usage. No language-game needs to be "justified" before it can be played; the playing of the game *is* its justification, and what we call "justification" is itself one language-game.

Therefore, modernity's penchant for creating a totalizing architectonic that explains "everything" is only evidence that its adherents are too close to see how they are playing: "The chief trouble with our grammar is that we don't have a *bird's eye view* of it."[46] In this statement we see Wittgenstein scold himself for his former attempt to view the world as a limited whole—the hope of finding an ahistorical, alinguistic place to stand from which we can see the world from the aspect of eternity (*sub species aeternitatis*) is but a pipedream.[47] As a result, the best we can do is describe the linguistic calculus in the play of its "games." Yet we thirst for a grand unification schema: "What people are after is something quite different. A certain paradigm hovers before their mind's eye and they want to bring the calculus *into line with this paradigm*."[48]

By 1932, Wittgenstein not only objected to the myth of objectivity, he also sought to expose the totalizing pretensions of general theories of language. For example, in *Philosophical Grammar* he observed that we are unable even to give a precise definition for the term "proposition." It is a concept with no clear boundaries. Even a gesture can function as a proposition. Because we cannot define "proposition," all our attempts to define "language" in terms of propositions are idle. Languages at best share a family resemblance. That being the case, there are no grounds for asserting a set of "super-rules" which govern the use of all the linguistic rules (grammars) of all languages. What counts as a sentence is whatever *functions* as a sentence in the system of expressions in which it occurs. Furthermore, to say that a proposition is "senseless" does not imply that the critique possesses a single criterion of falsifiability. Rather, to recognize a proposition as senseless is only to say that it doesn't belong to "the particular game its appearance makes it seem to belong to."[49]

Wittgenstein's opposition to general theories of language can be illustrated by his pedagogical style. He remarked in a letter to Russell regarding the *Blue and Brown Books* that

> Two years ago I held some lectures in Cambridge and dictated some notes to my pupils so that they might have something to carry home with them, in their hands if not in their brains. — (I think it is very difficult to understand them as so many points are just hinted at.)[50]

What made his lectures so enigmatic was the care with which he framed them so as to not be misunderstood. He explained to Drury, "My type of thinking is not wanted in this present age, I have to swim so strongly against the tide. Perhaps in a hundred years people will really want what I am writing."[51] Apparently Wittgenstein saw his philosophy of language as belonging to a different system of description than that held by his contemporaries. Through his dealings with the Vienna Circle, Wittgenstein came to be all too painfully aware that any statement which has the appearance of a general explanation will inevitably be mistaken for the sort of theorizing rampant in his day. This was the sort of mistake made by logical positivists who simply appropriated the *Tractatus* as their own, in total disregard of Wittgenstein's stated intentions.[52] In subsequent works Wittgenstein sought to outfox the would-be plagiarists by skillfully weaving a tapestry of remarks so tight that no thread could be unraveled and sewn into the warp and weft of another conceptual fabric.

Of course, it was not the speculative character of musings over language that Wittgenstein opposed per se. He himself was occasionally guilty of expressing himself in quasi-theoretical fashion: "perhaps it is like this. . . ." But what exonerates him of inconsistency is the fact that he provisionally offered a *large number* of such claims, each of which runs slightly against the grain of the others—a fact that shows what he is really up to. As we shall see shortly, Wittgenstein expressed himself aporetically in order to create a conversation, the limits of which would only make sense to those who had been sufficiently engaged so as to become fluent interlocutors. This conversation, in an important sense, created and fulfilled the conditions of its own meaningfulness, namely, the formation of a community which, by virtue of its language practices and form of life, shared Wittgenstein's outlook.

What Wittgenstein explicitly opposed was the totalizing tendency present in nearly all system-builders—especially in those who crave a general explanation of language. This resistance resonates with the two other ways of narrating the evolution of his philosophical method. On the one hand, once the human subject had migrated to the very center of Wittgenstein's thinking, he could not envision a privileged status for any totalizing system. Of chief importance is not the putative status of general explanations as repositories of "objective" truths (as if meaning were something that could simply be siphoned off by individuals in isolation), but rather the way ordinary people migrate toward mutual understanding by virtue of the endless interplay of language and life. "What we call 'understanding' is related to countless things that happen before and after the reading of *this* sentence."[53] Since he held that understanding hinges on the entire fabric of human subjectivities, Wittgenstein can be seen as siding with Kierkegaard who disdained theoretical *technē* for its "objective tendency, which proposes to make everyone an observer, and in its maximum to transform him into so objective an observer that he becomes almost a ghost . . . [a tendency which] naturally refuses to know or listen to anything except what stands in relation to itself."[54]

On the other hand, Wittgenstein's atheoretical stance is symptomatic of the journey his conception of form has taken. Wittgenstein's heavy reliance on the participation of language in logical form made plausible the logical positivists' claims that the *Tractatus* is commensurable with structuralism.[55] But later works, beginning perhaps as early as 1930, show ways in which Wittgenstein displayed a growing attention to the form of communal life. The lack of translingual criteria to guarantee understanding—a role formerly filled by the Tractarian notion of form—created a space which conventionalism was to fill for him: "The calculus is as it were autonomous.—Language must speak for itself."[56]

"Back to the rough ground!"

If production can be distinguished from praxis by the way *technē* is able to conceive and specify its ends "objectively"—which is to say, needing no assistance from sound judgment—the third way Wittgenstein unintentionally mimicked Aristotle's preference for *phronēsis* is shown by the challenge he posed to those who think it possible to specify what *ideal* language might amount to.

Recall that in the *Tractatus* Wittgenstein indicated that a sentence can be at risk of meaninglessness either for lack of content or for lack of form.

Because philosophical theses are sentences formed in ordinary language, they are vulnerable to the same dangers. Of course, Wittgenstein opposed both the kind of theorizing that affirms (as in the case of medieval metaphysics) and the kind that denies (as in the case of logical positivism) putatively straightforward claims about the beyond-the-world realm, because such theories are doubly troubled: they are both formless and contentless.

A further danger emerges in the sort of theorizing that is so formally enchanting that one is tempted to see content where there is none. One of Wittgenstein's favorite examples of this sort of theoretics run amok is found in Plato's *Theaetetus*. In *Philosophical Grammar* Wittgenstein reported the passage from 189A as follows:

> SOCRATES: "And if you have an idea must it not be an idea of *something*?
> THEAETETUS: "Necessarily."
> SOCRATES: "And if you have an idea of something, mustn't it be of something real?"
> THEAETETUS: "It seems so."
> SOCRATES: "So if someone has an idea of what is not, he has an idea of nothing?"
> THEAETETUS: "It seems so."
> SOCRATES: "But surely if he has an idea of nothing, then he hasn't any idea at all?"
> THEAETETUS: "That seems plain."[57]

Here the error lies in presupposing that the verb "to think" functions in the same way as the verbs "seeing," "hearing," and "touching."[58] Plato's account reified all objects of thought by assuming that the transitive verb "to think" required a concrete object to receive the verb's action. But by this line of reasoning one might conclude (erroneously) that *purple, love*, and *equity* all "exist" in a physical sense. But we cannot seriously maintain that other concrete properties hold as they do for physical existents. For example, can purple be said to pass out of existence?[59] Or, if we think about the dog that happens at this moment to be missing from the back yard, does it follow that we are not thinking at all, since there is no "something" (namely, Fido) to correspond to our judgment? In effect, Plato's Socrates, by concluding that all intentional objects are real in the same sense that physical objects are real, has mistaken a type II proposition (senseless and form-bearing) for a type I proposition (sensible and form-bearing).

Wittgenstein lamented this common response to type II propositions because, first, it mistakenly assumed that all propositions are empirical ones, and second, it seemingly supported the idea that the scientific-empirical world view was able to engulf all language use under its domain. In contrast, if we are clear about the kind of criteria embedded in the pictorial character of ordinary language, type II propositions must be dealt with as type II propositions. Rather than posit an object where there is none, we ought to be asking ourselves, "What is the legitimate way to *use this term?*" In striking contrast to Socrates' line of reasoning, Wittgenstein concluded, "Questions about 'existence' are really requests for a rule about the proper way to *speak* of something."[60]

I have already outlined some of the ways in which Wittgenstein's notion of "form" underwent drastic transformation. The further down this road he traveled, the more he associated form with the practice of ordinary language. Originally, he conceived ordinary language as "limited," which is to say, too coarse a tool for philosophy, especially philosophy of language.[61] But by 1931 he had concluded that this limit was not a "limitation" in the sense that it could be fixed by the invention of an *ideal* language. He wrote, "How strange if logic were concerned with an 'ideal' language and not with ours. For what would this ideal language express?"[62] Rather, the real problem lay in the inevitable finitude of human existence. In his journal he mused, "A curious analogy could be based on the fact that even the hugest telescope has to have an eye-piece no larger than the human eye."[63] The problem is not so much that language is limited as it is that language-*users* are limited! All that which we can sensibly talk about is inextricably bound up with the general shape of human experience.[64] And with this insight Wittgenstein began to see *human living*—rather than logical form—as fundamental to language. To put the same point differently, Wittgenstein after 1931 exhibited a growing tendency to identify the form which governs language as none other than "form of life," which is to say, the weave of life lived in human community.

Consequently, Wittgenstein's growing objection to general explanation had to do with the way system-building divorces language from life: "In the theories and battles of philosophy we find words whose meanings are well-known to us from everyday life used in an ultraphysical sense."[65] Perhaps nowhere is the urge to sublime the logic of language more prevalent than in the philosophy of Wittgenstein's contemporary, Polish mathematician Alfred Tarski.[66] For example, Tarski theorized that terms such as "true" and "corresponds to," when applied to other sentences, belong to a higher class of language called metalanguage. And, of course, judgments about the "truth" of metalinguistic claims would be sentences belonging to an even higher class of languages (meta-metalanguage). The only way to avoid an infinite regress of metalanguages is the axiomatizing of metalanguage at some point.[67] But then, what can be the cash value of assuming, as Tarski has done, that the word "true" is an adjective that qualifies sentences in a manner similar to the way the adjective "orange" qualifies material objects such as my son's basketball? What kind of *objects* are sentences? Perhaps this practice is on the same order as Socrates' assumption that thinking a negation ("There are no deer in my bathtub") is not really thinking at all.

In discussing mathematics, Wittgenstein was quick to deny the possibility of metamathematics and, therefore, the possibility of a "hierarchy of proofs," because in mathematics everything is of the same type or class.[68] In Wittgenstein's view, a recursive "proof" cannot drive to a particular generalized conclusion, but rather "the recursion shows nothing but itself," which is to say, a recursion shows a recursive *procedure*.[69] Thus Wittgenstein's account of mathematics was able to avoid the problem that, in Aristotle's eyes, productive reasoning (*technē*) could never solve, namely, that of bridging from universals to particulars. And similarly for language: we can stop at the recursion itself and feel no compulsion to generalize beyond it so long as we understand what is *shown* in the recursion, namely, a procedural rule. Thus the assertion "The sentence 'p' is true" is not the translation of p into metalanguage M. Nor does the claim "The sentence 'the sentence "p" is true' is true" belong to the meta-metalanguage M'. Rather, each string of words, despite their complexity, serves as a linguistic variable which substitutes for the simple sentence 'p'. To say "'p' is true" is to say nothing more than "p."[70]

What Wittgenstein objected to in approaches like Tarski's was the fact that we have no resource for talking about words and sentences except by using the language of ordinary life.

> When I talk about language (words, sentences, etc.) I must speak the language of every day. Is this language somehow too coarse and material for what we want to say? Then how is another one to be constructed?—And how strange that we should be able to do anything at all with the one we have![71]

If philosophy in general, and philosophy of language in particular, are built on the back of ordinary language, then the sense of each linguistic term will be of the same order of magnitude as that of ordinary language. If ordinary words get their meaning from the use to which humans put them, then a word such as "sentence" or "true" has no privileged status but only a sense that terminates in the application that ordinary language-users give it. The important difference between Wittgenstein and Tarski, then, is that for Wittgenstein the sense of both "kinds" of sentences is derived from what human being do with words:

> In reflecting on language and meaning we can easily get into a po-sition where we think that in philosophy we are not talking of words and sentences in quite a common-or-garden sense, but in a sublimated and abstract sense. —As if a particular proposition wasn't really the thing that some person utters, but an ideal entity (the "class of all syn-onymous sentences" or the like). But is the chess king that the rules of chess deal with such an ideal and abstract entity too?
>
> (We are not justified in having any more scruples about our lan-guage than the chess player has about chess, namely none.)[72]

In conclusion, Wittgenstein's third objection to theorizing stems from the nature of ordinary language. Since all explanations are framed in lan-guage, we have no extra-linguistic means for explaining, validating, or jus-tifying the way we use language: "What is spoken can only be explained in language and so in this sense language itself cannot be explained."[73] Theo-ries about how language functions reduce to mere descriptions of use, be-cause grammatical conventions can neither be justified nor refuted without using these same conventions.[74]

Realism without Empiricism

Finally, the fourth way Wittgenstein's polemic against theoretics is analo-gous to Aristotle's preference for *phronēsis* over *technē*, relates to the way that ends (*teloi*) of technical production are something identifiable in them-selves, distinct from both technique and technician. When one approaches language in a way akin to *technē*, one assumes that language can be dis-cussed and described as an entity that exists in its own right in distinction from both its speakers and their world. In contrast, Wittgenstein became captivated by the importance of phronetic-like linguistic judgment precisely because we lack the means for making intelligible claims about an *external* relation between language and world. What Wittgenstein espoused, there-fore, was not the bipolar opposite of critical realism, as many have assumed, but an alternative to the picture that holds both realists and nonrealists in its grip: "Not empiricism and yet realism in philosophy, that is the hardest thing."[75]

Paradoxically, the natural sciences have flourished under the assumption that there is an extra-linguistic world of objects "out there" to which scientific hypotheses (at least provisionally) correspond. However, this flourishing came at a price. The German Romantics (1790–1820) a generation before Wittgenstein bemoaned the way the scientific view alienated human beings from a dead material world. As they understood the problem, "the only solution appeared to be to reconceptualize the relationship between man and nature, and let a higher, more subtle philosophy repair the damage that analytical crudities had inflicted."[76] Wittgenstein provided this more subtle reconceptualization by forging a philosophical method that dealt with our world as *internally* related to our language. When I use the term "internally related" I am not stipulating yet another picture of how language and world are related. Rather, I am making what Wittgenstein would call a "grammatical remark" about the limits of what can intelligibly be said about the world. Wittgenstein himself used the term partly in reaction to his teacher, Bertrand Russell. In Russell's day, Hegelian idealism was the reigning paradigm in British thought. Russell identified the doctrine of internal relation as central to idealism. This doctrine conceived all relations between objects as internal to the nature of each object and, hence, as the co-participation of each object in each other's nature. Under the influence of G. E. Moore, Russell rejected this notion of internal relations and substituted in its place a version of Platonic realism that took both objects and relations as objectively real in their own right. Wittgenstein's genius, as Russell's student, was to recover the notion of internal relations without making it liable to the problems that faced the Hegelians—among other things, the inability to say something truthful short of saying everything. In particular, Wittgenstein's notion of internal relations did not purport to describe relations between objects in the world (as it had for the Hegelians) but rather gestured toward the irreducibly linguistic character of the "world." Now while it might appear that the speaking of a sentence requires mastery of the entire language in which it is embedded, and hence of an entire linguistic world to which it is internally connected (a claim that rivals the Hegelian demand for comprehensive knowledge en route to conveying absolute truth), in Wittgenstein's mind, boundary conditions for using language need to be specified neither in advance nor comprehensively; one merely needs sufficient knowledge of how to go on, that is, make the next linguistic move(s), in a particular case.[77] We can begin to get a glimpse of the scope of Wittgenstein's revolution by seeing, first, how he challenged representationalism as a general explanation of language, and second, the ways in which Wittgenstein came to view language as socially constituted.

Wittgenstein began his intellectual journey with the notion that somehow language pictured or modeled the world in such a way that language and world stood in agreement. Confusion ensued when logical positivists thought that we could draw up the terms of this agreement, as it were, by "lines of connection" or "representation." What kind of connection could this be? Mechanical? Electrical? Psychological? But mechanical, electrical, and psychological connections can fail. So the search was for an *infallible* connection unlike anything else in the world. The positivists were tempted to think, further, that this connection "authorized" the sense of a given word; the object on the table full of coffee somehow validates the word "cup." However, postulating a causal connection between sign and signified is not satisfying because we have no criterion by which we can judge when the effect goes awry. Nor is positing a psychological explanation any more satisfactory. For example, suppose that I stipulate that a word corresponds to an object if and only if both the word and the object give rise to the identical "idea" in my mind. This hypothesis is a description that *uses* the very words it is attempting to describe as the *means* for making the description. Thus, it becomes evident that we can get no deeper than this description; we cannot get outside the language to make our understanding of language any more fundamental than language itself. "It is in language that it is all done."[78]

Wittgenstein concluded that the chief problem with representationalism is that there is no way to talk about what language gets compared with without *talking* about it; there is no criterion for knowing I've got the right "this" (this effect, this referent, this object, this sensation, this word) unless language is already in place. Therefore, the "meaning" of a word can only be determined by its place in the linguistic system.[79] Investigation into meaning is grammatical, as is the explanation of meaning: "The connection between 'language and reality' is made by definition of words, and these belong to grammar so that language remains self-contained and autonomous."[80] If, then, we have no criterion by which the "connection" between language and world can be evaluated, the talk of "connection" becomes senseless.

Although there is ample evidence in the corpus that Wittgenstein abandoned the notion that language somehow corresponds to the world, this abandonment cannot be pinpointed historically, because nowhere does he explicitly refute this idea. And for good reason: a refutation would require

appealing to the very picture he wants to disabuse us of.[81] And this begins
to get at the heart of what turn-of-the-century empiricists (contemporary
empiricists prefer to go by the name "critical realists") found so maddening
about Wittgenstein. In *Philosophical Grammar* Wittgenstein wrote, "Here
instead of harmony or agreement of thought and reality one might say: the
pictorial character of thought."[82] Wittgenstein dropped the noun "picture"
(as in "picture theory") and suggested in its place the adjective "pictorial."
Why? The substitution signifies a marked shift in his outlook. With the insight that neither form nor method of projection can be specified except
in terms of the other, Wittgenstein realized that there is a conventionalism
that enables pictures of various sorts to adequately and successfully represent the experiential world. This insight contributed to his growing conviction that pictures are not something we look at, but something we look
with.[83] From here it is a very short step to realizing that not only are linguistic pictures of the world governed by convention, but indeed the entire
empiricist notion of "language-link-world" is itself just such a conventional
picture!

Wittgenstein's Tractarian picture theory of language presupposed a particular picture by means of which reality was conceived. So long as this presupposition went unrecognized, the theories born of it appeared to have
universal sovereignty. But Wittgenstein resisted this pretense by exposing
the arbitrariness of pictorial thought. Consider the following passage.

> The sense of a proposition and the sense of a picture. If we com-
> pare a proposition with a picture, we must think whether we are com-
> paring it to a portrait (a historical representation) or to a genre-picture.
> And both comparisons have point.
> Sentences in fiction correspond to genre-pictures.
> "When I look at a genre-picture, it 'tells' me something even
> though I don't believe (imagine) for a moment that the people I see
> in it really exist, or that there have really been people in that situation."
> Think of the quite different grammar of expressions:
> "This picture shows people in a village inn."
> "This picture shows the coronation of Napoleon."[84]

The Tractarian picture theory easily explains how the coronation of Napo-
leon could be painted, because portraits—even flawed ones—are what the
picture theory is all about. But the picture theory cannot account for the
meaningfulness of a genre-picture (depictions of ordinary objects arranged
realistically but with no actual referent state of affairs). Genre-pictures refer

only to themselves. The world is, as it were, contained within the bounds of the painting. So too with literary fiction—it creates its own world. In this example Wittgenstein challenges the assumption that language is necessarily externally related to the world. He could have mustered many more examples, and in other places he does allude to the "multifariousness of what we call 'language'."[85] But the fact that he only provides one counterexample to portraits shows as much as if he had multiplied the number of his examples. By offering an alternative model (genre-picture) to the representationalist's model (portrait), he is not claiming that this new model is really the way things are. Rather, he is robbing representationalists of the right to say that theirs is the only view possible, that reality "must" match their description. In one swift stroke he excised the "must" out of the representationalist's picture of things and relativized the "necessity" of any general explanation of language based on this, or any other single, picture.

If representationalists conceive of the world and language as externally related, then Wittgenstein's alternative has been said to treat language as internally related to the world, although what this amounts to, beyond being simply a grammatical remark, is difficult to describe without violating it with terminological sloppiness. Wittgenstein expressed the linguistic organization and grammatical parameters of this world with the following metaphor:

> If we imagine the expression of a wish as the wish, it is rather as if we were led by a train of thought to imagine something like a network of lines spread over the earth, and living beings who moved only along the lines. . . .
>
> You might as it were locate (look up) all of the connections in the grammar of the language. There you can see the whole network to which a sentence belongs.[86]

The grammar of our language determines the kind of world we inhabit by establishing the lines along which humans move (speak, think, act). Before we press ahead, let me attempt to remove the mystery of the phrase by illustrating the concept in two ways.

First, the internal relation between language and world is analogous to perichoresis. Literally this term means "to dance around," and there is a sense in which world and language are inseparable dance partners. But "perichoresis" is most notable for its theological use. For early Greek theologians, the term expressed the belief in the reciprocal inherence (circumincession) of the divine Persons of the Godhead. Now if we look past the metaphysical assumptions regarding divine nature and ontological essence, we can extract what George Lindbeck has called the "doctrinal rule" expressed by this ancient term. We might say today that the doctrine of perichoresis reminds Christians that it is not proper to speak about the actions of God the Father without also mentioning those of the Son and the Spirit in the same breath. Much the same was intended by Augustine's dictum that divine actions outside of the Trinity are indivisible (*opera trinitatis ad extra indivisa sunt*). The only distinctions that can be made regarding "Persons" of the Godhead are those which describe relations internal (*ad intra*) to the Trinity. To apply this term to Wittgenstein's view of the language-world relation means that language is the model in terms of which the world of experience is conceptually accessible. In this way the world is "made" by the linguistic model and it is only by means of this model that we experience at all.[87] The phenomenal world (at which all human perception terminates)[88] is linguistically shaped. If we had no language, we would simply be unaware of the world that we were thereby unable to perceive.

Wittgenstein himself saw that the inseparability of language and world could be alluded to by this theological metaphor. When asked by Waismann about the connection between the world (i.e., in-the-world) and the ethical (i.e., beyond-the-world), he responded:

> Men have felt that here there is a connection and they have expressed it thus: God the Father created the world, the Son of God (or the Word that comes from God) is that which is ethical. That the Godhead is thought of as divided and, again, as one being indicates there is a connection here.[89]

We speak of language and world separately. But this is a semantic distinction, one which is on the same level as that made between God the Father (creator of the world) and God the Son (the Word). The reluctance of the ancients to separate Word and world is another mark of their advantage over "Enlightenment" thinkers.

Language cannot be prized off the world of experience because language is *performative*. Language doesn't simply photograph the world in a way that leaves everything as it is. Language contributes to the world of experience. Consider a second example, this one taken from Annie Dillard's novel *The Living*, about the settling of Whatcom, Washington at the end of the nineteenth century. We meet Beal Obenchain, a bear of a man living as a hermit in a hollowed-out Sequoia stump who feasts his staggering, though demented, intellect on the works of Nietzsche. Obenchain decides that he will select one Whatcom citizen and "take his life." Not take his life by killing him—that merely would hasten death—but *possess* his life by threatening to kill him and then taking pains to do nothing but watch him writhe as if he were "stuck upon [my] bayonet and flailing."[90] The likable and carefree Clare Fishburn is randomly selected to become Obenchain's target and the following exchange takes place one midnight when Clare opens his front door to Obenchain.

> The big man, whom Clare recognized, ducked under the doorway to enter. He pushed into the parlor, blinked in the lamplight, and stopped abruptly in the middle of the room. . . .
>
> "What do you want?"
>
> Obenchain told him. He said, looking sideways at Clare and then idly at the tops of the lace parlor curtains, "I am going to kill you . . . as it happens." Both men stood in the decorated parlor, their arms tense at their sides—Obenchain coiled in his loose stained clothes, and Clare attentive in his wrinkled suit. Obenchain pressed his jaws together. Clare held himself still.
>
> "I am going to kill you, shortly . . . for my own reasons . . . with which you need not concern yourself." . . .
>
> "What are you saying man?"
>
> "I have considered it a part of . . . justice, to impart this knowledge to you." . . .
>
> Clare tried to concentrate on what the man was saying; he wanted to learn his place in this scheme. He could not, however, follow it. ". . . always by your side," he was saying, "waking and sleeping, early and late." His dark lips were askew, and his voice was urgent.
>
> "It need not have been you, but it . . . was you, delivered up to me this evening. You"—his voice surged and fell, his high crowned derby bobbed—"whose life I hereby take." Clare could see only that Obenchain believed himself. He was uttering a creed. Clare hoped to get him out of the house—mighty carefully—so he could think, or sleep on it.[91]

When Obenchain speaks these words, "Your life Mr. . . . Fishburn is in my hands," he instills a deeper and more profoundly disorienting fear than had he simply drawn a gun. Clare Fishburn never does die at the hand of Beal Obenchain, but neither can his life ever be the same: "Clare closed the door. He heard Obenchain's heavy tread descend the steps. Clare had been so young, ever since he could remember—so young and full of ideas."[92] Had been? Indeed!

"Words are deeds," Wittgenstein wrote in 1932; language is part of the event-network that constitutes the world of human experience. Wittgenstein's conception of world and language as internally related constituted nothing less than a revolution in philosophy.

Since the Enlightenment, a chief concern of philosophers has been to solve the "knowledge problem" by providing "justification" for beliefs and truth claims. What went unquestioned, for the most part, was this project's assumption that what justifies one bit of knowledge is *itself* a bit of knowledge. Wittgenstein's subtle change of metaphors is an allusion to the fact that he surrendered all battles for knowledge-based justification. Where generalizing explanations govern beliefs, as it were, from "above," Wittgenstein prefers to speak of understanding as "deep" (or, conversely, "shallow"). At the bottom, what justifies one belief over another is not theory but *practice*.

Requests for justification, in Wittgenstein's eyes, are examples of philosophical puzzlement. Puzzles of this kind are not overcome by general explanation but rather are dissolved by pointing out where wrong turns were made. For example, Frege thought that meaning was paired with a string of marks or sounds called "a sentence." But imagine that I overhear two people speaking, such that what I hear are unintelligible clicks and grunts and howls, while what they hear is a conversation. I might conclude that what is missing for me is the "meaning" that accompanies these sounds. This might even suggest to me a general explanation of how sentences work: "So what distinguishes a proposition from mere sounds is the thought that it evokes." But Wittgenstein prods me to ask whether I have really succeeded in explaining what makes a string of sounds "meaningful." In addition to an orderly series of sounds, I have posited another series, a parallel series of mental events. That simply duplicates the difficulty of language with something else that is equally problematic. The wrong turn made in this case was the assumption that "the sentence . . . plays a melody (the thought) on the instrument of the soul."[93] This picture presumes meaning to be something paired with vocables residing in my head. Ironically, when we are asked to describe the meaning of the sentence we can do so only by using more words. What work is done by the elusive "mental" element? Isn't the problem dissolved by simply taking language itself as basic? In other words, the expression of meaning is the act of expressing a sentence; the expression of a wish is the act of wishing; the expression of an intention is the act of intending—there is no need to posit an extra-lingual mental event.[94]

Wittgenstein came to understand language as a web of operations or actions which, in ways like mathematics, constituted a calculus. The only "theory" that was required to explain the calculus was the calculus itself.[95] The calculus motif in Wittgenstein's discussions of language was prominent in his 1930 writings compiled as *Philosophical Remarks*. There he wrote that propositions are *instructions*—specifically, instructions for making models. A proposition is not understood until the hearer does something with it. Understanding, therefore, terminates in action.[96]

To insist that a calculus must first be defended or justified—for fear that the calculus itself is disengaged from reality—would miss Wittgenstein's point entirely. Wittgenstein conceived language as performative in, and coterminous with, the world. Only if one conceives language as separated from the world does its *modus operandi* need justification by means of a theory of the most sublime variety: a general explanation of language. But on Wittgenstein's view, no theory can ever bridge the gap between the language-independent world on the one hand, and a world-independent language on the other, because it is in language that all theorizing is done.[97] As Richard Rorty commented, Wittgenstein's conception of language as one set of operations entangled in a vast matrix of human actions does not allow the question of whether the linguistic calculus is "disengaged" from reality.

> For one will feel in touch with reality *all the time*. Our language— conceived as the web of inferential relationships between our uses of vocables—is not, on this view, something 'merely human' which may hide something which 'transcends human capacities'. Nor can it de- ceive us into thinking ourselves in correspondence with something like that when we are not. On the contrary, using those vocables is as direct as contact with reality can get (as direct as kicking rocks, e.g.). The fal- lacy comes in thinking that the relationship between vocable and reality has to be piecemeal (like the relation between individual kicks and individual rocks), as a matter of discrete component capacities to get in touch with discreet hunks of reality.[98]

For Wittgenstein, the inability of language to supply its own justifica- tion was not troubling. After all, "explanations of signs come to an end somewhere."[99] In these words he once again conveyed the view that the cal- culus itself was basic. Not surprisingly, Wittgenstein illustrated this claim from the field of mathematics. What goes as basic in mathematics is the arithmetic (the calculus) and not the algebraic "proofs" of arithmetic rela- tions.[100] Proofs do not justify arithmetic, they simply show in symbolic form what arithmetic shows using particular numbers.[101] In this regard "proof" only means the application of rules to special cases.[102] Mathematics *is* the grammar (rules) of the calculus and not an ontology of special entities we call "numbers." Therefore, the gulf between arithmetic and algebra is not bridged by an ontological connection (such as the nature of numbers) but by stipulation of an agreement between the rules of arithmetic and the rules of algebra.[103]

In Wittgenstein's mind, then, either one must *stipulate* an agreement between language and world (correspondence theories) or one must relinquish the picture of an externally related language and world. But insofar as language and world are internally related, then understanding a word is necessarily also an understanding of how it "meshes" with life.[104] What counts as understanding is the tacit skill called "going on," which is to say, going beyond the kinds of behaviors (ostensive and otherwise) by which the linguistic calculus is learned, and calculating by means of language alone.[105] If language is internally related to world, then linguistic skill puts one into direct contact with the world at every point.

> "I arrive in Vienna on the 24th of December." They aren't mere words! Of course not: when I read them various things happen inside me in addition to the perception of the words: maybe I feel joy, I have images, and so on.—But I don't just mean that various more or less inessential concomitant phenomena occur in conjunction with the sentence; I mean that the sentence has a definite sense and I perceive it. But then what is this definite sense? Well, that this particular person, whom I know, arrives at such and such a place etc. Precisely: when you are giving the sense, you are moving around in the *grammatical background* of the sentence. You are looking at the various transformations and consequences of the sentence as laid out in advance; and so they are, in so far as they are embodied in a grammar. (You are simply looking at the sentence as a move in a given game.)[106]

Here the "grammatical background" is indistinguishable from the shape of one's contact with the "world" and moving around in it is enabled by one's fluency in a particular conceptual language. No intermediary link between a language-independent world and a world-independent language is necessary because the two coinhere in the living of our lives. We might say that the justification for the way language adequately "links up" with the "world" is shown in the measure of skill we possess in using language as a map for navigating through our world.[107] But the deeper point is that if language and

world are internally, or perichoretically, related, then requests for justification of the putative language-world link are wrongheaded. Does language
need justification? No. Yet persons may become lost and need help in order
to "go on." Do we *infer* the reality of the world from our fluent use of language? No; we do not infer from the one to the other. In fact, Wittgenstein
will even go so far as to say that inference does not enter at all. Certainly we
think, but we think *with* language.[108] And as thinking utilizes language,
thinking itself is a basic action. The "link" between thinking and acting
needs no more justification than the putative one between language and
world. We think, and we act; we think over our actions and then we do
them. But this process is neither "governed" nor "justified" by laws of inference. Thinking and acting are internally related so that we are constrained to act in accordance with our thinking in the same way that "we
are impelled to get out of the way of a car, to sit down when we are tired,
to jump up if we have sat on a thorn."[109]

In many ways Wittgenstein challenges the common assumption that
a request for justification always makes sense—as if the nature of human
life were irreducibly inductive. In some instances justification comes to a
full stop in the statement of reasons, rather than causes, where reasons go
shorthand for the following of rules internal to a particular linguistic calculus.[110] This following of rules is indistinguishable from a particular way
of living in the world. An understanding of this calculus, then, is not inferred from a standard set of theories about how language works in general.
Rather, understanding the calculus amounts to a particular public application of it.[111]

In summary, saying that Wittgenstein conceived language as internally
related to world is to say three things. First, it is to deny the intelligibility
of speaking about language as if it were externally related to the world. Second, it is to say that neither language nor world is conceivable by human
beings prior to, or independently of, the other. Third, it is to say that language-users are not spectators of the world but performers in it and creators
of it; language-use constitutes a world.

What may be gestured toward with a change of metaphors (e.g., from
"picture" to "perichoresis") cannot be discussed with any degree of speci-
ficity apart from the possession of the very linguistic skill that Wittgenstein
wants to cultivate in his readers. That Wittgenstein conceived language and
world as internally related can be deduced from his rejection of representationalism as a general theory of language. But Wittgenstein sees more
than one set of internal relations preventing our hurly-burly from suc-

cumbing to systematization. First, human beings are internally related to the human condition: "Nothing is so difficult as not deceiving oneself."[112] The "objectivity" necessary for representationalism to work is simply unavailable to humans. Second, Wittgenstein's model is itself internally related to ordinary language. Thus, he escapes the inconsistency of which the ideal language theorists are guilty. For, any "ideal" language constructed by means of work done with ordinary language will always be parasitic upon ordinary language for its sense. Not so for Wittgenstein. His views begin and end with ordinary language. Third, Wittgenstein describes the rules of games—including language-games—as internal to the playing of the game. How high is "high enough" when tossing the tennis ball for a serve? Rules of thumb may be formulated, but only a player is able to understand how such a rule is to be applied and in understanding the application of the rule, which is to say, in mastering a form of judgment, will discard the rule itself.

In some ways, "internal relation" is simply a grammatical remark: it is an observation about the impossibility of speaking about some things without talking about some other things. And yet even in this respect, Wittgenstein's understanding of language bears striking resemblance to what Aristotle calls *phronēsis*. *Phronēsis* is internally related to experience (a person in possession of sound judgment is called "experienced"), to character (in Aristotle's mind, one cannot "possess" sound judgment without using it; to "have" sound judgment but not use it is what is meant by lacking sound judgment), and to the ends of praxis (to exercise sound judgment in a case that requires kindness cannot be separated from the doing of the kind act). In retrospect, we might extend the analogy even further: for Wittgenstein, to be in possession of *phronēsis* is to be in possession of fluency in the (conceptual) language that constitutes the world.

The internal relationship between language and world had important consequences for Wittgenstein's views on knowledge, theoretical or otherwise. For, if the world was irreducibly linguistic in character, then knowledge ("of the world") was inevitably a function of this or that conceptual language wielded by this or that speaker. Modern "technological" philosophers had hoped to objectivize knowledge by systematizing doubt and turning epistemological justification into a technique (*technē*) that could be mastered by anyone who operated in isolation from the putatively corrupting influences of local language, custom, or culture. However, Wittgenstein moved in the opposite direction, concerning himself with the quality of judgment of particular human subjects who may, or may not, "know their way about."[113] Practical reasoning, in other words, became Wittgenstein's obsession. As we shall see shortly, the prominence that Wittgenstein accorded to specific instances of knowing by particular human subjects (described above as "the migration of the subject") manifested itself both in his religious opposition to scientism and in the aporetic character of his philosophical method.

THE SICKNESS OF A TIME AND THE ILLUSION OF CONTROL

Wittgenstein's fundamental shift in philosophy was shown by his repudiation of the sort of theoretical formalism exemplified by early-twentieth-century philosophy of language. However, Wittgenstein objected not only to the way system-building tempts us to say what can only be shown, but also to the way it seemingly legitimated one particular totalitarian *Weltanschauung*; namely, that of modern science. Wittgenstein mourned the fatal fascination with science in modern culture:

> The truly apocalyptic view of the world is that things do *not* repeat themselves. It isn't absurd, e.g., to believe that the age of science and technology is the beginning of the end for humanity; that the idea of great progress is a delusion, along with the idea that the truth will ultimately be known; that there is nothing good or desirable about scientific knowledge and that mankind, in seeking it, is falling into a trap. It is by no means obvious that this is not how things are.[114]

His whole project, under this light, can be seen as an attempt to relieve contemporary culture of the putative "must" of the scientific worldview. Of course, he could not refute the modern paradigm without entailing his own self-defeat, because the defect he sought to cure was precisely the craving for a general system; neither a systematic science nor a systematic refutation of *technē* could cure this constant craving. In fact, by 1929 Wittgenstein had begun to see that his Tractarian project had backfired; its severe architectonics had actually contributed to the problem. Ironically, those turn-of-the-century formalists who, by reading the *Tractatus* one way concluded "it *must* be this way," had, in fact, misread it. But to undo the damage required Wittgenstein to surrender his own human urge to construct a universal system and settle for a particularist therapy that unraveled one confusion at a time.

Although some speak of Wittgenstein's later "theory" of language, in view of his consistent antipathy toward global theorizing, it is more fitting to speak in terms of Wittgenstein's "model" [*Darstellung*] or, better yet, his "method" in philosophy of language. Just as language-games are "governed" by rules which do not exist prior to or independent of the playing of the game, but are partially constitutive of the game and therefore must be read off its play, so too, Wittgenstein maintained that no general theory of language governs our speaking, as it were, from above. Rather, the term "language" names a vast family of activities whose particularities can be described (but not predicted) by players. Throughout his life, Wittgenstein struggled for ways to formulate these descriptions without resorting to a version of "metalanguage" that engendered the very philosophical confusion (namely, the bifurcation of language and world) his descriptions were intent on avoiding. The temptation, of course, would have been to "refute" this confusion but, in so doing, Wittgenstein inevitably would have resorted to the very parasitic mode of discourse he claimed we do best without. Therefore, Wittgenstein's later philosophy ought not be construed as proposing a general theory of language, or even a theory about the status of theorizing. Rather, his later work intentionally employs a tangled net of aporias in order to engage his students in conversation. However, in the conversations which he conducted with himself—recorded in notes which he never intended to publish—we see a series of laments against the way *technē* had been enshrined by contemporary culture, laments that betray Wittgenstein's own "religious point of view."

Wittgenstein's Religious Point of View

In 1949 Wittgenstein confided to Drury: "I am not a religious man but I cannot help seeing every problem from a religious point of view."[115] How is this remark to be understood? Wittgenstein's words are open to multiple readings, an ambiguity whose primary benefit lies in the struggle his readers must undertake in order to understand him.

Norman Malcolm, in his posthumously published essay *Wittgenstein: A Religious Point of View?*, suggested four analogies for understanding Wittgenstein's comment. First, religious problems can be imagined as analogous to philosophical problems in the sense that explanation in both cases comes to an end before human craving for explanation may be satisfied. There is such a thing as explanation *within* the respective language-games of religion and philosophy but not explanation *of* religion or philosophy.

An explanation is *internal* to a particular language-game. There is no explanation that *rises above* our language-games, and explains *them*. This would be a *super-concept* of explanation—which means that it is an ill-conceived fantasy.[116]

Thus, for both religious belief and philosophy, Wittgenstein's view entailed a willingness to stop seeking explanation. Second, Malcolm suggested there may be an analogy between religious wonder at the existence of the world[117] and the astonishment we experience in the face of the inexplicable givenness of our language-games and the human agreement (in primitive reactions, in form of life, in judgments) from which our language-games emerge. Third, Malcolm saw the possibility of an analogy between the diagnosis of an illness in the religious person and the "disease" of philosophical confusion that may beset a person or a culture. That Wittgenstein attached great seriousness to this condition explains, in part, the passion of his therapeutic approach.[118] Finally, Malcolm suggested that Wittgenstein's comment to Drury expressed his conviction that just as religion originates in a way of living and acting, so too, the genesis of language is to be found in a groundless, instinctive way of acting.

In a response essay, Peter Winch reminded us that if one thing can be learned from Wittgenstein, it is that we ought always to attend to *differences*. Given the difference between religious practice and the practice of philosophy, Winch advised that great caution be exercised before we assume that an analogy can be formed between them on the basis of something *common* to both religion and philosophy. While he conceded many of Malcolm's points and chided him on others, Winch sketched a different way to read Wittgenstein's remark to Drury. For Winch, Wittgenstein's religious outlook, in the main, was an expression of Wittgenstein's stance toward life both as a gift and as a given that imposed certain duties on the living.[119]

What is remarkable in their respective analyses is that both authors take the first half of Wittgenstein's remark ("I am not a religious man") as evidence that Wittgenstein purposefully distanced himself from religion.[120] Although Malcolm did express some ambivalence in this regard when he wrote, "I am inclined to think that he was more deeply religious than are many people who correctly regard themselves as religious believers," he nevertheless followed Roy Holland's view that Wittgenstein's "stiff knees" toward religion referred to the way Wittgenstein resisted an impulse to pray in order to "maintain that mental concentration, that drawing together of his powers into a single burning point, which was demanded by his philosophical commitment."[121] Winch went further than Malcolm, insisting that Wittgenstein's stiffness manifested a bitter internal conflict that Wittgenstein was unable to overcome in his lifetime.[122] Their discussion proceeds, then, to ponder the ways in which Wittgenstein's *non*-religious philosophical enterprise resembled religion.

In contrast to Malcolm and Winch, I contend that Wittgenstein's claim not to be a religious man is good evidence that he was. Wittgenstein did not pretend that a truthful self-appraisal was easily attained. In 1937 he wrote,

> You cannot write anything about yourself that is more truthful than you yourself are. That is the difference between writing about yourself and writing about external objects. You write about yourself from your own height. You don't stand on stilts or on a ladder but on your bare feet.[123]

Yet, the possession of just such a truthful self-awareness was viewed by Wittgenstein as crucial to a philosopher's work:

> A man can see what he has, but not what he is. What he is can be compared to his height above sea level, which you cannot for the most part judge without more ado. And the greatness, or triviality, of a piece of work depends on where the man who made it was standing.
>
> But you can equally say: a man will never be great if he misjudges himself: if he throws dust in his eyes.[124]

The importance of a religious outlook, Wittgenstein thought, was its ability to check human pretensions regarding one's self-importance. Look at how he described the religious person:

> People are religious to the extent that they believe themselves to be not so much imperfect, as ill.
>
> Any man who is half-way decent will think himself extremely imperfect, but a religious man will think himself wretched.[125]

In other words, one of the marks of the person whose life is progressively religious is an increasingly severe judgment of just how sick he or she really is. This self-evaluation is evidence not of a deteriorating character but of an increasingly clarified self-perception that is manifested in one's autobiographical statements. Such a pattern of harsh self-evaluation is present in Augustine's *Confessions*—a work that Wittgenstein greatly admired and with which he was eminently familiar.[126] Augustine's writings manifest the way in which his twelve-year religious quest culminated in a (painfully) truthful self-perception:

> Ponticianus told us this story, and as he spoke, you, O Lord, turned me back upon myself. You took me from behind my back, where I had placed myself because I did not wish to look upon myself. You stood me face to face with myself, so that I might see how foul I was, how deformed and defiled, how covered with stains and sores. I looked, and I was filled with horror, but there was no place for me to turn my gaze from myself. . . .
>
> Thus was I gnawed within myself, and was overwhelmed with shame and horror. . . .[127]

It is not surprising in this regard that Wittgenstein himself found it a natural expression of his own religious commitment in 1931 to craft and deliver his own confession—at great emotional cost to him—to a circle of family and friends whose friendship he valued most.[128]

I am suggesting, then, that Wittgenstein's claim not to be religious was not a denial of his religious commitment but characteristic evidence that religious commitment had precipitated a profound change in self-evaluation. This change is evident already in his 1920 correspondence with Engelmann in which he lamented his "baseness and rottenness," and, convinced that he had sunk to the lowest level of abasement [*Ich bin ganz und gar gesunken*], contemplated afresh taking his own life.[129] Such self-critical remarks parallel a growing religious pattern in his life: that he gave away his own personal fortune in imitation of Jesus' Gospel; as a young man from the family of a prominent Viennese millionaire he so preferred the company of poor folk that onlookers remained baffled;[130] his life displayed a growing pacifism;[131] and, *pace* Malcolm, he bent his stiff knees *often* in prayer.[132] Wittgenstein claimed Christianity as his own at least in the sense that his manner of life had changed, for now he tried to be helpful to people. He reminds Drury,

> But remember that Christianity is not a matter of saying a lot of prayers; in fact we are told not to do that. If you and I are to live religious lives, it mustn't be that we talk a lot about religion, but that our manner of life is different. It is my belief that only if you try to be helpful to other people will you in the end find your way to God.
> . . . There is a sense in which you and I are both Christians.[133]

What, precisely, is this helpful manner of living? As a philosopher, Wittgenstein sought to help others according to his unique giftedness, by doing philosophical therapy. On the one hand, his therapy aimed at increasing the phronetic-linguistic skill of particular individuals as the means of disabusing them of their particular philosophical confusions. On the other hand, his therapeutic philosophy aimed at disabusing an entire culture of the *technē* of philosophical theorizing that ignored such human illness altogether.[134]

Technē as Symptomatic of Human Illness

As a religious person, Wittgenstein saw disease not only in himself,[135] but also in the culture around him:

> The sickness of a time is cured by the alteration in the mode of life of human beings, and it is possible for the sickness of philosophical problems to get cured only through *a changed mode of thought and life*, not through a medicine [i.e., a metaphysical system] invented by an individual.[136]

Just as religious conversion required adopting a different manner of living, so too, a culture can be cured, but only by an alteration in its corporate mode of life.

The mode of living that plagues western culture, and from which it seems hopelessly unable to extricate itself, is one which embodies a constant craving for generalized explanation: "Our disease is one of wanting to explain."[137] Malcolm noted that "The assumption that everything can be explained filled Wittgenstein with a kind of fury."[138] What is especially maddening about this condition is its self-reinforcing character. For example, we blindly assume that rational speculation and analysis are the means for discovering a cure. But why assume that analysis—rather than obedience, or ritual, or trial and error—is a superior means of self-treatment? In Wittgenstein's eyes, *the manner in which the search for a cure to this condition is conducted is simply another manifestation of the diseased condition itself.*[139]

The craving for explanation is the antithesis of the humility that characterizes the religious outlook. This craving kicks against the reminders of *phronēsis* that human knowledge is finite, that human existence is contingent, and that human language is limited. To the extent that explanation breeds the illusion of control, human craving for explanation turns out to be an expression of will-to-power.

Although Wittgenstein did not diagnose this condition in explicitly Nietz-schean terms, the family resemblance is unmistakable. As early as the *Tractatus*, Wittgenstein insisted that it was only by acknowledging the limits of human language (and hence, the limits of human knowledge) that any hope of apprehending *das Mystiche* could be entertained. Engelmann wrote,

> Wittgenstein passionately believes that all that really matters in human life is precisely what, in his view, we must be silent about. When he nevertheless takes immense pains to delimit the unimportant, it is not the coastline of that island which he is bent on surveying with such meticulous accuracy, but the boundary of the ocean.[140]

The optimism that presumes that human craving for totalizing systems and generalized explanations can and will be fulfilled is the very thing that obscures the shoreline. One who is unaware of the proximity of the shoreline will remain landlocked as surely as one "will be imprisoned in a room with a door that's unlocked and opens inwards; as long as it does not occur to him to pull rather than push it."[141] Ironically, the Tractarian view of things was beset by its own totalizing claims: there *must* be simple objects;[142] the analysis of any complex proposition into simple ones *must* be possible;[143] there *must* be something in common to all instances of language (namely, the general assertorial form) which validates each sentence as an instance of "language."[144]

In these examples we see that the word "must" (in phrases such as "it *must* be this way") is the primary symptom of living in the grip of some grand explanatory scheme. Wittgenstein confessed that his own conceptual revolution began with the realization that he had written the *Tractatus* while under the illusion of "a false and idealized picture of the use of language."[145] He returned to philosophy armed with a method of doing philosophy that aimed at freeing human subjects from the idolatrous grip of all such pictures. For, when we are under the sway of such pictures, we quest all the more eagerly for totalizing theoretical systems.

This aim comes out most strongly in *Remarks on the Foundations of Mathematics*. The entire collection of remarks, written between 1934 and 1944, is an *a fortiori* argument. By likening language to mathematics[146] and then showing the social-conventional character of mathematics, Wittgenstein hoped to more easily persuade readers of the irreducibly social and conventional character of all conceptual (linguistic) systems. The most difficult case for making this point is when we are faced with the apparent coercive power of mathematical proofs. But in what does a proof consist? On Wittgenstein's view, a proof does no more work than express a paradigmatic *manner* of conceiving such-and-such type of problem. In other words, we are constrained to conceive the world by means of conceptual paradigms or pictures. And yet, "We do not judge the pictures, we judge by means of the pictures. We do not investigate them, we use them to investigate something else."[147] On Wittgenstein's view, proofs simply standardize the picture that ordinary mathematical propositions manifest. The goal of mathematical proofs, therefore, is not the justification of mathematical particulars but the fostering of a skill in seeing.

Admittedly, it is very tempting to think of mathematics as grounded in empirical realities. But Wittgenstein observed that what we call "empirical propositions" are simply statements which we can imagine otherwise. In contrast, the propositions with which we do the conceiving are those that we cannot imagine otherwise—lest we be incapable of conceiving at all. Accordingly, paradigmatic propositions function much differently than empirical propositions.[148] It is the cannot-be-conceived-otherwise character of mathematical propositions that deliver to the proof its "mustness" or apparent necessity.[149]

Another way of putting it would be to say that mathematical proofs do not compel us to accept the truth status of a conclusion, but rather persuade us by guiding us in the use of a particular way of looking at things.[150] He wrote,

> The spectator sees the whole impressive procedure. And he becomes convinced of something; that is the special impression he gets. He goes away from the performance convinced of something. . . .
>
> But he does not say: I realized that *this* happens. Rather: that it must be like that. This "must" shews what kind of lesson he has drawn from the scene.
>
> The "must" shews that he has gone in a circle. . . .
> The *must* shews that he has adopted a concept.[151]

This comment makes clear Wittgenstein's conviction that a person's use of "it *must* be this way" can only guarantee that he or she sees things under a certain aspect. To say, "it must be like this, does not mean: it will be like this. On the contrary: 'it will be like this' chooses between one possibility and another. 'It must be like this' sees only one possibility."[152] In other words, the presence of words like "must," "necessarily," "demands," and "cannot be otherwise" in one's conversation betrays the fact that the person is only able to see by means of *one* picture. Debra Aidun summarizes,

> The person who is convinced that things must be this way is unable to see certain [other] characteristics of grammar (see, e.g., PI, 122). The recognition that what seems necessarily so belongs to our grammar and need not be the case may be like the sudden "dawning of an aspect" on a person who formerly saw an object in one way only.[153]

Wittgenstein's entire therapeutic strategy, therefore, consisted simply in describing alternatives to totalizing pictures which have bewitched human subjects. In *Remarks on the Foundations of Mathematics*, each instance where Wittgenstein says, "But we could imagine . . . ," is immediately recognizable as a devastating attack on the "hardness of the logical 'must'" because he posits an incommensurable alternative to the regnant picture that denies the possibility of other pictures.[154] By means of his grammatical mischief, Wittgenstein sought to dismantle the totalizing claims of mathematics, psychology, history, and theology. But above all, he strove to offer alternatives to the scientific picture of mechanical causality that had been so thoroughly ingested by twentieth-century western culture.

Scientism as Idolatry

Many academic disciplines appear dominated by a mechanical picture of the world, one which shows itself in the instinctive search for explanatory causes behind every contingent event.

> The insidious thing about the causal point of view is that it leads us to say: "Of course, it had to happen like that." Whereas we ought to think: it may have happened *like that*—and also in many other ways."[155]

As Wittgenstein observed, the causal picture does not guarantee what it asserts. Rather, it only guarantees that we are committed to using this, and only this, picture of the world. In Wittgenstein's words, "'Must': that means we are going to apply this picture come what may."[156]

Wittgenstein's religiousness, therefore, shows itself in his patient undermining of those explanatory systems that demand an allegiance that can be idolatrous in the following two senses. On the one hand, an explanatory scheme may occupy the space in one's life that God occupies in the life of a religious believer. Wittgenstein confessed:

> Jeans has written a book called *The Mysterious Universe* and I loathe it and call it misleading. Take the title. . . . I might say the title *The Mysterious Universe* includes a kind of idol worship, the idol being Science and the Scientist.
>
> I am in a sense making propaganda for one style of thinking as opposed to another. I am honestly disgusted with the other. Also I'm trying to state what I think. Nevertheless I'm saying: "For God's sake don't do this."[157]

On the other hand, a people can easily labor under the illusion that mastery of the explanatory scheme divinizes them. The thirst for general explanation is, in this case, none other than the will-to-power.

In what appears to be an autobiographical statement, Wittgenstein wrote in 1950:

> If someone who believes in God looks round and asks "Where does everything I see come from?", "Where does all this come from?" he is *not* asking for a (causal) explanation; and his question gets its point from being the expression of a certain request. He is, namely, expressing an attitude to all explanations.[158]

The best way to read this remark, it seems to me, is to see belief in God as entailing the shunning of certain forms of explanation. This can be illustrated by a comparison of the craving for "mustness" to Wittgenstein's philosophical method: "In philosophy we do not draw conclusions. 'But it must be like this!' is not a philosophical proposition. Philosophy only states what everyone admits."[159] And again,

> And we may not advance any kind of theory. There must not be anything hypothetical in our considerations. We must do away with all *explanation*, and description alone must take its place. And this description gets its light, that is to say, its purpose, from the philosophical problems. . . .
>
> Philosophy simply puts everything before us, and neither explains nor deduces anything.[160]

In these remarks Wittgenstein does not express an attitude toward explanation that is merely analogous to religion in general. Rather, *pace* Malcolm, he expresses an attitude in philosophy (namely, anti-theory) that is isomorphic with the Christian stance (namely, renunciation of will-to-power). Wittgenstein's "religious point of view" is internally related to his own philosophical outlook.

The resemblance between Wittgenstein's anti-theoretical bent and a theological doctrine of sin is striking. Theologians claim that part and parcel of the human illness is a rebelliousness against, rather than acceptance of, the givens of life. For Wittgenstein, the ethical life is the life lived within the limits of the world.[161] This point comes out clearly in Philip Shields's *Logic and Sin in the Writings of Ludwig Wittgenstein*.[162] Shields argues that the notion of "transgressing against the limits of language" played the same role in Wittgenstein's understanding of the human predicament as the concept of sin plays in the theological outlook. Robert Roberts wonders whether Shields's interpretation of Wittgenstein isn't a bit fanciful.[163] And in a sense, Roberts's objection is justified. What the "limits" of language meant for the later Wittgenstein underwent transformation; somewhere in the 1930s Wittgenstein stopped viewing language as a cage against whose bars humans kick.[164] Yet, in another sense, Shields points to something very deep in Wittgenstein. Wittgenstein is consistently distraught over the state of modern western civilization. Stephen Toulmin describes Wittgenstein's milieu in this way: "In the 1920's and 1930's philosophers of science in Vienna returned to the earlier monopolistic position" formerly maintained by the neo-Platonists as the "demand for a single universal 'method'."[165] The scientific method, one which offered explanations of the kind "This is really only this,"[166] offered to the modern world the promise of explaining everything (given enough time) and, consequently, the promise of power over everything. But, contended Wittgenstein, after the "stupid" scientist dissects and neatly wraps everything in tidy "cellophane" packages, no greater perspicuity has been attained than that of "soapy water."[167] Wittgenstein enjoyed parodying the modern scientific worldview as maximally pompous: "What a curious attitude scientists have—: 'We still don't know that; but it is knowable and it is only a matter of time before we get to know it!' As if that went without saying."[168] Yet, in more serious moments, he clearly considered the modern outlook as the death of a culture. To recall the quotation with which I began this section:

> The truly apocalyptic view of the world is that things do *not* repeat themselves. It isn't absurd, e.g., to believe that the age of science and

technology is the beginning of the end for humanity; that the idea of great progress is a delusion, along with the idea that truth will ultimately be known; that there is nothing good or desirable about scientific knowledge and that mankind, in seeking it, is falling into a trap. It is by no means obvious that this is not how things are.[169]

What Wittgenstein hoped for, clearly, was the birth of a new culture. "Perhaps in a hundred years," he had said to Drury.[170] In the meantime he planted seeds of this new culture in the form of students.

> If I say that my book is meant only for a small circle of people (if it can be called a circle), I do not mean that I believe this circle to be the élite of mankind; but it does comprise those to whom I turn (not because they are better or worse than others but) because they form my cultural milieu, my fellow citizens as it were, in contrast to the rest who are foreign to me.[171]

The Vienna Circle epitomized the old order and the decay of culture. But Wittgenstein had formed a new circle comprised of those who could learn to speak *his* language in the present age and, by becoming fluent, understand how to go on in the same way despite his eventual absence. And, as we shall see, he intended to bring this circle to maturity by means of an aporetic style of conversation, by which he sought to cultivate his readers' sensitivity to the grammar of ordinary language. Such fluency, he hoped, would cure them of their craving to escape the contingency of the human condition.

APORIAS IN PHILOSOPHY

Wittgenstein's working model [*Darstellung*] presumed language to be internally related to the world. In order to cultivate the sort of good judgment that Wittgenstein was after in his students, he could not resort to generalized theories as if he stood outside of both language and world. Rather, he had to somehow engage his students in the sort of conversation that, precisely because misunderstanding was so easy, students would struggle to make sure they understood properly. Wittgenstein utilized aporias to this end.

For example, in one passage, Wittgenstein spoke of language as an extension of the way human animals instinctively react to their environment.[172] Yet in another passage he insisted on the groundlessness of phronetic-linguistic judgment (since the experiential world and language are internally related).[173] These two claims, each of which resembles a general philosophical thesis, appear to constitute a logical contradiction. Nor is this the only occurrence of apparent contradiction: Wittgenstein's entire corpus seems to be a endless tangle of contradictions. However, these are not logical contradictions but *pedagogical aporias*.[174] Each side of a given aporia does not hold "in general." However, each given aporetic claim does hold in a *limited* way. The skill required for understanding the (grammatical) limits within which such a claim may be legitimately spoken was part and parcel of what Wittgenstein sought to cultivate in his readers and students. Wittgenstein's aporetic philosophy, therefore, was his means of engaging his readers in conversation, the goal of which was an increase in the reader's fluency and simultaneously an increase in appreciation for the inevitable limits attending any and all statements in philosophy. This "limit-recognition" is none other than linguistic fluency, which is to say, the phronetic skill by which one apprehends the manner and extent of an appropriate next move in a conversation. Thus, Wittgenstein waged a battle against the embodiment of *technē* in contemporary culture in piecemeal fashion — one conversation partner at a time.

Language as a Groundless Way of Acting

Scattered throughout Wittgenstein's later writings is a handful of terms that, despite their relative scarcity, are basic to his discussions of language. Chief among these are *primitive reaction, language-game, form of life*, and *aspect-seeing*. Since an understanding of these notions is crucial for a correct reading of Wittgenstein, let me illustrate the relations between these concepts with citations from his later writings. The four propositions that follow appear to be logically circular. In fact, they form a pedagogical spiral: with each turn of the spiral the reader's concepts are transformed so that one never ends up where one began.

P1: Agreement in primitive reactions constitutes a community's form of life. Language did not originate by some form of ratiocination but through an extension of the way human animals instinctively reacted to their environment. "Does a [nursing] child believe that milk exists? Or does it know that milk exists?"[175] Of course not. Rather, the newborn's behavior (crying) is an instinctive reflex, or *primitive reaction*, to the tactile, olfactory, and visual stimuli in his or her environment. Similarly, it belongs to the primitive reactions of the mother to attend to the pain behavior of her child. Her hugging, rocking, and humming are on the same order as speaking the sentence: "There, there. I know it hurts." Both types of behaviors are outgrowths of her prelinguistic primitive reactions. Yet Wittgenstein asked,

> What, however, is the word "primitive" meant to say here? Presumably, that the mode of behavior is *pre-linguistic:* That a language-game is based *on it:* that it is the prototype of a mode of thought and not the result of thought.[176]

In other words, language becomes possible because one person's instinctive reactions are mostly congruous with those of others. Thus, "if he is to play a lang[uage-] game, the possibility of this will depend upon his own and other peoples' reactions. The game depends upon the agreement of these reactions. . . ."[177]

Even in the language-games of science, what lies at the bottom is not a regularity of phenomena, but a regularity in the ways human beings react to phenomena. For example, concerning the language of cause and effect, Wittgenstein wrote:

> Certainly there is in such cases a genuine experience which can be called "experiences of the cause." But not because it infallibly shows us the cause; rather because one root of the cause-effect language-game is to be found here, *in our looking out for a cause.*[178]

The language-games that have to do with cause and effect do not depend upon an intuitive grasp of the occult connection between putative causes and effects but upon the way "we intuitively look from what has been hit to what has hit it."[179] If we have been struck, we invariably turn our attention from the pain toward the striking blow. It is the certainty of *this* regularity—a regularity in human ways of acting—that enables another regular behavior (in this example, the utterance of words such as "cause" and "effect") to take root. Thus, "The primitive form of the language-game is certainty, not uncertainty. For uncertainty could never lead to action."[180] Because human beings act and react without hesitation (in many cases), the use of language that becomes paired with the action itself takes on the character of certainty.

In this context it makes sense to see language as the extension or refinement of other more primitive behavior for which language goes proxy:

The origin and the primitive form of the language game is a reaction; only from this can more complicated forms develop.

Language—I want to say—is a refinement. "In the beginning was the deed."[181]

Thus, the most determinative ingredient for the shape of language behavior is the unmistakable "patterns in the weave of life."[182] On this he wrote:

I want to say it is characteristic of our language that the foundation on which it grows consists in steady ways of living, regular ways of acting. Its function is determined above all by action, which it [i.e., the language-game] accompanies.[183]

This regular way of acting—including the regularity of pairing vocables with nonverbal behavior—is what Wittgenstein settled on describing as a "form of life."

P2: A community's form of life conditions the shape of its language-games. Out of the regularity of more primitive behaviors emerges a regularity of vocal behaviors. "It is very fundamental to the game we play that we utter certain words and regularly act according to them."[184] Because of the conventional link between verbal and nonverbal behavior, it is ridiculous to stare at a word hoping to discover its meaning. Rather, meaning is a question of "what game I intend to be played with this sentence; e.g., who is allowed to say it and in what way are those to whom it is said to react to it?"[185] The key to understanding a sentence is understanding where this particular act of speaking it fits in the shared life of the speakers and hearers; "practice gives the words their sense."[186]

On the one hand, Wittgenstein used the term "practice" to signify a pattern of nonverbal behavior, woven from social conventions and primitive reactions, in which language becomes seamlessly enmeshed. Yet on the other hand, the term "practice" also included *linguistic* practice, that is, what we *do* with words. In Wittgenstein's eyes, we perform actions by use of words: "we *act* in such-and-such ways, e.g., *punish* certain actions, *establish* the state of affairs thus and so, *give orders*, render accounts, describe colors, take an interest in others' feelings."[187] Each of these actions (scolding, establishing, ordering, and the like), which are taken by means of speaking or writing sentences, Wittgenstein called a "language-game."[188] So completely does this linguistic behavior permeate human living that one cannot imagine a language without simultaneously imagining a common form of life.[189]

Thus, the relationship between "form of life" and "language-game" is complex. In one sense, we can imagine that the shape of a group's common life (for instance, whether their warfare is inter-tribal, guerrilla, or economic in nature) "determines" which language-games this group plays as well as the shape those language-games take. However, in another important sense, we can see that the form of a community's life is irreducibly linguistic in its texture; participation in *this* form of life necessarily requires the playing of *these* particular language games. In the first sense language-games are determined by, or an "extension" of, a given form of life.[190] In the second sense language-games contribute to, or are "auxiliary" to, a correlative form of life.[191]

P3: The language-games a community plays determine the way it conceives the world.

As children learn language, they simultaneously pick up the conceptual hardware necessary for sorting their world, because the language they are learning to speak is internally related to a "way of living."[192] Regularity within a form of life (which amounts to congruity of instinct and agreement in actions and reactions)[193] becomes "agreement in judgments," precisely because language is the means by which we think.[194] We may speak without thinking but never think without speaking.[195] Wittgenstein wrote, "when I think in a language, there aren't 'meanings' going through my mind in addition to the verbal expressions: the language itself is a vehicle of thought."[196] Therefore, concepts have no prelinguistic reality; "a concept is in its element within a language-game."[197] It is all done in language:

> Why can a dog feel fear but not remorse? Would it be right to say "Because he can't talk?" . . .
>
> There is nothing astonishing about certain concepts' only being applicable to a being that e.g. possesses a language.[198]

> Can only those hope who can talk? Only those who have mastered the use of a language. That is to say, the phenomena of hope are modes of this complicated form of life. . . .
>
> How do I know that this color is red? — It would be an answer to say: "I have learned English."[199]

As a result of the linguistic texture that Wittgenstein detects in human living, human ability to understand (i.e., adequately conceive) the world is tantamount to being able to describe it in a language. So nuanced is language as a medium, that simple narrative descriptions are superior to any other theoretical form of explanation. He concluded,

> It is possible to describe a painting by describing events; indeed that's the way it would be described in almost every instance. "He's standing there, lost in sorrow, she's wringing her hands . . . " Indeed, if you could not describe it in this way you wouldn't understand it, even if you could describe the distribution of color units in minute detail.[200]

Of course, with different "conceptual glasses," one may get an entirely different picture of the world.[201] When these different pictures, or different worlds, collide, what is often overlooked is the human bias "which forces us to think that the facts *must* conform to certain pictures embedded in our language."[202] In other words, when we are fluent in only one set of concepts, we assume that this set is the only set possible, that our way of seeing the world *must* be correct. We presume this necessity even in the face of opposing claims that are just as intractable as our own: "Where two principles do meet which cannot be reconciled with one another, then each man declares the other a fool and a heretic."[203] Wittgenstein views such a stalemate not simply as a disagreement of concepts, but more fundamentally as a variance of language-games precisely because the language-games determine the way speakers conceive the world.[204]

P4: The way a community conceives the world shapes the primitive reactions of its members.

Taken one way, P4 may be trivial: When I stub my toe, my speech reflex is "Ouch!" while another's may be "Aïe!" But this trivial difference points to a deeper difference in the way two groups may evidently *see different worlds.*

The way in which we see the world is fixed—not in the sense that we necessarily have the conceptual system we do, but in the sense that the conceptual system we do have stands firm for us.

> The child learns to believe a host of things. I.e., it learns to act according to these beliefs. Bit by bit there forms a system of what is believed, and in that system some things stand unshakably fast and some are more or less liable to shift. What stands fast does so, not because it

is intrinsically obvious or convincing; it is rather held fast by what lies around it.[205]

In the acquisition of a conceptual scheme we rarely realize that some beliefs are more deeply ingressed than others, sometimes to the point of invisibility: "It may be for example that *all enquiry on our part* is set so as to exempt certain propositions from doubt, if they are ever formulated. They lie apart from the route traveled by enquiry."[206] If such a basic proposition is ever formulated, because of its central role in the manner of our thinking, it will strike us as "self-evident," which is to say, "we also release it from all responsibility in the face of experience."[207]

Somewhat surprisingly, Wittgenstein thought that *any* proposition could conceivably play this central role. He wrote, "Every empirical proposition may serve as a rule if it is fixed, like a machine part, made immovable, so that now the whole representation turns around it and it becomes part of the coordinate system, independent of facts."[208] For example, what we call the "laws of logic" only have the force they do because of the place we have granted them in our corporate life. Similarly, continuing a simple mathematical series is a matter of convention.[209] To this claim Wittgenstein's imaginary interlocutor objects: "Then according to you everybody could continue the series as he likes; and so infer *any*how!" Wittgenstein responds in a rare summary,

> In that case we shan't call it "continuing the series" and also presumably not "inference." And inferring (like continuing) is of course bounded for us, not by arbitrary definition, but by natural limits corresponding to the body of what can be called the role of thinking and inferring in our [corporate] life.
>
> For we are at one over this, that the laws of inference do not compel him to say or to write such and such like rails compelling a locomotive. . . .
>
> Nevertheless the laws of inference can be said to compel us; in the same sense, that is to say, as other laws in human society. The clerk who infers . . . *must* do it like that; he would be punished if he inferred differently. If you draw different conclusions you indeed get into conflict, e.g., with society. . . .[210]

What fixes a "whole way of seeing"[211] is a social *paideia*: training, instruction, upbringing, and education by which we learn to link certain gestures, pictures, and reactions with a "constantly practiced use."[212] Children thus can be acclimated to a linguistic system only by force of habit: "Under what circumstances pointing can explain, i.e., convey the use of a word. Not to a baby. *It* learns by being drilled."[213]

I once observed my eight-year-old niece apparently trying to teach her three-year-old brother his numbers by quizzing him with a deck of playing cards. Showing him a ten of spades she asked, "What is this?" He was stumped. So she hinted, "What comes after nine?" Still stumped. So she added, "Can you *count* them?" I was struck by the fact that Julia's hints were at least as sophisticated as her initial question. No amount of Socratic dialogue could ever help Robert intuit that the number before him was a "10." He could only learn to sight-read a "10" by a merciless training regimen.

Forms of behavior like sight-reading Arabic numerals, multiplying two numbers, deducing the conclusion of an argument, and picking out red from a color chart, eventually become habituated beyond one's ability to question them. "Any other arrangement would strike us as incorrect. Through custom these forms of behavior become a paradigm; they acquire so to speak the force of law ('the power of custom')."[214]

Such a training not only shapes a way of seeing, but conditions human reflexes to instantly react to various stimuli in conformity with the practices of one's group. For example, we react to the symbol "→" by instinctively looking to the right, simply because we have been trained to do so.[215] Thus, "I have been trained to react to this sign in a particular way, and now I do so react. . . . I have further indicated that a person goes by a sign-post in so far as there is a regular use of sign-posts, a custom."[216] But not only do we exhibit physically conditioned reflexes to proper stimuli, we also may be trained to exhibit *linguistically* conditioned behavior.

> If I am drowning and shout "Help!", how do I know what the word Help means? Well, that's how I react in this situation. — Now *that* is how I know what 'green' means as well and also how I have to follow a rule in a particular case.[217]

Wittgenstein summarized,

> By nature and by particular training, a particular education, we are disposed to give spontaneous expression to wishes in certain circumstances. . . . In this game the question whether I know what I wish

before my wish is fulfilled cannot arise at all . . . If I have learned to talk, then I do know.[218]

In other words, our use of language is itself a set of (sometimes) spontaneous reactions to situations that arise within the life we lead.

Now it is clear that primitive reactions can be trained (e.g., the drowning person cries "Help!"), but we must not overlook the fact that the means by which this training takes place may also be language itself. Not only does the burned child fear the fire, but the child flees from the shout "Fire!" with equal urgency. He or she has been conditioned to react *to the speaking of these words.* From this, Wittgenstein reasoned that members of a tribal group whose language lacks resources to express what we call pain, will likely have differently trained reactions, and thus different experiences, than we:

> Imagine that a people of a tribe were brought up from early youth to give no expression of feeling of any kind. . . .
> For here life would run on differently. — What interests us would not interest them. Here different concepts would no longer be imaginable. In fact, this is the only way in which essentially different concepts are imaginable.[219]

> I want to say: an education quite different from ours might also be the foundation for quite different concepts.[220]

In such a case our reactions to the world would be so different from theirs that even were we to master their language, we would discover that "we do not *understand* the people. (And not because of not knowing what they are saying to themselves. We cannot find our feet with them.)"[221] Clearly, understanding this rival culture could not be accomplished by a phrase-by-phrase same-saying. Rather, understanding would require immersion into the life and language of the rival culture deeply enough to have one's primitive reactions trained to run along the same rails as those of natural speakers, to the end that one is able "to bicker with the native like a brother."[222]

Circular or Self-Consuming?

Although any short summary of Wittgenstein's later work is bound to do him an injustice, I have tried to retain one feature of his work that shows more than it says. Taken one way, the "theses" I have put in Wittgenstein's mouth form a hopeless circle:

P1   Agreement in primitive reactions constitutes a community's form of life.
P2   A community's form of life conditions the shape of its language-games.
P3   The language-games a community plays determine the way it conceives the world.
P4   The way a community conceives the world shapes the primitive reactions of its members.

Yet, is the reasoning viciously circular or is it *self-consuming* by virtue of a conceptual transformation it engenders along the way? If one gets too close to Wittgenstein's work, one easily gets the impression from an analysis of the relation between any two of his central concepts (between "primitive reactions" and "form of life," between "form of life" and "language-game," and so on) that Wittgenstein has constructed a linear philosophical argument which drove toward a general explanation of how language works. But this flies in the face of his explicit refusal to seek general explanations. In 1950 he wrote,

> We could say people's concepts show what matters to them and what doesn't. But it's not as if this explained the particular concepts they have. It is only to rule out the view that we have the right concepts and other people the wrong ones.[223]

In other words, explanation is not what he is after. Rather, he wants to free us from the grip of totalizing claims that the world *must* be such-and-such by showing us the origin of specific claims in particular conceptual systems. Thus,

> All testing, all confirmation and disconfirmation of a hypothesis takes place already within a system. And this system is not a more or less arbitrary and doubtful point of departure for all our arguments: no, it belongs to the essence of what we call an argument. The system is not so much the point of departure, as the element in which arguments have their life.[224]

The conceptual system Wittgenstein speaks of is a linguistic system and therefore an irreducibly social one. Within a socio-grammatical system there can be no way to question "reality" or "other minds" or "the world" of which we jointly speak. Thus Wittgenstein evades some of the perennial problems that have plagued analytic philosophy for three hundred years and gestures toward something new: a realism without empiricism.

Near the end of his life he wrote:

> Because it seems so to me—or to everybody—it does not follow that it is so.
>
> Therefore: from the fact that this table seems brown to everyone, it does not follow that it is brown. But just what does it mean to say, 'This table isn't really brown after all'?
>
> Don't we *call* brown the table which under certain circumstances appears brown to the normal-sighted? We could certainly conceive of someone to whom things seemed sometimes this color and sometimes that, independently of the color they are.
>
> That it seems so to men is their criterion for its *being* so.[225]

In other words, that we call the table brown is indistinguishable to us from it being brown. The world we inhabit is a linguistic one, and our employment of language for thinking and speaking is internally related to this world. That is why "It is simply the normal case, to be incapable of mistake about the designation of certain things in one's mother tongue."[227] This is also why skepticism fizzles. How can a philosopher standing in a downpour wonder, "But how do I *know* that I am really wet?" so long as he or she correctly uses the word "wet"? After all, the philosopher did not ask, "How do I know I'm bleen?" (or honest, or cylindrical, or . . .). In such cases there would be a real puzzle! But so long as the skeptic correctly uses the word "wet," he or she has already conceded the doubting game, for the term "wet" is inextricably bound up with things like standing in the rain.[227]

Wittgenstein's concern, therefore, was to free his readers from the choking grip of totalizing theoretical systems (such as philosophical skepticism) by showing us the contingency of the concepts by which we think. Of course, he could not simply describe the way language "really" works without artificially bifurcating language-in-general from descriptions of language-in-general. To avoid dichotomizing language and the world-of-facts, Wittgenstein proposed doing philosophy of language in a way that showed (rather than stated) the manner in which language functions: "We can't expect by describing language to penetrate to depths deeper than language itself reveals: for it is by means of language that we describe language."[229] Consequently, the "circularity" of P1–P4 is not meant to turn the full circle, but merely meant to show that the relations between "language-games," "form of life," "primitive reactions," and "aspect-seeing" are *internal* relations, and that the whole description of language, like all instances of language, is *ungrounded*.[230]

Certainly Wittgenstein was guilty of giving a provisional definition to the term "language-game" in the *Blue Book*, but he did so there for purely pedagogical reasons.[231] Despite the incompleteness of his examples, Wittgenstein was inviting the student to imagine language-games as "languages complete in themselves, as complete systems of human communication" because to do so would prove "useful" for keeping in mind his point that any given linguistic system is complete in itself.[232]

As his present-day readers, we find that we can only learn Wittgenstein's philosophical language-game as a child learns a native tongue. Once we've played the game enough (i.e., gone 'round the circle enough times), we realize that by gaining fluency in *this* language-game, our own way of seeing has been remodeled. Where at first we may have been tempted to think of "primitive reactions" as prelinguistic human experience in which language originates (P1), our admission that one's conceptual system shapes one's primitive reactions (P4) leads us to concede that a "primitive reaction may have been a glance or a gesture, *but it may also have been a word*."[232]

At this point it may dawn on us that Wittgenstein was never offering us a new brand of foundationalism or genetic theory of language, because the recognition of these primitive reactions is made from within the very language-games thought to emerge from these reactions![233] The importance of Wittgenstein's pedagogy may be summarized: If Wittgenstein's instruction succeeds, readers will undergo a shift in aspect, and the language which was once imagined externally related to the world thereafter will be perceived internally related to it.

Once we have come to see language and world under the aspect of internal relations, we thereby perceive what Wittgenstein saw, namely, that this view is not diaphanous, as if we needed something more substantial. No, our employment of language provides contact with the world as real as kicking rocks.

> If I say, 'Of course I know that that's a towel' I am making an utterance. I have no thought of a verification. For me it is an immediate utterance. . . .
>
> It is just like directly taking hold of something as I take hold of my towel without having doubts.[234]

The concepts embodied in one's language can no longer be thought to *reflect* a life. Rather, "they stand in the middle of it."[235]

If the first trip round the circle (P1–P4) transforms a reader's concept of primitive reaction, a second trip round may prove to alter the reader's notion of language-game. At the end of his life Wittgenstein used the term in the singular to refer to the whole of language.[236] This is not to say that Wittgenstein changed his mind (for in the *Investigations* [§23] he speaks of "countless" kinds of language-games). Rather, he hoped to have changed our minds; at the end of the day, readers ought to be able to recognize the family resemblance between discreet language-games (like praying, thanking, cursing) and the whole of language.

Subsequent wrestling matches with the aporia embodied in P1–P4 will inevitably refashion others of a reader's concepts. But the main point is this: When viewed as a totality, Wittgenstein's later writings show that philosophical clarity is not the property of a text, but a function of the linguistic mastery the reader brings to texts. Cultivation of this skill in himself and others was Wittgenstein's preeminent goal.

The task which remains is to examine the ways in which Hauerwas did ethics through Wittgenstein's lens—that is, in a phronetic way—as one who had been cured of modernity's ills by serious engagement with Wittgenstein's aporias. What Wittgenstein did for philosophy of language (namely, turn it toward phronetic skill), Hauerwas did for ethics; Hauerwas turned ethics toward the ordinary language skills of one believing community in particular. And in so doing, Hauerwas was enabled by grace to surmount the aporias with which Wittgenstein was constrained to express himself.

SIX

ETHICS AS GRAMMAR

Now if arguments were in themselves enough to make men good,
they would justly . . . have won very great rewards . . . but as things
are . . . they are not able to encourage the many to nobility and
goodness. For these . . . have not even a conception of what is
noble and truly pleasant, since they have never tasted it. What
argument would remould such people?
—Aristotle, *Nicomachean Ethics*

Although I was not anxious to learn what [Ambrose] said, but
merely to learn how he said it—for such bootless concern
remained with me, although I had no hope that any way lay open
for a man to come to You—yet at the same time with the words,
which I loved, there also entered into my mind the things
themselves to which I was indifferent. Nor was I able to separate
them from one another, and when I opened up my heart to receive
the eloquence with which he spoke, there likewise entered,
although only by degrees, the truths that he spoke.
—Augustine, *Confessions*

In many ways Stanley Hauerwas does theological ethics *through* Wittgenstein. The migration of the subject in Wittgenstein's philosophy receives concrete expression in Hauerwas's treatment of ethics as an aesthetic task, and Wittgenstein's preoccupation with a linguistic community's form of life informs the political approach of Hauerwas to ethics. One more feature remains to be described in order for the family resemblance to be manifest. In this chapter we will see how Hauerwas, precisely because he takes Wittgenstein seriously, is able to surmount the aporias with which Wittgenstein felt constrained to speak. Hauerwas does so by grace, which is to say, by the gift of the particular community called Christian. I begin by sketching how reading Wittgenstein has enabled Hauerwas to conceive (1) the Christian world as internally related to Christian discourse; (2) Christian doctrine as internally related to Christian praxis; and (3) individual Christians as internally related to the communal whole.

THE WORLD AS INTERNALLY RELATED
TO CHRISTIAN DISCOURSE

Wittgenstein wrote that part of the grammar of "chair" is our sitting in them.[1] As I discussed at length earlier, in this memorable illustration is hidden a wealth of philosophy of language. By the notion of "grammar" Wittgenstein intended us to realize that there is no way to extract the complicated matrix of all our behavior (in short, *our world*) from our use of language. Thus, the word "chair" does not correspond with some mind-independent platform with four legs, or even with sense impressions such as "fourness," "platformness," "brownness," or "hardness." Rather, the word "chair" is put to use within the context of a community whose common life is constituted, in part, by actions such as chair-sitting, chair-fetching, chair-imagining, chair-upholstering, and chair-counting. That linguistic behavior is paired with nonverbal behavior simply shows that all life can be described under the aspect of "behavior." However, because descriptions cannot be given apart from language, human behavior is also seen to be a function of language: "It is in language that it is all done."[2] Recall that by "language" Wittgenstein did not mean merely natural languages such as English or French. Rather, by "language" Wittgenstein also meant the sorts of possibilities (vocable, behavioral, social, etc.) that enable natural languages. The matrix of these possibilities is expressed by the term "grammar," which connoted for Wittgenstein the world-permeating character of language, or better, the world-*constituting* character of language.

We must take care not to confuse Wittgenstein's account with the idealism in general or antirealism in particular. In contemporary philosophy, realists posit a world "out there" and haggle over what it means for language to "fit" or "fail to fit." Wittgenstein's conception of the internal relation of language and world is not as much a denial of realism's theses about descriptions (and knowledge) of the world "out there" as it is a questioning of the representationalists' ability to intelligibly conceptualize *in their own terms* the "fit" of language and world. As D. Z. Phillips laments,

> The core of the complaint against the representationalist theories is that in claiming that epistemic practices must adequately represent Reality or Truth, the notion of "adequate representation" hangs in metaphysical limbo, cut off from any context which could give it sense.
>
> We can ask whether Tom is in pain, but what does it mean to ask whether the language in which we talk of pain itself accurately represents what is Real or what is True? We can ask whether it is true or false that there are chairs in the next room, but what would it mean to ask whether the language in which we speak of physical objects is itself true or false? We can ask whether the curtains are blue, but what would it mean to ask whether the language of colours refers to anything real? Our various uses of language show us what "contact with reality" comes to in these contexts: what it means to speak of real pain, real chairs and real colours.[3]

In order to get the point of ordinary sentences about chairs and curtains we need only know what to do (and here both verbal and nonverbal behavior is included in the "doing") in response to our hearing such sentences. The "real" world that our language is *about* is necessarily a socially-constituted one.

On Wittgenstein's account, the form of life we share in human community is linguistic in shape, and some aspects of our lives are most naturally described as functions of our use of language. For example, what does "waiting expectantly" amount to if not thinking some sentences rather than others, accompanied (sometimes, though not always) by various nonverbal behavior such as lifting one's eyebrows, sighing heavily, drumming the table, or glancing repeatedly at one's watch?[4]

All this Hauerwas has gathered up into his own particularly theological outlook. For Hauerwas the theologian, the internal relation of world and language implies that those who have learned to speak the Christian language inhabit a world aeonically different than that inhabited by nontheists, precisely because conflicting (and, at some points, incommensurable) descriptions are rendered by each. In St. Paul's words: ὥστε εἴ τις ἐν χριστω καινὴ κτίσις — "When anyone is united to [the body of] Christ, there is a new world."[5] The "world" under consideration is not the empiricists' world comprehended *sub specie aeternitatis*, but a *manner of being* which is itself qualified by one's "fluency." In Hauerwas's eyes, "no practice more determines a church's being than how we have learned to speak the church's language."⁶ For Hauerwas, the practice of language training is a type of *paideia*. Thus, *paideia* is how the word "world" gains a pejorative sense for Christians (as in 1 John 2:15). Hauerwas explains, "Learning to speak as a Christian is to acquire habits that will put me at odds with the world. Indeed the very linguistic habits of describing the world as 'world' is a practice."⁷ For example, the old Calvinist put-down ("What did Calvin say when he fell down the stairs? . . . 'Glad to get that over with!'") has bite precisely because the Calvinists' response to misfortune has been schooled by the vocabulary of divine providence. In Hauerwas's view, linguistic training is the central component of the church's primary task, namely, being the church (rather than something else).

> The first task of the church . . . becomes more intelligible once we understand that morally you can only act in the world that you can see, and you can only see *by learning to say*. In other words, our understanding of what it means to be Christian is to submit ourselves to the discipline of learning how to speak a foreign language. The church's language is not a natural language, but it is a language that requires the self to be part of that language. . . . [L]anguages are languages in use. Language is a set of practices rather than a collection of words.⁸

Of course, as Wittgenstein has taught, learning a new language is never a straightforward task. Rather, it is a dialectical process of speaking and acting, of acting and speaking, until it becomes true of us that the two moments can no longer be separated. The activity which perhaps best illuminates the practical character of our language and the linguistic character of our practices is prayer. In 1996 Hauerwas wrote with Willimon,

> Learning to pray is the way Christians discover how to speak. The primary language of the church is the language of prayer—because in prayer the practice and the language are inseparable. Of course, it is not easy to learn to pray well. And that is why we do well to imitate those who have prayed before us. So we say prayers whose words we may not even well understand because in the saying we discover that we have become part of an understanding we can only later make our own. So by becoming skilled speakers of that language called Christian, through prayer we discover the skills necessary for Christians not only to survive but also to resist the world that would destroy us.⁹

The acquisition of the Christian language that constitutes a whole new world is more commonly called "conversion." However, conversion can only be recognized retrospectively, for "what is crucial for Christian formation is to have people engaged in activities through which they learn the habits that shape them before they can name what the shaping is about."[10] Thus it is the world-making power of language that makes theology itself a battle over which language rules.[11] Hauerwas writes that when he began his career,

> I thought that ethics provided an intellectual opportunity to explore the differences Christian speech could and should make. I did not anticipate then the ways in which this project would force me to (re)discover the significance of the church as the primary set of language games not in which Christians learn to speak, but in which our speech is already a practice with a significant difference.[12]

For this reason, a central challenge facing theology today is to

> reclaim a voice that speaks with authority, a voice those power compels without coercion and persuades without denigration. Accomplishing such a feat requires, at the very least, a competence in writing and speaking in such a manner that our language as Christians actually does some work. By "doing work" I mean that our language is not simply a means of "saying what everyone already knows," but is deploying and engendering linguistic practices that enable Christians to discuss and simultaneously to bear witness to a reality that we (and all that is) are God's good creation. In short, theological language that "does work" consists of those discourse practices that truly make a difference. (Language that "makes" a difference, of course, does so precisely because it also "reveals" important differences.)[13]

Hauerwas admits freely that the attempt to discover and explicate such differences has always been the animating center of his work. My point is simply this: since Hauerwas conceives language as internally related to world, Christian ethics begins and ends with a grammatical task; there is no way to describe the difference that Jesus makes without resorting to the language Christians have habitually employed. Moreover, it is precisely attention to this particular set of linguistic practices that train us to see the "point" Christians have always claimed to see. One can only begin to understand prayer by attending to the language of prayer. But as one cannot understand a language without participation in the speakers' form of life, one cannot understand the language-game of prayer without praying. But in speaking the words "Dear God," believers assume the posture of subordination, from which position alone prayer can begin to be understood as making a difference.

If the world is best understood as internally related to language, then clearly the world stands in a similar relation to those narratives which train a community's use of language and constitute that community's form of life.[14] The church's *canonical* narrative, of course, cannot be easily distinguished from the *historical* narrative of the church. In fact, the great training manuals for Christian speech include the historical creeds which habituate Christians both to forms of speaking that are "canonical" and to the way of living which is commensurate with the pattern of life that constitutes the present-day identity of the "historical" church.[15] Hauerwas admits that his early conception of "narrative" may have been too narrow for making this point. He has recently tried to redress the situation by using "narrative" as a gesture toward a mode of rationality more akin to *phronēsis* than *technē*. Hauerwas cites with approval John Milbank's description of narrative as

> a more basic category than either explanation or understanding: unlike either of these it does not assume punctiliar facts of discrete meanings. Neither is it concerned with universal laws, nor universal truths of the spirit. Yet it is not arbitrary in the sense that one can repeat a text in just any fashion, although one can indeed do so in any number of fashions. . . . If reading texts means that we renarrate them or repeat them, and if, as we have seen, textuality is the condition of all culture, then narration—of events, structures, institutions, tendencies as well as of lives—is the final mode of comprehension of human society.[16]

Hauerwas echoes Milbank's affirmation that "narrative is our primary mode of inhabiting the world, and it characterizes the way the world happens to us, not, primarily, the cultural world which humans make."[17] This statement marks a broadening of the concept of narrative since Hauerwas's early period. As a result, Hauerwas takes narrative to be the primary, perhaps even the only, form truth claims can take.[18] Christians ought to object on theological grounds to "any correspondence theory of truth that presumes that an isolated proposition must fit an equally isolated fact,"[19] because Christian claims about the world only achieve clarity when they are offered "thickly." Sentences cannot be verified in isolation, since the sense of each sentence depends on the rest of the narrative discourse. And if Christian discourse depends for its sense upon the determinative form of life of actual Christians, then the only thing that needs to be verified is the presence of a community whose praxis embodies its deepest theological convictions and whose deep theological convictions are embodied in a discourse that brings the world into proper focus. Thus, for example,

> the doctrine of creation only makes Christian sense as part of the doctrine of the Trinity. For Christians, the doctrine of the Trinity is necessary if we are to render the world intelligible as we find it and as we hope it will be. Such a claim is "empirical," not in the sense of being verifiable, but in the sense that it requires a tradition-determined community to narrate the way the world is, and, given the way the world is, how Christians must be in such a world.[20]

When narrative is seen as the fundamental mode of inhabiting the world and, hence, as the fundamental mode of rationality, the fact that the rivalry between Christian and secular truth claims, at bottom, consists in a struggle between stories is manifest. But also visible is the irreducibly contingent character of claims made by both sides (where "contingent" claims are those whose contrary is intelligible). Although Hauerwas is rightly suspicious of Milbank's self-proclaimed victory over the secular theorists, supposedly procured by his "out-narrating" liberalism, there is a point to Milbank's claim that only the Christian story, which is framed in the language of grace, can account for the contingent character of the rivalry. Hauerwas finds this analysis very appealing: "Milbank . . . observes that to be part of the church is to have 'the moral luck to belong to the society that overcomes moral luck'."[21] According to Hauerwas, Milbank's profundity lies in the fact that

> our violence is often the attempt to render certain and necessary contingent moral commitments that we have made and for which others have paid the price — i.e., our attempt to rid our life of luck is the source of our greatest violence. The word Christians use to describe how our lives are constituted by such luck is grace. Yet grace does not remove, as the Greeks tried to remove through theory, the contingency of our existence.[22]

Does Christianity's superior ability to account for the contingent character of truth claims chalk up points for the home team? That depends on who
is keeping score.

In a later essay, Hauerwas continues to explore the bearing which narrative, contingency, and violence have upon the status of the debate between rival conceptual frameworks by attending to the writing of Iris
Murdoch, especially *Metaphysics as a Guide to Morals*. Murdoch opposes
much in Christianity because she thinks that it, like all religions, forms a
totalizing theoretical system that misrepresents as necessity the contingent
character of human life. Human depravity, in her estimation, can be seen
in our penchant for self-delusion, which takes the form of theoretical systems. She suggests, in contrast, that human morality requires the prior
nonexistence of a God, for only in the absence of a sovereign being is life
truly contingent, and only when the genuinely contingent is redeemed
by moral artistry can divinity be incarnated in human knowledge, human
work, and human love.[23]

What Hauerwas finds persuasive is not Murdoch's conclusion, but the
genre of her argument. Happily, she does not oppose theoretical systems
with a system of her own. Rather, she recounts a story. In particular, Murdoch takes her cues from Plato's myth of the Demiurge and offers the Demiurge as "the paradigmatic artist making beauty out of [apparent] necessity."[24]
Murdoch understands that at stake are narratives that provide us with the
ability to see the contingent as just that—contingent. Hauerwas's response
is, appropriately, a re-telling of the story. With special reference to Aquinas,
Hauerwas renarrates the Christian story of creation *ex nihilo* in a way that
better shows the contingency of human existence than does Murdoch's appropriation of Plato's myth. The presence of a *telos* in the Christian story of
creation *ex nihilo*, *pace* Murdoch, is not warrant for an exclusionary violence by which the sovereign being always gets his or her own way. Rather,
the *telos* in the Christian story of creation is a reminder of what Christians
call their "creatureliness."

> In contrast to Murdoch's account of the absolute pointlessness of
> existence, Christians believe that God means for all creation to wor-
> ship God. Such a "purpose," however, does not mean that all we do is
> guaranteed to "come out all right." "Purpose" understood doxologically
> can only be displayed by a narrative that is subject to constant retelling
> given the contingent character of our existence. . . . The "purpose" that
> sustains the Christian is eschatological because we believe that creation

names not just a beginning but God's continuing providential care of creation. Creation for us is not only "in the beginning" but continuing.

The telos that characterizes the Christian understanding of morality is not that of a single overriding purpose that violently forces all we do into a preestablished hierarchy. Rather it is a telos of hope that gives us the confidence to believe that we are not fated by our collective or individual pasts. We know that we cannot avoid being creatures of history, but that very way of putting the matter presumes we should desire, if possible, an alternative. Such a desire cannot help but appear to the Christian as a sinful attempt to escape our creatureliness. Our only alternative is not a salvation that mystically frees us from history, from our past, but rather an alternative history made possible by a community of people across time who maintain a memory of God's hope for us and for the world.[25]

In many ways Hauerwas's response to Murdoch runs parallel to Milbank's grand narrative in *Theology and Social Theory*. In both cases the internal relation between world and language means that, ultimately, the intercommunal rivalry over competing and incommensurable truth claims boils down to differences in story. As such, no non-narrative (i.e., theoretical) appeals to necessity can settle the matter.[26] In Hauerwas's estimation, Milbank has shown that "liberal political and social theory is unable to imagine any society able to control violence except through counterviolence" because the *mythos* that begat the *saeculum* presumes an ontology of violence.[27] As a result,

> The positing of a permanent chaotic material realm of violent conflict, means that it is finally hard to account for this realm without either retreating to a foundationalist metaphysics, or else making an arbitrary, violent difference itself the ultimate principle.[28]

But neither Thomas Hobbes's foundationalism nor Friedrich Nietzsche's violent difference is the story that Christians tell.

> For Christians, violence is always a "secondary willed intrusion," which is known only because of a profounder peace. Such a peace is not driven to hegemonic or totalizing accounts of existence, since God's creation is the ongoing actualization of harmonious difference displayed in the Trinity.[29]

Not only does the form of Jesus' life shape the polity of the church, but the story of human creation in the image of the God who is one-and-yet-three implies a human sociality that is neither coercively totalitarian (in which differences are lost) nor dispassionately tolerating (in which unity is never attained). For this reason Nietzsche astutely singled out Christianity for attack, because Nietzsche "rightly saw that Christianity was the only viable alternative to his agonistic world."[30] What is currently touted as the problem of relativism is not the result of a backlash against failed forms of epistemological foundationalism, but the offspring of a much older *practical* problem about how to order political life.[31]

Other insights of Milbank corroborate Hauerwas's insistence that pacifism is not an eccentric doctrine that is inconsequential for the "truth claims" made by Christians. On the one hand, since the world is internally related to language, the term "pacifism" goes proxy for a host of Christian practices—indeed, for an entire form of life—upon which depends the sense of the language in which Christian truth claims are framed. On the other hand, since the Christian world is internally related to Christian *narrative*, pacifism is simultaneously the embodiment of a radically different story, one that is incommensurate with secular versions of human origins and existence, and yet one that *shows* the way to transcend the apparently lamentable human condition of having no theoretical means for adjudicating between rival conceptual frameworks and their respective claims to true descriptions. Running against the grain of human craving for demonstrating superiority, the pacifism of Jesus counsels Christians to (1) reconceive matters in nonagonistic ways and (2) embody a radical alternative to the greater society's way of relating to others. This "sociality of harmonious difference" succeeds where theoretical accounts since Plato have failed, since theoretical solutions inevitably resort to violence. Early on, Hauerwas wrote that

> pacifism . . . is the very form of moral rationality since it is a pledge that we can come to common agreement on the basis of discussion rather than violence. What the nonviolent witness denies is that such agreement is possible by argument abstracted from the kind of people who have learned that even their enemy may be speaking the truth.[32]

That Hauerwas espouses a "grammatical" model of ethics is reflected, in the first place, in his conception of language and world as internally (i.e., grammatically) related. The claims made from within one linguistic community may not translate into claims made from within another.[33] Yet this does not imply that conflicting claims struggle to displace each other on the basis of mutually exclusive depictions of a language-independent reality; we have no way of speaking intelligibly about such a thing.[34] On the contrary, multiple linguistic practices constitute multiple worlds, each of which can occupy the same space, just as multiple music scores can simultaneously fill a room. To the extent that Christians resist this multiplicity of worlds—either by coercing others into "agreement" (as is the temptation when Christians are in power) or by resisting martyrdom (when Christians are not in power)—they resort to a form of life quite alien to the Christian story, a move which, in the end, can only be an admission that rival truth claims *are* settled by violent means. But in contrast, to the extent Christians embody a pacifist form of life, the need to *conquer* relativism is shown to be a false option arising from a conceptual framework that is as arbitrary and non-Christian as it is violently hegemonous.[35]

MORAL REASONING AND THEOLOGICAL ETHICS AS INTERNALLY RELATED TO PRACTICE

If the first way to understand ethics-as-grammar follows from conceiving Christians' language and world as internally related, the second aspect under which ethics-as-grammar can be brought into focus is related to Wittgenstein's stance that, given the conventional nature of language, rules are read off the play of the game. When applied to ethics, such a conventionalism concedes, on the one hand, that there is no way to talk about moral behavior except from within a community whose form of life admits to the logical possibility of certain patterns of behavior. On the other hand, because of the internal relation between practice and discourse, there can be no way to talk about practice-independent criteria for adjudicating between rival moral schemes. At first blush this sounds very problematic; how are we to decide between rivals if we are left without a theoretical fulcrum? But Hauerwas's point goes even deeper: not only are there no practice-independent criteria for adjudication, adjudication itself is not a practice-independent theoretical exercise, but rather an exercise of practical reason requiring for its excellence training within some particular tradition or other. This is not to downplay the very real tensions which exist between rival moral traditions. But it does transcend the putative problem of relativism as it is commonly expressed; relativism is not a theoretical problem requiring a theoretical solution, but a series of practical problems requiring embodied solutions: "What we require, therefore, is not an argument that provides an a priori defeat of relativism, but an interpretation of and the corresponding skills to live in a world where others exist who do not share my moral history."[36] As we shall see, Hauerwas conceives both forms of Christian discourse—first-order speech-acts involved in moral reasoning and theological ethics, and second-order reflections on the grammar of first-order claims—as internally related to Christian praxis.

Escaping modernity's craving for an account of ethics that resembles *technē* requires nothing less than a "conversion." Hauerwas himself underwent such a conversion under the influence of Wittgenstein. In the *Tractatus*, Wittgenstein's explicit intent was to help cultivate in his readers the skill of seeing the world rightly, where "seeing" meant understanding both that language was limited to depiction of facts which constituted the world, and that the very limits of language expressed a trans-world reality of ultimate importance.[37] Of course, Wittgenstein retreated from this account of language as he realized that language could do its "picturing" in innumerable ways. In the end, Wittgenstein's attention shifted to the ways in which people actually used language. Thus, his concern became the explication of the grammar of ordinary language. However, Wittgenstein never retreated from his intent to shape his readers into skillful language users. The genius of his later therapeutic philosophy lay in his seeing that this skill could be cultivated by helping others gain perspicuity about the grammar of ordinary language. Hauerwas espouses a similar agenda in the following confession.

> By suggesting . . . that my task is to change lives, I am attempting to make what Wittgensteinians call a "grammatical point." Christian discourse is not a set of beliefs aimed at making our lives more coherent; rather it is a constitutive set of skills that requires the transformation of the self to rightly see the world.[38]

The Christian's moral vision is made adequate to the task of seeing the world rightly by means of gaining fluency in Christian discourse.

Hauerwas's intention to cultivate truthful speakers of Christian discourse requires him to swim against the tide of common approaches to "applied ethics." Commenting on Alasdair MacIntyre's essay "Does Applied Ethics Rest on a Mistake?," Hauerwas notes that modern ethical approaches assume that theory is the prior activity that generates the rules or principles that only subsequently are applied in practical matters.[39] But, if Wittgenstein is correct, rules do not exist prior to their embodiment in concrete applications. Moreover, whenever theoretical reasoning claims to proceed according to "first principles" reputed to be intelligible regardless of context, it inevitably rests on practices so familiar that they are invisible. Such an exercise yields conclusions that can never challenge the form of life constituted by these practices but rather will serve only to mask the way theorizing protects those who currently have the upper hand.[40]

Hauerwas finds precedent for his refusal to engage in ethics as a form of *theoria* in Aristotle, for whom "ethics is not a theory but a mode of inquiry that shapes skills necessary for those who would live well." In other words, "in contrast to ethics done in the theoretical mode of modernity that tries to begin from nowhere, Aristotle begins his ethics decidedly from 'somewhere'," namely, the sort of moral judgments that can only be made from within a concrete community.[41] Following Wittgenstein very closely, Hauerwas suggests that our moral judgments come to a "full stop" in the exercise of a tradition-trained perception. According to Wittgenstein, a fitting defense to give when asked "How do you know this is red?" is simply to say "Because I speak English." Similarly for Hauerwas, the moral status of an action is identifiable by those who are conversant in Christian discourse on the subject.

> It is therefore a philosophical mistake to ask what is wrong with murder. If we rightly understand the grammar of the word murder, we understand that the only issue is whether this or that killing is a case of murder.
>
> But, of course, the attempt to explain or to give a further reason why murder is wrong has been one of the besetting temptations of modern moral philosophy. Fearing that if morality is based on the "intuition" that murder is wrong then such judgments are arbitrary, it became the philosophical task to find a single principle that could "ground" such "intuitions." That is the reason, moreover, that modern moral philosophy has tended to corrupt our morality through the attempt to give reasons when no reason is required and has the effect of undercutting our true judgments.[42]

In other words, the true moment of ethical perception (what Aristotle meant by *aisthēsis*) comes in the skillful application of Christian discourse to a given situation. Christian discourse, therefore, supplies the ultimate particular which enables practical reasoning to lead to action.

Yet moral reasoning is not a tidy linear syllogism. For Hauerwas, the discourse which precipitates concrete action is dependent upon Christian praxis for its own meaningfulness. No matter how tempting it is for the theological ethicist to conceive of ethics as a theoretical enterprise, Hauerwas's model of ethics-as-grammar reminds us that

> in fact, the work of the theologian is parasitical on the faithful practice of Christian people. That does not mean that theologians reflect on what most Christians are currently doing, but what Christians have done through the centuries. Such an appeal to the "past" does not mean that Christians will be faithful today by doing what was done in the past, but by attending to *how* Christians did what they did in the past we hope to know better how to live now.[43]

The work of the theological ethicist as grammarian is therefore part language tutor and part (hi)story-teller. But never is it one of system-builder, for the conversation continues and the story has not yet ended.

> I do not know how the story will end. . . . I do not have a finished theological system nor do I believe in such a thing. I do not know what a finished theological system would look like, and if I knew, I am pretty sure that I would not want it. My suspicion is that the desire to have such a system may indicate the theologian's lack of faith in the church. Indeed, the church across the centuries and through the communion of the saints believes more than any theologian could possibly say. The theologian is therefore free to wander and wonder, knowing that the truth of what the church believes is not threatened by the "theologians" who "put it all together."[44]

Thus, because moral reasoning and Christian praxis are conceived as internally related, theological ethics is revealed to be none other than an explication of the form of life of the actual community, which is to say, the grammar of Christian discourse. Wittgenstein paved the road here, conducting therapeutic philosophy by attending to the actual use of ordinary language. Hauerwas in the same way shows that theologians and ethicists have no purchase on their respective disciplines except by means of their descriptions of the pattern of life displayed by the historical believing community. Thus Hauerwas attends to the lives of historical saints (Augustine, Bernice, Thomas More) and contemporary saints (Martin Luther King, Jr., as well as "Gladys" of *Resident Aliens* fame). He recounts church history in broad strokes and details moments of crisis in real church communities.[45] He organizes his university ethics course around Christian liturgy[46] and never tires of drawing our attention to other grammarians of the faith whose theologies constitute "training manuals" for the saints.[47] While he is not overly hesitant to do constructive theology, which is to say, make concrete recommendations for what it means to speak faithfully as Christians today,[48] more often than not Hauerwas centers his work on the moral significance of everyday Christian practices such as confession, reconciliation, peacemaking, and worship, because Christian theology begins and ends in these practices.[49] Hauerwas summarizes his model of ethics:

> Learning to be moral is much like learning to speak a language. You do not teach someone a language (at least nowhere except in language courses at a university!) by first teaching that person rules of grammar. The way most of us learn to speak a language is by listening to others speak and then imitating them. Most of the time we act as if morality is a matter of rules to be learned. We seem to believe that, after we have learned all the right rules (Think for yourself. First be sure you're right, then go ahead. Let your conscience be your guide. Abortion is wrong. Love your neighbor), we can go act morally.
>
> No. You learn to speak by being initiated into a community of language, by observing your elders, by imitating them. The rules of grammar come later, if at all, as a way of enabling you to nourish and sustain the art of speaking well. Ethics, as an academic discipline, is simply the task of assembling reminders that enable us to remember how to speak and to live the language of the gospel. Ethics can never take the place of community any more than rules of grammar can replace the act of speaking the language. Ethics is always a secondary enterprise and is parasitic to the way people live together in community.[50]

Of course, it might be objected that the model of ethics (and theology) as grammar lacks the objectivity necessary for getting descriptions right. Hauerwas's response is straightforward:

> The attempt to make theology attain quasi-scientific "objectivity"— even in science attaining objectivity is more an image than an actual activity—by providing it with a firm foundation (intended or not) could not help but produce a domesticated theology. Such theology is but the mirror image of empire, inasmuch as it seeks to put everything in its place, to secure all the loose ends, in the interest of order and security. By providing a rational basis for theology, by finding the essential core to determine the meaning of all theological discourse, theology could pretend to be for anyone.

Architectonic theology is but the mirror image of Christianity as a system that "explains things." It is a theology for people who believe that faith in God is meant to put us firmly in control of our existence. It is a theology that attempts to take the surprise out of the resurrection. Accordingly, architectonic theology tends to a reductionistic display of the various loci of Christian doctrine, trying to show that insofar as the various doctrines are rational, they all "mean" the same thing.[51]

In other words, because human reasoning depends upon language skills, even theological system-building is internally related to practice. Consequently, any attempt to theorize in isolation from all contextual considerations can in the end only reinforce one form of life in particular — perhaps the very form of life which needs to be called into question but cannot be, because it has been rendered invisible by the system-builder's pretension to "objectivity." What is likewise invisible when ethics adopts the mode of *technē*, is the implicit assumption that God's *telos* for humanity is our escape from the contingency that marks the human condition, by gaining the mastery over our lives that *technē* promises (but cannot deliver). And there is something profoundly un-Christian about such a promise.

Some have objected that liberalism marginalizes practices by relegating them to the realm of the private sphere. Hauerwas rightly counters with alternative conceptions of practices as "intrinsic to theological convictions."[52] Nevertheless, a grammatical model of theological ethics, some complain, fails to be anything more than mere anthropology, and for this reason fails to be a *radical* alternative to liberalism after all. As Barth feared in the case of Schleiermacher, isn't Hauerwas's "theological" ethics simply anthropology in a loud voice? Well, yes and no. Hauerwas *is* exegeting the form of life of a particular historical community — but this is not all that he is doing. The mistake made by those who would attempt to do ethics apart from attention to human praxis lies in their assumption that it makes perfect sense to speak about rules that (1) exist independently of their embodiment in concrete historical communities and (2) are, in principle, knowable by anyone and everyone. What can this two-fold claim mean? If we take it to be a picture of the way things really are, then lacking criteria for this picture's application, the claim is idle. If this two-fold claim attempts to make a grammatical point — for example, "objectivist ethics is meaningful as an embodiment of reverence for the divine command" — then its sense still depends on the prior existence of some concrete community that is doing the revering. In contrast, Hauerwas sees both first-order Christian discourse and second-order grammatical statements about Christian discourse emerging from the community's attendant form of life (I have called this second-order discourse "ethics-as-grammar") as *simultaneously* about God and humanity. It is precisely a Wittgensteinian notion of the internal relation between language and world that enables theology to properly envision God's immanence: descriptions about God supervene on descriptions of the form of life of the believing community.[53] Thus, the church witnesses to the salvation of God by being an axiological alternative to rival worlds of discourse, for rules are embodied in practice. Hauerwas exegetes the works of James McClendon to make a similar point:

> He [McClendon] does not let us begin with God, for such a God cannot be other than an abstraction—even as Trinity. Instead he forces us to focus on learning the story through becoming servants to the rule of God found in Christ. Accordingly, he even treats sin and salvation prior to treating the identity of Christ.
>
> I mention this point because I have to acknowledge that it makes me nervous. I worry that such an order can underwrite an anthropological account of sin and salvation that subsequently determines the meaning of Christ (rather than an account of salvation learned from Christ). . . .
>
> Raising this issue, however, helps us see the power of McClendon's execution of the structure of the church's teaching. For he does not assume that he is displaying theological language as if that language were a primitive metaphysics separate from the practices of the concrete people called church and whose very lives tell us the nature of the world. McClendon can treat salvation and sin prior to Christology precisely because there is in fact no "priority" other than the story-formed practices of the church. By doing so he reminds us that questions of Christ's identity (e.g., speculation concerning the "two natures") are in service to the church's faithful practice. In effect, the structure of his theology is to force us to remember that theology is not an end in itself. Theology is not, in other words, a speculative endeavor.[54]

Liberal theology after Schleiermacher became increasingly aware that theological statements could not refer to God per se and therefore opted to think of them as mere expressions of human sentiments. But post-liberal theology in the vein of McClendon and Hauerwas reminds us that claims about God *are* claims about God. However, in order for these claims to be intelligible, they must find a home in the context of practices (for example, confession, worship, and witness) which give to all forms of Christian language their sense. Such a vision does not simply repeat the worry that theological language is disengaged from its object (God)—for language does not represent reality, it constitutes reality—but rather reminds us that theological language can only do work when it is self-consciously framed within the context of actual church living.

In consequence of the internal relation between theological ethics and practice, Hauerwas is untroubled by the demand to locate practice-independent criteria for adjudicating rival modes of moral description—there simply are no such criteria. But more profoundly, Hauerwas's understanding of moral reasoning's dependence upon practice means that he is able to ignore as nonsensical the call for theological ethics as a form of *technē* to be performed prior to, and independent of, attention to historical Christian praxis. Indeed, it is incumbent upon Hauerwas to ignore such calls, for the theoretical mode of reasoning inevitably entails a totalizing pretension that distorts our worship of God. For this reason Hauerwas challenges the "architectonic" strand in theologians such as Milbank and, more recently, Oliver O'Donovan:

> we see no reason (as O'Donovan does) to privilege the concept of God's rule over creation and history predominantly in monarchical terms. In short, monarchs always desire architectonics, but we believe that what is crucial is the character of the church's witness to God's rule. That is to say, because the church assumes the role of a servant to the world, such architectonic ambitions must be kept at bay.[55]

The servile form of church life (a minority status that stems not from its withdrawal but from the fact that it is surrounded and outnumbered on every flank!) reminds us not to acknowledge the moral particularity of the people called Christian as a *theoretical* problem, however insistently we are urged to do so by architectonic systems that insist that it "must" be such-and-such a way.

INDIVIDUAL CHRISTIANS AS INTERNALLY RELATED TO THE COMMUNAL WHOLE

A third aspect under which Hauerwas's model of ethics-as-grammar may be viewed is his eschewal of the subject-object dichotomy. By this I mean that ethics-as-grammar takes seriously the inability of the theologian (the subject) to describe the church's life (the object of the theologian's grammatical analysis) without simultaneously being aware of the inextricability of his or her own life from the collective whole. Each member of the moral community called the church is internally related to others. Each person is a part of the living grammar of the whole.

This way of understanding human relations runs against the grain of the story liberalism tells. As noted above, the story of political liberalism embodies an irreducibly violent ontology. History, on the liberal view, is simply the playing out of the struggle within a complex matrix of material beings that are externally related to one another as causes to effects. However, this reductive physicalist assumption undermines the other pillar of the liberal platform. How can one be truly free if, from the side of the social world, there are innumerable agents that each seek to impose their will on one's own? Most versions of the story try to accommodate the conviction that humans are completely free by positing the human individual as a *self*-causing agent in a way that guarantees human autonomy while leaving unchanged the description of social life as a matrix of cause and effects. But it is precisely at this point that Hauerwas challenges the liberal story on two counts.

First, subject and object are not externally related, but internally related; creation is apocalyptic rather than mechanical; the apparently unbreakable matrix of causes and effects is susceptible to the inbreaking of something new. In this regard Hauerwas finds allies in both Wittgenstein and William Stringfellow. To recall a quotation used earlier, Wittgenstein wrote,

> The truly apocalyptic view of the world is that things do not repeat themselves. It isn't absurd, e.g., to believe that the age of science and technology is the beginning of the end for humanity; that the idea of great progress is a delusion, along with the idea that the truth will ultimately be known; that there is nothing good or desirable about scientific knowledge and that mankind, in seeking it, is falling into a trap. It is by no means obvious that this is not how things are.[56]

In Wittgenstein's words Hauerwas hears echoes of Stringfellow, for whom the term "apocalyptic" was but a "way of reminding us that history is not a seamless web of causal relations."[57] Hauerwas comments:

> Both the "liberal" American academy and "conservative" American politicians are committed, of course, to the opposite propositions — that it *is* obvious that things repeat themselves, that the social world is a sealed network of causally determined functions, that ultimately there

can be neither sin nor hope. As Wittgenstein also noted: "The insidious thing about the causal point of view is that it leads us to say: 'Of course, it had to happen like that.' Whereas we ought to think: it may have happened *like that*—and also in many ways." Stringfellow's apocalypticism enabled him—and demands of us—that we reject the "causal point of view" for a construal of "how things are" as the creation of God who cannot be excluded from creating new possibilities for our lives through our lives.[58]

Not only does the conception of creation as apocalyptic challenge the mechanical view of "world-as-nature" found in Oswald Spengler, but in addition, the Christian view of history construes relationships between human individuals as constituting a story with a *telos*. Of course, liberalism insists on a non-teleological account of human relations in order to protect the autonomy of human subjects.[59] But throughout his academic career Hauerwas has consistently opposed liberalism's notion of persons as those who are merely externally related. Beginning with *Character and the Christian Life*, Hauerwas showed his conviction that agency cannot be reduced to an explanation of causation any more than sentences of the form "I did X" reduce without remainder to "X happened." In stark contrast to the liberal vision, Hauerwas came to think of human existence as irreducibly narrative in texture and of each individual as no more than a co-author in the story of his or her own life. Nevertheless, "narrative web" proved to be a relatively brief stopping point in Hauerwas's longer conceptual journey. On the one hand, the notion of "story" seemed too flimsy to fully express the ways in which the believing community constitutes the material condition of Christian convictions. And, as I have shown, his evolving views of language eventually enabled him to augment the concept of "narrative" to include practices, history, practical reasoning, speech, and theological convictions as threads from which the tapestry of human existence is woven.[60] On the other hand, Hauerwas also backed away from "narrative web" for fear that his readers might misconstrue this locution as *merely* metaphorical. In fact, the language of theology demands far more determinative intracommunal relations than a figure of speech could adequately express. This accounts for some of the fire in his rhetoric against descriptions of the church as a "voluntary" community.[61] The church is not *like* a body; it *is* a body.[62]

The third way to understand Hauerwas's model of ethics-as-grammar, then, is to recognize that, contrary to metaphysically reductionistic versions of human persons—such as those held by Hobbes, Locke, and Kant, who viewed human beings as ontologically prior to community—Hauerwas conceives of the human individual as constituted by his or her relations to others. Milbank asserts that it was Aquinas's genius to describe *friendship* as the apex of virtue, since this entailed the view that human virtues were relational rather than metaphysical. In other words, character is possessed in relation, not in isolation.[63] Much the same move is made by Hauerwas in his recent book, *Christians among the Virtues*.[64] Hauerwas and co-author Charles Pinches argue that the Good, virtue, and community cannot be understood except in terms of each other. However, there is a problem with Aristotle's account of friendship. While Aristotelian friendship excludes difference (on Aristotle's view, friends are those who share the same character traits), it also describes the *best* friend as one in possession of such lofty character that he or she is virtually self-sufficient—a condition that makes for a very poor friend. In contrast, the friendship Jesus commands "is a friendship made possible because through His life a new order has come into being. An order that makes friendship possible not because we are alike, but because we are different."[65] This new order is the eschatological community whose *telos* is none other than friend-forming. Moreover, in salvation, we have been given a constancy and unity of self (by virtue of having found ourselves in God's story and in the community that embodies it) that is sufficient for friendship. Therefore, *self*-sufficiency is not a prerequisite for friendship; we come to each other vulnerable, needy, and interdependent.

The contingency of human existence (or what Hauerwas in other places calls the temporality of human existence),[66] toward which the internal relation between human subjects points, that indicates the third way Hauerwas's model of ethics-as-grammar transcends the liberal story of individualism. Clearly the language of choice dominates the liberal paradigm. Liberalism in the likeness of Kant "can be characterized as the presumption that you should have no story other than the story you *chose* when you had no story."[67] It is inconceivable, to the nonbeliever who has been schooled in Enlightenment thinking, that conversion could be understood as anything other than a choice made by an individual in isolation. However, Christian conversion is so radical that it actually trains us, by immersion in a different community with a different set of constitutive practices than those of liberalism, to see a whole new world. In this way, then, Hauerwas transcends the liberal vision by himself inhabiting a world in which the transfer of citizenship from one conceptual framework to another does not proceed on the basis of choice but rather comes by grace.

The language of "gift" and the gift of language together enable this new self-description. To the extent that we use the language of "choice" in our self-description, we are insufficiently Christian in our practices:

> To be Christian means we must be embedded in practices so materially constitutive of our communities that we are not tempted to describe our lives in the language offered by the world, that is, the language of choice. Only then will Christians be able to challenge an all too tolerant world that celebrates many gods as alternatives to the One alone who is worthy of worship.[68]

But by a *gift* we are trained to see ourselves as "sinners" and "creatures":

> both the notions of creature and sinner require that we find ourselves constituted by narratives we did not create.
>
> As I indicated earlier, that is to put us at deep odds with modernity. For the very notion that our lives can be recognized as lives only as we find ourselves constituted by a more determinative narrative that has been *given* to us rather than created by us, is antithetical to the very spirit of modernity.[69]

The extent of this incommensurability is easy to minimize or overlook. Pluralism is undoubtedly troubling to the modern mind because the onus is on the modern self to "choose" the story that must be deemed true prior to the choosing. But Hauerwas notes that liberalism's way of putting the matter gets things wrong: "For the truth is that since we are God's good creation we are not free to choose our own stories. Freedom lies not in creating our lives, but in recognizing our lives as a gift."[70] Christians take themselves to be individuals whose lives are internally related to each other in such a substantial way that this relation can, at best, be described as "grammatical." Christians do *not* take themselves to be autonomous choosers. But this does not leave us with our heads in the sand or at the mercies of the powers that be, for the Christian language of grace constitutes the real world.

REALISM WITHOUT EMPIRICISM

Wittgenstein once summed up the difficulty he faced: "Not empiricism and yet realism in philosophy, that is the hardest thing."[71] As has been frequently noted, Wittgenstein seems to be a relativist of the most vicious sort: on his view, one cannot apply the notion of "true" to the conceptual framework in which it arises, since conceptual frameworks are neither true nor false but brute givens.[72] In Wittgenstein's defense, D. Z. Phillips and others have claimed that such views do not make Wittgenstein a relativist, since Wittgenstein simply shows that the charge of relativism *fails to be intelligible*: there is no way to measure the "fit" between descriptions of the world and "reality." Lacking a criterion of correspondence, the battle between rival conceptual frameworks must, therefore, be determined on more pragmatic grounds.

However, Wittgenstein's point may have been more subtle: he conceded that deep misunderstanding *may* occur between two or more persons, so deep, in fact, that neither can "find his feet" with the other. But this is a far cry from the use to which some want to put works such as his *On Certainty*. It is very tempting to appeal to Wittgenstein in order to proclaim that "language does *not* correspond to reality" or "the battle between rival conceptual frameworks *must* be decided on pragmatic grounds," as if these sentences were themselves accurate pictures! Our temptation to misuse Wittgenstein in this way runs very deep. For example, when Wittgenstein says that those who "know" and those who don't are separated by a "difference in understanding,"[73] it is very tempting to think that this difference could be overcome by "getting it right," where "getting it right" means having an objective grasp of reality "out there." Yet all of *On Certainty* is an attempt to defuse the putative necessity of realism, at least realism as conceived by G. E. Moore. Moore claimed that from the assertion "I *know* that *p*" it necessarily follows that *p*. Wittgenstein denudes this simplistic form of realism by showing that in ordinary language the sentence "I know that *p*" is not an assertion that *p* corresponds to some reality "out-there." Rather, saying "I know" constitutes a next move in a language-game, a move which goes proxy for "you can rely on it" or "I have reasons that . . . ," and so on.[74] Yet if Moore's empiricism unravels in this way, in what sense can "true" or "truth," "real" or "reality," be legitimately used in ordinary language?

Hauerwas's later works embody an answer to this question. On the one hand, there is no place to stand from which the putative correspondence (or lack thereof) between language and language-independent reality (whatever that is thought to mean) can be measured. Yet on the other hand, the affirmation that language and world are internally (rather than externally) related does not obligate us to abandon all attempts to claim Christian beliefs as true.[75] On the contrary, Hauerwas avers (with Willimon) that

"Beyond the present relativism, even beyond the past confessionalism, we came to feel that theology really does make true or false claims about the way things are. . . ." Consequently, "the Christian faith is intellectually 'imperialistic,' a contentious competitor with all other claimants for truth."[76] As we shall see, Hauerwas's model of ethics-as-grammar indicates two ways his work is moving in the direction of the sort of "realism-without-empiricism" which Wittgenstein sought.

At the outset I wish to be clear that the epistemological realism that Hauerwas envisions does not rely upon a concept of "reality" as something "'out there' waiting to be seen."[77] On the contrary, he eschews representationalism in no uncertain terms: "I am simply calling into question any correspondence theory of truth that presumes that an isolated proposition must fit an equally isolated fact."[78] However, this comment, made in 1997, may mask the conceptual journey Hauerwas has taken to arrive at his current conception of "truth."

Hauerwas's earliest writings betray some ambiguity surrounding his notion of truth. On the one hand, he distanced himself from representationalism with these words (from 1976):

> Put more directly, we often think that a true story is one that provides an accurate statement, a correct description. However, I am suggesting that a true story must be one that helps me to go on, for, as Wittgenstein suggested, to understand is exactly to know how to go on.[79]

Hence, the truthfulness of a story is not understood in terms of its "fit" onto "reality." Yet, on the other hand, the true story is one which equips the reader to handle what Hauerwas calls "the basic ontological invariables of our lives, e.g., fate, anxiety, tragedy, hope and so on."[80] Unfortunately, this way of putting matters shows that Hauerwas had only succeeded in avoiding a language-world dichotomy by virtue of a dichotomy of the *same magnitude* between subject (the one who handles) and object (the basic ontological invariables which appear to exist independent of knowing subjects).

Hauerwas may have tried to escape this ambiguity by pressing the word "true" into multiple uses. For example, in 1976 he wrote, "For at least part of what it means to claim the convictions of Christians are *true* is that they must produce *truthful* lives."[81] Convictions are "true" in the sense that they are pragmatically reliable for "changing the self,"[82] and lives are "truthful" in the sense of being "faithful to our ancient vision."[83] Unfortunately, the multiple ways Hauerwas employed the notion did little to clarify, much less settle, in which sense or senses he thinks the Christian story is "true."

Despite our inability to get any clearer on just what sort of realism Hauerwas envisioned at the inception of his career, one thing is undeniable: he never thought that questions of truth could be abstracted from questions of skillful judgment. In 1977 he wrote,

> But if the story we find in Christ is true, this contemporary story [of political liberalism] cannot be true. For what we must come to recognize is that we are all formed by stories (including the story that we have no story) which we have not chosen. The question is not just what sense of identity is correlated with certain notions of goodness, but which stories that form our identity are true. In this sense every ethic is ultimately judged by how it makes us "available to reality," but "reality" is not "out there" waiting to be seen. Rather to know reality truthfully requires the ability to discriminate between true (good) and false (bad) stories.[84]

Apparently, the question "Which story is true?" cannot be answered prior to the development of skillful discrimination. But since discriminating judgment is cultivated by encountering stories of the true sort, there appears no way to evaluate truth claims in Enlightenment fashion, which is to say, in isolation from a particular community.

In his middle period, Hauerwas's writing displayed a different sort of ambiguity regarding "truth." For example, he insisted that there was "no way to deal with the question of 'truth as such' but only the question of the veracity of this or that claim."[85] Read charitably, these words might be taken as an indication of Hauerwas's refusal, in Wittgenstein's words, to apply the notion of "true" to the system within which the word is used. However, there is a persistent tendency in this period for Hauerwas to argue for the superiority of Christianity *as a whole*.

> I assume that Christian theology has a stake in a qualified epistemological realism. I certainly do not believe, nor did Wittgenstein, that religious convictions are or should be treated as an internally consistent language game that is self-validating. What Wittgenstein has taught me, however, is that if we attend to the diversity of our language we learn to appreciate what a marvelously diverse world we inhabit and how complex claims about the way the world is will inevitably be.[86]

Claims about the world are complex, yes, but apparently not unintelligible. Hauerwas maintained that we are justified in speaking about the way the world is and in thinking that there is some basis, however complex, for our

confidence that Christianity is superior to rival claimants. During this period, Hauerwas looked to MacIntyre's essay, "Objectivity in Morality and
Objectivity in Science," and eventually to his longer treatments, *Whose Justice? Which Rationality?* and *Three Rival Versions*, for clues as to how this
superiority might be established. It is not without reason, therefore, that
Hauerwas sheepishly later admitted to a latent imperialism in these middle-
period writings that stemmed from a hankering after a theology that is able
to silence all comers by having the most comprehensive story.[87]

In his middle period, Hauerwas was not so brash as to claim that Christianity overcomes the "ontological invariables" of human existence, as he
did in his earliest works. However, he exhibits a lingering tendency to think
of human existence in overly generalized terms—for example, as irreducibly *narrative* in shape. Thus, narrative served as the fulcrum for measuring the strength of rival traditions. In various places, Hauerwas tried to
spell out criteria of superiority while simultaneously trying to avoid the sort
of entanglements which haunt Lindbeck's unhappy model of "correspondence with Ultimate Reality."[88] Unfortunately, he was overly enamored with
estimating Christianity's superiority on theoretical grounds. And this misses
the point of his best insights regarding the central role *phronēsis* ought to
play for both the Christian and the Christian ethicist.

More recently, Hauerwas has come to realize that there is a profound
difference between making universal truth claims (e.g., "All have sinned
and fallen short of the glory of God") and claims about the superiority (narrative or otherwise) of Christianity as a whole. He has come to acknowledge
that the latter is misguided for appealing to "narrative" in the abstract;[89] for
catering to human lust for control in the "out-narrating" of all rivals;[90] and
for speaking in a voice that pretends to have gained a bird's-eye view of matters. Perhaps he was able to ease his grip on the project to demonstrate the
progressive superiority of Christianity after he has spotted these same ten-
dencies in John Cobb and learned better how to describe himself in opposite terms:

> Accordingly, I do not desire nor would I know how to give Chris-
> tian reasons for being "progressive." I seek, rather, to know how to go
> on when I do not know where I am. I assume this is not a new condi-
> tion for Christians to be in, as being a member of the church becomes
> necessary exactly because the claims of Jesus are meant to put us out
> of control. However, once we Christians learn how to tame our pen-
> chant for control (or, to put it bluntly, our felt need to run the world),
> to pretend that we know not only where we are but where everyone else

is or should be, maybe we will live such joyful lives that others may actually be attracted to the celebration we call worship.[91]

Hauerwas's transition toward realism-without-empiricism is aided, of course, by his coming to acknowledge the internal relation between subject and object, praxis and theory, and especially between language and world. In short, because language is conceived as internally related to the world that it constitutes, *claims about that world cannot but be realistic for the speakers of that language.* The question, therefore, is no longer realism vs. something else, but "Whose realism?"

> For example, Christians are well aware of how easy it is to live as if the world has no creator. It is easy to live in a world where pieces of wood are just pieces of wood. But to live in such a way is not to live in the world "as it is." For to live in the world "as it is" is to be the kind of people who can see that everything has been created to glorify its creator. To fail to live in such a way is to deny the way the world "is." This is why Christians believe that imagination formed by the storied practices of the church constitute the ultimate realism.[92]

I am not convinced that Hauerwas ever quite escapes the temptation to specify ways in which Christianity is demonstrably superior to rival traditions. For example, recently he has wondered whether Christian *speech* can be shown to be superior to rival languages (such as science).[93] And perhaps such optimism is part and parcel of what it means to be a believer. Nevertheless, his version of realism does have the advantage of reflecting one of Hans Frei's crucial insights:

> In philosophical terms Frei's appeal to the church as the *subject* of the narrative as well as the *agent* of the narrative is a reminder that the narrative does not refer but rather people do. To isolate the biblical narratives in and of themselves would be equivalent to considering the truth and falsity of sentences separate from their context of utterance. Once this is understood, Frei's proposal cannot be seen as an attempt to avoid realist claims but rather an attempt to situate the context of those claims.[94]

These two aspects of Christian claims—that the church is both the speaker of the claims as well as the content of the claims—conspire to form a realism of the nonempirical sort. In order to better understand this, consider

the following sentence: "English is a living language." This sentence, com-
posed in English, (1) is realistic in the ordinary language sense that what it
is "about," namely the fact that some people today speak English, is being
affirmed. Yet, this sentence (2) cannot be realistic in the empirical sense,
since its veracity cannot be determined by an investigation into whether the
sentence "accords" with "facts" that can be apprehended nonlinguistically;
there is no such vantage point from which to measure such a putative correspondence.[95] However, this sentence (3) is realistic in a nonempirical
sense. The "realism" of this sentence is not a property of the sentence *qua*
sentence. Rather, its "realism" names an aspect under which a given human
language-user may, or may not, come to see such-and-such a particular sentence. In short, "realism" can only be ascribed to the sentence, "English is
a living language," by someone who understands the sentence. In the absence of a convincing theory of truth (such as the theory of correspondence), conditions for the truth of a sentence become closely tied (in this
case, identical) with the intelligibility of the sentence. In other words, if
theories about truth are unavailable (for whatever reason), then sentences
in the form "*p* is true" have roughly the same function as the simple assertion "*p*." However, "*p*" is dependent for its intelligibility upon the particular language-game (and the correlative form of life) in which it was framed.
The statement "You may not castle while in check" has prior dependence
upon there being instances of the game of chess being played. To put a finer
point on it, only in such practical contexts could sentences about chess ever
emerge.

In the case of "English is a living language," the practical context which
gives this sentence its intelligibility includes, among other things, the actual speaking of English sentences, of which the example sentence is a crucial instance. Thus, the person who is in the position to evaluate the truth
of the sentence "English is a living language" must be one who understands
this sentence and one whose understanding therefore constitutes conditions
for the truth of this sentence precisely because, in understanding it, the
reader is included in the group of English speakers whose reality is both presupposed and affirmed by the assertion itself. This is realism, but of a nonempirical sort.

Hauerwas claims that the church is both the subject and the object of
the Christian claims about the way the world really is. Christianity is the
language in which these claims are framed, and such a language presupposes for its intelligibility the existence of a community of speakers whose
correlative form of life gives the utterances their sense. Simultaneously, the

Christian claims of the gospel are "about" salvation, which, as discussed in chapter 4, is irreducibly political in nature. In other words, the gospel is about the Christian community, inclusion into which—by virtue of becoming a practitioner of its form of life and language—constitutes salvation. Christian claims are realist in the nonempirical sense, therefore, not because conditions for their truth rely upon "correspondence with reality" but rather because the utterance of the claims *creates and fulfills* its own conditions for being true. Another way to put it is that the speaking of the gospel creates the world which the speaker and hearer—insofar as they speak and hear—automatically inhabit. This occurs in two ways. First, the utterance— insofar as it is an utterance of a sentence—is correlative with the reality of a community of speakers. Second, the utterance, insofar as it is intelligible, enfolds comprehending hearers into this community.

Hauerwas himself is engaged in several different types of Christian discourse. His recent *Prayers Plainly Spoken*[96] contain many examples of first-order Christian speech (namely, prayers), as do his sermons collected in *Unleashing the Scripture* and *Sanctify Them in Truth*. On other occasions he writes as a Christian theologian, which is to say, he elucidates the grammar of first-order Christian speech. On yet other occasions, as he traces the grammar of theological language (i.e., the grammar of grammatical analyses of first-order speech), he writes as a philosopher of religion. My point is this: the three types of Christian discourse (piety, theology, philosophy)[97] he practices are not related as language to meta-language to metametalanguage but as a variety of language-games played within the sphere of the language of ordinary Christians. In every case, despite his sometimes enigmatic and convoluted style, the sense of his words rests upon the praxis of the believing community. Granted, his engagement of others in these forms of Christian discourse augments the conversation. But his own inclusion into the community of the faithful was not, nor could it ever have been, of his own doing. For this reason, despite the endless torrent of words from his pen, that his words mean anything at all is a gift of grace.

SURMOUNTING APORIAS BY GRACE

Uncovering the family resemblance between Wittgenstein and Aristotle (explored in chapter 5) has been made possible in part by a relatively recent rebirth in Aristotelian studies by followers of Wittgenstein. Moreover, not only has Wittgenstein occasioned a revised reading of Aristotle, his work has also seemed to open up the space both for a recovery of Aristotle's best ethical insights and for a robust appropriation of these insights by distinctively Christian ethicists. It is in this space that Hauerwas finds a home.

Hauerwas, in a recent essay, notes that before the Reformation, theological ethics could not have been identified as an academic discipline, which is to say, as having its own distinctive domain, because ethics was thought to encompass the entirety of human affairs. Not only would earlier church fathers have found the modern distinction between ethics and other disciplines (such as theological doctrine) puzzling, they probably would have considered it a profound theological mistake.[98] Yet it was precisely the Protestant Reformers' polemic against "works," together with a zeal to distance themselves from any sort of holistic understanding of the church as a political entity, that produced the eventual distinction between doctrine and ethics, on the one hand, and between personal and social ethics, on the other. Since then, ethics has become an especially perplexing task.

> The birth of modernity is coincident with the beginnings of "ethics" understood as a distinguishable sphere or realm of human life. Faced with the knowledge of the diversity of moral convictions modern people think of themselves as haunted by the problem of relativism. If our "ethics" are relative to time and place, what, if anything, prevents our moral opinions from being "conventional?" If they are conventional some assume they must also be "arbitrary." But if our morality is conventional how can we ever expect to secure agreements between people who disagree? Is it our fate to be perpetually at war with one another? "Ethics" becomes that quest to secure a rational basis for morality so we can be confident that our moral convictions are not arbitrary.[99]

In the modern period it was assumed that there could be only two options for convincing oneself that morality was not arbitrary. If one tried to do ethics (or theology) from below, by appeal to human experience, one would merely reproduce sociology and be left puzzled as to how to move from "is" to "ought." If one attempted to do ethics from above, one could not avoid reproducing the confused assumptions about language that modernity has been wont to surmount.[100] Both approaches are lamentably problematic for theological ethics:

> By starting from the 'bottom up,' by trying to show the intelligibility of morality in itself, we cannot help but give an account of a world in which God does not finally matter. . . . But if we begin from the

'top-down,' that is, with God the Commander, then the God who commands risks appearing arbitrary or at best external to God's own creation.[101]

The impasse that resulted from modernity's assumption that ethics *must* be done either from "the bottom up" or from "the top down" was surmounted by Wittgenstein, who labored to show that language and world were internally related; one cannot begin from either the top or the bottom. One must begin in the middle of a particular, concrete community whose identity-constituting form of life is determinative for the proper application of the means by which ethics and theology take place at all, namely, their common language.

In saying that Wittgenstein opened up the space for ethics to be Christian, I am not saying simply that he trumpeted the need for something like sound judgment (*phronēsis*) in a world lacking objective moral norms, or that he tried to show that the inescapable contingency of the human condition ought to discipline the hubris embodied in our quest to make all forms of learning a matter of *technē*, or that he eschewed general explanations in favor of a philosophical therapy that equipped particular human subjects with the responsiveness and fluency to "go on." I am saying all this and more, for these are but reminders that ethics, insofar as it is "done" at all, is done with a language. Such a language cannot be simply an instrument, as a scalpel is in the hand of surgeon. Rather, language use is constitutive of the speaker and the speaker's world as well as a reflection of a community's form of life.

Hauerwas has come to think of Wittgenstein's startlingly profound alternative as illuminating the proper appoach to ethics and theology (proper in the sense of being commensurate with the narratively- and linguistically-shaped identity of those called Christian). He has done so precisely because Wittgenstein pointed the way to overcoming the long-standing division between natural revelation (including observations of the ways human creatures live together) and the divine revelation that comes by grace: our access to either depends upon a language whose meaningfulness is the function of the concrete practices of a particular community.

By concretely situating the relationship between nature and grace within the ethical practices of everyday Christian life (the content and shape of which are stipulated in the Decalogue), I want to show that the proper way to construe knowledge of God is neither from 'the bottom up' nor from 'the top down' (insofar as this strategy merely reproduces the epistemological dualisms upon which modernity founders) but is according to the mutual interpenetration of grace and nature as exhibited in the inescapably analogical and historically ordered uses of language by which God's relation to God's creation is articulated.[102]

Thus Hauerwas admits, "I try to do theology in a manner that exposes the politics, the material conditions, of Christian speech,"[103] because "theology gains its intelligibility through the practices of the church."[104] What he achieves by this attention to the grammar of theology is the realism-without-empiricism that Wittgenstein tried to show was possible if only the pretensions of modernity were first surrendered. Hauerwas offers two premodern precedents that exemplify what Wittgenstein and he are after.

First, Hauerwas notes the curious connection that St. Paul sees between stealing and truth-telling:

> So then, putting away falsehood, let all of us speak the truth to our neighbors, for we are members of one another. Be angry but do not sin; do not let the sun go down on your anger, and do not make room for the devil. Thieves must give up stealing; rather let them labor and work honestly with their own hands, so as to have something to share with the needy. Let no evil talk come out of your mouths, but only what is useful for building up, as there is need, so that your words may give grace to those who hear. And do not grieve the Holy Spirit of God. . . . (Eph. 4:25–30, NRSV)

So long as we remain bewitched by representational theories of language, it seems self-evident that one might speak a true sentence (defined as corresponding to a state of affairs in view) entirely untainted by the character of the speaker. But stealing, to name a behavioral example, undermines our ability to speak the truth. Now it is trivially obvious that the truth value of the sentence "All men are evil brutes!" is a function of the speaker's identity. Consider the difference it makes whether Gloria Steinem or Billy Graham were to speak it! But this example alludes to the deeper point that truthful speech requires orthopraxy, since the sense of a sentence depends upon the pattern of human relationships in the community from which it is spoken. Thus the Pauline assertion of a close connection between Christian behavior and the quality of Christian speech is nothing less than the requirement that Christians "be a community capable of speaking the truth."[105] Of course stealing is connected with speaking the truth; if our intracommunal praxis is distorted, the sense of our speech is likewise twisted. Speaking truthfully about the way things are (realism) depends upon the kind of people we are—a dependency that disregards the unattainable demands for "objectivity" and "correspondence" foisted upon us by well-intentioned empiricists. What is this if not realism-without-empiricism?

Hauerwas finds a second example in the use that both Aquinas and Luther make of the Decalogue. Since the Enlightenment, it has become commonplace to think of the second table of the law as expressing the baseline for a universal morality that can be perceived by reason under the light afforded by nature. That this view is yet another distortion of modernity can be shown by the way both Luther (who wrote just prior to modernity) and Aquinas (the putative champion of *natural* theology) uniformly presume that the so-called "moral" commandments (4–10) are conceptually inseparable from the so-called "religious" commandments (1–3). This does not mean that the obligations of a common morality should be expanded to include worship of YHWH. Rather, the interconnectedness of all the commandments signifies that love of neighbor is simultaneously love of God, and, conversely, that admonitions to love one's neighbor are unintelligible apart from love of God. Taken this way, the Decalogue does not express a minimum or baseline common morality but the political constitution of a particular historical community. The Decalogue ordered Israel's communal form of life, an ordering which enabled sentences (such as those of ethics and theology) spoken from within this determinative form of life to have a sense.

> Aquinas' and Luther's accounts of the Decalogue help us see how any attempt to tell the truth about God is unavoidably connected with our ability to speak the truth about the world. Truth about the way things are, accordingly, cannot be isolated from the kind of people capable of acknowledging [or better, speaking] the way things are. For the way things are, the God who creates the way the world is, is revealed by a people trained to be truthful. Holiness and truth are inseparable, which means that no metaphysics is or can be sufficient if a community has lost the [linguistic] skill to recognize lies. Such a skill, moreover, requires constant attention since truth at one time or in one context can so quickly become the lie.[106]

Once again, speaking truthfully (realism) depends upon the kind of people we corporately are. The socially constituted world that we inhabit allows us to speak truthful descriptions to each other without needing to subject our sentences to mythical criteria for correctness such as "correspondence with reality." This is realism-without-empiricism. And to live in this world is to see why the description "without empiricism" is not a lamentable deficiency.

It should be evident from this discussion that it was only possible for Hauerwas to conceive ethics as grammar after he had been trained to "go on in the same way" by a regiment of reading Wittgenstein. And yet despite the inevitable similarities between the two, there is one glaring difference. Wittgenstein's style in philosophy—an achievement of which he was understandably proud—was intentionally and thoroughly aporetic.

By "aporetic" I allude once again to the irreconcilable tensions throughout Wittgenstein's corpus that fairly beg for some sort of reaction from his readers. When I first noticed these tensions, I grew increasingly uncomfortable—not just because these tensions were terribly knotty (which, of course they were), but because Wittgenstein had succeeded in changing the nature of problem-solving for me: I knew I could not search for *general* solutions to these tensions without abandoning what Wittgenstein had already taught me. I grew more hopeful under the assumption that these tensions might be overcome in MacIntyrean fashion. Following *Whose Justice? Which Rationality?* I fancied that Wittgenstein was the authoritative voice that had established a "postmodern" tradition superior to modernity.[107] As I initially conceived it, there were three problems that constituted his distinctive "epistemological crisis": ethical individualism, fideism, and relativism. I had hoped to find in Hauerwas someone who had traveled further along the trajectory established by Wittgenstein and arrived at a position that was, therefore, superior to Wittgenstein on precisely these three issues.[108] However, I was haunted by the way my project thus conceived— both in form as well as content—subsumed Wittgenstein's work under a more general theory (in this case, what I took to be MacIntyre's theory of historicism). And I feared that there was something terribly un-Wittgensteinian about the way I had framed the task.

What follows is my attempt to surmount these difficulties with the help of a suggestion made by David Burrell. The provisional character of my ending place may simply reflect my own lack of fluency, But I invite others to further the conversation begun here. Burrell's suggestion made to me was that there may be a family resemblance between the appropriation Hauerwas makes of Wittgenstein and what Edward Booth describes as Aquinas's surmounting of aporias in Aristotle.[109]

The term "aporia" is really more of a comment on the genre or style of a philosopher's writing than on the epistemological status of specific theses he or she sets forth. Taken one way, statements which comprise an aporia may appear contradictory. For example, in *Metaphysics*, Aristotle rejected Plato's view that Forms have an eternal and immutable self-subsistence, insisting that form only exists insofar as it exists *in re*, in particular things. Instead of a separable Form, Aristotle claimed that the primary substrate of a thing is its substance. But which of the three aspects—matter, form, or their combination—is most determinative of a thing's identity? Brute matter cannot be substance, since formless matter lacks the individuation and "whatness" required for knowable identity. Nor can the form-matter complex be regarded as fundamental, since a combination is always posterior to its component parts. But that seems to leave Form as the primary substrate—the very option espoused by Plato that Aristotle was intent on rejecting.

Yet taken another way, a set of dissonance-producing statements may be seen as moments in a pedagogical conversation. In Aristotle's case, the statements he offered each opposed general theses asserted by Plato. However, since each of Aristotle's statements must be understood in light of the whole discussion, they each retain a sense of tentativeness that is uncharacteristic of universal theses. The tension that persists between them cannot be solved in general. In fact, the aporias cannot be solved, dissolved, or removed, because they are essential to Aristotle's philosophical pedagogy. In other words, Aristotle utilizes aporias in order to press the ambiguity of language into a pedagogical direction: aporias that emerge from the way language is susceptible to multiple senses are useful for schooling students in the fluency necessary for perceiving which sense applies, at which time, to which extent, and under which conditions. Thus for Aristotle, aporias do not assert general philosophical theses, but engage students in a self-consuming conversation. As Booth explains,

> The metaphysics of Aristotle consists of a series of deeply thought-out philosophical figures, coincident in outline but not in detail; hence the impression of obscurity and difficulty. At first sight the acknowledged and unacknowledged aporias seem to be nothing but a statement of insoluble difficulties; but this is not the whole case: the aporias are artfully exposed so that the reader may be led by them into ontology, or epistemology, itself. To appreciate the aporia *from within* is a mark of competence; like an initiate he then perceives what kind of problem

the philosopher again and again attempts to resolve, what limits the factors that refuse to come together, their area of operation and their area of independence; and what kind of partial answer is temporarily tolerable.[110]

When one proceeds according to the path of the aporias, one becomes fluent in the grammar of them; one develops an appropriate familiarity with the kinds of problems that are involved, as well as the inherent conceptual limits of the discussion, with the result that deceptively complete, though partial, theoretical answers are not mistaken for final ones.[111]

Clearly what Booth has identified as an aporetic methodology in Aristotle resembles the philosophical therapy we have already met in Wittgenstein, who by such therapy strove to cultivate the "taste" of his students.[112] Both thinkers hoped for others who, having taken the trouble to travel the aporetic route, would come to possess the skill necessary to carry on the conversation. What neither fully anticipated were the ways in which fully trained apprentices might also surmount the aporias by means of a creative responsiveness made possible by their own particular concrete contexts. For Aristotle, this apprentice was, of course, Thomas Aquinas.

Booth utilizes the German *Aufhebung* to denote the sort of transformative appropriation Aquinas made of Aristotle. The term, for which there is no tidy English equivalent,

> indicates a supervening unity such that its antecedents figure as "moments." Although the "logic" of such an integration of consequent unity and antecedent moments is explicit in Hegel only, it may be clear enough to say that, in *Aufhebung*, the antecedents are viewed as contributive to the consequent unity; they are in a sense functional with respect to a unity surpassing them. It is essential in this connection that the unity in question is treated as more "true" than its antecedents.[113]

In Thomas's case, his *Aufhebung* was neither simple eclecticism nor syncretism but a response that sprung from a mastery of Aristotle's conceptual language and a creativity born of a context vastly different than that of Aristotle.

It is a matter of historical fact that Thomas did not *refute* Aristotle's aporias (although such an option may have been tempting to him), a move that would have rendered him even more Neoplatonic than his theological predecessors, Boethius and Pseudo-Dionysius. But neither did Thomas embrace Aristotle so completely that he undertook to "solve" the aporias (were that even possible); that would have rendered Thomas *simply* Aristotelian. Rather, Thomas moved further from Plato by extending the Aristotelianization of Neoplatonism that had already begun at the hands of Boethius and Pseudo-Dionysius.[114] In the process, Thomas manifested the sort of skilled judgment that Aristotle's aporias aimed at cultivating in his readers. However, Thomas went on to make a move that was not open to Aristotle in his Athenian context: Thomas offered positive theological content that rendered Aristotle's aporias no longer germane to the conversation.

> And here Thomas's own method of dealing with the Aristotelian material is important. His doxographic reduction of the Aristotelian material to its characteristic points, which demanded the solution, or at least omission, of whatever was aporetic, and the fundamentality of his conception of *esse* as a locus of union with it, allowed two ontologies to be brought together with the least disturbance to the concepts of each, their relationship facilitated by his own overall uniform stylistic treatment. The search for a total interpretation of Thomas's philosophy as Aristotelian is a vain one; as also the search for a partial Neoplatonist ontology within it, in the sense of integral wholes and parts: neither proposal discerns the way in which it was intended to bring the two elements together.[115]

The aporias, which Aristotle had purposed for the reader's struggle, were, in the end, subordinated by Thomas to the philosophy of being (*esse*) that he had been graced with by his theological forbears (especially, Boethius and Pseudo-Dionysius). Thomas was neither Aristotelian nor Neoplatonist, but Christian—a fact that required him not only to transform some conceptions (because of their pagan origins) but also to introduce a particular notion of God into the discussion, thus changing the very questions that framed the original conversation.[116] Thomas's context—namely, thirteenth-century Catholic Christianity—enabled him to knit together voices from both the Aristotelian and Neoplatonist traditions, and while he maintained similarities to both of these camps, strictly speaking, Thomas belonged to neither camp. Thomas surmounted the Aristotelian aporetic—not by a general explanation that "solved" Aristotle's aporetic objections to Plato's doctrine of Form in a way that would surely have pleased both sides, but by changing the terms of the conversation (of which he had become a fluent interlocutor) through the introduction of the theologically derived conviction regarding the direct dependence of every creature upon their Creator for their existence. This theologically rich notion of God's being (*esse*), when rightly understood, has totalizing ramifications, for by it "everything is placed in the theological context of the knowledge proper to the divine Word."[117] As this conviction was not of Thomas's own making, but one that he was given by simple virtue of his inclusion in the community of Christ-followers, we can properly say that Thomas scaled Aristotle's aporias in order to subsequently surmount them by grace.

I come at last to the consideration of Hauerwas's relation to the aporetic methodology of Wittgenstein, by means of which he has claimed to have gained a degree of clarity he could not have possessed apart from wrestling with Wittgenstein's writings. In 1981, Hauerwas expressed his own hope that his essays, like Wittgenstein's aphorisms, should engage the reader in a similar self-consuming struggle.[118] Nearly two decades later he mused:

> Do I represent a method for others to use? Recently a student who is doing her PhD with me was told by another graduate student: "Hauerwas will never be able to establish a school because after he is gone it will never hold together. The only reason the contradictions in his position are not more apparent than they are is because they are part of the same body." An extraordinarily astute remark that is all the more important given the account of the body I develop in this book. Of course, I hope it is not the case that the way I try to do theology is filled with contradictions, but I know that if what I have been trying to do is even close to being right, then everything yet remains to be done. And because everything remains to be done, of course, I hope the work [i.e., conversation] will be shared and continued.[119]

Hauerwas would be the first to admit that the style of his writing falls far short of the power displayed by Wittgenstein and that the tensions his own work engenders may simply be the fault of his own inelegance. And yet, Hauerwas does not simply parrot Wittgenstein's aporias, tailoring them slightly for a new generation. In stark contrast to Wittgenstein, Hauerwas seems almost driven to make explicit claims that are universal in scope (e.g., "Jesus is Lord"). How can one so thoroughly schooled by Wittgenstein make so many nonaporetic statements?

The answer, at least in part, is embedded in the passage just cited. Hauerwas compliments the graduate student's complaint for being particularly astute in light of "the account of the body I develop in this book." The term "body" turns out to have a surprising referent, for it is Hauerwas's conviction that a believer's physical body is constituted by the Body of Christ, the church, and not the other way around. Since the Body of Christ is not of one's own making, neither are our lives our own. We receive our lives only by grace. I suggest, without implying that Hauerwas can be compared to Aquinas, that the manner in which Hauerwas has "gone on" in relation to Wittgenstein is analogous to the manner of Thomas's *Aufhebung*.

Wittgenstein sought to counter confusions engendered by a philosophical method gone awry, namely, the giving of general explanation. However, he could not refute the method (or the theses born of it) without becoming guilty of the very same confusion. Nor could he persuasively counter the totalizing pretensions of general schemes by offering some given particularist response (such as has been offered by Marxists or Thomists); the fact that philosophy, when conceived as a form of *technē*, so easily subsumes particular views under a broader theoretical rubric is part of its enchanting power. Rather, Wittgenstein confounded the generalists on their own terms. He appropriated their overly mundane language (a language purged of all reference to history, culture, morality, and religion) and constructed aporias that *could not* be solved in general. It was not the aporias that changed when they were successfully encountered, but rather the reader's own conceptions. Thus, as Wittgenstein intended, the aporias would be lasting ones, standing as the obstacles by which novices were trained to skillfully navigate a course through and, hopefully, beyond modernity. The unsolvable character of these aporias makes them fitting responses for Wittgenstein to have made to his own mid-twentieth-century Anglo-American context. And yet, while his aporias could not be solved in general, they can be obviated in particular.

Hauerwas was schooled by Wittgenstein. His diagnosis of modernity was that the ethical concepts we have inherited from Enlightenment thinkers—concepts such as "human rights" and "the categorical imperative"—are far too abstract to provide the tutelage that concrete human beings require.[120] Consequently, he can see no reason for theology or ethics to mimic the approach of *technē* as modern philosophy has done. He cautions,

> theology has lost its way when it attempts to provide a *theory* of the meaningfulness of religious convictions. The task of theology is primarily finding the means to remind us what we are or should be doing when we profess adherence to the claim that God has acted graciously through Israel and Christ.[121]

Christian discourse is so rich that attention to it provides us with all the resources we need to skillfully inhabit the world in a Christianly way.

Indeed only a community that has properly learned to honor mothers and fathers, to share rather than steal, to speak truthfully and to respect what rightfully belongs to one another, and, equally important, to recognize through all these lessons what constitutes idolatry—only a community so formed is capable of, and more important, desires to worship the one true God truly.[122]

Hauerwas's ethics-as-grammar is at once descriptive and prescriptive, and both tasks are necessary if theologians are "to help the church produce adequate speakers of the faith."[123] In that the *descriptive* task belongs to Christian discourse, each description, if rightly done, is an exercise that schools the reader's fluency. And since the sense of Christian discourse is a function of the linguistic community's praxis, the *prescriptive* task simply calls for believers to maintain the proper sense of their speech by sustaining the community's identity-constituting form of life.

Hauerwas has recently written,

> I have always hoped that my work might exhibit Cardinal Suhard's claim: "To be a witness does not consist in engaging propaganda nor even in stirring people up, but in being a living mystery. It means to live in such a way that one's life would not make sense if God did not exist."[124]

As we have seen, for Hauerwas "to live in such a way" is a widely ramified concept. To be a Christian is to be a witness; to be a witness is to skillfully engage in Christian discourse; skillful engagement in Christian discourse requires time-intensive participation in particular historical practices; such historical practices constitute a political reality over which we, as individuals, exercise little or no control and yet in which we find salvation. For by means of this community we are schooled to speak of, for, and to God.

> Gracious God, humble us through the violence of your love so we are able to know and confess our sins. We want our sins to be interesting, but, God forgive us, they are so ordinary: envy, hatred, meanness, pride, self-centeredness, laziness, boredom, lying, lust, stinginess and so on. You have saved us from "and so on" to be a royal people able to witness to the world that the powers that make us such ordinary sinners have been defeated. So capture our attention with the beauty of your life that the ugliness of sin may be seen as just that—ugly. God, how wonderful it is to be captivated by you. AMEN.[125]

NOTES

INTRODUCTION

1. Personal correspondence, 25 March 1998.

2. See Nancey Murphy and Brad J. Kallenberg, "Anglo-American Postmodern Theology," in *Cambridge Companion to Postmodern Theology*, ed. Kevin J. Vanhoozer (Cambridge, UK: Cambridge University Press, forthcoming).

3. Fergus Kerr, *Theology after Wittgenstein* (Oxford, UK: Basil Blackwell, 1986).

4. Joseph Dunne, *Back to the Rough Ground: Practical Judgment and the Lure of Technique* (Notre Dame, IN: University of Notre Dame Press, 1993).

5. PI, p. 227e.

6. "Yes, I have reached a real resting place. And I know that my method is right." M. O'C. Drury, "Conversations with Wittgenstein," in *Recollections of Wittgenstein*, ed. Rush Rhees (Oxford, UK: Oxford University Press, 1984), 125.

7. See, for example, the works of D. Z. Phillips such as *Interventions in Ethics* (Albany, NY: State University of New York Press, 1992) or *Wittgenstein and Religion* (London, UK: St. Martin's Press, 1993).

8. See CV [1931], 11e, [1950], 86e.

9. Søren Kierkegaard, *Concluding Unscientific Postscript*, with introduction and notes by Walter Lowrie, trans. David F. Swenson (Princeton, NJ: Princeton University Press, 1968), 165–16.

10. Words of Wittgenstein's former student, G. E. M. Anscombe, cited in Kerr, *Theology after Wittgenstein*, 32.

11. Paul Engelmann, *Letters from Ludwig Wittgenstein, with a Memoir* (Oxford, UK: Blackwell, 1967), 97.

12. For robust theology in this vein, see Nicholas Lash, *Theology on the Way to Emmaus* (London: SCM Press, 1986).

13. CV [1931], 18e.

14. Friedrich Waismann, *Wittgenstein and the Vienna Circle: Conversatios Recorded by Friedrich Waismann*, trans. Joachim Schulte and Brian McGuinness (New York: Barnes and Noble, 1979), 118.

15. RFM §116, pp. 80-81.

16. Z §455.

17. PR, p. 319.

18. OC §475.

19. OC §478.

20. Cf. PI §96.

21. Stanley Hauerwas, *The Peaceable Kingdom: A Primer in Christian Ethics* (Notre Dame, IN: University of Notre Dame Press, 1983), xxi.

22. "Situation Ethics, Moral Notions, and Moral Theology," in *Vision and Virtue* (Notre Dame, IN: Fides Publishers, 1974; repr., Notre Dame, IN: University of Notre Dame Press, 1981), 29.

23. WL, 21.

24. This term is Wallace Matson's. See *A New History of Philosophy*, 2 Vols. (San Diego, CA: Harcourt Brace Jovanovich, 1987), 2:275f.

CHAPTER ONE   **WORKING ON ONESELF**

1. Ludwig Wittgenstein, *Zettel*, ed. G. E. M. Anscombe and G. H. von Wright, trans. G. E. M. Anscombe (Berkeley and Los Angeles: University of California Press, 1970).

2. Wittgenstein's life and thinking is typically divided into two periods. The early period culminates in the publication of the *Tractatus* in the early 1920s. His later period begins with his return to philosophy nearly a decade later, in 1929, and ends with his death in 1951.

3. Lars Hertzberg, "Primitive Reactions-Logic or Anthropology?" in *The Wittgenstein Legacy*, ed. Peter A. French, Theodore E. Uehling, Jr., and Howard K. Wettstein, Midwest Studies in Philosophy, vol. 17 (Notre Dame, IN: University of Notre Dame Press, 1992), 24.

4. Bernard Williams, "Wittgenstein and Idealism," in *Understanding Wittgenstein*, ed. Godfrey Vesey (Ithaca, NY: Cornell University Press, 1974), 76–95; Norman Malcolm, "Wittgenstein and Idealism," in *Wittgensteinian Themes: Essays 1978–1989*, ed. Georg Henrik von Wright (Ithaca, NY: Cornell University Press, 1982), 87–108.

5. James C. Edwards, *Ethics without Philosophy: Wittgenstein and the Moral Life* (Tampa, FL: University Presses of Florida, 1982); Kerr, *Theology after Wittgenstein*.

6. Perhaps only those who undergo a similar conceptual transformation as Wittgenstein can thereby overcome that which makes his realism-without-empiricism seem so elusive at the outset of the journey.

7. See NB 2.9.16, p. 82.

8. D. Z. Phillips, "The World and 'I,'" *Philosophical Investigations* 18, no. 3 (1995): 237.

9. PR, §§57–58. For a helpful exegesis of this passage see David G. Stern, *Wittgenstein on Mind and Language* (New York: Oxford University Press, 1995), 79–87.

10. TLP 5.47, 3.315.

11. The one notable exception to this pattern is 5.6; but there Wittgenstein uses "my" in a specially restricted sense; in no way does it refer to L. W., but rather, to the generic metaphysical subject.

12. Cited in Ray Monk, *Ludwig Wittgenstein: The Duty of Genius* (New York: Viking Penguin, 1990), 271.

13. TLP 5.6, 4.12.

14. TLP, preface, p. 27.

15. TLP 6.45.

16. See TLP, 6.53, 6.54. Gottlob Frege was the first to differentiate between sense and reference. However, Frege all but ignored the significance of this distinction when he anchored meaning primarily to reference. Similarly, the early Wittgenstein played down the distinction and regarded reference as the ultimate ground of meaning. Wittgenstein's logical atomism was the view that the sense of every significant proposition *must* terminate in some combination of simple objects lest propositions have no determinate meaning at all. This was not so much proved by his logical atomism as it was the presupposition of it. See Stern, *Wittgenstein on Mind and Language*, 53–60.

17. TLP 3.31, 4.023, also N, 14.10.20, p. 16.

18. It is important to note that Wittgenstein did not consider mere lack of reference to be that which makes a sentence senseless, as the logical positivists (e.g., Ayer) did. Rather, both "*p*" and "*~p*" derive their opposing senses from the same source. What gives a proposition its sense is its correspondence to logical space, which is the range of all possible arrangements of simple objects (TLP 4.0621). Thus, some particular complex named by *p* may be logically possible but, in fact, nonexistent. In this case *p* is not nonsensical but simply false (TLP 3.24). A senseless proposition, on this view, is a proposition that attempts to describe a nonexistent simple or something lying outside logical space.

19. TLP 6.54 reads "*dann sieht er die Welt richtig.*" Here "*sehen*" can only be taken to refer to the attitude of the transcendental will toward the world *sub specie aeternitatis*.

20. *Phaedrus*, lines 277–278. Citations from *Phaedrus and The Seventh and Eighth Letters*, translated with introductions by Walter Hamilton (New York: Viking Penguin, 1973), 101.

21. Stanley Fish, "Literature in the Reader: Affective Stylistics," in *Is There a Text in This Class?* (Cambridge, MA: Harvard University Press, 1980), 38.

22. Fish, "Literature in the Reader: Affective Stylistics," 38.

23. Fish, "Literature in the Reader: Affective Stylistics," 38–39.

24. J. L. Austin, *How to Do Things with Words*, ed. J. O. Urmson and Marina Sbisà, 2d ed. (Cambridge, MA: Harvard University Press, 1962, 1975).

25. Fish, "Literature in the Reader: Affective Stylistics," 40.

26. Emphasis added.

27. LW-BR, 19.8.19, in Brian McGuinness and Georg Henrik von Wright, eds., *Ludwig Wittgenstein: Cambridge Letters* (Oxford, UK, and Cambridge, MA: Blackwell, 1995), 124.

28. Michael Dummett, "Frege, Gottlob," in *The Encyclopedia of Philosophy*, ed. Paul Edwards (New York: Macmillan Publishing and The Free Press, and London, UK: Collier Macmillan Publishing, 1968), 225–237.

29. Cited in Monk, *Ludwig Wittgenstein*, 175.

30. *[D]ann sieht er die Welt richtig*; TLP 6.54.

31. Z §457.

32. Lawrence M. Hinman, "Philosophy and Style," *Monist* 63 (1980): 523.

33. Monk, *Ludwig Wittgenstein*, 174–180.

34. The only footnote Wittgenstein made in the *Tractatus* appears at the bottom of the first page of text and contains these sober words: "The decimal figures as numbers of the separate propositions indicate the logical importance of the propositions, the emphasis laid upon them in my exposition."

35. "The work is strictly philosophical and at the same time literary, but there is no babbling in it." Letter to Ficker, cited in Monk, *Ludwig Wittgenstein*, 177.

36. Wittgenstein is explicitly indebted to Heinrich Hertz (and to a lesser degree, Fritz Mauthner) for a conception of representation as a type of model-making that can only be evaluated on social and pragmatic grounds. He clearly does not hold to the type of naive realism espoused by fellow Viennese thinker Ernst Mach. For a discussion of Wittgenstein's conceptual heritage in this regard see Allan Janik and Stephen Toulmin, *Wittgenstein's Vienna* (New York: Simon & Schuster, 1973), 120–166.

37. TLP 4.0621.

38. TLP 5.61 concludes: "What we cannot think, that we cannot think: we cannot therefore *say* what we cannot think."

39. Hinman, "Philosophy and Style," 519–520.

40. Frege's comment cited in Monk, *Ludwig Wittgenstein*, 176.

41. PHIL, 161–199. This selection was one of four from the *Big Typescript* not included in the edited work *Philosophical Grammar*. Citation from 179.

42. Hinman, "Philosophy and Style," 520.

43. After serving in the Austrian army in WWI, Wittgenstein began teaching elementary school in rural Austria in 1920. In 1921 Kegan Paul agreed to publish the English version of TLP the following year. Wittgenstein did not formally return to philosophy until his admittance into Cambridge as an "advanced student reading for Ph.D." in 1929.

44. Cited in Monk, *Ludwig Wittgenstein*, 177.

45. The correlation of the *Notebooks* with the *Tractatus* was done by the editors of the *Notebooks* (G. H. von Wright and G. E. M. Anscombe), who supplied

the corresponding Tractarian decimals in brackets after each pertinent *Notebooks* entry.

46. It might be possible to build a case that the absence of entries between these dates indicates a marked shift in Wittgenstein's thinking triggered by, for example, the influence of Tolstoy. That Tolstoy's influence was profound is not doubted (e.g., see Henry LeRoy Finch, "Wittgenstein's Long Journey: Logical Ideal to Human Norm," *International Philosophical Quarterly* 23 [1983]: 3–11). But to argue for specific causal links between his biography and philosophy is more than I need to make a case for the narrative continuity of his philosophy.

47. I discuss this in more detail in chapter 5. See Russell Nieli, *Wittgenstein: From Mysticism to Ordinary Language* (Albany, NY: State University of New York Press, 1987).

48. PG, 487.

49. Wittgenstein provided the table of contents for "Part II, On Logic and Mathematics." Rush Rhees tried to imitate this for the table of contents of "Part I, The Proposition and Its Sense." It could be argued that the absence of a table of contents in the *Big Typescript* was not an oversight that Wittgenstein intended to correct. Rather, he may have purposely left it off to prevent a reader from thinking that the material could be understood by any means short of working through each page in the order it was written. See p. 489 of PG for further explanation.

50. PG §14.

51. From notes taken by D. A. T. Gasking and A. C. Jackson, cited by Michael Nedo and Michele Ranchetti in *Wittgenstein: Sein Leben in Bildern und Texten* (Suhrkamp, 1983), 270.

52. CV [1931], 17e.

53. CV [1933–34], 24e.

54. M. O'C. Drury, "Some Notes on Conversations with Wittgenstein," in *Recollections of Wittgenstein*, ed. Rush Rhees (Oxford, UK: Oxford University Press, 1984), 96.

55. WL, 21.

56. See PI §133.

57. Rush Rhees, ed., *Recollections of Wittgenstein* (Oxford, UK: Oxford University Press, 1984), 110. Cited in Monk, *Ludwig Wittgenstein*, 297.

58. Drury, "Some Notes on Conversations," 173.

59. Wittgenstein told Malcolm that he always considered the delivery of his lectures a form of publication, but clearly one that was restricted to a particular audience. Norman Malcolm, *Ludwig Wittgenstein: A Memoir*, with a Biographical Sketch by G. H. von Wright (London: Oxford University Press, 1958), 56.

60. Drury, "Some Notes on Conversations," 155.

61. Monk notes that of all the writings of the *Nachlaß*, only this section is free from later emendations. That Wittgenstein withdrew it from publication at the last minute testifies to his fear that his writing might be once again misconstrued as a general theory of language.

62. Drury, "Some Notes on Conversations," 173. The year Wittgenstein finished editing §§1–188 of PI, he had this to say about the energy he invested in writing: "If I am thinking about a topic just for myself and not with a view to writing a book, I jump all around it; that is the only way of thinking that comes naturally to me. Forcing my thoughts into an ordered sequence is a torment for me. Is it even worth attempting now?

"I squander an unspeakable amount of effort making an arrangement of my thoughts which may have no value at all." CV [1937], 28e.

63. Drury, "Some Notes on Conversations," 104.

64. St. Augustine, *The Confessions of St. Augustine*, translated with an introduction and notes by John K. Ryan (Garden City, NY: Doubleday, 1958), vii.20.

65. CV [1939–40], 35e.

66. CV [1939–40], 35e.

67. Citing Lessing's *Theologische Streitschriften*, "Eine Duplik" in Drury, "Some Notes on Conversations," 149 (and 173). See also CV, 16e, 44e, 77e.

68. CV [1932–34], 23e.

69. Jane Heal, "Wittgenstein and Dialogue," in *Philosophical Dialogues: Plato, Hume, Wittgenstein*, ed. Timothy Smiley, Proceedings of the British Academy, 85, Dawes Hicks Lectures on Philosophy (Oxford: Oxford University Press, 1995), 63–83.

70. In favor of this interpretation are statements like the following from 1931: "Perhaps what is inexpressible (what I find mysterious and am not able to express) is the background against which whatever I could express has its meaning." CV [1931], 16e. Consider also the passage from 1946: "An observation in a poem is overstated if the intellectual points are nakedly exposed, not clothed from the heart." CV [1946], 54e.

71. Heal, "Wittgenstein and Dialogue," 73–80. See also Edwards, *Ethics without Philosophy*, 48–60. Edwards claims that Wittgenstein construed the truths of logical as a species of practical reasoning as early as the *Tractatus* (57).

72. Heal, "Wittgenstein and Dialogue," 78.

73. CV, 4, 24, 39.

74. Hinman, "Philosophy and Style," 521.

75. Stanley Cavell, A *Pitch of Philosophy: Autobiographical Exercises* (Cambridge, MA: Harvard University Press, 1994), 10.

76. I have teased out similarities between Wittgenstein and the reader-response theory of literary criticism. For an alternative account see Walter Glannon, "What Literary Theory Misses in Wittgenstein," *Philosophy and Literature* 10 (1986): 263–272.

77. "I ought to be no more than a mirror, in which my reader can see his own thinking with all its deformities so that, helped in this way, he can put it right." CV [1931], 18e.

78. See Robert C. Roberts, "The Philosopher as Sage," *Journal of Religious Ethics* 22, no. 2 (1994): 409–431.

79. Engelmann, *Letters from Ludwig Wittgenstein, with a Memoir*, 126. See also an explanation of Kraus's social-critical views in Janik and Toulmin, *Wittgenstein's Vienna*, 67–91.

80. Engelmann, *Letters from Ludwig Wittgenstein, with a Memoir*, 126.

81. PR, p. 7; emphasis added.

82. For contrasting views of Wittgenstein's "religious point of view" see chapter 5.

83. This received its harshest expression under A. J. Ayer. See Alfred Jules Ayer, *Language, Truth and Logic* (New York, NY: Dover Publications, 1952), 35, 107, 115.

84. D. Z. Phillips, *Interventions in Ethics* (Albany, NY: State University of New York Press, 1992).

85. Roberts, "The Philosopher as Sage," 417. So too, James Wm. McClendon, Jr., has argued persuasively that we must look to the religious character of Wittgenstein's life for what it shows if we are to fully understand his later work. See James Wm. McClendon, Jr., *Witness: Systematic Theology*, vol. 3 (Nashville, TN: Abingdon Press, 2000). B. R. Tilghman seems to have Phillips in mind when he speaks of philosophers who are "vertically" related to the position they criticize and therefore disengaged from the very form of life necessary for them to make interventions that are both intelligent and intelligible. Roberts succinctly observes that such a stance for professional philosophers is out of step with Wittgenstein himself, who as "a deeply ethical man . . . has a particular ethical outlook which he regards as *right* . . . and seeks to *communicate and commend* to other people."

86. Wittgenstein wrote in 1930 that "it is a great temptation to try to make the spirit explicit," CV [1930], 8e. Apparently Wittgenstein maintained after 1930 that philosophy could accomplish the same sort of world-manifesting descriptions as art. See CV [1930], 5. Regarding Wittgenstein's notion of "spirit," Tilghman argues that, early on, Wittgenstein displayed a Cartesian dualism-one which he would later repudiate-when he discriminated between *Geist* (the inner life) and the body which manifests it. While Wittgenstein rejected a causal connection between mind and body, conversely, he also was unwilling to construe bodily action as purely arbitrary. Instead, he settled for describing the two as "internally related."

87. Benjamin Tilghman, *Wittgenstein, Ethics and Aesthetics: The View from Eternity* (Albany, NY: State University of New York Press, 1990), 54, emphasis added. Tilghman is expressing Wittgenstein's appropriation of Spinoza's distinctive sense of "essence," namely, the place of a thing in a whole scheme. For Wittgenstein, essence means "connections" rather than "internal nature." See, CV, 4–5.

88. CV [1930], 4e.

89. Tilghman, *Wittgenstein, Ethics and Aesthetics*, 58.

90. Tilghman, *Wittgenstein, Ethics and Aesthetics*, 85.

91. LC, 11.

92. Cited in G. E. Moore, "Wittgenstein's Lectures in 1930-33," in *Philosophical Occasions, 1912-1952*, ed. James C. Klagge and Alfred Normann (Indianapolis and Cambridge: Hackett Publishing, 1993), 106.

93. RPP I §250.

94. See LC, 6.

95. Moore, "Wittgenstein's Lectures in 1930-33," 106.

96. Moore, "Wittgenstein's Lectures in 1930-33," 105.

97. "Remember how it was said of Labor's playing: 'He is *speaking*.' How curious! What was it about this playing that was so strongly reminiscent of speech? And how remarkable that we do not find the similarity with speech incidental, but something important, big! — Music, *some* music at least, makes us want to call it a language. . . ." CV [1947], 62e.

98. CV [1947], 58e. Emphasis added.

99. Moore, "Wittgenstein's Lectures in 1930-33," 105.

100. RFM I §§167, 168.

101. RFM I, Appendix 1 §2.

102. CV [1931], 17e.

103. Moore, "Wittgenstein's Lectures in 1930-33," 113.

104. Rush Rhees, ed., *Discussions of Wittgenstein* (New York: Schocken Books, 1970), 79.

105. Emphasis added.

CHAPTER TWO   **ETHICS AS AESTHETICS**

1. Stephen Toulmin, *Cosmopolis: The Hidden Agenda of Modernity* (Chicago: University of Chicago Press, 1990), 167, 172.

2. Toulmin, *Cosmopolis*, 40.

3. Toulmin, *Cosmopolis*, 190.

4. See Hauerwas's first chapter, entitled "Christian Ethics in a Fragmented and Violent World," in his *The Peaceable Kingdom*, 1–16.

5. Hauerwas, *The Peaceable Kingdom*, 11.

6. The fact that Hauerwas chose a pre-Enlightenment thinker (Aristotle) the anchor of his doctoral dissertation foreshadowed the way his entire career would be characterized by a polemic against the sort of political liberalism that was fashioned after the Enlightenment project.

7. See Iris Murdoch, *The Sovereignty of Good* (London: Routledge & Kegan Paul, 1970), 32.

8. See Stanley Hauerwas, *Character and the Christian Life: A Study in Theological Ethics* (San Antonio, TX: Trinity University Press, 1975; repr. Notre Dame and London: University of Notre Dame Press, 1994), 33–34.

9. CV [1937], 33e.

10. See *Character and the Christian Life*, 40, for Hauerwas's discussion of the following passage from *Nicomachean Ethics* 1105a27–32: "an act is not performed justly or with self-control if the act itself is of a certain kind, but only if in addition the agent has certain characteristics as he performs it: first of all, he must

know what he is doing; secondly he must choose to act in the way he does, and he must choose it for its own sake; and in the third place, the act must spring from a firm and unchangeable character."

11. Hauerwas, "Situation Ethics," 12–13. Internal citation from Julius Kovesi, *Moral Notions* (New York: Humanities Press, 1967), 111.

12. "Situation Ethics," 16–17.

13. "Situation Ethics," 18.

14. "Situation Ethics," 18 n. 16.

15. "Situation Ethics," 20.

16. Stanley Hauerwas, "The Significance of Vision," in *Vision and Virtue*, 31–32. Internal citation taken from Iris Murdoch, "Against Dryness: A Polemical Sketch," *Encounter* 16 (January 1961): 20.

17. For Hauerwas's self-evaluation see "To Be or Not to Be a Bricoleur," *Koinonia* 4, no. 1 (1994): 109.

18. See Jeffrey Stout, *Ethics after Babel* (Boston, MA: Beacon Press, 1988), 74–77.

19. In the opening pages of *Dispatches from the Front: Theological Engagements with the Secular*, Hauerwas confesses, "I use Trollope because I love Trollope" (Durham, NC: Duke University Press, 1994), 8. In a later note he goes on to say, "It is my hunch that the novel became our primary form for instruction of the moral imagination once we lacked the cultural consensus to make the kind of instruction exemplified by Samuel Johnson in the *Rambler* papers coherent. When I am asked who one should read for moral instruction, I recommend Ms. Manners" (192 n. 13). Other uses of narrative as a pedagogical tool include works by fiction authors Ann Tyler (see "Why Truthfulness Requires Forgiveness: A Commencement Address for Graduates of the Church of the Second Chance," in *Dispatches from the Front*, 80–88) and James David Duncan (see *In Good Company: The Church as Polis* [Notre Dame, IN: University of Notre Dame Press, 1995], 1–16); works by historical figures such as St. Augustine (see Hauerwas, with David Burrell, "From System to Story: An Alternative Pattern for Rationality in Ethics," in *Truthfulness and Tragedy* [Notre Dame, IN: University of Notre Dame Press, 1977], 15–39) and St. Bridget (see "Political Righteousness," *Perspectives: A Journal of Reformed Thought* 8, no. 6 [June 1993]: 8–9); and the stories of real churches (see the books written with William H. Willimon, *Resident Aliens: Life in the Christian Colony* [Nashville, TN: Abingdon Press, 1989] and *Where Resident Aliens Live: Exercises for Christian Practice* [Nashville, TN: Abingdon, 1996]; see also "Abortion Theologically Understood," in *The Church and Abortion: In Search of New Ground for Response*, ed. Paul T. Stallsworth [Nashville, TN: Abingdon, 1993], 44–66).

20. Alasdair MacIntyre, *After Virtue: A Study in Moral Theory*, 2d ed. (Notre Dame, IN: University of Notre Dame Press, 1984), 222.

21. "On Keeping Theological Ethics Theological," in *Revisions: Changing Perspectives in Moral Philosophy*, ed. Stanley Hauerwas and Alasdair MacIntyre (Notre Dame, IN: University of Notre Dame Press, 1983), 30.

22. History tends to serve as a variant of "narrative" for Hauerwas. In *Vision and Virtue* and *Truthfulness and Tragedy*, as well as in *A Community of Character* (Notre Dame, IN: University of Notre Dame Press, 1981), Hauerwas speaks of narrative as *tool* by means of which one interprets the world. For a prominent example of this see "Story and Theology," in *Truthfulness and Tragedy*, 71–81. While this resonates with Wittgenstein's limited use of "paradigm" in RFM I §105 and §158, eventually Hauerwas goes on to use "narrative" in a much more nuanced way. See chapter 6.

23. *Character and the Christian Life*, xviii.

24. This occurs repeatedly throughout the corpus. See, e.g., *The Peaceable Kingdom*, 99; *A Community of Character*, 40; *Christian Existence Today: Essays on Church, World, and Living in Between* (Durham, NC: Labyrinth Press, 1988), 101; *Resident Aliens*, 43.

25. "A Story-Formed Community: Reflections on *Watership Down*," in *A Community of Character*, 9–35. See also Hauerwas's article written with Philip D. Kenneson, "The Church and/as God's Non-Violent Imagination," *Pro Ecclesia* 1, no. 1 (Fall 1992): 76–88. The role stories play in Hauerwas's methodology, albeit limited, has historical precedence. Calvin argued that Scripture was for the Christian what spectacles were for the eyes (*Institutes*, I.14.1; I.6.1). Similarly Wittgenstein once spoke of a picture which could serve as a paradigm for understanding (RFM I §105).

26. Z §138.

27. Hauerwas observes, "it is only seldom that we have occasion to think of ourselves as 'persons'—when asked to identify myself, I do not think that I am a person, but I am Stanley Hauerwas, teacher, husband, father, or, ultimately, a Texan." ("Must a Patient Be a Person to Be a Patient? Or, My Uncle Charlie Is Not Much of a Person But He Is Still My Uncle Charlie," in *Truthfulness and Tragedy*, 129). Moral obligation follows from the *telos* of human life, which is communicated to us by our moral tradition via the stories that identify who we are and how we fit into the scheme of things. Part and parcel of our identity is where we find ourselves in relation to others. Moral obligation, therefore, is internally related to our identity. Spelling out the "we" is a strategy Hauerwas frequently employs and is occasionally the central focus of an entire essay. See, e.g., "Who Is the We?" *Sojourners* 22, no. 3 (April 1992): 15; "Whose Conscience? Whose Emotion?: Review of Sidney Callahan's *In Good Conscience: Reason, Emotion, and Moral Decision Making*," *Hastings Center Report* 22, no. 1 (January/February 1992): 48–49; and "Whose 'Just' War? Which Peace?," in *Dispatches from the Front*, 136–152. For a later account of moral obligation which is tied to thick description of Christian identity see Hauerwas with Charles Pinches, *Christians among the Virtues: Theological Conversations with Ancient and Modern Ethics* (Notre Dame, IN: University of Notre Dame Press, 1997), 166–178.

28. This latter phrase first occurs in 1972: "The Future of Christian Social Ethics," in *That They May Live: Theological Reflections on the Quality of Life*, ed. George Device (Staten Island, NY: Alba House, 1972), 131.

29. *The Peaceable Kingdom*, 30–31. For a later account see *After Christendom? How the Church Is to Behave If Freedom, Justice, and a Christian Nation Are Bad Ideas* (Nashville, TN: Abingdon Press, 1991), 107–111.

30. Rush Rhees explains that perception of family resemblance is not a matter of seeing what all the examples in a given set have in common, as if each example were a fumbling attempt to express the same thing. Rather, "variety is important— not in order to fix your gaze upon the unadulterated form, but to keep you from looking for it." See Rush Rhees, "Some Developments in Wittgenstein's View of Ethics," in *Discussions of Wittgenstein*, 102.

31. Hauerwas, *Truthfulness and Tragedy*, 3.

32. CV [1947], 61e. Cf. the similar remark in CV [1948], 66.

33. The foreword to the *Philosophical Remarks* reads: "This book is written for such men as are in sympathy with its spirit. This spirit is different than the one which informs the vast stream of European and American civilization in which all of us stand. *That* spirit expresses itself in an onwards movement, in building ever larger and more complicated structures; the other in striving after clarity and perspicuity in no matter what structure." PR, 7.

34. PI §201: "This was our paradox: no course of action could be determined by a rule, because every course of action can be made out to accord with a rule."

35. See Saul Kripke, *Wittgenstein on Rules and Private Language* (Cambridge, MA: Harvard University Press, 1982). See also Peter Winch's criticisms of Kripke in "Facts and Superfacts," in *Trying to Make Sense* (Oxford, UK: Basil Blackwell, 1987), 54–63.

36. Edwards, *Ethics without Philosophy*, 188–192.

37. See any of the essays in D. Z. Phillips, *Wittgenstein and Religion* (London, UK: St. Martin's Press, 1993) or *Interventions in Ethics* (Albany, NY: State University of New York Press, 1992).

38. D. Z. Phillips and H. O. Mounce, *Moral Practices* (London, UK: Routledge & Kegan Paul, 1970), 61–78.

39. "The Demands of a Truthful Story: Ethics and the Pastoral Task," *Chicago Studies* 21, no. 1 (Spring 1982): 65–66.

40. "Story and Theology," 80.

41. Strangely, this crime is something for which he regularly takes Gustafson to task. E.g., see "On Keeping Theological Ethics Theological," 16–42.

42. "The Moral Limits of Population Control," in *Truthfulness and Tragedy*, 116–126. For other examples see "Suffering, Medical Ethics and the Retarded Child," 164–168, and "The Demands and Limits of Care: On the Moral Dilemma of Neonatal Intensive Care," 169–183.

43. "Medicine as a Tragic Profession," in *Truthfulness and Tragedy*, 190–191. For another positive example see "Care," in *Encyclopedia of Bioethics* (New York: Free Press, 1978), 145–150.

Whatever is the source of these early tensions, they are clearly resolved by the time of his 1995 essay "How Christian Ethics Became Medical Ethics," in *Religion and Medical Ethics: Looking Back, Looking Forward*, ed. Alan Verhey (Grand Rapids, MI: W. B. Eerdmans, 1995), 61–80. This essay captures especially well the ambiguity of medicine from a Christian perspective. On the one hand, because medicine is a practice it constitutes training in morality, at least at some level. On the other hand, insofar as the story of medicine is not the Christian story, medicine itself threatens to be idolatrous.

44. A *Community of Character*, 6.

45. A *Community of Character*, 3. Cf. Wittgenstein's comment in 1932 that he restrained himself to giving students only "a hint" (BB, 60). Out of this practice grew the later maxim: "Anything your reader can do for himself leave to him" (CV [1948], 77e).

46. LW II, 84e.

47. See chapter 6 for my discussion of Edward Booth, *Aristotelian Aporetic Ontology in Islamic and Christian Thinkers* (Cambridge, UK: Cambridge University Press, 1983).

48. Drury, "Some Notes on Conversations with Wittgenstein" and "Conversations with Wittgenstein," in *Recollections of Wittgenstein*, ed. Rush Rhees, 94.

49. Søren Kierkegaard, *Fear and Trembling*, with an introduction by Alastair Hannay, trans. Alastair Hannay (New York: Viking Penguin, 1985), 62.

50. Søren Kierkegaard, *Purity of Heart Is To Will One Thing* (New York: HarperCollins, 1956 [1846]), 184–197. For an account of "rebellious ethics" see Stanley Hauerwas, "Self-Deception and Autobiography: Reflections on Speer's *Inside the Third Reich*," in *Truthfulness and Tragedy*, 82–98.

51. See Karen L. Carr, "The Offense of Reason and the Passion of Faith: Kierkegaard and Anti-Rationalism," *Faith and Philosophy* 13, no. 2 (1996): 226–251, and Alastair McKinnon, "Søren Kierkegaard," in *Nineteenth Century Religious Thought in the West*, ed. Ninian Smart et al. (Cambridge, UK: Cambridge University Press, 1985), 181–213.

52. Søren Kierkegaard, "The Sickness Unto Death," in *Fear and Trembling and Sickness Unto Death*, translated with introductions and notes by Walter Lowrie (Princeton, NJ: Princeton University Press, 1941[1849]), 146.

53. See *Purity of Heart*, 177–196.

54. See Paul L. Holmer, "Wittgenstein and the Self," in *Essays on Kierkegaard and Wittgenstein*, ed. Richard H. Bell and Ronald E. Hustwit (Wooster, OH: College of Wooster, 1978), 10–31.

55. Janik and Toulmin, *Wittgenstein's Vienna*, 161, 179.

56. Janik and Toulmin, *Wittgenstein's Vienna*, 164.

57. Janik and Toulmin, *Wittgenstein's Vienna*, 162.

58. WVC, 117.

59. WVC, 117.

60. M. O'C. Drury, "Conversations with Wittgenstein," 117.

61. See my chapter 1. See also Edwards, *Ethics without Philosophy*, 215, 208.

62. Edwards, *Ethics without Philosophy*, 235–236, 251.

63. Cited in Rush Rhees, "Some Developments in Wittgenstein's View of Ethics," 100.

64. Rhees, "Some Developments in Wittgenstein's View of Ethics," 100.

65. Rhees, "Some Developments in Wittgenstein's View of Ethics," 101.

66. Rhees, "Some Developments in Wittgenstein's View of Ethics," 103.

67. Waismann, *Wittgenstein and the Vienna Circle*, 118.

68. RFM §116, pp. 80–81.

69. Edwards, *Ethics without Philosophy*, 251.

70. Edwards, *Ethics without Philosophy*, 206.

71. Edwards, *Ethics without Philosophy*, 235–236. See also 243. *Pathos* is Edwards's shorthand for "a "deep impressiveness in things," 233.

72. See Edwards, *Ethics without Philosophy*, 211–214, 216.

73. Edwards, *Ethics without Philosophy*, 216, emphasis added.

74. Edwards, *Ethics without Philosophy*, 255.

75. *Character and the Christian Life*, 7–8.

76. See *Character and the Christian Life*, 33.

77. Søren Kierkegaard, *The Prayers of Kierkegaard*, edited with a New Interpretation of His Life and Thought by Perry D. LeFevre (Chicago, IL: University of Chicago Press, 1956), §30.

78. *Character and the Christian Life*, 169.

79. For Bultmann one's past is the sinfulness from which one must be freed. God's divine command comes to one *in the moment* and therefore calls him or her into action which is now. Bultmann's conception of forgiveness as the *denial* of the past implies that the future is both radically open and the only thing in terms of which the self can be defined. See *Character and the Christian Life*, 157–169.

80. See *Character and the Christian Life*, 36–45.

81. *Character and the Christian Life*, 11.

82. *Character and the Christian Life*, 21.

83. *Character and the Christian Life*, 28. Cp. BB, 38, 42.

84. *Character and the Christian Life*, 26.

85. *Character and the Christian Life*, 21; emphasis added.

86. *Character and the Christian Life*, 27.

87. See *Character and the Christian Life*, 115–128.

88. See *Character and the Christian Life*, 107–115.

89. *Character and the Christian Life*, 109.

90. *Character and the Christian Life*, 96.

91. *Character and the Christian Life*, 106.

92. *Character and the Christian Life*, 105. See also "Judgment and the New Morality," *New Blackfriars* 53 (May 1972): 210–221.

93. See "Agency: Going Forward by Looking Back," in *Christian Ethics: Problems and Prospects*, volume in honor of James Gustafson, ed. Lisa Sowle and J. F. Childress (Cleveland: Pilgrim Press, 1996), 64–79.

94. MacIntyre, *After Virtue*, 209–210.

95. L. Gregory Jones, "Alasdair MacIntyre on Narrative, Community, and the Moral Life," *Modern Theology* 4 (October 1987): 53–69.

96. "Judgment and the New Morality," 215; emphasis added.

97. "Abortion: The Agent's Perspective," in *Vision and Virtue*, 148.

98. "From System to Story," 22.

99. "The Ethicist as Theologian," *Christian Century* 92, no. 15 (April 23, 1975), 409.

100. See "Abortion: Why the Arguments Fail," in *A Community of Character*, 212–229 and "Why Abortion Is a Religious Issue," 196–211.

101. PI §373; Hauerwas, "Story and Theology," 72.

102. "Story and Theology," 73.

103. In the *Confessions* he writes, "Yet for all that I did not think that the Catholic way must be held to by myself, even though it could have its learned defenders who would fully and not absurdly refute objections made to it. Nor did I think that what I had previously held was to be condemned, for both parties seemed to be equal in their defenses. Thus while the Catholic position did not seem to be overthrown, neither did it appear to be the victor. I then earnestly applied my mind to see if it were possible, by means of sure arguments, to convict the Manicheans of falsity. . . . But this I was unable to do." And again, "That they were false *afterwards* became clear to me." St. Augustine, *The Confessions of St. Augustine*, 5.14, p. 131; 6.4, p. 137. Emphasis added.

104. "From System to Story," 33–34.

105. "From System to Story," 24.

106. "The Demands of a Truthful Story," 63.

107. "From System to Story," 34.

108. "Character, Narrative, and Growth in the Christian Life," in *A Community of Character*, 144–145.

109. PI §583. Wittgenstein gives us no reason to limit the temporal context of these "surroundings"; the plot of our lives may be what Wittgenstein has in mind when he muses: "—this particular and not at all simple pattern in the drawing of our life." LW II, 26–27e.

110. John Milbank, *Theology and Social Theory beyond Secular Reason* (Oxford, UK: Basil Blackwell, 1990), 291.

111. "Ethics and Ascetical Theology," *Anglican Theological Review* 16, no. 1 (January 1979), 96.

112. "From System to Story," 29, 30.

113. "The Demands of a Truthful Story," 65–66.

114. "Story and Theology," 225 n. 31; see also 80–81.

115. *The Peaceable Kingdom*, 1–49.

116. *The Peaceable Kingdom*, 11.

117. *The Peaceable Kingdom*, 8–9.

118. *The Peaceable Kingdom*, 37.

119. "The Self as Story," in *Vision and Virtue*, 74.

120. *The Peaceable Kingdom*, 42.

121. *Truthfulness and Tragedy*, 12. The intuition that suffering somehow makes us real is present in Hauerwas's thinking from the very beginning. See "Aslan and the New Morality," in *Vision and Virtue*, 96; and "Judgment and the New Morality," 210, 217. For a mature treatment on owning tragedy, one that uses narratives rather than theorizing about them, see *Naming the Silences: God, Medicine, and the Problem of Suffering* (Grand Rapids, MI: Wm. B. Eerdmans, 1991).

122. Hauerwas writes that "Every community locates and names certain kinds of behavior that are prohibited, but the prohibition is not an end in itself. Rather, such prohibitions 'fit' within the community's sense of its 'telos', that is what it is about, and are justified because the community has learned that it cannot sustain its life and the necessary virtues of its citizens if such behavior is approved or even thought indifferent" ("The Demands of a Truthful Story," 65). For an account of the teleological character of Christian ethics in this vein, see Nancey Murphy, Brad J. Kallenberg, and Mark Thiessen Nation, eds., *Virtues and Practices in the Christian Tradition: Christian Ethics after MacIntyre* (Harrisburg, PA: Trinity Press International, 1997).

CHAPTER THREE   **THIS COMPLICATED FORM OF LIFE**

1. TLP 2.16, 2.2.
2. TLP 4.12.
3. TLP 2.025.
4. TLP 1.1, 2.01.
5. See NB, 83; see also Tilghman, *Wittgenstein, Ethics and Aesthetics*, 52–53.
6. TLP 2.0121.
7. TLP 2.0131.
8. TLP 2.014, 2.0141. Note that even in 1922, Wittgenstein cannot be considered in the critical realist camp; "objects" cannot be construed as mind-independent realities.
9. See TLP 1.1.
10. NB entries dated 31.5.15 and 1.6.15, p. 53.
11. TLP 2.022.
12. TLP 6.13.
13. Models which are externally related to their subject matter must be evaluated by criteria that are outside the model. This is what rendered the correspondence theory of language so problematic: one presumably must stand outside both language and the world to measure their fit. In contrast, Wittgenstein mimicked Heinrich Hertz's methodological genius and devised a model of language that was internally related to language, hence, accountable to criteria internal to the model (i.e., language) itself. On the contrast between Ernst Mach's externally related modeling and Hertz's internally related modeling see Janik and Toulmin, *Wittgenstein's Vienna*, 120–166.

14. TLP 6.41.

15. Ludwig Wittgenstein, *Briefe an Ludwig von Ficker*, Brenner Studien vol. 1, ed. G. H. von Wright, in collaboration with Walter Methagl (Salzburg: Otto Müller, 1969), 35; cited in Janik and Toulmin, *Wittgenstein's Vienna*, 193.

16. TLP 6.41–6.421, 6.432.

17. TLP 3.032; see NB, pp. 12–13, TLP 3.02–3.021.

18. TLP 4, 4.022, 4.063, 4.0641, 4.003, 3.3, 3.315, 3.322–3.323, 3.334; see also NB 20.10.14, p. 16.

19. TLP 4.012–4.013; see also NB, pp. 21–23, 25, 46, 47.

20. NB 77.10.14; 28.10.14, p. 20; TLP 5.47–5.473.

21. NB 24.11.14, p. 32e; see also p. 38.

22. TLP 5.551.

23. PG §107, p. 156. Wittgenstein also wrote, "I am my world," in TLP 5.63. See also 5.631; 5.641.

24. TLP 5.6. See also TLP 3.

25. In this remark "reality" is only a broader variation on the concept "world." The world is everything that is the case while "reality" is everything that is the case together with everything that is not the case, but might have been. TLP 2.04, 2.06.

26. In 1914 projection is still an activity of the mind: "the projection *of the picture* on to reality" (emphasis added, NB, 30e). Yet the idea of projection became for Wittgenstein an increasingly passive notion (e.g., he will speak of lines of projection) that begins to sound like an external relation between language and world.

27. TLP 3.11–3.12, 4.0141.

28. See NB, 21, 46–47.

29. See NB, 23.

30. See NB, 25.

31. NB 1.11.14, p. 23e.

32. NB 18.6.15, p. 63e; cf. TLP 3.23.

33. See TLP 3.11; see also NB, 30.

34. NB 20.6.15, p. 68e.

35. NB, 64. Wittgenstein later declared that even one's perception of a patch of color was a socially trained technique. See RPP II §296.

36. See Monk, *Ludwig Wittgenstein*, 273–274. Ramsey's initial praise and criticism of TLP was published as "Critical Notice of Ludwig Wittgenstein's 'Tractatus Logico-Philosophicus'," *Mind* 32, no. 128 (October 23, 1923): 465–478. For a more general account of the tension between Wittgenstein's conception of logical space and his insistence that elementary propositions are not truth-functionally complex, see Peter Winch, "Introduction: The Unity of Wittgenstein's Philosophy," in *Studies in the Philosophy of Wittgenstein*, ed. Peter Winch (London, UK: Routledge & Kegan Paul, 1969), 1–19.

37. NB, 50, 61–62.

38. SRLF, 34, emphasis added.

39. SRLF, 30.

40. The reliability of conversations can be measured by correlative passages in the *Philosophical Remarks*. Since my intent was to tell the story of Wittgenstein's conceptual transformation, I found WVC much easier to follow next than the constipated self-talk of PR. At least the occasional question asked by Schlick and Wittgenstein's own awareness that he must make himself intelligible to other human beings give WVC a life that PR lacks.

41. WVC, 73–74. Moore reports that ". . . he said . . . that he had made a mistake (I think he meant in the *Tractatus*) in supposing that a proposition must be complex. He said that truth was that we can replace a proposition by a simple sign, but that the simple sign must be 'part of a system'." Moore, "Wittgenstein's Lectures in 1930-33," 54–55.

42. WVC, 220.

43. See PR §81, p. 109.

44. WVC, 77–78.

45. WVC, 89.

46. TLP 2.1512; WVC, 63, see also PR §§54, 82.

47. See PR §17. See also Moore, "Wittgenstein's Lectures," 52–53.

48. TLP 6.341–6.342.

49. WVC, 88–89.

50. WVC, 97.

51. WVC, 90.

52. PR §54.

53. SRLF, 30–31; also PR §93.

54. See PG §13.

55. WVC, 220.

56. WVC, 126.

57. WVC, 126.

58. Rules may be violated, but there cannot be a "hidden" contradiction between rules within that system. WVC, 119, 124.

59. WVC, 76.

60. PR §§82, 83.

61. WVC, 126.

62. WVC, 75, 76.

63. WVC, 74–76, 220; PR §§23, 10.

64. PR §1.

65. PR §§40, 24, 21.

66. RFGB, 118–155. Citation from 131.

67. Oswald Spengler, *Decline of the West*, 2 vols. (New York: Knopf, [1926–28] 1946), 2:23.

68. Spengler, 2:32.

69. Spengler, 2:33. Here Spengler is more in keeping with early-twentieth-century emergentism than with present-day biological sciences.

70. Spengler, 1:5–6.

71. Spengler, 1:97.

72. Drury, "Conversations with Wittgenstein," 127.

73. CV [1930], 6, 5.

74. CV [1931], 14.

75. RFGB, 133. Internal citation is from Goethe's "Metamorphosis of Plants."

76. Jer. 18:7–9, NEB, emphasis added.

77. RFGB, 133.

78. RFGB, 133.

79. PR, foreword, p. 7 [ca. 1930].

80. M. W. Rowe, "Goethe and Wittgenstein," *Philosophy* 66 (1991): 283–303.

81. Johann Wolfgang Goethe, "The Metamorphosis of Plants," in *The Poems of Goethe* (New York: Lovell, Coryell, & Co., 1882), 289.

82. RFGB, 133.

83. PHIL, 163, 175; PG §87.

84. PG §113.

85. PR §217.

86. PG, 211.

87. PHIL, 199.

88. CV [1931], 15e; see also PHIL, 185.

89. See PG §85.

90. PG §16.

91. PG, 213.

92. PG §60.

93. PG §29, p. 65.

94. CV [1931], 10e; emphasis added.

95. PG §46, p. 89.

96. PG §32, p. 68.

97. PG §45, p. 88.

98. PHIL, 187, emphasis added.

99. PG, 476.

100. See PG §101.

101. PG §34.

102. The term "stage-setting" occurs in PI §257. The more frequent way Wittgenstein expresses linguistic background is with the term "surroundings." See BB, p. 44; RC III §341; Z §§97, 99, 159, 162, 164, 170, 175, 527, 533, 534, 567; RPP II §501; RPP I §§314, 335, 337, 339, 878, 881; RFM VII §§47, 70; PI §§540, 583.

103. RPP I §433; Z §24. See also Z §§134–175.

104. RPP I §780.

105. LW II, 42 and 40.

106. Malcolm, *Ludwig Wittgenstein: A Memoir*, 69.

107. RFM VI §48, p. 352.

108. Z §227.

109. RPP II, §§625, 626.

110. PI §244. See also PI §257.

111. OC §476.

112. RFM IV §36.

113. "But this is important, namely that this reaction [here, pupil behavior], which guarantees one's claim to understand, presupposes as a surrounding particular circumstances, particular forms of life and speech. (As there is no such thing as a facial expression without a face.)" RFM VII §47.

114. PI §43.

115. See Z §32 and OC §56.

116. PI §529.

117. See, for example, H. Richard Niebuhr, *The Responsible Self; An Essay in Christian Moral Philosophy* (New York, NY: Harper and Row, 1963).

118. PI §539.

119. RPP I §381; RPP II §§382–386; CV [1946], 47, 51–52; [1948], 68; [1949], 81–82.

120. "I should like to say: conversation, the application and further interpretation of words flows on and only in this current does a word have its meaning." RPP I §240. See also LW II, 7; and Z §289: "If the meaning-connection can be set up before the order, then it can also be set up afterwards."

121. PI §373.

122. PI §371.

123. RPP I, §§960, 961.

124. RPP I, §339. Here one senses strongly Wittgenstein's movement away from Russellian realism toward a position which might be called an idealism of the non-Hegelian sort or a realism of the nonempirical sort. On internal relations see RFM VII §72.

125. Sometimes Wittgenstein emphasizes this skill as something *trainable* (e.g., Z §186 or RFM VII §47), and other times he emphasizes the fact that we are at the mercy of whatever aspects under which, and according to which, we see.

126. CV [1948], 74e. Also 83.

127. RFGB, 147.

128. It would be entirely appropriate to apply the notion of incommensurability to Wittgenstein's insistence that some language-games (e.g., the language-game of "soul" and that of "body") cannot be mixed without perpetuating unresolvable confusion. But by this he is not claiming that fluency in one language-game necessarily precludes fluency in another. See RPP II §§394, 395.

129. "Forms of behavior may be incommensurable. And the word 'behavior', as I am using it, is altogether misleading, for it includes in its meaning the external circumstances-of the behavior in a narrower sense." RPP I §314.

130. LW II, 30e. Also Z §173. It is very difficult to not construe "form of life" as if it were a pattern of activities distinct from language use. Rather, language itself is one of the activities that constitutes what Wittgenstein means by "form of life."

131. Z §144.

132. Drury, "Some Notes on Conversations with Wittgenstein," 105.

133. CV [1950], 85. For descriptions of Wittgenstein's religious practices see chapters 4 and 5 of McClendon, *Witness: Systematic Theology*, vol. 3; James Wm. McClendon, Jr., with Brad J. Kallenberg, "Ludwig Wittgenstein: A Christian in Philosophy," *Scottish Journal of Theology* 51, no. 2 (1998): 131–161.; Frederick Sontag, *Wittgenstein and the Mystical: Philosophy as an Ascetic Practice* (Atlanta, GA: Scholars Press, 1995); Norman Malcolm, *Wittgenstein: A Religious Point of View?*, edited with a response by Peter Winch (Ithaca, NY: Cornell University Press, 1993).

134. Malcolm, *Wittgenstein: A Religious Point of View?*, 92.

CHAPTER FOUR   **ETHICS AS POLITICS**

1. William Willimon and Stanley Hauerwas, with Scott C. Saye, *Lord, Teach Us: The Lord's Prayer & the Christian Life* (Nashville, TN: Abingdon, 1996), 16.

2. *The Peaceable Kingdom*, xxv.

3. See McClendon, Jr., with Kallenberg, "Ludwig Wittgenstein: A Christian in Philosophy," 131–161.

4. Kai Nielsen, "Wittgensteinian Fideism," *Philosophy* 42, no. 161 (July 1967): 191–192.

5. Judith Genova, *Wittgenstein: A Way of Seeing* (New York and London: Routledge, 1995), 87.

6. NB 8.3.15, p. 40e. Also 22.11.14, 31.

7. OC §§400, 51.

8. Nieli, *Wittgenstein: From Mysticism to Ordinary Language*, 168–169.

9. PI, p. 227e; emphasis added.

10. CV [1947], 61e.

11. Z §455. On another occasion he remarked to Drury, "I think one of the things you and I have to learn is that we have to live without the consolation of belonging to a church." Drury, "Conversations with Wittgenstein," 129.

12. Drury, "Conversations with Wittgenstein," 136.

13. Nieli, *Wittgenstein: From Mysticism to Ordinary Language*, 91, 123.

14. See OC §422.

15. Z §401.

16. See James Gustafson, "The Sectarian Temptation: Reflections on Theology, the Church and the University," *Proceedings of the Catholic Theological Society* 40 (1985): 83–94.

17. Gustafson, "The Sectarian Temptation," 94; emphasis added.

18. Hauerwas is explicitly opposed to the notion of "translatability" which is so prominent in Davidson's views. See "On Witnessing Our Story: Christian Education in Liberal Societies," in *Schooling Christians*, ed. Stanley Hauerwas and John H. Westerhoff (Grand Rapids, MI: Wm. B. Eerdmans, 1992), 214–234, and his essay written with William Willimon, "Embarrassed by God's Presence," *Christian Century* 102, no. 4 (January 30, 1985): 98–100. Hauerwas's "anti-translation" stance

is maintained in his later writings as well. See, e.g., *Wilderness Wanderings: Probing Twentieth-Century Theology and Philosophy* (Boulder, CO: Westview Press, 1997), 3.

19. Donald Davidson, "On the Very Idea of a Conceptual Scheme," in *Inquiries into Truth and Interpretation* (Oxford, UK: Clarendon Press, 1984), 183–198.

20. *Wilderness Wanderings*, 2–3.

21. Alasdair MacIntyre, "The Fate of Theism," in *The Religious Significance of Atheism* (New York: Columbia University Press, 1969), 25–26. See also Hendrikus Berkhof, *Two Hundred Years of Theology: Report of a Personal Journey*, trans. John Vriend (Grand Rapids, MI: Wm. B. Eerdmans, 1989).

22. For a detailed analysis of Davidson see my "The Gospel Truth of Relativism," *Scottish Journal of Theology* 53, no. 2 (2000), 177–211.

23. Hauerwas, "On Witnessing Our Story," 215.

24. "On Witnessing Our Story," 216.

25. "On Witnessing Our Story," 216 n. 4.

26. RPP II §720.

27. Z §173.

28. PI §381.

29. Z §144.

30. CV [1950], 85.

31. Cited in Phillips, *Belief, Change, and Forms of Life* (Atlantic Highlands, NJ: Humanities Press International, 1986), 9.

32. Phillips, *Belief, Change, and Forms of Life*, 10.

33. See PI §441.

34. See PI. p. 223. On translation and training cf. Z §191 with §186.

35. BB, 24.

36. Ger. *Lebensform*. See PI §§ 19, 23, 241, and p. 226.

37. Lindbeck builds on Wittgenstein's insistence that language and world mutually permeate each other. This view is also at the heart of Hans Frei's *The Eclipse of Biblical Narrative: A Study in Eighteenth- and Nineteenth-Century Hermeneutics* (New Haven, CT: Yale University Press, 1974). Since it does not make sense to think of language in correspondence with the world, neither can texts be thought to stand to one side and describe a world that is ontologically prior to the text. Rather, texts embody a use of language which *creates* a world. In this regard, "understanding" names the skill one achieves from within such texts and text-defined communities, i.e., intratextually.

38. "How to Go On When You Know You Are Going to Be Misunderstood or How Paul Holmer Ruined My Life or Making Sense of Paul Holmer," in *Wilderness Wanderings*, 145, emphasis added. Internal citations from Holmer's *Theology and the Scientific Study of Religion* (Minneapolis, MN: T. S. Denison, 1961).

39. "How To Go On When You Know You Are Going To Be Misunderstood," 144–145.

40. *The Peaceable Kingdom*, 76.

41. See chapter 5 below.

42. Hauerwas, with Burrell, "From System to Story, 39.

43. Hauerwas, "The Virtues and Our Communities: Human Nature as History," in A Community of Character, 115. For Hauerwas on linguistic skill see "Reconciling the Practice of Reason: Casuistry in a Christian Context," in Christian Existence Today, 67–88; and Against the Nations: War and Survival in a Liberal Society (Notre Dame, IN: University of Notre Dame Press, 1992), 1–22, esp. 1–12. For further discussion of the role of canonical stories see "The Moral Authority of Scripture: The Politics and Ethics of Remembering," in A Community of Character, 53–71. It is no secret that Hauerwas parallels MacIntyre closely on this point. See, e.g., MacIntyre's definition of "tradition" in Whose Justice? Which Rationality? (Notre Dame, IN: University of Notre Dame Press, 1988), 12.

44. See "A Story-Formed Community: Reflections on Watership Down," in A Community of Character, 9–35; and "The Church in a Divided World: The Interpretive Power of the Christian Story," in A Community of Character, 89–110.

45. Hauerwas and L. Gregory Jones, eds., Why Narrative? (Grand Rapids, MI: Wm. B. Eerdmans, 1989), 5; also 308. See also Christian Existence Today, 10; The Peaceable Kingdom, 24–44.

46. Hauerwas is content early on to think of narrative as that which binds the communities together (See The Peaceable Kingdom, 96–97). But he will move from here to a much less metaphorical description of Christian interconnectedness within the Body of Christ. See "A Tale of Two Stories: On Being Christian and a Texan," in Christian Existence Today, 25–47. See also "The Virtues and Our Communities," 115–116; "The Church in a Divided World"; "God, Medicine, and the Problems of Evil," Reformed Journal 38, no. 4 (April 1988): 16–22, and the resulting book, Naming the Silences; The Peaceable Kingdom, 1–49, and 135–151.

47. Hauerwas remarks, "my emphasis on the narrative character of Christian convictions has not been an attempt to avoid truth-claims but to understand better how claims about God entail fundamental assumptions about the narrability of the world and our lives." "Why the Truth Demands Truthfulness: An Imperious Engagement with Hartt," in Why Narrative?, 308.

For more on narrability see also Hauerwas's essay "On Keeping Theological Ethics Theological," in which he desists from argument and simply tells the story of Christian ethics as an ongoing conversation. This reveals the inescapable historical conditionedness of the practice of Christian ethics and undermines liberal assumptions about universality and translatability; in Revisions, ed. Hauerwas and MacIntyre, 16–42.

48. For accounts on the role of stories in training analogy-recognition see Thomas S. Kuhn, The Structures of Scientific Revolution; and David Burrell, Analogy and Philosophy of Language (New Haven, CT: Yale University Press, 1973).

For more on training see also "On Keeping Theological Ethics Theological" and The Peaceable Kingdom, 29–30.

49. "Why the Truth Demands Truthfulness," 304–305.

50. See William J. Wainwright, *Reason and the Heart: A Prolegomenon to a Critique of Passional Reason* (Ithaca, NY, and London, UK: Cornell University Press, 1995), 7–107 for accounts of Jonathon Edwards, John Henry Newman, and William James regarding the role that character plays in the reliability of religious knowledge.

51. Hauerwas, "Why the Truth Demands Truthfulness," 308 n. 15.

52. "Failure of Communication or A Case of Uncomprehending Feminism," *Scottish Journal of Theology* 50, no. 2 (1997), 229. The bone of contention between them stems clear back to Albrecht's reaction to Hauerwas's *A Community of Character*. Emerging in 1981, Hauerwas's model of ethics-as-politics constitutes a second enduring strand in his thinking, which can be illustrated from both middle- and late-period essays.

53. Gloria Albrecht, "Myself and Other Characters: A Feminist Liberationist Critique of Hauerwas's Ethics of Christian Character," in *The Annual of the Society of Christian Ethics*, ed. Harlan Beckley (Washington, DC: Georgetown University Press, 1992), 110.

54. Albrecht, "Myself and Other Characters," 99–100.

55. Albrecht, "Myself and Other Characters," 103.

56. Albrecht, "Myself and Other Characters," 111.

57. Albrecht, "Myself and Other Characters," 107.

58. Albrecht, "Myself and Other Characters," 108.

59. Gloria Albrecht, *The Character of Our Communities: Toward an Ethic of Liberation for the Church* (Nashville, TN: Abingdon Press, 1995), 227.

60. "Failure of Communication or A Case of Uncomprehending Feminism," 228.

61. "Failure of Communication or A Case of Uncomprehending Feminism," 229. Hauerwas notes that MacIntyre has been the brunt of similar misunderstanding: "Many who criticize MacIntyre's work fail to understand that he is not suggesting that Thomism provides a better epistemology than the encyclopaedist or genealogist, but rather Thomism rightly displaces epistemology" (229 n. 4).

62. Gloria Albrecht, "Stanley Hauerwas's *In Good Company: The Church as Polis*," *Scottish Journal of Theology* 50, no. 2 (1997): 224.

63. See Albrecht, "Stanley Hauerwas's *In Good Company*," 224; *The Character of Our Communities*, 84–97; "Myself and Other Characters," 104–106.

64. "Failure of Communication or A Case of Uncomprehending Feminism," 230.

65. "Failure of Communication or A Case of Uncomprehending Feminism," 234–235.

66. "Failure of Communication or A Case of Uncomprehending Feminism," 231; emphasis added.

67. Sharon Welch, "Review of Gloria Albrecht's *The Character of Our Communities: Toward an Ethic of Liberation for the Church*," *Scottish Journal of Theology* 50, no. 2 (1997): 251.

68. See Iddo Landau, "What's Old in Derrida?" *Philosophy* 69 (1994): 279–290; and R. R. Reno, "Feminist Theology as a Modern Project," *Pro Ecclesia* 5, no. 4 (Fall 1996): 405–426.

69. Albrecht, "Myself and Other Characters," 100; see also *The Character of Our Communities*, 11, 12, 32.

70. Hauerwas has contended throughout his writing that the church is obligated to be "relevant" but the assumption that this obligation can be fulfilled by translating the Gospel confuses the demands of the Gospel with the regnant ideology of contemporary culture. See his 1972 essay "Theology and the New American Culture," in *Vision and Virtue*, 241–260

71. "Failure of Communication or A Case of Uncomprehending Feminism," 231. I develop these thoughts into an argument that defuses relativism in my essay "The Gospel Truth of Relativism."

72. "For I have argued that the very content of Christian convictions requires the self be transformed if we are adequately to see the truth of convictions—e.g., that I am a creature of a good creator yet in rebellion against my status as such. Talk of our sin, therefore, is a claim about the way we are, but our very ability to know we are that way requires that we have already begun a new way of life. That is why the Christian doctrine of sanctification is central for assessing the epistemological status of Christian convictions. Assessing the truthfulness of religious convictions cannot be separated from the truthfulness of the persons who make those claims." *Christian Existence Today*, 10.

73. *Christian Existence Today*, 11. This makes a fitting response to Janik and Toulmin's lament of the absence of a *Lebensform* commensurate with the expression (and formation) of skillful ethical judgment. In their eyes, contemporary society is as unstable as the society of pre-war Vienna. See Janik and Toulmin, *Wittgenstein's Vienna*, 266.

74. Alasdair MacIntyre, *A Short History of Ethics* (New York, NY: Collier Books, 1966). Charles Taylor's account of social leveling is discussed by Hauerwas in his essay "Killing Compassion," in *Dispatches from the Front*, 164–176.

75. See "Faith in the Republic: A Frances Lewis Law Center Conversation between Stanley Hauerwas, Sanford Levinson, and Mark Tushnet," *Washington and Lee Law Review* 45, no. 2 (Spring 1988): 467–534.

76. "Preaching As Though We Had Enemies," *First Things* 53 (May 1995): 47.

77. Cited in "On Doctrine and Ethics," in *The Cambridge Companion to Christian Doctrine*, ed. Colin E. Gunton (Cambridge, UK: Cambridge University Press, 1997), 30.

78. *Against the Nations*, 18; emphasis added.

79. See Ronald Beiner, *What's the Matter with Liberalism?* (Berkeley, CA: University of California Press, 1992), 21–26.

80. "Whose Conscience? Whose Emotion?: Review of Sidney Callahan's *In Good Conscience: Reason, Emotion, and Moral Decision Making*," *Hastings Center Report* 22, no. 1 (January/ February 1992): 49.

81. "Killing Compassion," 166–167; emphasis added.

82. Hauerwas discusses Martha Nussbaum's suggestion that Aristotle provides profound advice on friendship to tired liberals who are condemned to live out the Enlightenment project they no longer believe in. Nussbaum's crucial error, in Hauerwas's estimation, is her own latent liberalism: unlike Aristotle she separates friendship from the context of community. See *Christians among the Virtues*, 70–88; and "Can Aristotle Be a Liberal? Nussbaum on Luck," *Soundings: An Interdisciplinary Journal* 72, no. 4 (Winter 1989): 675–691.

83. *After Christendom? How the Church Is to Behave If Freedom, Justice, and a Christian Nation Are Bad Ideas* (Nashville, TN: Abingdon Press, 1991), 105; emphasis added.

84. See "Christian Practice and the Practice of Law in a World without Foundations," *Mercer Law Review* 44, no. 3 (Spring 1993): 743–751; "Virtue and Character," in *Encyclopedia of Bioethics* (New York: Macmillan Library Reference, 1995), 2525–2532; "Authority and the Profession of Medicine," in *Suffering Presence: Theological Reflections on Medicine, the Mentally Handicapped, and the Church* (Notre Dame, IN: University of Notre Dame Press, 1986 [1982]), 39–62; and "Medicine as a Tragic Profession," in *Truthfulness and Tragedy*, 184–202.

85. "Christian Practice and the Practice of Law in a World without Foundations," 748. For an example of Hauerwas's argument that "rights" are fictions invented to fill the vacuum created by the breakdown of morally rich notions, see "Rights, Duties, and Experimentation on Children," in *Suffering Presence*, 125–141.

86. That the medieval notion of just desert had been reduced to brute equality can be seen by the shape theodicy was forced to take as a result of the changing forms of description used in social and intellectual life after 1700. See *Naming the Silences*, esp. 48–49.

87. "To Be or Not to Be a Bricoleur," 106.

88. "A Non-Violent Proposal for Christian Participation in Culture Wars," *Soundings* 75, no. 4 (Winter 1992): 487.

89. "Flights in Foundationalism, or Things Aren't As Bad As They Seem: Review of Stout's *Ethics after Babel*," *Soundings* 71, no. 4 (Winter 1988): 690.

90. "Flights in Foundationalism," 690.

91. See "Communitarians and Medical Ethicists: Or, 'Why I Am None of the Above'," in *Dispatches from the Front*, 156–163; "Why I Am Neither a Communitarian Nor a Medical Ethicist," *Hastings Center Report* 23, no. 6 (November/December 1993): S9–S10; "A Communitarian Lament: A Review of *The Good Society* by Robert Bellah," *First Things* 19 (January 1992): 45–46.

92. ". . . liberalism is not simply a theory of government but a theory of society that is imperial in its demands." *Against the Nations*, 18.

93. "Christian Practice and the Practice of Law," 748. See also "Preaching As Though We Had Enemies"; "Killing Compassion"; and *Dispatches from the Front*, 5–28

94. Kerr, *Theology after Wittgenstein*, esp. 3–27.

95. See George A. Lindbeck, *The Nature of Doctrine* (Philadelphia, PA: Westminster Press, 1984).

96. See "The Kingship of Christ: Why Freedom of 'Belief' is Not Enough," in *In Good Company*, 199–216. See also "The Democratic Policing of Christianity," in *Dispatches from the Front*, 92, 106.

97. Both fundamentalists and biblical critics "assume an objectivity of the text in order to make the Bible available to anyone, and that 'anyone' is assumed to be the citizen of democratic polities." *Unleashing the Scripture: Freeing the Bible from Captivity to America* (Nashville, TN: Abingdon Press, 1993), 36.

98. Despite Hauerwas's self-confessed admiration for, and appropriation of, the work of John Howard Yoder, he fears that even Yoder has not escaped a voluntaristic account of the church. See "Whose Church? Which Future? Whither the Anabaptist Vision?" in *In Good Company*, 65–78.

99. "Faith in the Republic," 480. Hauerwas leans heavily on Yoder's description of "constantinianism." For Yoder's account see *The Original Revolution* (Scottdale, PA: Herald Press, 1971), 148–182; and *The Priestly Kingdom* (Notre Dame, IN: University of Notre Dame Press, 1984), 135–147.

100. "Faith in the Republic," 479.

101. "Faith in the Republic," 496.

102. See Hauerwas's essay with Michael Broadway, "The Irony of American Christianity: Reinhold Niebuhr on Church and State," *Insights: A Journal of the Faculty of Austin Seminary* 108 (Fall 1992): 33–46. See also "The Democratic Policing of Christianity"; "A Christian Critique of Christian America," in *Christian Existence Today*, 171–190; and chapter 2, "Walter Rauschenbusch and the Saving of America," in his ethics textbook (in progress): *History of Christian Ethics in America* (unfinished book mss., n.d.).

103. "The Democratic Policing of Christianity," 93.

104. "Preaching As Though We Had Enemies," 48.

105. "The Kingship of Christ: Why Freedom of 'Belief' Is Not Enough," 210.

106. Max L. Stackhouse, "Liberalism Dispatched vs. Liberalism Engaged. Review of *Dispatches from the Front: Theological Engagements with the Secular* by Stanley Hauerwas," *Christian Century* 112 (October 18, 1995): 963.

107. Michael Himes and Kenneth Himes, *Fullness of Faith: The Public Significance of Theology* (New York: Paulist Press, 1993).

108. Stackhouse explains "conciliar denominationalism" as proto-democracy in his essay "The Continuing Importance of Walter Rauschenbusch," which is his introduction to Walter Rauschenbusch's *The Righteousness of the Kingdom*, ed. Max L. Stackhouse (New York: Abingdon, 1968), 13–59. Stackhouse attempts to extend Rauschenbusch's program in constructive Protestantism in his own *Creeds, Society, and Human Rights: A Study in Three Cultures* (Grand Rapids, MI: Wm. B. Eerdmans, 1984). Although Hauerwas makes only passing reference to Stackhouse in *Christian Existence Today* (175–176), he sustains a longer argument against him

in "The Non-Violent Terrorist: In Defense of Christian Fanaticism," in *Sanctify Them in Truth: Holiness Exemplified* (Edinburgh, UK: T&T Clark, 1998), 177–190.

109. Stackhouse, "Liberalism Dispatched," 963.

110. Cited in Hauerwas, "The Non-violent Terrorist," 182.

111. Stackhouse, "Liberalism Dispatched," 963.

112. *In Good Company*, 8; emphasis added.

113. *A Community of Character*, 1.

114. "Jesus: The Story of the Kingdom," in *A Community of Character*, 51.

115. *The Peaceable Kingdom*, 76.

116. Because of its internal relation to the form of Jesus' life, pacifism is a prominent theme in Hauerwas's works. See especially "Peacemaking: The Virtue of the Church," in *Christian Existence Today*, 89–97; "Pacifism: A Form of Politics," in *Peace Betrayed? Essays on Pacifism and Politics*, ed. Michael Cromartie (Washington: Ethics and Public Policy Center, 1990), 133–142; "Epilogue: A Pacifist Response to the Bishops," in *Speak Up for Just War or Pacifism: A Critique of the United Methodist Bishop's Pastoral Letter "In Defense of Creation"* by Paul Ramsey (University Park, PA and London, UK: Pennsylvania State University Press, 1989), 149–182; "The Church and/as God's Non-Violent Imagination," *Pro Ecclesia* 1, no. 1 (Fall 1992): 76–88; and "Should War Be Eliminated?" in *Against the Nations*, 169–208.

117. "Epilogue: A Pacifist Response," 160.

118. *The Peaceable Kingdom*, 76.

119. "A Tale of Two Stories: On Being Christian and a Texan," 29; "Political Righteousness," *Perspectives: A Journal of Reformed Thought* 8, no. 6 (June 1993): 9.

120. Stackhouse, "Liberalism Dispatched," 964; emphasis added.

121. "I think that the Protestant churches have, more than any other single force, generated modern democratic polity out of their intrinsically proto-democratic, conciliar ecclesiology, and that in consequence faithful believers ought also to be responsible participants in civil society." Stackhouse, "Liberalism Dispatched," 964.

122. Stackhouse, "Liberalism Dispatched," 965.

123. Stackhouse, "Liberalism Dispatched," 966.

124. "The Non-Violent Terrorist," 182 n. 9.

125. "Eschatology and Nuclear Disarmament," *New Catholic World* 226, no. 1356 (November/December 1983): 249. See also Yoder, *The Original Revolution*, 56, and *The Politics of Jesus*, 2d ed. (Grand Rapids, MI, and Carlisle, UK: Wm. B. Eerdmans and Paternoster Press, 1994).

126. "Epilogue: A Pacifist Response," 160; "The Sermon on the Mount: Just War and the Quest for Peace," *Concilium* 195 (1988): 38.

127. 2 Cor. 5:17, NEB.

128. *Resident Aliens*, 88.

129. Samuel Wells, "How the Church Performs Jesus' Story: Improvising on the Theological Ethics of Stanley Hauerwas" (Ph. D. Diss. University of Durham, NC, 1996), 172–179. A version of this dissertation appears as *Transforming Fate into*

Destiny: The Theological Ethics of Stanley Hauerwas (Carlisle, UK: Paternoster Press, 1998).

130. Phillip D. Kenneson, "Taking Time for the Trivial: Reflections on Yet Another Book From Hauerwas. Review of *Christian Existence Today: Essays on Church, World and Living in Between* by Stanley Hauerwas," *Asbury Theological Journal* 45, no. 1 (Spring 1990): 65–74. For a discussion of the eschatological dimension in Hauerwas's work see Wells, "How the Church Performs Jesus' Story," 145–190. Unfortunately, Hauerwas himself is ambiguous. Sometimes he uses the term as a temporal metaphor, as in "Taking Time for Peace," *Religion and Intellectual Life* 3, no. 3 (Spring 1986): 87–100. Other times he cannot resist thinking of eschatology in spatial terms. See Hauerwas, with Mark Sherwindt, "The Reality of the Kingdom: An Ecclesial Space for Peace," in *Against the Nations*, 107–121.

131. "The Need for an Ending," *Modern Churchman* 28, no. 3 (1986): 6.

132. My appeal to the way Christians ordinarily speak is essential for understanding what "inhabiting a different time" might mean. First, confusions over the concept of "time" abound, and yet we use the term fluently in ordinary speech. Wittgenstein's debunking of confusions over the "flow" of time (e.g., BB, 107–109) are but reminders that distinctions concerning time do not have metaphysical bases but are linguistically discerned. This is another way of saying that there is no way to understand the eschatological nature of salvation except by learning this new language.

133. Wells, "How the Church Performs Jesus' Story," 168.

134. "Taking Time for Peace: The Ethical Significance of the Trivial," in *Christian Existence Today*, 256–257.

135. Stackhouse, "Liberalism Dispatched," 965.

136. Stackhouse, "Liberalism Dispatched," 962.

137. Max L. Stackhouse, *Apologia: Contextualization, Globalization, and Mission in Theological Education* (Grand Rapids, MI: Wm. B. Eerdmans, 1988), 75.

138. "Jesus: The Story of the Kingdom," 50.

139. "The Future of Christian Social Ethics," in *That They May Live: Theological Reflections on the Quality of Life*, ed. George Devine (Staten Island, NY: Alba House, 1972), 125; "Natural Law, Tragedy and Theological Ethics," in *Truthfulness and Tragedy*, 60, 35; *The Peaceable Kingdom*, 96.

140. "The Demands of a Truthful Story: Ethics and the Pastoral Task," *Chicago Studies* 21, no. 1 (Spring 1982): 62.

141. "The Reality of the Kingdom: An Ecclesial Space for Peace," 112–119.

142. "What Could It Mean for the Church to Be Christ's Body? A Question without a Clear Answer," in *In Good Company*, 24.

143. "The Church and the Mentally Handicapped: A Continuing Challenge to the Imagination," in *Dispatches from the Front*, 184. I cannot resist mentioning the similarity in Hauerwas's inversion of metaphysical reductionism (that the whole-the church-is nothing but the sum of the parts) to a similar move made by Wittgenstein in PI §§47–50.

144. "The Sanctified Body: Why Perfection Does Not Require a 'Self'," in *Sanctify Them in the Truth*, 77–92.

145. "What Could It Mean for the Church to Be Christ's Body?" 25.

146. See "A Homage to Mary and to the University Called Notre Dame," in *In Good Company*, 83. See also "The Church's One Foundation Is Jesus Christ Her Lord; Or, In a World without Foundations: All We Have Is the Church," in *Theology without Foundations: Religious Practice and The Future of Theological Truth*, ed. Stanley Hauerwas, Nancey Murphy, and Mark Nation (Nashville, TN: Abingdon Press, 1994), 147–149.

147. Beiner, *What's the Matter with Liberalism?*, 25.

148. *Resident Aliens*, 46–47.

149. Hauerwas and William Willimon, *Where Resident Aliens Live*, 45, citing Raymond Brown.

150. See "Faith in the Republic," 486.

151. Col. 1:13.

152. Gustafson takes this in a different direction than does Hauerwas. Rather than use this claim to soften the respective hegemonies of rival claims to "objective" knowledge (such as those often made by science), Gustafson locates the significance of historical conditioning in the fact that theology can never escape from being tainted by culture; see "A Response to My Critics," *Journal of Religious Ethics* 13 (Fall 1985): 196. The fact of human situatedness in history and creation, which Gustafson thinks ought to fill us with caution when making normative claims, gives his work a stoic texture; see 205. For an early account of Gustafson's particularism see his *Treasure in Earthen Vessels: The Church as Human Community* (New York: Harper Brothers, 1961). For a later indication of his thinking see *Ethics from a Theocentric Perspective*, Vol. 1, *Theology and Ethics* (Chicago, IL: University of Chicago Press, 1981), 124–125, 317–318 (cf. 151). For an account of the growing tension between Gustafson's acknowledgment of the inescapability of our historical situatedness and his hankering after universality in ethics see Hauerwas's "God as Participant: Time and History in the Work of James Gustafson," in *Wilderness Wanderings*, 62–81.

153. Gustafson lumps this under the notion of Edwardsian "piety," which he defines as "an attitude of reverence, awe, and respect" which implies "a sense of devotion and duties and responsibilities." *Ethics from a Theocentric Perspective*, 1:164, 257. See also "Response to My Critics," 188–189.

154. See Hauerwas's "Christian Ethics in America: Beginning with an Ending," in *History of Christian Ethics in America* (unfinished book mss., n.d.), 44. For Hauerwas's analysis of Gustafson's criticism of anthropocentrism see "God the Measurer. Review of James Gustafson's *Ethics from a Theocentric Perspective*. Vol. 1, *Theology and Ethics*," *Journal of Religion* 62, no. 4 (1982): 402–411.

155. Gustafson, *Ethics from a Theocentric Perspective*. 1:81, 317–318; "Response to My Critics," 186. For Hauerwas's contention that voluntarism is killing the church see "In Defense of Cultural Christianity: Reflections on Going to Church," in

Sanctify Them in Truth, 164–167; see also "The Importance of Being Catholic: Unsolicited Advice from a Protestant Bystander," in *In Good Company*, 99–100.

156. Gustafson, *Ethics from a Theocentric Perspective*, 1:3–16.

157. James Gustafson, "Sectarian Temptation," 83–94.

158. *Christian Existence Today*, 10.

159. Gustafson, *Ethics from a Theocentric Perspective*, 1:251–257. See also "Response to My Critics," 192, 194.

160. "Response to My Critics," 185. See also "Sectarian Temptation," 85, 88, 92.

161. "Sectarian Temptation," 93; see also "Response to My Critics," 197.

162. "Sectarian Temptation," 85.

163. Gustafson, *Ethics from a Theocentric Perspective*, 1:236.

164. "Response to My Critics," 198. However, he notes that piety rightly gives rise to an impulse to *test* theological claims despite their nonempirical status; 194.

165. "Response to My Critics," 192.

166. Gustafson, *Ethics from a Theocentric Perspective*, 1:195. Also 129.

167. Gustafson, *Ethics from a Theocentric Perspective*, 1:237. Similarly, see "Response to My Critics," 193.

168. Ayer, *Language, Truth and Logic*.

169. The fact that the lion's share of the debate between self-proclaimed liberal and conservative theologians in the twentieth century turns on their respective views of language is discussed at length in Nancey Murphy, *Beyond Liberalism and Fundamentalism* (Philadelphia, PA: Trinity Press International, 1996).

170. See Berkhof, *Two Hundred Years of Theology*. Gustafson completes a trend begun in H. Richard Niebuhr to professionalize the discipline of Christian ethics. Hauerwas summarizes: "For it has been one of Gustafson's projects to write about Christian ethics in a manner acceptable to the developing canons of knowledge underwritten by the modern university." Taken from ms. "Christian Ethics in America: Beginning with an Ending," 39.

171. "Response to My Critics," 194. See *Ethics from a Theocentric Perspective*, 1:153–154.

172. "A Homage to Mary," 86.

173. *Christian Existence Today*, 10.

174. *Christian Existence Today*, 10–11.

175. Clement tells of Roman Christians who sold themselves into slavery in order to gain money to ransom others and feed the poor (2 Clement 55:2). Similarly, Athenagoras writes, "But among us you will find uneducated persons and artisans, and old women who, if they are unable in words to prove the benefit of our doctrine, yet by their deeds exhibit the benefit arising from their persuasion of its truth: they do not rehearse speeches, but exhibit good works; when struck, they do not strike again; when robbed, they do not go to law; they give to those who ask of them, and love their neighbors as themselves." Cited in Athenagoras, "A Plea for Christians," in *Classical Readings in Christian Apologetics A.D. 100–1800*, ed. L. Russ Bush (Grand Rapids, MI: Academie Books, Zondervan Publishing House, 1983), 44.

176. This decline is noted by Alasdair I. C. Heron, in *The Holy Spirit* (Philadelphia, PA: Westminster Press, 1983), 63. See also Hauerwas, "The Ministry of a Congregation: Rethinking Christian Ethics for a Church-Centered Seminary," in *Christian Existence Today*, 101–110.

177. "Epilogue: A Pacifist Response," 163.

178. *After Christendom*, 35.

179. *After Christendom*, 37.

180. See *In Good Company*, 8; "The Kingship of Christ: Why Freedom of 'Belief' is Not Enough," 199–216. For a later account see "In Defense of Cultural Christianity."

181. See "The Church as God's New Language,"in *Christian Existence Today*, 47–66; and "Virtue in Public," in *Christian Existence Today*, 191–198.

CHAPTER FIVE   **THIS COMPLICATED FORM OF LIFE**

1. Dunne, *Back to the Rough Ground*, 263.
2. Dunne, *Back to the Rough Ground*, 247.
3. *Nicomachean Ethics*, 1109a28–29.
4. *Nicomachean Ethics*, 1180b20–22.
5. Dunne, *Back to the Rough Ground*, 253.
6. *Nicomachean Ethics*, 1141b15.
7. Dunne, *Back to the Rough Ground*, 296.
8. Cited in Dunne, *Back to the Rough Ground*, 299.
9. Dunne, *Back to the Rough Ground*, 312.
10. Dunne, *Back to the Rough Ground*, 313.
11. PHIL, 181; PG, p. 380.
12. PR, p. 336.
13. PHIL, 175.
14. CV [1937], 31.
15. E.g., PG §§28, 34, 37, 39.
16. LE, 41.
17. cited in CV [1938], 34.
18. PR §1.
19. PR §7.
20. TLP 6.375, 6.3751.
21. PR §230.
22. PR §225.
23. PR §230.
24. PR §225.
25. TLP 5.132.
26. PHIL, 193.
27. RFM VI §23, p. 325.

28. Nieli, *Wittgenstein: From Mysticism to Ordinary Language*, 62.

29. Rudolph Carnap, "Die Überwindung der Metaphysik durch logische Analyse der Sprach," *Erkenntnis* Band 2, Heft 4 (1932). English translation by Arthur Pap appears in A. J. Ayer, ed., *Logical Positivism* (New York: The Free Press, 1959), 60–81.

30. Cited in Nieli, *Wittgenstein*, 7.

31. RPP II §296.

32. Cited in Monk, *Ludwig Wittgenstein*, p. 244.

33. Cited in Nieli, *Wittgenstein*, 109.

34. Nieli, *Wittgenstein*, 83.

35. Nieli, *Wittgenstein*, xii, 69. In addition, Nieli points out that Wittgenstein's metaphor of "ladder" is not uncommon in mystical literature (118).

36. WVC, 69.

37. Engelmann, *Letters from Ludwig Wittgenstein, with a Memoir*, 97.

38. Nieli, *Wittgenstein*, 116. See also Sontag, *Wittgenstein and the Mystical*. For the chronology of this experience, see Monk, *Ludwig Wittgenstein*, 115–116. For an account of Wittgenstein as a "quiet" Christian believer see McClendon, Jr., with Brad J. Kallenberg, "Ludwig Wittgenstein: A Christian in Philosophy."

39. TLP 6.41. See WVC 68–69

40. Janik and Toulmin, *Wittgenstein's Vienna*, 179–184.

41. Heinrich Hertz, *The Principles of Mechanics*, trans. D. E. Jones and J. T. Walley (New York: Dover Publications, 1956), 427, cited in Wayne C. Myrvold, "Tractatus 4.04: (Compare Hertz' Mechanics, on Dynamical Models)," in *Wittgenstein Eine Neubewertung: Akten des 14. International Wittgenstein-Symposiums, Feier des 100. Geburtstages, 13. bis 20. August 1989, Kirchberg as Wechsel (Österreich)*, ed. Rudolph Haller and Johannes Brandl, Schriftenreihe der Wittgenstein-Gesellschaft (Vienna: Hölder-Pichler-Tempsky, 1990), 42.

42. Myrvold, "Tractatus 4.04," 43.

43. PR, p. 324.

44. PR, pp. 318–319.

45. On the impact of conventionalist H. J. Brouwer's 1929 lecture on Wittgenstein see John T. E. Richardson, *The Grammar of Justification* (New York: St. Martin's Press, 1976), 18.

46. PR §1, p. 52.

47. For an account of Wittgenstein's thought as primarily a turn from rationality-as-representation to rationality-as-practice see James C. Edwards, *Ethics without Philosophy: Wittgenstein and the Moral Life* (Tampa, FL: University Presses of Florida, 1982).

48. PR, p. 346.

49. PG §§69, 72, 73, 78, 81.

50. Cited in the preface to BB, v.

51. Drury, "Conversations with Wittgenstein," 173.

52. I.e., TLP 6.54.

53. PG §34.

54. Kierkegaard, *Concluding Unscientific Postscript*, 118.

55. Jules David Law, "Wittgenstein, Ludwig," in *The John Hopkins Guide to Literary Theory and Criticism*, ed. Michael Groden and Martin Kreiswirth (Baltimore, MD: Johns Hopkins University Press, 1994), 738.

56. PG §27, p. 63.

57. PG §114 and §90.

58. Plato, *Theaetetus*, edited, with introduction, by Bernard Williams, translated by M. J. Levett, revised by Myles Burnyeat (Indianapolis, IN: Hackett Publishing, 1992), 187–189.

59. Of course, just this sort of reasoning led to belief in the eternality of universals.

60. PHIL, 173; emphasis added. For a recent application of this to Christian theology see Lindbeck, *The Nature of Doctrine*. See also Paul Holmer's works such as *The Grammar of Faith* (San Francisco, CA: Harper and Row, 1978) or "Learning to Theologise," in *Wittgenstein: Attention to Particulars: Essays in Honour of Rush Rhees (1905–89)*, ed. D. Z. Phillips (New York and Frankfurt am Main: St. Martin's Press and Suhrkamp, 1989), 194–200.

61. TLP 5.6; LE 7, 11–12.

62. PR §3.

63. CV [1931], 17e.

64. Some examples are given in PR §§214, 217.

65. PHIL, 193.

66. Alfred Tarski, "The Semantic Conception of Truth," in *Readings in Philosophical Analysis*, ed. Herbert Feigl and Wilfrid Sellars (New York: Appleton-Century-Crofts, 1949), 52–84.

67. A. N. Prior, "Correspondence Theory of Truth," in *The Encyclopedia of Philosophy*, ed. Paul Edwards (New York: Macmillan Publishing and The Free Press, 1965), 2:231. Convention T is, after all, called a *convention* for good reason. Tarski writes that "the problem of the definition of truth obtains a precise meaning and can be solved in a rigorous way only for those languages whose structure has been exactly specified" (58). Since ordinary language does not yield such an exact structural description, the stopping place for justification of this definition of truth will inevitably be governed by convention. Tarski seeks to simply catch hold and specify a very old notion of truth that he thinks is implicit in language (53).

68. PR §§148, 153.

69. PG, p. 406.

70. PG §79, pp. 123–124. For Tarski's response to the claim that semantic terms (e.g., 'true') do no real work, see Tarski, "The Semantic Conception of Truth," 68–69.

71. PG §77.

72. PG §77.

73. PG §2.

74. PR §7.

75. RFM VI §23.

76. M. W. Rowe, "Wittgenstein's Romantic Inheritance," *Philosophy* 69 (1994): 334.

77. See Paul Edwards, William P. Alston, and A. N. Prior, "Russell, Bertrand Arthur William," in *The Encyclopedia of Philosophy*, ed. Paul Edwards (New York: Macmillan Publishing and The Free Press, 1965), 7:235–258. See also P. M. S. Hacker, *Wittgenstein's Place in Twentieth-Century Analytic Philosophy* (Oxford, UK, and Cambridge, MA: Blackwell, 1996), 1–32.

78. PG §§95, 33.

79. This conclusion is especially troubling for empirical realists who assume that by this claim Wittgenstein is using "linguistic system" as something separable from the world. But that misses the point Wittgenstein is trying to make. Meaning belongs to the linguistic system because the linguistic system and the world of experience coinhere.

80. PG §55.

81. See, for example, PR §§23, 43, 47 and PG §33.

82. PG §113.

83. PHIL, 199.

84. PG §114.

85. PG §129.

86. PG §§101–102.

87. For a contemporary account see Nelson Goodman, *Ways of Worldmaking* (Indianapolis, IN: Hackett Publishing, 1978).

88. See PR §225.

89. WVC, 118.

90. Annie Dillard, *The Living: A Novel* (New York: HarperPerennial, 1992), 171.

91. Dillard, 183–184.

92. Dillard, 185.

93. PG §104.

94. PG §§101–104.

95. See WVC, 126.

96. PR §§10, 14, 27.

97. PG §95, p. 143; §55.

98. Richard Rorty, "Pragmatism, Davidson, and Truth," in *Objectivity, Relativism, and Truth: Philosophical Papers*, vol. 1 (Cambridge, UK: Cambridge University Press, 1991), 145–146.

99. PG §52.

100. PG, p. 470.

101. See PG, pp. 395–459.

102. PG, p. 454.

103. PG, p. 449.

104. PG §29.

105. PG §43.

106. PG §104; emphasis added.

107. PG §21.

108. PG §§66, 95, 71.

109. PG §67, also §68.

110. PG §§57, 61, 32.

111. PG §40.

112. CV [1938], 34.

113. PHIL, 181; PG, p. 380.

114. CV [1947], 56.

115. Drury, "Some Notes on Conversations with Wittgenstein," 94.

116. Malcolm, *Wittgenstein: A Religious Point of View?*, 78.

117. See LE; also TLP 6.44.

118. James F. Peterman, *Philosophy as Therapy: An Interpretation and Defense of Wittgenstein's Later Philosophical Project* (Albany, NY: State University of New York Press, 1992).

119. Malcolm, *Wittgenstein: A Religious Point of View?*, 125–127.

120. See Malcolm, *Wittgenstein: A Religious Point of View?*, 20, 22, 89, 108, 126, and 119.

121. Malcolm, *Wittgenstein: A Religious Point of View?*, 20–23. See also CV [1946], 56.

122. Malcolm, *Wittgenstein: A Religious Point of View?*, 119, 89, 108, 126.

123. CV [1937], 33e.

124. CV [1946], 49e.

125. CV [1944], 45e. Likewise Kierkegaard claimed that remorse is not only a wonderful friend, it is a measure of one's spiritual health. Furthermore, an admission of reticence to pray may be nothing other than a confession that one is not wise, for wisdom comes through prayer. See Kierkegaard, *Purity of Heart Is To Will One Thing*, 39, 46, 55.

126. Drury, "Some Notes on Conversations with Wittgenstein," 104.

127. *Confessions*, viii.7.

128. See Rhees, *Recollections of Wittgenstein*, 190–219; Monk, *Ludwig Wittgenstein*, 361–384.

129. This particular letter, dated May 30, 1920, is reprinted in Engelmann, *Letters from Ludwig Wittgenstein, with a Memoir*, 33. In this letter Wittgenstein also comments that he wished he might completely empty himself *again*-presumably an allusion to the sense of catharsis he enjoyed as a result of his conversion upon encountering Tolstoy's *Gospels in Brief*, ca. 1915. Other letters to Engelmann bear a similar theme of Wittgenstein's discontent with his own lack of decency. For example, in a letter dated October 23, 1921 he wrote, "Here everything is as it was. I am as stupid and rotten as ever. Nothing stirs in me that could be taken to indicate a better future" (47). Evidently, Wittgenstein considered his own moral flaws as preventing him from making more significant philosophical progress.

130. Engelmann, *Letters from Ludwig Wittgenstein, with a Memoir*, 62.

131. Engelmann notes that, early on, his own pacifist urges were incommensurable with Wittgenstein's views on the matter. Clearly Wittgenstein was no pacifist when they first met (*Letters from Ludwig Wittgenstein, with a Memoir*, 68, 71–73). Yet by life's end, Wittgenstein is reported to have told Drury in anticipation of impending military tour of duty, "If it ever happens that you get mixed up in hand to hand fighting, you must just stand aside and let yourself be massacred." Drury, "Conversations with Wittgenstein," 163.

132. The centrality of prayer is noted by Wittgenstein in 1931 and again in 1948. See, e.g., Drury, "Conversations with Wittgenstein," 135, and Monk, *Ludwig Wittgenstein*, 534.

133. Drury, "Conversations with Wittgenstein," 129–130. On the centrality of practice to genuine religion see CV [1950], 85.

134. PI §§133, 593, 255; CV [1944], 44: "If in life we are surrounded by death, so too in the health of our intellect we are surrounded by madness."

135. "A philosopher is a man who has to cure many intellectual diseases in himself before he can arrive at the notions of common sense." CV [1944], 44e.

136. RFM II §23.

137. RFM VI §31. The term "craving for generality" was first used by Wittgenstein in BB, 17.

138. Malcolm, *Wittgenstein: A Religious Point of View?*, 85. Winch concurs, 110.

139. This is not unlike the heart condition described by the prophet Jeremiah: "The heart is more deceitful than all else and is desperately sick; who can understand it?" Jer. 17:9 NASB. The ultimate deception of the human heart is, of course, its ability to convince itself that it is not liable to deception.

140. Engelmann, *Letters from Ludwig Wittgenstein, with a Memoir*, 97.

141. CV [1942], 42e.

142. See TLP 2.02, 2.021, 2.0211, 2.0212.

143. TLP 3.25; also NB, p. 67.

144. NB 23.11.16, p. 90.

145. PG, p. 211.

146. RFM VII §18; OC §38.

147. RFM IV §12; see also PI § 352.

148. See RFM IV §4. Here Wittgenstein anticipated the discussion in OC that some propositions are so deeply ingressed that they, in practice, stand fast for a *Weltbild*.

149. See RFM IV §§29–30. Similar points are made in PI §§97, 101–107, 112, 122, 115.

150. "Do not look at proofs as a procedure that *compels* you, but as one that *guides* you. —And what guides is your *conception* of a (particular) situation." RFM IV §30. And, "The mathematical Must is only an expression of the fact that mathematics forms concepts. And concepts help us to comprehend things. They

correspond to a particular [i.e., paradigmatic] way of dealing with situations."
RFM VII §67.

151. RFM VI §§7, 8.

152. RFM IV §31.

153. Debra Aidun, "Wittgenstein, Philosophical Method and Aspect-Seeing,"
Philosophical Investigations 5 (1982): 114.

154. RFM VI §49. The phrase is also used in PI §§352, 356.

155. CV [1940], 37.

156. CE, 375. See CV 64, 85.

157. LC, 27–28.

158. CV [1950], 85e.

159. PI §599.

160. PI §§109, 126.

161. Tilghman, *Wittgenstein, Ethics and Aesthetics*, 53, 74–5.

162. Philip R. Shields, *Logic and Sin in the Writings of Ludwig Wittgenstein*
(Chicago and London: University of Chicago Press, 1993). Shields argues that Wittgenstein has a religious viewpoint which underlies and unifies all his writings. For example, the sort of force which logic has upon us is akin to "the will of God." Attempts
to transgress the limits of language are manifestations of pride, sin, and idolatry.

163. Roberts, "The Philosopher as Sage," 409–431.

164. See Edwards, *Ethics without Philosophy*, 103–159.

165. Toulmin, *Cosmopolis*, 154.

166. LC, 24. In contemporary philosophy of science this methodology is some-
times referred to pejoratively as "metaphysical reductionism." See Nancey Murphy,
"Nonreductive Physicalism: Philosophical Issues," in *Portraits of Human Nature*
(Philadelphia, PA: Fortress Press, forthcoming), and Nancey Murphy and James
Wm. McClendon, Jr., "Distinguishing Modern and Postmodern Theologies." See
also works by Arthur Peacocke such as *Creation and the World of Science*, Bampton
Lecture Series, 1978 (Oxford, UK: Oxford University Press, 1979), esp. 112–118.

167. RFGB, 155; RFM III §81; CV [1946], 49.

168. CV [1941], 40e.

169. CV [1947], 56e.

170. Drury, "Some Notes on Conversations with Wittgenstein," 94; also "Conversations with Wittgenstein," 173.

171. CV [1931], 10e.

172. OC §§475–478.

173. OC §130.

174. See Booth, *Aristotelian Aporetic Ontology in Islamic and Christian
Thinkers*.

175. OC §478.

176. RPP I §916. Also Z §541.

177. PESD, 234.

178. CE, 373, emphasis added.

179. CE, 373.
180. CE, 397.
181. CE, 395. Also CV [1937], 31.
182. LW II, 43e.
183. CE, 397.
184. CE, 379. See also RFM IV §34.
185. PESD, 257.
186. CV [1950], 85e.
187. RPP I §630.
188. See the long list of examples of language-games in PI §23.
189. See PI §§19, 241, 23, and pt. II, p. 226.
190. RPP I §151.
191. Z §545.
192. LW II, 43e. Also RFM IV §36: "A proposition may describe a picture and this picture be variously anchored in our way of looking at things, and so in our way of living and acting."
193. RPP II §632; RFM IV §39.
194. RFM VI §639. Also PI §242.
195. This is not identical to saying we must think with words. Rather, Wittgenstein conceives of our thought as sharing the linguistic texture that is internal to all human experience (see PI §§329–442). For example, we can think a sequence of images (a red ball bouncing), but to take these images in a way that is meaningful to humans, which is to say, meaningful within our complicated form of life rather than within that of a family of beavers, depends on the possession of adequate linguistic resources to describe the images in words. There is a tension between Wittgenstein's apparent view that some experience (e.g., experience of *das Mystiche*) is ineffable—shown, not said—and his belief that the richness (or poverty) of human experience is internally related to the richness (or poverty) of one's language. This tension is somewhat reduced for us when we recall Wittgenstein's use of "language" as a technical term that expresses the logical possibilities necessary for there being natural languages.
196. PI §329.
197. RPP II §632 and Z §391. Also PI §§383, 384.
198. Z §§518, 520.
199. PI, p. 174e; PI §381.
200. RPP II §385.
201. RPP II §481, 525. See also RFM IV §§29–35.
202. BB, 43.
203. OC §611.
204. "If we call this 'wrong' aren't we using our language-game as a base from which to *combat* theirs?" OC §609.
205. OC §144.
206. OC §88.

207. RFM IV §30.

208. RFM VII §74.

209. See Z §197. What makes a solution a solution is not an explanation of why I call my answer a "solution," but the fact that it passes for a solution in the playing of the game.

210. RFM I §116.

211. OC §291.

212. See Z §186; RPP II §568; OC §279; RFM I §§9, 10, 14.

213. Wittgenstein continues, "There is therefore, no occult act of naming an object that in itself can give a word a meaning." NPL, 447.

214. RPP I §343. See also OC §39; RFM IV §35.

215. "Training" is a common topic in PI. See §§189, 197–199, 202, 206–208.

216. PI §198.

217. RFM VI §35.

218. PI §441.

219. RPP II §§706, 708.

220. RPP II §707.

221. PI, p. 223e.

222. I owe this memorable phrase to W. V. O. Quine. Cited in Richard Rorty, "Hesse and Davidson on Metaphor," in *Objectivity, Relativism, and Truth: Philosophical Papers*, vol. 1, 166 n. 17.

223. RC III §293.

224. OC §105.

225. RC III §§96–98.

226. OC §630. See also §528.

227. See OC §595.

228. PG, pp. 283–284.

229. See OC §110.

230. In BB, 17, he defines language-game as "the forms of language with which a child begins to make use of words. The study of language-games is the study of primitive forms of language or primitive languages."

231. BB, 81.

232. PI, p. 218e, emphasis added.

233. OC §475. See Rush Rhees, "Language as Emerging from Instinctive Behavior," *Philosophical Investigations* 20, no. 1 (1997): 4.

234. OC §510.

235. LW II, 72e.

236. OC §609.

CHAPTER SIX   THIS COMPLICATED FORM OF LIFE

1. BB, 24.

2. PG §95, p. 143.

3. D. Z. Phillips, "Reclaiming the Conversations of Mankind," *Philosophy* 69, no. 267 (January 1994): 36.

4. See discussion surrounding PI, p. 174.

5. 2 Cor. 5:17 NEB.

6. Hauerwas and Willimon, *Where Resident Aliens Live*, 58.

7. *Where Resident Aliens Live*, 78.

8. *Where Resident Aliens Live*, 59, emphasis added.

9. *Where Resident Aliens Live*, 42.

10. *Where Resident Aliens Live*, 82. This account of conversion appears open to the charge of logocentricity. However, such a charge misses the point of how broadly Hauerwas, like Wittgenstein before him, conceives language. Mastering the Christian language does not mean simply "talking the talk." Rather, it involves gaining the sort of fluency that can only come by self-transforming participation in the believing community's praxis (form of life).

11. See "Remembering Martin Luther King Jr. Remembering; A Response to Christopher Beem," *Journal of Religious Ethics* 23, no. 1 (Spring 1995): 145. See also *In Good Company*, 12–13.

12. *Wilderness Wanderings*, 3.

13. *Wilderness Wanderings*, 2.

14. Hauerwas remains indebted to Frei for teaching him that narratives are not pictures of the world, but creators of it. See Hans Frei, *The Eclipse of Biblical Narrative*.

15. *Where Resident Aliens Live*, 107.

16. Cited in "Creation, Contingency, and Truthful Nonviolence: A Milbankian Reflection," in *Wilderness Wanderings*, 191

17. Milbank, *Theology and Social Theory beyond Secular Reason*, 359.

18. "Creation, Contingency, and Truthful Nonviolence," 188.

19. *Wilderness Wanderings*, 20 n. 17.

20. *Wilderness Wanderings*, 9.

21. "Creation, Contingency, and Truthful Nonviolence," 193.

22. "Creation, Contingency, and Truthful Nonviolence," 198 n. 10.

23. "Murdochian Muddles: Can We Get Through Them If God Does Not Exist?," in *Iris Murdoch and the Search for Human Goodness*, ed. Maria Antonaccio and William Schweiker (Chicago and London: University of Chicago Press, 1996), 200–201.

24. "Murdochian Muddles," 200. See Iris Murdoch, *Metaphysics as a Guide to Morals* (London: Penguin Books, 1993), 477.

25. Murdochian Muddles," 205–206.

26. Cf. "Creation, Contingency, and Truthful Nonviolence," 194, to Milbank, *Theology and Social Theory*, 375.

27. "Creation, Contingency, and Truthful Nonviolence," 190.

28. Milbank, *Theology and Social Theory*, 374.

29. "Creation, Contingency, and Truthful Nonviolence," 190.

30. "Creation, Contingency, and Truthful Nonviolence," 190.

31. See Milbank, *Theology and Social Theory*, 337.

32. Hauerwas, "Pacifism: Some Philosophical Considerations," *Faith and Philosophy* 2, no. 2 (April 1985): 103.

33. "I have a number of theological and philosophical misgivings about the very idea of translation. The notion that Christian speech can or must be translated if it is to be acceptable to modern people too often embodies simplistic views regarding the nature of language. For instance, such views of the linguistic character of the theological task fail to understand that the theologian should be trained as an adequate, skillful speaker of a language." *Wilderness Wanderings*, 3.

34. For helpful discussions of the linguistic character of the world, see Hilary Putnam, *The Many Faces of Realism* (LaSalle, IL: Open Court, 1987), 3–40, and *Reason, Truth and History* (Cambridge, UK: Cambridge University Press, 1981), 49–74.

35. For more on pacifism as the form of Christian community, see Hauerwas's "Pacifism: A Form of Politics;" "Peacemaking: The Virtue of the Church;" "A Tale of Two Stories: On Being Christian and a Texan;" "The Sermon on the Mount: Just War and the Quest for Peace;" and, with Sherwindt, "The Reality of the Kingdom: An Ecclesial Space for Peace."

36. "The Church in a Divided World," 104. Hauerwas's response to relativism, i.e., that he exposes it as a non-theoretical problem, is isomorphic with his defusing of the "theoretical" problem of evil. See "God, Medicine, and the Problems of Evil" and *Naming the Silences: God, Medicine, and the Problem of Suffering* (Grand Rapids, MI: Wm. B. Eerdmans, 1991).

37. TLP 6.54.

38. "Introduction: Positioning: In the Church and University but Not of Either," in *Dispatches from the Front*, 7.

39. This discussion occurs in "Casuistry in Context: The Need for Tradition," in *In Good Company*, 169–184. See also Alasdair MacIntyre, "Does Applied Ethics Rest on a Mistake?," *Monist* 67 (1984): 501–503.

40. For Hauerwas's take on these matters see "Casuistry in Context," 171–172; "Can a Pacifist Think about War?," in *Dispatches from the Front*, 135; also 223 n. 42.

41. *Christians among the Virtues*, xiii.

42. "Casuistry in Context," 177.

43. *Dispatches from the Front*, 188 n. 2.

44. *Wilderness Wanderings*, 5.

45. In addition to *Where Resident Aliens Live*, see the first book in this series, *Resident Aliens*. See also "Abortion Theologically Understood;" "Creation, Contingency, and Truthful Nonviolence," 195–196; "In Defense of Cultural Christianity."

46. "The Liturgical Shape of the Christian Life: Teaching Christian Ethics as Worship," in *In Good Company*, 153–168.

47. E.g., "Reading James McClendon Takes Practice: Lessons in the Craft of Theology," in *Wilderness Wanderings*, 171–187; see also, with James Fodor, "Remaining in Babylon: Oliver O'Donovan's *Defense of Christendom*," in *Wilderness Wanderings*, 199–224.

48. E.g., "A Trinitarian Theology of the Chief End of All Flesh," in *In Good Company*, 185–198.

49. "Christian theology begins in ecclesiology, in church practices, not in something called 'systematic theology'. Theology begins in church and works its way out, rather than beginning in a university department of religion and dribbling back to the church as the practical application of great thoughts." *Where Resident Aliens Live*, 57.

50. *Resident Aliens*, 97.

51. "Reading James McClendon Takes Practice," 177.

52. Stanley Hauerwas, "Christians in the Hands of Flaccid Secularists: Theology and 'Moral Inquiry' in the Modern University," in *Sanctify Them in the Truth*," 215.

53. N.B.: This is *not* an ontological claim; *descriptions* supervene upon *descriptions*. See my "Human Finitude and the Supervenience of God" (paper presented at the AAR/SBL, Nashville, TN, 2000. See also my "Unstuck from Yale: Theological Method after Lindbeck," *Scottish Journal of Theology* 50, no. 2 (1997): 191–218, and my "All Suffer the Affliction of the One: Metaphysical Holism and the Presence of the Spirit," *Christian Scholars Review* (forthcoming).

54. "Reading James McClendon Takes Practice," 180–181.

55. "Remaining in Babylon: Oliver O'Donovan's *Defense of Christendom*," 213.

56. CV [1947], 56e.

57. Hauerwas, with Jeff Powell, "Creation as Apocalyptic: A Tribute to William Stringfellow," in *Dispatches from the Front*, 109.

58. "Creation as Apocalyptic: A Tribute to William Stringfellow," 109. Internal citation from CV [1940], 37e.

59. See "How Christian Ethics Became Medical Ethics," 79. Coincidentally, the hegemony of the liberal tale of human history hinges upon the presupposition that human subjects are only externally related to their surroundings. This external relation, which lies at the heart of the liberal story, is the putative warrant for both human autonomy and the logical possibility of an objective record of history. In Hauerwas's view, to the extent we have failed to challenge the myth of objectivity, we have likewise failed to be truthful. See "On Witnessing Our Story." 216–226.

60. For Hauerwas's self-confessed "postmodern" account of his journey toward a narratively-constituted conception of agency see "Agency: Going Forward by Looking Back," 64–79.

61. See "In Defense of Cultural Christianity."

62. "The Sanctified Body: Why Perfection Does Not Require a 'Self'," in *Sanctify Them in the Truth*, 77–92; "What Could It Mean for the Church to Be Christ's Body? A Question without a Clear Answer," in *In Good Company*. See also

Hauerwas and Joel Shuman, "Cloning the Human Body," in *Human Cloning: Religious Responses*, ed. Ronald Cole-Turner (Louisville, KY, Westminster John Knox Press, 1997), 58–65. In this essay Hauerwas and Shuman argue that Christians oppose cloning, not because Christians oppose nonsexual reproduction, but because the real human body—the one which constitutes each of our own—is the body of Christ. This body is reproduced by nonsexual means. Once again Hauerwas drives home the point that St. Paul's "parenting" of the Corinthian church was not metaphorical but paradigmatic.

63. Milbank, *Theology and Social Theory*, 360.

64. This book, written with Charles Pinches, grew out of Hauerwas's Asbury lectures entitled "Happiness, the Life of Virtue, and Friendship," printed in *Asbury Theological Journal* 45, no. 1 (Spring 1990): 5–48.

65. "Happiness, the Life of Virtue, and Friendship," 43–44.

66. See *Christians among the Virtues*, 4–16. Hauerwas relates this notion to fragility and tragedy; see 20–88.

67. "Christian Practice and the Practice of Law in a World without Foundations," 748; emphasis added.

68. "Not All Peace Is Peace: Why Christians Cannot Make Peace with Tristam Engelhardt's Peace," in *Wilderness Wanderings*, 116–117. See 113–118 generally.

69. *After Christendom*, 109; emphasis added.

70. "Preaching As Though We Had Enemies," 48.

71. RFM VI §23, p. 325.

72. OC §105.

73. OC §563.

74. See OC §564.

75. "Creation, Contingency, and Truthful Nonviolence," 188.

76. Hauerwas, with Willimon, "Embarrassed by God's Presence," 99.

77. "Ethics and Ascetical Theology," 97.

78. *Wilderness Wanderings*, 20 n. 17.

79. "Story and Theology," 80.

80. "Story and Theology," 225 n. 31.

81. "Story and Theology," 80; emphasis added.

82. "Story and Theology," 81. See also "Ethics and Ascetical Theology," 97.

83. Citing McClendon, "Story and Theology," 81.

84. "Ethics and Ascetical Theology," 97; Emphasis added.

85. *Christian Existence Today*, 8.

86. *Christian Existence Today*, 10.

87. See "Testament of Friends: How My Mind Has Changed," *Christian Century* 107, no. 7 (February 28, 1990): 213; *Dispatches from the Front*, 188 n. 2; "Reading James McClendon Takes Practice," esp. 184.

88. See Hauerwas, with Burrell, "From System to Story," 15–39; Hauerwas, "The Church in a Divided World, 89–110; and Hauerwas and Jones, *Why Narrative?*, 1–18. For comparison see Lindbeck, *The Nature of Doctrine*, 63–72.

89. See "The Eyes Have It," *Second Opinion* 17, no. 4 (April 1992): 41–43. See also "Remembering Martin Luther King Jr. Remembering," 135–148.

90. See *Wilderness Wanderings*, 12.

91. "Knowing How to Go On When You Do Not Know Where You Are: A Response to John Cobb," in *Wilderness Wanderings*, 31.

92. Hauerwas, with Kenneson, "The Church and/as God's Non-Violent Imagination," 83. See also Hauerwas, "The Church as God's New Language," in *Christian Existence Today*, 60.

93. See his appreciative remark concerning Nancey Murphy's project (*Theology in the Age of Scientific Reasoning*) in his *Wilderness Wanderings*, 15 n. 4. Hauerwas himself may be moving in a similar direction in his essay "Timeful Friends: Living with the Handicapped," in *Sanctify Them in the Truth*, 143–156.

94. "The Church as God's New Language," 59, emphasis added.

95. Hauerwas is very clear that the truth of Christian claims does not depend on theories of truth. Such theories (unlike Christian claims themselves) do no work since they are abstracted from any basis in praxis which might give them a sense. Being disengaged from actual living renders these theories liable to misappropriation in the service of violence.

"Christians do not believe in an 'eternal truth or truths' that can be known apart from the existence of the people of Israel and the church. We know that the witness that we are called to make is such exactly because that to which we witness is unavailable apart from its exemplification in the lives of a community of people. That such a witness takes the form of nonviolence is necessary because we believe that the God who makes such a witness necessary is a God who would not be known otherwise.

"For many, that seems to be an invitation to relativism and, correlatively, war and violence. If we lack a standpoint that at least promises to secure agreement between people who otherwise share nothing in common, what chance do we have of making war less likely? Yet from my perspective, just such theories have made war likely. Christians do not promise the world a theory of truth that will resolve conflict. Rather, we promise the world a witness that we think is the truth of our existence. That witness requires the existence of a body of people who provide an alternative so that we may be able to see the violence that so grips our lives." "Can a Pacifist Think about War?," in *Dispatches from the Front*, 135.

96. (Downers Grove, IL: InterVarsity Press, 1999).

97. The discourse of piety is constituted by first-order confessional statements. "Theology" refers to second-order statements, namely, those that are formed by reflection upon first-order discourse in its proper context. Since both first- and second-order statements are "insider" statements, conflicts which arise between them can be settled only by appealing to the authority of the linguistic system; to remain on the inside, one must play the game in such-and-such a manner. Philosophy constitutes third-order discourse that seeks only to elucidate the grammar of first- and

second-order statements and draw attention to points in the conversation where the grammar has been ignored and confusion has thereby entered. Compare Phillips, "Philosophy, Theology and the Reality of God," in *Wittgenstein and Religion*, ed. Phillips, 22–31, and Hans Frei, *Types of Christian Theology* (New Haven, CT: Yale University Press, 1992), 46–55.

98. Hauerwas, "On Doctrine and Ethics," in *The Cambridge Companion to Christian Doctrine*, ed. Gunton, 25.

99. "On Doctrine and Ethics," 29.

100. That is, doing theology or ethics from "top down" hinges upon the wrong-headed view of language as corresponding with reality, only in this case, we are told, *God* guarantees the fit between world and language. Unfortunately God must still convey truth by utilizing human propositions, and so we are stuck with wondering how good is the fit between truth divinely conceived and that which is expressed by means of propositions in human language.

101. Hauerwas, "The Truth about God: The Decalogue as Condition for Truthful Speech," in *Sanctify Them in Truth*, 53–54.

102. "The Truth about God," 44.

103. Hauerwas, "Introduction," in *Sanctify Them in Truth*, 5.

104. "On Doctrine and Ethics," 34–35.

105. Hauerwas, "'Salvation Even in Sin': Learning to Speak Truthfully about Ourselves," in *Sanctify Them in Truth*, 72; emphasis added.

106. "The Truth about God," 44.

107. MacIntyre, *Whose Justice? Which Rationality?*

108. See my "Changing the Subject in Postmodernity: Narrative Ethics and Philosophical Therapy in the Works of Stanley Hauerwas and Ludwig Wittgenstein" (Ph.D. Diss. Fuller Theological Seminary, 1998).

109. Booth, *Aristotelian Aporetic Ontology in Islamic and Christian Thinkers*, esp. 1–35, 205–270.

110. Booth, *Aristotelian Aporetic Ontology*, 2; emphasis added.

111. Booth, *Aristotelian Aporetic Ontology*, 25.

112. CV (1931), 17.

113. Booth, *Aristotelian Aporetic Ontology*, 205 n. 1, citing Klaus Hartmann.

114. Booth, *Aristotelian Aporetic Ontology*, 227.

115. Booth, *Aristotelian Aporetic Ontology*, 216.

116. Booth writes, "Platonist conceptions of participation [i.e., the participation of a particular thing in a Form] are . . . more transformed than related Aristotelian ones; though to these is added the explicit dimension of *esse*, in which the ultimate reality of participation is the direct dependence of every creature on God. Compared with this, all other participation can only be aspects of its content." *Aristotelian Aporetic Ontology*, 220.

117. Booth, *Aristotelian Aporetic Ontology*, 241.

118. Hauerwas, *A Community of Character*, 6.

119. "Introduction," *Sanctify Them in Truth*, 7.
120. "On Doctrine and Ethics," 33.
121. "Story and Theology," 224–225 n. 26.
122. "The Truth about God," 57.
123. "Introduction," *Sanctify Them in the Truth*, 6.
124. "The Truth about God," 38.
125. *Prayers Plainly Spoken*, 64.

Bibliography

Wittgenstein and Hauerwas

WORKS BY LUDWIG WITTGENSTEIN

The Blue and Brown Books. New York, NY: Harper and Brothers, 1958.

"Cause and Effect: Intuitive Awareness." In *Philosophical Occasions, 1912–1952.* Edited by James C. Klagge and Alfred Normann, 370–426. Indianapolis and Cambridge: Hackett Publishing, 1993.

Culture and Value. Translated by Peter Winch. Edited by G. H. von Wright and Heikki Nyman. English translation with the amended 2d ed. Oxford, UK: Basil Blackwell, 1980.

Last Writings on the Philosophy of Psychology. Vol. 1. *Preliminary Studies for Part II of the Philosophical Investigations.* Translated by C. G. Luckhardt and M. A. E. Aue. Edited by G. H. von Wright and Heikki Nyman. Chicago, IL: University of Chicago Press, 1982.

Last Writings on the Philosophy of Psychology. Vol. 2. *The Inner and the Outer, 1949–1951.* Translated by C. G. Luckhardt and M. A. E. Aue. Edited by G. H. von Wright and Heikki Nyman. Cambridge, MA, and Oxford, UK: Blackwell, 1992.

"A Lecture on Ethics." In *Philosophical Occasions, 1912–1952.* Edited by James C. Klagge and Alfred Normann, 37–44. Indianapolis and Cambridge: Hackett Publishing, 1993.

Lectures & Conversations on Aesthetics, Psychology, and Religious Belief. Edited by C. Barrett. Oxford: Oxford University Press, 1966.

Ludwig Wittgenstein: Wiener Ausgabe/Vienna Edition: Einfuhrung/Introduction. Edited by Michael Nedo. Vienna and New York: Springer-Verlag, 1993.

Notebooks, 1914–1916. With an English translation by G. E. M. Anscombe and an index prepared by E. D. Klemke. Edited by G. H. von Wright and G. E. M. Anscombe. Chicago: University of Chicago Press, 1961.

"Notes for Lectures on 'Private Experience' and 'Sense Data'." In *Philosophical Occasions, 1912–1952*. Edited by James C. Klagge and Alfred Normann, 202–288. Indianapolis and Cambridge: Hackett Publishing, 1993.

"Notes for the Philosophical Lecture." In *Philosophical Occasions, 1912–1952*. Edited by James C. Klagge and Alfred Normann, 447–58. Indianapolis and Cambridge: Hackett Publishing, 1993.

On Certainty. Translated by Denis Paul and G. E. M. Anscombe. Edited by G. E. M. Anscombe and G. H. von Wright. New York, NY: Harper Torchbooks, 1969, 1972.

Philosophical Grammar. Translated by Anthony Kenny. Edited by Rush Rhees. Berkeley and Los Angeles: University of California Press, 1974.

Philosophical Investigations. Translated by G. E. M. Anscombe. Edited by G. E. M. Anscombe and Rush Rhees. New York: Macmillan, 1953.

Philosophical Occasions, 1912–1952. Edited by James C. Klagge and Alfred Normann. Indianapolis and Cambridge: Hackett Publishing, 1993.

Philosophical Remarks. Translated by Anthony Kenny. Edited from his posthumous writings by Rush Rhees and translated into English by Raymond Hargreaves and Roger White. Chicago, IL: University of Chicago Press, and Oxford, UK: Basil Blackwell, 1974.

"Philosophy." In *Philosophical Occasions, 1912–1952*. Edited by James C. Klagge and Alfred Normann, 161–199. Indianapolis and Cambridge: Hackett Publishing, 1993.

Remarks on Colour. Translated by Linda L. McAlister and Margarete Schättle. Edited by G. E. M. Anscombe. Berkeley and Los Angeles, CA: University of California Press, 1977.

Remarks on the Foundations of Mathematics. Translated by G. E. M. Anscombe. Edited by G. H. von Wright, Rush Rhees, and G. E. M. Anscombe. Cambridge, MA, and London, UK: MIT Press, 1978.

"Remarks on Frazer's Golden Bough." In *Philosophical Occasions, 1912–1952*. Edited by James C. Klagge and Alfred Normann, 118–155. Indianapolis and Cambridge: Hackett Publishing, 1993.

Remarks on the Philosophy of Psychology. Two Volumes. Translated by C. G. Luckhardt and M. A. E. Aue. Edited by G. H. von Wright and Heikki Nyman. Chicago, IL: University of Chicago Press, 1980.

"Some Remarks on Logical Form." In *Philosophical Occasions, 1912–1952*. Edited by James C. Klagge and Alfred Normann, 29–35. Indianapolis and Cambridge: Hackett Publishing, 1993.

Tractatus Logico-Philosophicus. Translated by D. F. Pears and B. F. McGuinness. London and New York: Routledge, 1961.

Tractatus Logico-Philosophicus. German text with an English translation by C. K. Ogden and introduction by Bertrand Russell. London and New York: Routledge, [1921] 1992.

Wittgenstein's Lectures: Cambridge, 1930–32. Edited by Desmond Lee. Chicago: University of Chicago Press, 1980.

Wittgenstein and the Vienna Circle: Conversations Recorded by Friedrich Waismann. Translated by Joachim Schulte and Brian McGuinness. Edited by B. F. McGuinness. New York: Barnes and Noble, 1979.

Zettel. Translated by G. E. M. Anscombe. Edited by G. E. M. Anscombe and G. H. von Wright. Berkeley and Los Angeles: University of California Press, 1970.

BOOKS BY STANLEY HAUERWAS

After Christendom? How the Church Is to Behave If Freedom, Justice, and a Christian Nation Are Bad Ideas. Nashville, TN: Abingdon Press, 1991.

Against the Nations: War and Survival in a Liberal Society. Notre Dame, IN: University of Notre Dame Press, 1992.

Character and the Christian Life: A Study in Theological Ethics. San Antonio, TX: Trinity University Press, 1975. Notre Dame and London: University of Notre Dame Press, 1994.

Christian Existence Today: Essays on Church, World, and Living in Between. Durham, NC: Labyrinth Press, 1988.

Christians among the Virtues: Theological Conversations with Ancient and Modern Ethics. Stanley Hauerwas with Charles Pinches. Notre Dame, IN: University of Notre Dame Press, 1997.

A Community of Character. Notre Dame, IN: University of Notre Dame Press, 1981.

Dispatches from the Front: Theological Engagements with the Secular. Durham, NC: Duke University Press, 1994.

In Good Company: The Church as Polis. Notre Dame, IN: University of Notre Dame Press, 1995.

Naming the Silences: God, Medicine, and the Problem of Suffering. Grand Rapids, MI: Wm. B. Eerdmans, 1991.

The Peaceable Kingdom: A Primer in Christian Ethics. Notre Dame, IN: Notre Dame University Press, 1983.

Prayers Plainly Spoken. Downers Grove, IL: InterVarsity Press, 1999.

Resident Aliens: Life in the Christian Colony. Stanley Hauerwas and William H. Willimon. Nashville, TN: Abingdon Press, 1989.

Revisions: Changing Perspectives in Moral Philosphy. Edited by Stanley Hauerwas and Alasdair MacIntyre. Notre Dame, IN: Notre Dame University Press, 1983.

Sanctify Them in the Truth: Holiness Exemplified. Nashville, TN: Abingdon Press, 1998.

Schooling Christians. Hauerwas, Stanley, and John H. Westerhoff, eds. Grand Rapids, MI: Wm. B. Eerdmans, 1992.

Suffering Presence: Theological Reflections on Medicine, the Mentally Handicapped, and the Church. Notre Dame, IN: University of Notre Dame Press, 1986.

Theology without Foundations: Religious Practice and the Future of Theological Truth. Edited by Stanley Hauerwas, Nancey Murphy, and Mark Thiessen Nation. Nashville, TN: Abingdon Press, 1994.

Truthfulness and Tragedy. Stanley Hauerwas with David Burrell. Notre Dame: University of Notre Dame Press, 1977.

Unleashing the Scripture: Freeing the Bible from Captivity to America. Nashville, TN: Abingdon Press, 1993.

Vision and Virtue. Notre Dame, IN: Fides Publishers, 1974; repr., Notre Dame, IN: University of Notre Dame Press, 1981.

Where Resident Aliens Live: Exercises for Christian Practice. Stanley Hauerwas and William Willimon. Nashville, TN: Abingdon, 1996.

Why Narrative? Edited by Stanley Hauerwas and L. Gregory Jones. Grand Rapids, MI: Wm. B. Eerdmans, 1989.

Wilderness Wanderings: Probing Twentieth-Century Theology and Philosophy. Boulder, CO: Westview Press, 1997.

ESSAYS BY STANLEY HAUERWAS

The year in parentheses following an essay title represents the date of first publication.

"Abortion: The Agent's Perspective." (1973). In *Vision and Virtue*, 147–165. Notre Dame, IN: Fides Publishers, 1974; repr., Notre Dame, IN: University of Notre Dame Press, 1981.

"Abortion: Why the Arguments Fail." In *A Community of Character*, 212–229. Notre Dame, IN: University of Notre Dame Press, 1980/1981.

"Abortion and Normative Ethics." (1971). In *Vision and Virtue*, 127–146. Notre Dame, IN: Fides Publishers, 1974; repr., Notre Dame, IN: University of Notre Dame Press, 1981.

"Abortion Theologically Understood." In *The Church and Abortion: In Search of New Ground for Response*. Edited by Paul T. Stallsworth, 44–66. Nashville, TN: Abingdon, 1993. Also in *Virtue and Practices in the Christian Tradition: Christian Ethics after MacIntyre*. Edited by Nancey Murphy, Brad J. Kallenberg, and Mark Thiessen Nation, 221–238. Harrisburg, PA: Trinity Press International, 1997.

"Agency: Going Forward by Looking Back." In *Christian Ethics: Problems and Prospects*, volume in honor of James Gustafson. Edited by Lisa Sowle and J. F. Childress, 64–79. Cleveland: Pilgrim Press, 1996.

"Aslan and the New Morality." (1972). In *Vision and Virtue*, 93–110. Notre Dame, IN: Fides Publishers, 1974; repr., Notre Dame, IN: University of Notre Dame Press, 1981.

"Athens May Be a Long Way from Jerusalem but Prussia Is Even Further." *Asbury Theological Journal* 45, no. 1 (Spring 1990): 59–64.

"Authority and the Profession of Medicine." (1982). In *Suffering Presence: Theological Reflections on Medicine, the Mentally Handicapped, and the Church*, 39–62. Notre Dame, IN: University of Notre Dame Press, 1986.

"Beyond 'Political Correctness,' Left or Right." *New Oxford Review* 58, no. 8 (October 1991): 9–11.

"Can a Pacifist Think about War?" In *Dispatches from the Front: Theological Engagements with the Secular*, 116–135. Durham, NC: Duke University Press, 1994.

"Can Aristotle Be a Liberal? Nussbaum on Luck." *Soundings: An Interdisciplinary Journal* 72, no. 4 (Winter 1989): 675–691.

"Can Ethics Be Theological?" *Hastings Center Report* 8, no. 5 (October 1978): 47–49.

"Capital Punishment: It's a Rite of Vengeance." *Notre Dame Magazine* 8, no. 4 (October 1979): 67–68.

"Care." In *Encyclopedia of Bioethics*, 145–150. New York: The Free Press, 1978.

"Casuistry in Context: The Need for Tradition." In *In Good Company: The Church as Polis*, 169–184. Notre Dame, IN: University of Notre Dame Press, 1995.

"Character, Narrative, and Growth in the Christian Life." (1980). In *A Community of Character*, 129–152. Notre Dame, IN: University of Notre Dame Press, 1981.

"Characterizing Perfection: Second Thoughts on Character and Sanctification." In *Wesleyan Theology Today: A Bicentennial Theological Consultation*. Edited by Theodore Runyon, 251–263. Nashville, TN: Kingswood Books, 1985.

"A Christian Critique of Christian America." (1986). In *Christian Existence Today: Essays on Church, World, and Living in Between*, 171–190. Durham, NC: Labyrinth Press, 1988.

"Christian Ethics in America: Beginning with an Ending." In *History of Christian Ethics in America*, unfinished book mss., n.d.

"Christian Practice and the Practice of Law in a World without Foundations." *Mercer Law Review* 44, no. 3 (Spring 1993): 743–751.

"The Christian, Society and the Weak: A Meditation on the Care of the Retarded." (1972). In *Vision and Virtue*, 187–194. Notre Dame, IN: Fides Publishers, 1974; repr., Notre Dame, IN: University of Notre Dame Press, 1981.

"Christianity: It's Not a Religion, It's an Adventure." *U.S. Catholic* 56, no. 6 (June 1991): 6–13.

"Christianity and Democracy: A Response." *Center Journal* 1, no. 3 (Summer 1982): 42–51.

"Christians in the Hands of Flaccid Secularists: Theology and 'Moral Inquiry' in the Modern University." In *Sanctify Them in the Truth: Holiness Exemplified*, 201–218. Nashville, TN: Abingdon, 1998.

"The Church and Liberal Democracy: The Moral Limits of Secular Polity." In *A Community of Character*, 72–86. Notre Dame, IN: University of Notre Dame Press, 1981.

"The Church and the Mentally Handicapped: A Continuing Challenge to the Imagination." In *Dispatches from the Front: Theological Engagements with the Secular*, 177–186. Durham, NC: Duke University Press, 1994.

"The Church and/as God's Non-Violent Imagination." With Philip D. Kenneson. *Pro Ecclesia* 1, no. 1 (Fall 1992): 76–88.

"The Church as God's New Language." (1986). In *Christian Existence Today: Essays on Church, World, and Living in Between*, 47–66. Durham, NC: Labyrinth Press, 1988.

"The Church in a Divided World: The Interpretive Power of the Christian Story." (1980). In *A Community of Character*, 89–110. Notre Dame, IN: University of Notre Dame Press, 1981.

"The Church's One Foundation Is Jesus Christ Her Lord; Or, In a World without Foundations: All We Have Is the Church." In *Theology without Foundations: Religious Practice and the Future of Theological Truth*. Edited by Stanley Hauerwas, Nancey Murphy, and Mark Nation, 143–162. Nashville, TN: Abingdon Press, 1994.

"Clerical Character." In *Christian Existence Today: Essays on Church, World, and Living in Between*, 133–148. Durham, NC: Labyrinth Press, 1986/1988.

"Cloning the Human Body." Stanley Hauerwas and Joel Shuman. In *Human Cloning: Religious Responses*. Edited by Ronald Cole-Turner, 58–65: Louisville, KY: Westminster John Knox Press, 1997.

"A Communitarian Lament: A Review of *The Good Society* by Robert Bellah." *First Things* 19 (January 1992): 45–46.

"Communitarians and Medical Ethicists: Or, 'Why I Am None of the Above'." In *Dispatches from the Front: Theological Engagements with the Secular*, 156–163. Durham, NC: Duke University Press, 1994.

"Community and Diversity: The Tyranny of Normality." (1977). In *Suffering Presence: Theological Reflections on Medicine, the Mentally Handicapped, and the Church*, 211–217. Notre Dame, IN: University of Notre Dame Press, 1986.

"Constancy and Forgiveness: The Novel as a School for Virtue." (1983). In *Dispatches from the Front: Theological Engagements with the Secular*, 31–57. Durham, NC: Duke University Press, 1994.

"Creation as Apocalyptic: A Tribute to William Stringfellow." With Jeff Powell. In *Dispatches from the Front: Theological Engagements with the Secular*. Edited by Stanley Hauerwas, 107–115. Durham, NC: Duke University Press, 1994.

"Creation, Contingency, and Truthful Nonviolence: A Milbankian Reflection." (1995). In *Wilderness Wanderings: Probing Twentieth-Century Theology and Philosophy*, 188–198. Boulder, CO: Westview Press, 1997.

"The Cruelty of Peace." (1995). In *Sanctify Them in the Truth*, 245–248. Nashville, TN: Abingdon Press, 1998.

"Daring Prayer: A Review." *Princeton Seminary Bulletin* II, no. 1, new series (1978): 50–51.

"The Demands and Limits of Care: On the Moral Dilemma of Neonatal Intensive Care." (1975). In *Truthfulness and Tragedy*, 169–183. Notre Dame, IN: University of Notre Dame Press, 1977.

"The Demands of a Truthful Story: Ethics and the Pastoral Task." *Chicago Studies* 21, no. 1 (Spring 1982): 59–71.

"The Democratic Policing of Christianity." In *Dispatches from the Front: Theological Engagements with the Secular*, 91–106. Durham, NC: Duke University Press, 1994.

"The Difference of Virtue and the Difference It Makes: Courage Exemplified." *Modern Theology* 9, no. 3 (July 1993): 249–264.

"Don't Let Them Eat Cake: Reflections on Luck, Justice, and Poor People." *Notre Dame Magazine* 10, no. 5 (December 1981): 24–25.

"Embarrassed by God's Presence." With William Willimon. *Christian Century* 102, no. 4 (January 30, 1985): 98–100.

"Embodied Memory." *Journal for Preachers* 19/3 (Easter 1996): 20–24.

"Epilogue: A Pacifist Response to the Bishops." in *Speak Up for Just War or Pacifism: A Critique of the United Methodist Bishop's Pastoral Letter 'In Defense of Creation'*, by Paul 149–182. University Park, PA, and London, UK: Pennsylvania State University Press, 1989.

"An Eschatological Perspective on Nuclear Disarmament." (1983). In *Against the Nations: War and Survival in a Liberal Society*, 160–168. Notre Dame, IN: University of Notre Dame Press, 1992.

"Eschatology and Nuclear Disarmament." *New Catholic World* 226, no. 1356 (November/December 1983): 249–253.

"Ethical Issues in the Use of Human Subjects." In *Suffering Presence: Theological Reflections on Medicine, the Mentally Handicapped, and the Church*, 114–124. Notre Dame, IN: University of Notre Dame Press, 1975/1986.

"Ethics and Ascetical Theology." *Anglican Theological Review* 61, no. 1 (January 1979): 87–98.

"The Ethicist as Theologian." *Christian Century* 92, no. 15 (April 23, 1975): 408–412.

"Ethics Christian." Stanley Hauerwas and D. Stephen Long. In *New Handbook of Christian Theology*. Edited by Donald Musser and Joseph Price, 160–167. Nashville, TN: Abingdon, 1992.

"The Ethics of Death: Letting Die or Putting to Death?" In *Vision and Virtue*, 166–186. Notre Dame, IN: Fides Publishers 1974; repr., Notre Dame, IN: University of Notre Dame Press, 1981.

"The Eyes Have It." *Second Opinion* 17, no. 4 (April 1992): 41–43.

"A Failure in Communication: Ethics and the Early Church: Review Essay of Sanders, *Ethics in the New Testament*, and Osborn, *Ethical Patterns in Early Christian Thought*." *Interpretation* 32, no. 2 (April 1978): 196–200.

"Failure of Communication or A Case of Uncomprehending Feminism." *Scottish Journal of Theology* 50, no. 2 (1997): 228–239.

"Faith and the Republic: A Frances Lewis Law Center Conversation between Stanley Hauerwas, Sanford Levinson, and Mark Tushnet." *Washington and Lee Law Review* 45, no. 2 (Spring 1988): 467–534.

"The Family: Theological and Ethical Reflections." In *A Community of Character*, 167–174. Notre Dame, IN: University of Notre Dame Press, 1981.

"The Family as a School for Character?" *Religious Education* 80, no. 2 (Spring 1985): 272–286.

"Flights in Foundationalism, or Things Aren't As Bad As They Seem: Review of Stout's *Ethics after Babel.*" *Soundings* 71, no. 4 (Winter 1988): 683–699.

"For Dappled Things." In *Sanctify Them in the Truth: Holiness Exemplified*, 227–233. Nashville, TN: Abingdon Press, 1998.

"Foreword." In *Basic Christian Ethics* by Paul Ramsey. With Stephen D. Long. Louisville, KY: Westminster John Knox Press, 1993.

"Forgiveness and Political Community." *Worldview* 23, no. 1–2 (January–February 1980): 15–16.

"From Conduct to Character: A Guide to Sexual Adventure." With Allen Verhey. *Reformed Journal* 36, no. 11 (November 1986): 12–16.

"From System to Story: An Alternative Pattern for Rationality in Ethics." With David Burrell. In *Truthfulness and Tragedy*, 15–39. Notre Dame: University of Notre Dame Press, 1977.

"The Future of Christian Social Ethics." In *That They May Live: Theological Reflections on the Quality of Life*. Edited by George Devine, 123–131. Staten Island, NY: Alba House, 1972.

"The Gesture of a Truthful Story." (1985). In *Christian Existence Today: Essays on Church, World, and Living in Between*, 101–110. Durham, NC: Labyrinth Press, 1988.

"God as Participant: Time and History in the Work of James Gustafson." (1985). In *Wilderness Wanderings: Probing Twentieth-Century Theology and Philosophy*, 62–81. Boulder, CO: Westview Press, 1997.

"God the Measurer. Review of James Gustafson's *Ethics from a Theocentric Perspective*. Vol. 1, *Theology and Ethics.*" *Journal of Religion* 62, no. 4 (1982): 402–411.

"God's Grandeur." n.d.

"God, Medicine, and the Problems of Evil." *Reformed Journal* 38, no. 4 (April 1988): 16–22.

"Happiness, the Life of Virtue, and Friendship." *Asbury Theological Journal* 45, no. 1 (Spring 1990): 5–48.

"Having and Learning to Care for Retarded Children." (1975). In *Truthfulness and Tragedy*, 147–156. Notre Dame: University of Notre Dame Press, 1977.

"History as Fate: How Justification by Faith Became Anthropology (and History) in America." In *Wilderness Wanderings: Probing Twentieth-Century Theology and Philosophy*, 32–47. Boulder, CO: Westview Press, 1997.

"The Holocaust and the Duty to Forgive." *Sh'ma* 10, no. 198 (October 3, 1980): 137–139.

"A Homage to Mary and to the University Called Notre Dame." (1994). In *In Good Company: The Church as Polis*, 81–90. Notre Dame, IN: University of Notre Dame Press, 1995.

"Hope Faces Power: Thomas More and the King of England." (1978). In *Christian Existence Today: Essays on Church, World, and Living in Between*, 199–220. Durham, NC: Labyrinth Press, 1988.

"How Christian Ethics Became Medical Ethics." In *Religion and Medical Ethics: Looking Back, Looking Forward*. Edited by Allen Verhey, 61–80. Grand Rapids, MI: W. B. Eerdmans, 1995.

"How Christian Universities Contribute to the Corruption of Youth." (1986). In *Christian Existence Today: Essays on Church, World, and Living in Between*, 237–252. Durham, NC: Labyrinth Press, 1988.

"How to Go On When You Know You Are Going to Be Misunderstood or How Paul Holmer Ruined My Life or Making Sense of Paul Holmer." (1996). In *Wilderness Wanderings: Probing Twentieth-Century Theology and Philosophy*, 143–152. Boulder, CO: Westview Press, 1997.

"The Humanity of the Divine." *Cresset* 35, no. 8 (June 1972): 16–17.

"If It Were Up to Me: Critics Choice." *Salt* 11, no. 10 (November / December 1991): 26–27.

"The Importance of Being Catholic: Unsolicited Advice from a Protestant Bystander." (1990). In *In Good Company: The Church as Polis*, 91–108. Notre Dame, IN: University of Notre Dame Press, 1995.

"In Defense of Cultural Christianity: Reflections on Going to Church." In *Sanctify Them in Truth: Holiness Exemplified*, 157–176. Edinburgh, UK: T&T Clark, 1998.

"Interpreting the Bible as a Political Act." With Steve Long. *Religion and Intellectual Life* 6, no. 3/4 (Spring/Summer 1989): 134–142.

"Introduction." In *Sanctify Them in Truth: Holiness Exemplified*, 1–18. Edinburgh, UK: T&T Clark, 1998.

"Introduction: Positioning: In the Church and University but Not of Either." In *Dispatches from the Front: Theological Engagements with the Secular*, 5–28. Durham, NC: Duke University Press, 1994.

"Introduction: Theological Interventions and Interrogations." In *Wilderness Wanderings: Probing Twentieth-Century Theology and Philosophy*, 1–21. Boulder, CO: Westview Press, 1997.

"The Irony of American Christianity: Reinhold Niebuhr on Church and State." With Michael Broadway. *Insights: A Journal of the Faculty of Austin Seminary* 108 (Fall 1992): 33–46.

"The Irony of Reinhold Neibuhr: The Ideological Character of Christian Realism." With Michael Broadway. (1992). In *Wilderness Wanderings: Probing Twentieth-Century Theology and Philosophy*, 48–61. Boulder, CO: Westview Press, 1997.

"Jesus: The Story of the Kingdom." (1978). In *A Community of Character*, 36–52. Notre Dame, IN: University of Notre Dame Press, 1981.

"Jews and Christians among the Nations: The Social Significance of the Holocaust." *Cross Currents* 31, no. 1 (Spring 1981): 15–34.

"Judgment and the New Morality." *New Blackfriars* 53 (May 1972): 210–221.

"Killing Compassion." In *Dispatches from the Front: Theological Engagements with the Secular*, 164–176. Durham, NC: Duke University Press, 1994.

"The Kingship of Christ: Why Freedom of 'Belief' Is Not Enough." (1992). In *In Good Company: The Church as Polis*, 199–216. Notre Dame, IN: University of Notre Dame Press, 1995.

"Knowing How to Go On When You Do Not Know Where You Are: A Response to John Cobb." (1995). In *Wilderness Wanderings: Probing Twentieth-Century Theology and Philosophy*, 25–31. Boulder, CO: Westview Press, 1997.

"Language, Experience, and the Life Well-Lived: A Review of the Work of Donald Evans." With Richard Bondi. *Religious Studies Review* 9, no. 1 (January 1983): 33–37.

"Learning Morality from Handicapped Children." *Hastings Center Report* 10, no. 5 (October 1980): 45–46.

"Learning to See Red Wheelbarrows: On Vision and Relativism." *Journal of the American Academy of Religion* 45, no. 2 (June 1977): 225, 644–655.

"Letter to the Editor: On Liberalism and Virtue." *Commonweal* 105, no. 24 (December 8, 1978): 790, 799.

"Like Those Who Dream: A Sermon." In *The Bible in Theology and Preaching*. Edited by Donald K. McKim, 134–136. Nashville, TN: Abingdon Press, 1994.

"The Liturgical Shape of the Christian Life: Teaching Christian Ethics as Worship." In *In Good Company: The Church as Polis*, 153–168. Notre Dame, IN: University of Notre Dame Press, 1995.

"Living on Dishonest Wealth." *Journal for Preachers* 20, no. 1 (Advent 1996): 15–17.

"Love's Not All You Need." (1972). In *Vision and Virtue*, 111–126. Notre Dame, IN: Fides Publishers 1974; repr., Notre Dame, IN: University of Notre Dame Press, 1981.

"The Meaning of Being Human." In *Selected Readings: Genetic Engineering and Bioethics*. Edited by Robert Paoletti, 129–133. New York: MSS Information, 1972.

"Medicine as a Tragic Profession." In *Truthfulness and Tragedy*, 184–202. Notre Dame, IN: University of Notre Dame Press, 1977.

"A Meditation on Developing Hopeful Virtues." In *The Return to Scripture in Judaism and Christianity: Essays in Post-Critical Scriptural Interpretation*. Edited by Peter Ochs, 308–324. New York: Paulist Press, 1993.

"Memory, Community, and the Reasons for Living: Reflections on Suicide and Euthanasia." (1976). In *Truthfulness and Tragedy*, 101–115. Notre Dame, IN: University of Notre Dame Press, 1977.

"Messianic Pacifism." *Worldview* 16, no. 6 (June 1973): 29–33.

"Ministry as More Than a Helping Profession." With Will Willimon. *Christian Century* 106, no. 9 (March 15, 1989): 282–284.

"The Ministry of a Congregation: Rethinking Christian Ethics for a Church-Centered Seminary." In *Christian Existence Today: Essays on Church, World, and Living in Between*, 101–110. Durham, NC: Labyrinth Press, 1988.

"*Moral Actions and Christian Ethics*, by Jean Porter, a Review." *Journal of Religion* 77/1 (January 1997): 172–173.

"The Moral Authority of Scripture: The Politics and Ethics of Remembering." (1980). In *A Community of Character*, 53–71. Notre Dame, IN: University of Notre Dame Press, 1981.

"The Moral Challenge of the Handicapped." (1981). In *Suffering Presence: Theological Reflections on Medicine, the Mentally Handicapped, and the Church*, 182–188. Notre Dame, IN: University of Notre Dame Press, 1986.

"The Moral Limits of Population Control." (1974). In *Truthfulness and Tragedy*, 116–126. Notre Dame: University of Notre Dame Press, 1977.

"The Moral Value of the Family." In *A Community of Character*, 155–166. Notre Dame, IN: University of Notre Dame Press, 1981.

"The Morality of Teaching." In *The Academic's Handbook*. Edited by A. Leigh DeNeeff, Craufurd D. Goodwin, and Ellen Stern McCrate, 19–28. Durham, N.C.: Duke University Press, 1988.

"Murdochian Muddles: Can We Get Through Them If God Does Not Exist?" In *Iris Murdoch and the Search for Human Goodness*. Edited by Maria Antonaccio and William Schweiker, 190–208. Chicago and London: University of Chicago Press, 1996.

"Must a Patient Be a Person to Be a Patient? Or, My Uncle Charlie Is Not Much of a Person but He Is Still My Uncle Charlie." (1975). In *Truthfulness and Tragedy*, 127–131. Notre Dame, IN: University of Notre Dame Press, 1977.

"Natural Law, Tragedy, and Theological Ethics." (1975). In *Truthfulness and Tragedy*, 57–70. Notre Dame, IN: University of Notre Dame Press, 1977.

"The Need for An Ending." *Modern Churchman* XXVIII, no. 3 (1986): 3–7.

"The Nonresistant Church: The Theological Ethics of John Howard Yoder." In *Vision and Virtue*, 197–221. Notre Dame, IN: Fides Publishers, 1974; repr., Notre Dame, IN: University of Notre Dame, 1981.

"A Non-Violent Proposal for Christian Participation in Culture Wars." *Soundings: An Interdisciplinary Journal* 75, no. 4 (Winter 1992): 477–492.

"The Non-violent Terrorist: In Defense of Christian Fanaticism." In *Sanctify Them in Truth: Holiness Exemplified*, 177–190. Edinburgh, UK: T&T Clark, 1998.

"Not All Peace Is Peace: Why Christians Cannot Make Peace with Tristam Engelhardt's Peace." In *Wilderness Wanderings: Probing Twentieth-Century Theology and Philosophy*, 111–123. Boulder, CO: Westview Press, 1997.

"Obligation and Virtue Once More." (1975). In *Truthfulness and Tragedy*, 40–56. Notre Dame, IN: University of Notre Dame Press, 1977.

"On Being a Christian and an American." 1998. Forthcoming in Bellah festscrift.

"On Being 'Placed' by John Milbank: A Response." In *Christ, Ethics and Tragedy*. Edited by Kenneth Surin, 197–201. Cambridge, UK: Cambridge University Press, 1989.

"On Being Professionally a Friend: Review of *Faith and the Professions* by Thomas Shaffer." *Christian Legal Society Quarterly* 9, no. 2 (Summer 1988): 24–26.

"On Doctrine and Ethics." In *The Cambridge Companion to Christian Doctrine*. Edited by Colin E. Gunton, 21–40. Cambridge, UK: Cambridge University Press, 1997.

"On God: Ethics and the Power to Act in History." In *Essays on Peace Theology and Witness*. Edited by Willard Swartley. Elkhart, IN: Institute of Mennonite Studies, 1988.

"On Honor: By Way of a Comparison of Karl Barth and Trollope." (1988). In *Dispatches from the Front: Theological Engagements with the Secular*, 58–79. Durham, NC: Duke University Press, 1994.

"On Keeping Theological Ethics Theological." (1983). In *Against the Nations: War and Survival in a Liberal Society*, 23–50. Notre Dame, IN: University of Notre Dame Press, 1992.

"On Learning Simplicity in an Ambiguous Age." *Katallagete* 10, no. 1–3 (Fall 1987): 43–46.

"On Medicine and Virtue: A Response." In *Virtue and Medicine*. Edited by Earl Shelp, 347–355. Dordrecht: D. Reidel Publishing, 1985.

"On Surviving Justly: Ethics and Nuclear Disarmament." (1983). In *Against the Nations: War and Survival in a Liberal Society*, 132–159. Notre Dame, IN: University of Notre Dame Press, 1992.

"On Taking Religion Seriously: The Challenge of Jonestown." (1982). In *Against the Nations: War and Survival in a Liberal Society*, 91–106. Notre Dame, IN: University of Notre Dame Press, 1992.

"On the Ethics of War and Peace: Review Essay of Walzer's *Just and Unjust Wars*, and Durnbaugh's *On Earth Peace*." *Review of Politics* 41, no. 1 (January 1979): 147–153.

"On the 'Right' to Be Tribal." *Christian Scholars Review* 16, no. 3 (March 1987): 238–241.

"On Witnessing Our Story: Christian Education in Liberal Societies." In *Schooling Christians*. Edited by Stanley Hauerwas and John H. Westerhoff, 214–234. Grand Rapids, MI: Wm. B. Eerdmans, 1992.

"Pacifism: A Form of Politics." In *Peace Betrayed? Essays on Pacifism and Politics*. Edited by Michael Cromartie, 133–142. Washington: Ethics and Public Policy Center, 1990.

"Pacifism: Some Philosophical Considerations." *Faith and Philosophy* 2, no. 2 (April 1985): 99–105.

"Pacifism, Just War, and the Gulf: An Exchange with Richard Neuhaus." *First Things* 13 (May 1991): 39–42.

"The Pastor as Prophet: Ethical Reflections on an Improbable Mission." (1985). In *Christian Existence Today: Essays on Church, World, and Living in Between*, 149–167. Durham, NC: Labyrinth Press, 1988.

"Peacemaking: The Virtue of the Church." (1985). In *Christian Existence Today: Essays on Church, World, and Living in Between*, 89–97. Durham, NC: Labyrinth Press, 1988.

"Political Righteousness." *Perspectives: A Journal of Reformed Thought* 8, no. 6 (June 1993): 8–9.

"The Politics of Charity." In *Truthfulness and Tragedy*, 132–142. Notre Dame, IN: University of Notre Dame Press, 1977.

"Politics, Vision, and the Common Good." (1970). In *Vision and Virtue*, 222–240. Notre Dame, IN: Fides Publishers, 1974; repr., Notre Dame, IN: University of Notre Dame, 1981.

"Practice Preaching." *Journal for Preachers* 18, no. 1 (Advent 1994): 21–24.

"Preaching As Though We Had Enemies." *First Things* 53 (May 1995): 45–49.

"Protestants and the Pope." *Commonweal* 107, no. 3 (February 15, 1980): 80–85.

"The Radical Edge of Baptism." With Brett Webb-Mitchell. *Reformed Liturgy & Music* 29, no. 2 (1995): 71–73.

"Rational Suicide and Reasons for Living." (1981). In *Suffering Presence: Theological Reflections on Medicine, the Mentally Handicapped, and the Church*, 100–113. Notre Dame, IN: University of Notre Dame Press, 1986.

"Reading James McClendon Takes Practice: Lessons in the Craft of Theology." In *Wilderness Wanderings: Probing Twentieth-Century Theology and Philosophy*, 171–187. Boulder, CO: Westview Press, 1997.

"The Reality of the Church: Even a Democratic State Is Not the Kingdom." (1982). In *Against the Nations: War and Survival in a Liberal Society*, 122–131. Notre Dame, IN: University of Notre Dame Press, 1992.

"The Reality of the Kingdom: An Ecclesial Space for Peace." (1982). With Mark Sherwindt. In *Against the Nations: War and Survival in a Liberal Society*, 107–121. Notre Dame, IN: University of Notre Dame Press, 1992.

"Reconciling the Practice of Reason: Casuistry in a Christian Context." (1986). In *Christian Existence Today: Essays on Church, World, and Living in Between*, 67–88. Durham, NC: Labyrinth Press, 1988.

"Reflections on Suffering, Death, and Medicine." (1979). In *Suffering Presence: Theological Reflections on Medicine, the Mentally Handicapped, and the Church*, 23–38. Notre Dame, IN: University of Notre Dame Press, 1986.

"Reflections on the Relation of Morality and Art: A Review Essay of R. W. Beardsmore's *Art and Morality*." *Cresset* 39, no. 5 (March 1976): 14–17.

"Reformation Is Sin." *Perspectives: A Journal of Reformed Thought* 11, no. 8 (October 1996): 10–11.

"Religious Concepts of Brain Death and Associated Problems." (1978). In *Suffering Presence: Theological Reflections on Medicine, the Mentally Handicapped, and the Church*, 87–99. Notre Dame, IN: University of Notre Dame Press, 1986.

"Religious Onlooks: A Review of *The Logic of Self-Improvement*." *Cresset* 34, no. 4 (February 1971): 22–23.

"Remaining in Babylon: Oliver O'Donovan's *Defense of Christendom*." With James Fodor. In *Wilderness Wanderings: Probing Twentieth-Century Theology and Philosophy*, 199–224. Boulder, CO: Westview Press, 1997.

"Remembering as a Moral Task." (1981). In *Against the Nations: War and Survival in a Liberal Society*, 61–90. Notre Dame, IN: University of Notre Dame Press, 1992.

"Remembering Martin Luther King Jr. Remembering; A Response to Christopher Beem." *Journal of Religious Ethics* 23, no. 1 (Spring 1995): 135–148.

"Resurrection, the Holocaust, and Forgiveness: A Sermon for Eastertime." In *Removing Anti-Judaism from the Pulpit*. Edited by Howard Clark Kee and Irvin J. Borowsky, 113–120. Philadelphia and New York: American Interfaith Institute and Continuum, 1996.

"The Retarded and the Criteria for the Human." (1973). In *Truthfulness and Tragedy*, 157–163. Notre Dame, IN: University of Notre Dame Press, 1977.

"The Retarded, Society, and the Family: The Dilemma of Care." (1982). In *Suffering Presence: Theological Reflections on Medicine, the Mentally Handicapped, and the Church*, 189–210. Notre Dame, IN: University of Notre Dame Press, 1986.

"Rev. Falwell and Dr. King." *Notre Dame Magazine* 10, no. 2 (May 1981): 28–29.

"Review Essay of *Christianity, Social Tolerance, and Homosexuality*, by John Boswell." *St. Lukes Journal* 28, no. 2 (March 1985): 228–232.

"Review Essay of Ellul's Violence: Reflections from a Christian Perspective." *American Journal of Jurisprudence* 18 (1973): 206–215.

"Review of Paul Lehmann's *The Transfiguration of Politics: The Presence and Power of Jesus of Nazareth In and Over Human Affairs*." *Worldview* 18, no. 12 (December 1975): 45–48.

"Review of *Soul in Society: The Making and Renewal of Social Christianity* by Gary Dorrien." *Modern Theology* 13, no. 3 (July 1997): 418–420.

"Review of *Violence Unveiled: Humanity at the Crossroads* by Gil Bailie." *Modern Theology* 12, no. 1 (January 1996): 113–115.

"Rights, Duties, and Experimentation on Children." In *Suffering Presence: Theological Reflections on Medicine, the Mentally Handicapped, and the Church*, 125–141. Notre Dame, IN: University of Notre Dame Press, 1986.

"Salvation and Health: Why Medicine Needs the Church." (1985). In *Suffering Presence: Theological Reflections on Medicine, the Mentally Handicapped, and the Church*, 63–83. Notre Dame, IN: University of Notre Dame Press, 1986.

"'Salvation even in Sin': Learning to Speak Truthfully about Ourselves." In *Sanctify Them in Truth: Holiness Exemplified*, 61–74. Edinburgh, UK: T&T Clark, 1998.

"The Sanctified Body: Why Perfection Does Not Require a 'Self'." In *Sanctify Them in the Truth*, 77–92. Nashville, TN: Abingdon Press, 1998.

"The Search for the Historical Yale School." Yale Divinity School Alumni Dinner, October 9, 1996.

"The Self as Story: A Reconsideration of the Relation of Religion and Morality from the Agent's Perspective." (1973). In *Vision and Virtue*, 68–89. Notre Dame, IN:

Fides Publishers, 1974; repr., Notre Dame, IN: University of Notre Dame Press, 1981.

"Self-Deception and Autobiography: Reflections on Speer's *Inside the Third Reich*." (1974). In *Truthfulness and Tragedy*, 82–98. Notre Dame, IN: University of Notre Dame Press, 1977.

"Self-Sacrifice as Demonic: A Theological Response to Jonestown." In *Violence and Religious Commitment*. Edited by Ken Levi, 152–162, 189–191. University Park, PA: Pennsylvania State University Press, 1982.

"The Sermon on the Mount: Just War and the Quest for Peace." *Concilium* 195 (1988): 36–43.

"Sex and Politics: Bertrand Russell and 'Human Sexuality'." *Christian Century* 95, no. 14 (April 19, 1978): 417–422.

"Sex in Public: Toward a Christian Ethic of Sex." (1980). In *A Community of Character*, 175–195. Notre Dame, IN: University of Notre Dame Press, 1981.

"Should War Be Eliminated?" (1983). In *Against the Nations: War and Survival in a Liberal Society*, 169–208. Notre Dame, IN: University of Notre Dame Press, 1992.

"The Significance of Vision: Toward an Aesthetic Ethic." (1972). In *Vision and Virtue*, 30–47. Notre Dame, IN: Fides Publishers, 1974; repr., Notre Dame, IN: University of Notre Dame Press, 1981.

"Situation Ethics, Moral Notions, and Moral Theology." (1971). In *Vision and Virtue*, 11–29. Notre Dame, IN: Fides Publishers, 1974; repr., Notre Dame, IN: University of Notre Dame Press, 1981.

"Some Theological Reflections on Gutierrez's Use of 'Liberation' as a Theological Concept." *Modern Theology* 3, no. 1 (1986): 67–76.

"The Sources of Charles Taylor. Review of *Sources of the Self: The Making of the Modern Identity* by Charles Taylor." With David Matzko. *Religious Studies Review* 18, no. 4 (October 1992): 286–289.

"Splendor of Truth: A Symposium." *First Things* 39 (January 1994): 21–23.

"Standing on the Shoulders of Murderers: The End of Sacrifice." *Preaching: A Professional Journal for Preachers* 10/5 (March–April 1995): 40, 42.

"Story and Theology." (1976). In *Truthfulness and Tragedy*, 71–81. Notre Dame, IN: University of Notre Dame Press, 1977.

"Story Telling: A Response to 'Mennonites on Hauerwas'." *Conrad Grebel Review: A Journal of Christian Inquiry* 13, no. 2 (Spring 1995): 166–173.

"A Story-Formed Community: Reflections on *Watership Down*." In *A Community of Character*, 9–35. Notre Dame, IN: University of Notre Dame Press, 1981.

"Suffering the Retarded: Should We Prevent Retardation?" (1984). In *Suffering Presence: Theological Reflections on Medicine, the Mentally Handicapped, and the Church*, 159–181. Notre Dame, IN: University of Notre Dame Press, 1986.

"Suffering, Medical Ethics and the Retarded Child." In *Truthfulness and Tragedy*, 164–168. Notre Dame, IN: University of Notre Dame Press, 1977.

"Taking Time for Peace." *Religion and Intellectual Life* 3, no. 3 (Spring 1986): 87–100.

"Taking Time for Peace: The Ethical Significance of the Trivial." (1986). In *Christian Existence Today: Essays on Church, World, and Living in Between*, 253–266. Durham, NC: Labyrinth Press, 1988.

"A Tale of Two Stories: On Being Christian and a Texan." (1981). In *Christian Existence Today: Essays on Church, World, and Living in Between*, 25–47. Durham, NC: Labyrinth Press, 1988.

"Testament of Friends: How My Mind Has Changed." *Christian Century* 107, no. 7 (February 28, 1990): 212–216.

"Theological Reflection on *In Vitro* Fertilization." In *Suffering Presence: Theological Reflections on Medicine, the Mentally Handicapped, and the Church*, 142–156. Notre Dame, IN: University of Notre Dame Press, 1986.

"Theology and the New American Culture." In *Vision and Virtue*, 241–260. Notre Dame, IN: Fides Publishers, 1974; repr., Notre Dame, IN: University of Notre Dame, 1972/1981.

"Timeful Friends: Living with the Handicapped." In *Sanctify Them in the Truth*, 143–156. Nashville, TN: Abingdon Press, 1998.

"To Be or Not to Be a Bricoleur." *Koinonia* 4, no. 1 (1994): 109.

"Toward an Ethics of Character." (1972). In *Vision and Virtue*, 48–67. Notre Dame, IN: Fides Publishers, 1974; repr., Notre Dame, IN: University of Notre Dame Press, 1981.

"A Trinitarian Theology of the Chief End of All Flesh." (1992). In *In Good Company: The Church as Polis*, 185–198. Notre Dame, IN: University of Notre Dame Press, 1995.

"The Truth about God: The Decalogue as Condition for Truthful Speech." In *Sanctify Them in Truth: Holiness Exemplified*, 37–59. Edinburgh, UK: T&T Clark, 1998.

"Truth and Honor: The University and the Church in a Democratic Age." In *Christian Existence Today: Essays on Church, World, and Living in Between*, 221–236. Durham, NC: Labyrinth Press, 1988.

"Truthful Difference, An Interview with Stanley Hauerwas." *Faith and Freedom: A Journal of Christian Ethics* 4, no. 3 (September 1995): 13–16.

"Understanding Homosexuality: The Viewpoint of Ethics." *Pastoral Psychology* 24, no. 3 (Spring 1976): 238–242.

"Veritatis Splendor: A Comment." *Commonweal* 120, no. 18 (October 22, 1993): 16–18.

"Virtue." In *The Westminster Dictionary of Christian Ethics*. Edited by James F. Childress and John Macquarrie, 648–650. Rev. ed. Philadelphia, PA: Westminster Press, 1986.

"Virtue and Character." In *Encyclopedia of Bioethics*, 2525–2532. New York: Macmillan Library Reference, 1995.

"Virtue, Description and Friendship: A Thought Experiment in Catholic Moral Theology." *Irish Theological Quarterly* 62, no. 2–3 (1996–97): 170–184.

"Virtue in Public." In *Christian Existence Today: Essays on Church, World, and Living in Between*, 191–198. Durham, NC: Labyrinth Press, 1988.

"The Virtues and Our Communities: Human Nature as History." In *A Community of Character*, 111–128. Notre Dame, IN: University of Notre Dame Press, 1981.

"Walter Rauschenbush and the Saving of America." In *History of Christian Ethics in America*: unfinished book mss., n.d.

"What About the Church?" With Will Willimon. *Christian Century* 106, no. 4 (February 1–8, 1989): 111, 128.

"What Can the State Ask?" *Christianity and Crisis* 43, no. 19 (November 1983): 458–459.

"What Could It Mean for the Church to Be Christ's Body? A Question without a Clear Answer." In *In Good Company: The Church as Polis*. Notre Dame, IN: University of Notre Dame Press, 1994/1995.

"When the Politics of Jesus Makes a Difference." *Christian Century* 110, no. 28 (October 13, 1993): 982–987.

"Who Is the We?" *Sojourners* 22, no. 3 (April 1992): 15.

"Whose Church? Which Future? Whither the Anabaptist Vision?" In *In Good Company: The Church as Polis*, 65–78. Notre Dame, IN: University of Notre Dame Press, 1994/1995.

"Whose Conscience? Whose Emotion?: Review of Sidney Callahan's *In Good Conscience: Reason, Emotion, and Moral Decision Making*." *Hastings Center Report* 22, no. 1 (January/February 1992): 48–49.

"Whose 'Just' War? Which Peace?" (1992). In *Dispatches From the Front: Theological Engagements With the Secular*, 136–152. Durham, NC: Duke University Press, 1994.

"Why Abortion Is a Religious Issue." In *A Community of Character*, 196–211. Notre Dame, IN: University of Notre Dame Press, 1981.

"Why Gays (as a Group) Are Morally Superior to Christians (as a Group)." In *Dispatches from the Front: Theological Engagements with the Secular*, 153–162. Durham, NC: Duke University Press, 1994.

"Why I Am Neither a Communitarian Nor a Medical Ethicist." *Hastings Center Report* 23, no. 6 (November/December 1993): S9–S10.

"Why Resident Aliens Struck a Chord." (1991). In *In Good Company: The Church as Polis*, 51–64. Notre Dame, IN: University of Notre Dame Press, 1995.

"Why the Truth Demands Truthfulness: An Imperious Engagement with Hartt." (1984). In *Why Narrative?* Edited by Stanley Hauerwas and L. Gregory Jones, 303–310. Grand Rapids, MI: Wm. B. Eerdmans, 1989.

"Why Truthfulness Requires Forgiveness: A Commencement Address for Graduates of the Church of the Second Chance." (1992). In *Dispatches from the Front: Theological Engagements with the Secular*, 80–88. Durham, NC: Duke University Press, 1994.

"Will The Real Sectarian Stand Up." *Theology Today* 14, no. 1 (April 1987): 87–94.

"Worship Is Evangelism." *Circuit Rider* 20, no. 10 (December–January 1996–97): 6–7.

General Index

INDEX
OF QUOTATIONS

QUOTATIONS BY STANLEY HAUERWAS

"a story is the material content which gives form to our character," 79
"a true story must be one that helps me to go on," 60, 240
"a truthful narrative is one that gives us the means to accept the tragic," 82
"attending to *how* Christians did what they did in the past," 230

"character . . . is the form of our agency," 72
"Christian convictions [require] that the self be transformed," 156
"Christian discourse is not a set of beliefs . . . rather it is a . . . set of skills," 228
"Christians do not believe in an 'eternal truth or truths' that can be known apart
	from the existence of . . . ," 300 n. 95
"Christians . . . attempt to translate their convictions," 55
"conversion as a long process," 150

"Ethics is always . . . parasitic to the way people live together in community," 231

"I learn the most . . . by attending . . . to how they say it," 56
"I never use the language of 'symbols' to characterize language," 130
"If truthfulness . . . is to be found, it will have to occur in and through stories," 76

"Language is a set of practices," 220
"learning to be moral is much like learning to speak a language," 231
"Learning to pray is the way Christians discover how to speak," 220
"liberalism is . . . a theory of society that is imperial in its demands," 281 n. 92
"'live in such a way that one's life would not make sense if God did not exist'
	[quoting Suhard]," 256